WHAT WE MOURN

Victorian Literature and Culture Series

Herbert F. Tucker, Editor
William R. McKelvy, Jill Rappoport, and
Andrew M. Stauffer, Associate Editors

What We Mourn

Child Death and the Politics of Grief in Nineteenth-Century Britain

Lydia Murdoch

University of Virginia Press
Charlottesville and London

The University of Virginia Press is situated on the traditional lands of the Monacan Nation, and the Commonwealth of Virginia was and is home to many other Indigenous people. We pay our respect to all of them, past and present. We also honor the enslaved African and African American people who built the University of Virginia, and we recognize their descendants. We commit to fostering voices from these communities through our publications and to deepening our collective understanding of their histories and contributions.

University of Virginia Press
© 2025 by the Rector and Visitors of the University of Virginia
All rights reserved
Printed in the United States of America on acid-free paper

First published 2025

1 3 5 7 9 8 6 4 2

LIBRARY OF CONGRESS CATALOGING-IN-PUBLICATION DATA
Names: Murdoch, Lydia, author
Title: What we mourn : child death and the politics of grief in nineteenth-century Britain / Lydia Murdoch.
Description: Charlottesville : University of Virginia Press, 2025. | Series: Victorian literature and culture series | Includes bibliographical references and index.
Identifiers: LCCN 2025021921 (print) | LCCN 2025021922 (ebook) | ISBN 9780813953816 hardback | ISBN 9780813953823 trade paperback | ISBN 9780813953830 ebook
Subjects: LCSH: Children—Death—Political aspects—Great Britain—History—19th century | Premature death—Political aspects—Great Britain—History—19th century | Bereavement—Political aspects—Great Britain—History—19th century | Child labor—Great Britain—History—19th century | Great Britain—Social conditions—19th century | Great Britain—Politics and government—19th century | BISAC: HISTORY / Europe / Great Britain / Victorian Era (1837–1901) | SOCIAL SCIENCE / Children's Studies
Classification: LCC HQ792.G7 M87 2025 (print) | LCC HQ792.G7 (ebook)
LC record available at https://lccn.loc.gov/2025021921
LC ebook record available at https://lccn.loc.gov/2025021922

Cover art: The Dying Child, Hans Heyerdahl, 1881 (dated 1882). Oil on canvas, 194 × 224 cm. (Musée Francisque Mandet, Riom)
Cover design: Joel W. Coggins

For Andy, Kit, and Henrik

What we miss—what we lose and what we mourn—isn't it this that makes us who, deep down, we truly are. To say nothing of what we wanted in life but never got to have.

—Sigrid Nunez, *The Friend*

CONTENTS

	List of Illustrations	xi
	Acknowledgments	xiii
	Introduction	1
1.	"National Grievances": Petitioning for the Dead and Dying Factory Child	11
2.	"Shrouding My Poor Children": The Transatlantic Antislavery Campaign	36
3.	"Suppressed Grief": Mourning the Death of British Children and the Memory of the 1857 Indian Rebellion	72
4.	"A Loud and Bitter Cry": The Mourned and Unmourned in Late Nineteenth-Century Urban Public Health Debates	100
5.	"A Life of Her Own": Women, Maternity, and the Politics of Grief	132
	Conclusion	157
	Notes	163
	Bibliography	229
	Index	257

ILLUSTRATIONS

1. Dying child in *The Good Little Boy* — 3
2. "Ignorance" and "Want" from *A Christmas Carol* (1843) — 9
3. "The Negro Mother's Appeal" (1829) — 44
4. Female Society for Birmingham abolitionist handbag (ca. 1827) — 49
5. *Leeds Anti-Slavery Juvenile Series* front cover (1860) — 54
6. Sarah Parker Remond — 66
7. "O God of Battles! Steel My Soldiers' Hearts!," *Punch* (1857) — 78
8. "Too 'Civil' by Half," *Punch* (1857) — 79
9. "The British Lion's Vengeance on the Bengal Tiger," *Punch* (1857) — 80
10. "Massacre of English Officers and Their Wives at Jhansi" (1858) — 80
11. "Massacre at Cawnpore" (1858) — 81
12. "Angel of the Resurrection" Memorial at Kanpur — 97
13. Portrait of Josephine Butler by George Frederic Watts (1895) — 110
14. Sculpture of Evangeline Butler — 117
15. Josephine Butler's carte de visite — 117
16. "Vaccination Act for Jenner-ation of Disease" (1886) — 121
17. "Fifteen Children, Four Living, Father an Iron-Moulder" (1915) — 147

MAP

1. 1833 British petitions for factory reform — 22

ACKNOWLEDGMENTS

I received generous funding for this project from the George A. and Eliza Gardner Howard Foundation and from the Vassar College Lucy Maynard Salmon Research Fund, the Elinor Nims Brink Fund, the Tatlock Fund, and a Faculty Conversation Grant. I benefited as well from the expertise and kindness of archivists and staff at Bishopsgate Institute, the British Library, London School of Economics Archives, the Women's Library, the National Archives, and Royal Holloway, University of London Archives. Mary Wilke went above and beyond in providing me materials from the Center for Research Libraries.

The community of scholars at Vassar enhanced my work at every stage, highlighting the best of the liberal arts. Judith Dollenmayer helped me craft the first of many grant proposals, and the Committee on Research, Lori Buckey, Gary Hohenberger, Chris Johnson, and Amanda Thornton worked with me to secure additional funding. This book would not have been possible without friends in the Vassar Library—Debra Bucher, Gretchen Lieb, Lydia Smith, and our beloved Carollynn Costella—and Ron Patkus and Dean Rogers in Special Collections and Archives. Neil Curri improved the book with his map-making skills. For inspiration, I couldn't imagine a better cohort than my History Department colleagues, past and present, notably Nancy Bisaha, Amanda Brennan, Bob Brigham, Yu-chi Chang, Maria Höhn, Daniel Mendiola, Quincy Mills, Leslie Offutt, Karen Perrucci, Izzy Plowright, Miki Pohl, Allison Puglisi, Ismail Rashid, Josh Schreier, Ashanti Shih, Noel Smyth, and Michelle Whalen, with heartfelt gratitude to Mita Choudhury, Miriam Cohen, Rebecca Edwards, Jim Merrell, and Tony Wohl for their help with this book. Members of Vassar's Global Nineteenth-Century Studies program (and formerly Victorian Studies) sparked new directions in my teaching and research and continue to host the best campus dinners. Thanks in particular to Beth Darlington, Wendy Graham, Susan Hiner, Christian Lewis, Brian Lukacher, Jeff Schneider, Elliott Schreiber, and Mark Taylor. My co-teacher, co-author, mentor, and friend Susan Zlotnick read selections of the manuscript, never failing to provide incisive comments and solutions when I felt stuck. I've been lucky to have Eva Woods and, from my first years at Vassar, Lisa Collins and Lee Bernstein as neighbors and friends with whom to share walks, food, and family.

Vassar students have also done much to shape the ideas of this book. It was a joy to work with Rachel Fuerstman, Ivanna Guerra, Aliya Hussain, and Ashish Patil, who died too young, as Vassar Ford Summer Scholars. Thanks as well to my amazing student research assistants and History interns who supported me during my term as Department Chair: Isabel Bielat, Katherine Cheatham, Cameron Daddis, Ivanna Guerra, Ben Papa, Andrea Selby, Jesse Schatz, Sara Shepherd, Ananya Suresh, Antar Thiam, and Ellie Vamos.

Since March 13, 2020, sharing daily haiku with my then senior thesis students—Philip Ahn, Isabel Bielat, Jen Jacobs, and Hanna Stasiuk—kept me writing. I've learned much and enjoyed good food and laughs while discussing British history books with Andy August, Polly Beals, Dina Copelman, Ren Pepitone, George Robb, Ellen Ross, Jennifer Tucker, and Judy Walkowitz. And my SUNY New Paltz Writing Buddies—Andy Evans, Jackie George, Jed Mayer, Cy Mulready, and Tom Olsen—gave me the support and structure I needed to finish this book. Terri Sabatos first showed me the power of Victorian images of death. For their insight and encouragement at key moments, thanks as well to the late Judith Allen, Mona Ali, Nick Barone, Rob Boddice, Anna Clark, Mary Jean Corbett, Nadja Durbach, Jeannette Estruth, Laura Kasson Fiss, Kit French, Ginger Frost, Debbie Gershenowitz, Durba Ghosh, Daniel Grey, Hannah Groch-Begley, Carol Engelhardt Herringer, Tracey Holland, Kathleen Jones, Bethan Johnson, David Kelly, Wilma King, Lara Kriegel, Amitava Kumar, Patrick Leary, Alison Lotto, Sarah Maza, Kay McAdams, Tamara Myers, Stephanie Olsen, Susan Pennybacker, Jeanne Peterson, Nicola Phillips, Jude Pitti, Linda Pollock, David Pomfret, Tom Prasch, Tim and Catherine Schmitz, Julia Shatz, Susie Steinbach, and Melissa Turoff. I've especially valued feedback from Ellen Ross on drafts of my work and have often returned to her scholarship as a model to which to aspire.

My sincere thanks to Eric Brandt of the University of Virginia Press for his early interest in the manuscript and to Angie Hogan, Ellen Satrom, and everyone at the press for bringing it to publication. I'm lucky to have had Seth Koven and Rohan McWilliam as readers of the entire manuscript and am grateful for the opportunity to acknowledge their contributions. Their insightful observations and notes made this a better book. I'm also immensely appreciative of the Victorian Literature and Culture Series editor Herbert Tucker and associate editors William McKelvy, Jill

Rappoport, and Andrew Stauffer for their close readings, detailed suggestions, and rich knowledge of the Victorians. Thanks as well to Colleen Romick Clark for her expert copyediting and to Rebecca McCorkle for the index.

As I completed the revisions for this book, my mother, Deborah Murdock, died from acute myeloid leukemia. I remain deeply indebted to the medical staff at the University of Virginia Hospital for their expert care of us both, and of course to my mother for her wit, intelligence, and endless curiosity in people's daily lives. Thanks to Robert, Alec, Kris, Will, and Sadie, and to Carolyn Evans, my father, Angus Murdoch, and stepmother, Alice Wakefield. And most of all thanks to Andy Evans for his historical counsel, ready pen, and loving partnership, and to our sons, Kit and Henrik, who make this life a joy.

A version of chapter 3 is reprinted with permission from the *Journal of British Studies* 51, no. 2 (April 2012): 364–92. Sections of chapter 4 were published in "Anti-Vaccination and the Politics of Grief for Children in Late-Victorian England," 242–60, in *Childhood, Youth and Emotions in Modern History: National, Colonial and Global Perspectives*, edited by Stephanie Olsen (London: Palgrave Macmillan History of Emotions Series, 2015) and in "'The Dead and the Living': Child Death, the Public Mortuary Movement, and the Spaces of Grief and Selfhood in Victorian London," *Journal of the History of Childhood and Youth* 8, no. 3 (Fall 2015): 378–402. I am grateful for permission to republish these works.

WHAT WE MOURN

Introduction

ONE OF the first texts purposely created for child readers instructed them on how to die. "My dear reader," concluded the Religious Tract Society pamphlet *The Good Little Boy,* "pray to God to make you like James, a good child; and then when you die He will take you to a good place, to live with Christ for ever."[1] The miniature booklet made for small hands advised children at the beginning of the nineteenth century that "there is nobody born good," yet though James was born sinful, God held the power to "take away his bad heart and give him a good heart."[2] James "cared most for reading good books, thinking about heaven and hell, and praying to Almighty God," unlike the "many children who spend all their time in eating and drinking, sleeping and playing."[3] Indeed, the author wrote, James "was fast ripening for heaven" (fig. 1).[4] When scarlet fever struck his family, it was the divine rather than the domestic realm that offered comfort: James "had none of his mother's kind attentions during his sickness," for she was already in the hospital, and "before she recovered" her child "was dead and buried." Still, the narrator assured, "though she did not see him he was in safe hands, for his soul was carried by the angels into Abraham's bosom, to live with a good God, and good men, and good angels, for ever and ever."[5]

Compare this death of *The Good Little Boy* published sometime in the first decades of the nineteenth century with the later, more famous imagined passing of Tiny Tim in *A Christmas Carol* (1843) by Charles Dickens. The second spirit of the night, "a jolly Giant," the Ghost of Christmas Present, greets Scrooge in his normally spartan room transformed with "living green," "a mighty blaze" awakening the "dull petrification of a hearth," a "throne" of delicacies piled on the floor.[6] Experiencing a corporeal rather than heavenly "ripening," Scrooge and the Spirit tour London's culinary delights before witnessing the Cratchits' more meager, yet joyful, feast. "Tell me if Tiny Tim will live," asks Scrooge, and the Spirit replies, "I see a vacant seat.... If these shadows remain unaltered by the Future, the child will die." "Oh no, kind Spirit! say he will be spared," cries Scrooge. Echoing Scrooge's earlier rebuke of the poor, the Spirit says, "If he be like to die, he had better do it, and decrease the surplus population." At this, "Scrooge hung his head to hear his own words quoted by the Spirit, and was overcome with penitence and grief."[7]

Dickens identified grief as the overwhelming response to a child's death and, moreover, politicized this grief by revealing Tiny Tim's demise to be the natural outcome of Scrooge's Malthusian support for the New Poor Law of 1834. In this most classic of Victorian texts, mourning for dead children becomes a means to critique prisons and the poor laws, to foreshadow a future without change, and ultimately to alter the present: Scrooge experiences an earthly transformation, and "to Tiny Tim, who did NOT die, he was a second father."[8] Through his expression of grief for the child, Scrooge embraces family and fellowship along with a vision of reproductive futurism tied to child life, and the man who had been as "solitary as an oyster" ends his days as a model local and global citizen.[9]

Dickens had tapped a profound change in responses to child death. The Religious Tract Society's method of targeting child readers proved new, but the message remained old. James's passing in *The Good Little Boy* underscored devotional triumph and heavenly resolution, while visions of Tiny Tim's early death conjured grief, regret, and worldly reform. *What We Mourn* explores the contours of this change. During the long nineteenth century, public mourning for dead and dying children gained new political significance and power within British, imperial, and transatlantic contexts. By combining concepts from histories of the family, childhood, emotions, and the state, this book weaves together the personal and political to argue that public grief for lost child life became a means to assert and even reimagine British rights and citizenship. The deaths of children unsurprisingly, and unevenly, took on greater public prominence as childhood came to be redefined during the nineteenth century as a life stage associated with innocence, domesticity, protection, and dependence. As Britain and the empire increasingly structured state powers around categories of age, particularly childhood, the focus on *child* death highlighted fears of the state's inability literally to reproduce itself. Calling attention to the loss of child life in political protests also became a means for everyday people shut out of standard definitions of liberal citizenship—the working class, women, colonial subjects, the formerly enslaved, and people of

FIGURE 1. A dying child in the Religious Tract Society pamphlet *The Good Little Boy* (n.d.). (Archives and Special Collections, Vassar College Library)

color—to assert the value of their lives and their rights. These rights often began with demands for full legal recognition by the state that came with citizenship, but extended to other areas: freedom from slavery, suffrage, improved labor conditions, bodily autonomy, housing, and health care.

These changes took place in an era of horrifically high child mortality. Dickens suffered the death of his beloved sister-in-law Mary Hogarth, who died at the age of seventeen in 1837, followed fourteen years later by the death of his eight-month-old daughter Dora. Charles Darwin wrote poignantly when his eldest daughter, Annie, died at the age of ten, "We have lost the joy of the Household, and the solace of our old age."[10] Thomas Malthus, Elizabeth Fry, Leigh Hunt, Mary Shelley, William Gladstone, Elizabeth Gaskell, Matthew Arnold, Margaret Oliphant, and Isabella Beeton all lost children, sometimes more than one, as did countless others. Memories of deceased youth filled nineteenth-century literature. The young girl in William Wordsworth's "We Are Seven" (1798) points to the churchyard resting place of her siblings, asserting, "Their graves are green, they may be seen."[11] The martydom, illness, and death of Helen Burns at Lowood School in Charlotte Brontë's *Jane Eyre* (1847) echoed the sorrows of Charlotte's eldest sister, Maria Brontë. The many deaths of children in Dickens's novels and stage reenactments—Little Nell, Paul Dombey, Jo the Crossing Sweeper, and others—alternately inspired praise for their realist accuracy from the *British Medical Journal* and criticism for their "mawkish" excess.[12] In nineteenth-century Britain, child death was a fact of literature and life.

British death rates fell over the course of the long nineteenth century, but the trend affected populations unevenly depending on region, class, age, gender, and other factors such as profession. In the particularly dangerous setting of mid-eighteenth-century London, nearly two-thirds of all children from wealthy as well as impoverished backgrounds had died before their fifth birthday.[13] Within the combined parish workhouse of St. George's Bloomsbury (decried by the philanthropist Jonas Hanway as "the greatest sink of mortality in these kingdoms") and St. Giles-in-the-Fields, 80 percent of children admitted in 1766 did not live to see their first birthday.[14] Infant mortality rates for London children under one year (the period of greatest risk) peaked in the 1740s at 450 deaths per thousand live births, declining to 250 in the 1770s and likely to under 200 by the turn of the nineteenth century.[15] Along with industrialization, urbanization, and the introduction of new diseases such as cholera, the first half of the nineteenth century brought an interval of worsening mortality from the 1820s to the 1860s, although life expectancy still remained better than during the extreme eighteenth-century lows.[16] In the second half of the nineteenth century, infant mortality rates averaged at around 150 per thousand live births for England and Wales and 120 for Scotland, meaning that roughly one out of every seven or eight children died before the age of one.[17] Urban areas proved more deadly than agricultural districts, and within cities the working classes and the very poor remained at greater risk. In the late 1850s and 1860s, for example, the city of Preston illustrated these geographical and class disparities: About one-fifth of all upper-class children, one-third of all middle-class children, and two-thirds of all working-class children in the Lancashire city died before the age of five.[18] Although average British life expectancy improved significantly after 1870, infant mortality rates remained stubbornly high in many communities and even worsened overall for a period in the 1890s. Only in the twentieth century did British death primarily align with old age rather than childhood. While nineteenth-century Britons faced better survival chances than they had a century before, child death remained a common experience among all classes, though particularly among the urban working poor.

Despite the pervasiveness of child mortality in the nineteenth century, scholars have only begun to trace its effects. The rise of demography and social history in the mid-twentieth century and, more recently, the history of emotions have provided historians with the tools to study child death. Scholarship on parental bereavement during the nineteenth century, for example, has done much to address what José Harris identified in 1993 as "a phenomenon that still awaits imaginative historical reconstruction."[19] M. Jeanne Peterson offered one of the earliest accounts of elite Victorian parents struggling with the death of children in her analysis of the gentry couple Catherine and Archibald Tait, who lost five of their seven children to scarlet fever in 1856—a case that Pat Jalland developed in detail in her foundational work, *Death in the Victorian Family* (1996).[20] Moving from elite to working-class families, Ellen Ross and Julie-Marie Strange have shown how working parents also deeply grieved the deaths of children in ways that voiced the language of fatalism and resignation, but also expressed "profound sorrow."[21] What these and other recent works on child mortality share is a common rejection of earlier theories claiming that high child death rates discouraged parents from developing affectionate bonds with children or from mourning their deaths.[22] These existing studies of child death also primarily concentrate on personal, private forms of grief within families, particularly parental grief.[23]

Mourning for children, however, took on ever more prominent public forms as childhood came to be redefined during the nineteenth century as a life stage associated with innocence, domesticity, and protection. Earlier religious and popular accounts often expressed overall fatalism toward child mortality of the kind illustrated in *The Good Little Boy*. For example, in his widely reproduced and performed *Divine and Moral Songs for Children* (1715), the Protestant dissenter Isaac Watts instructed his young subjects to remember

> There is an Hour when I must die,
> Nor do I know how soon 'twill come;
> A thousand Children young as I
> Are call'd by Death to hear their Doom.[24]

Watts's hymns supported the generally accepted Christian belief of original sin and encouraged children to prepare for their early deaths by learning to read and studying the Bible. Generations of youth memorized Watts's songs, giving thanks

> That I am brought to know
> The Danger I was in,
> By Nature and by Practice too
> A wretched Slave to Sin.[25]

During the late eighteenth and nineteenth centuries, however, such fatalism felt increasingly uncomfortable as members of the middle classes drew on the teachings of Jean-Jacques Rousseau, the Romantics, and the Evangelicals to reconceptualize childhood as a life stage characterized by innocence, education (with national elementary schools eventually established in 1870 for England and Wales, 1872 for Scotland), and in some cases playfulness rather than work.[26] Rousseau initially shocked readers with his declaration in *Émile, or On Education* (1762), "There is no original perversity in the human heart."[27] "Love childhood," he wrote, instructing readers to "look with friendly eyes on its games, its pleasures, its amiable dispositions.... Why steal from the little innocents the enjoyment of a time that passes all too quickly?"[28] The religious emphasis on original sin persisted, but by the late nineteenth century, a belief in child purity predominated. By 1886, the founder of what would become the National Society for the Prevention of Cruelty to Children (NSPCC), Benjamin Waugh, declared, "A child is not only made in the image of God, but of all His creatures it is the most like to Himself in its early purity, beauty, brightness, and innocence."[29] Yet, wrote Waugh, "death reigns over them even in their early innocence," leading him to call for additional state regulations that would ensure the "protection" of "the most helpless and defenceless of the creatures that God has made."[30] Above all, childhood came to be understood as a period characterized by protection and dependence—new ideals that sparked public mourning and grief over the death and suffering of children.

By the nineteenth century, these new ideals of childhood and chronological age more generally played ever more important roles in defining the constitution and bureaucratic tools of modern states.[31] As Holly Brewer has shown, over the course of the seventeenth and eighteenth centuries, legal codes gradually distinguished children from consenting adults in England and its North American colonies. Children in sixteenth-century England could sign apprenticeship agreements, marry at the age of seven, be hanged for felonies at the age of eight, serve in the military, and vote if they met property requirements.[32] By the early nineteenth century, however, stricter age limits more often served as a basis for legal rights and protections (though the last state hanging of a minor in Britain occurred in 1889). Youth continued to enlist in the military, but by the time of the Great War such service became categorized—and all too often overlooked—as "underage." The state's greater reliance on age classifications, particularly childhood, mirrored demographic trends. The relative decline in mortality of the eighteenth and early nineteenth centuries combined with a rapid rise in fertility to create an unusually young population for Britain. At the extreme end, nearly 40 percent of people in England were under fifteen years old in 1826, compared with 29 percent of the population in 1676.[33] These demographic changes not only influenced major historical developments such as industrialization by providing larger numbers of child workers, but also reshaped how individuals understood their identities in relation to their own and other age cohorts and in relation to the evolving state. During the long nineteenth century, British and colonial governments used chronological age to rule through censuses and compulsory vaccination, age of consent legislation and national education. And the particularly youthful population at the beginning of the century gave all the more weight to developing state powers based on emerging understandings of childhood. The case studies that follow explore this process, beginning with the campaigns for the abolition of slavery and the regulation of child labor and ending with demands for state-funded maternal and child health care at the dawn of the twentieth century. The threat of death—and particularly child death—served to justify new state interventions, but inherent in each of these battles was a tension between age-based protections and universal rights. *What We Mourn* thus offers both a history of children's experiences of life and death and what Sarah Maza identifies as a "history *through* children" focused on questions of political rights.[34]

Just as childhood took on new meanings in the long nineteenth century, so too did death and mourning. The "good death" envisioned by Romantic and Evangelical writers at the end of the eighteenth century was the Victorian ideal: a death that took place within the domestic setting in which the dying gave farewells to loved ones, endured suffering with grace, and ultimately displayed signs of union with God.[35] By the 1870s and 1880s, emotionally laden accounts of the moment of death became much less common as the decline of Evangelical Christianity and the rise of more secular outlooks marked a shift in focus from the state of the soul to the suffering of the body. Such mourning practices and conceptualizations of the dead—referred to by Thomas de Quincey as the "Parliament of ghosts"—carried political meaning.³⁶ *What We Mourn* is a history deeply influenced by Thomas Laqueur's "story of the ways in which the presence of the dead enchants our purportedly disenchanted world, of the reinvention of enchantment in more democratic forms."³⁷ This democratization of the dead is most perceptible in Laqueur's account of the shift from churchyards to cemeteries in the decades following the French Revolution. Unlike the small, crowded Christian churchyard of the old regime, the nineteenth-century suburban cemetery provided a more secular, "cosmopolitan place" within industrial capitalist societies that welcomed all the dead who could afford the cost of a plot alongside visitors who ambled through its parklike landscape; loosened from the control of the Church, the modern dead, asserts Laqueur, "could be mobilized to create new memorial communities, to make a new civic order, or to advance a particular political or social claim."³⁸ Like Laqueur's book, *What We Mourn* traces the democratization of public grief as factory hands and abolitionists, sanitation reformers and suffragists called upon the state to recognize their lives as part of a new, reinvented order.

By turning to the public and political understandings of grief for the dead and dying child, *What We Mourn* discovers the expression of new "emotional regimes" centered around child life and child death in the nineteenth century.³⁹ The book addresses questions raised by the feminist philosopher Judith Butler and others about how public forms of mourning mark particular lives as having value—and, by extension, represent generally unspoken views about whose lives are not valued. According to Butler, "Certain losses are not avowed as losses, and violence is derealized and diffused."⁴⁰ Thus, writes Butler, some "forms of grief become nationally recognized and amplified, whereas other losses become unthinkable and ungrievable."⁴¹ Or, as Sara Ahmed observes, grief takes on political value "by identifying those that *can be* loved, those that *can be* grieved, that is, by constituting some others as the legitimate objects of emotion."⁴² The proliferation and commercialization of Victorian mourning practices—the elaborate stages of mourning dress, postmortem photographs, death masks, hair jewelry, and costly funerals—therefore represented not only new expressions of private grief and selfhood but also new claims to political subjectivity, citizenship, and power.⁴³ The dead "dwell in us—individually and communally," notes Laqueur, as "they give meaning to our lives" and "structure public spaces, politics, and time."⁴⁴ Given these political as well as personal meanings attached to mourning rituals, it is understandable, as Julie-Marie Strange has argued, that working-class

FIGURE 2. John Leech's woodcut illustrating "Ignorance" and "Want" in Charles Dickens's *A Christmas Carol* (Boston: Charles E. Lauriat, 1924, a facsimile of the original 1843 edition). (Archives and Special Collections, Vassar College Library)

families might arrange burial services seemingly beyond their means in an effort to affirm their presence in the national community and claim their "right of citizenship."⁴⁵

What We Mourn follows a thematic, roughly chronological organization with chapters exploring popular responses to children's fatalities in the context of industrial factory labor, slavery and abolition, the 1857 Indian Rebellion, and late-Victorian urban housing and public health reforms (compulsory vaccination, the registration of births and deaths, and the state regulation of infectious diseases). A final chapter analyzes how, during the First World War, the Women's Co-operative Guild brought issues of maternal health and child mortality directly before Parliament and the public—with the support of prominent figures, most notably Virginia Woolf—to argue for greater national health care provisions. In each of these case studies, collective grief for dead and dying children became politicized. The acknowledgment and, alternately, the silencing of grief for children upheld the granting or denial of new rights and new models of governing. Reformers voiced their grief as a means to question the powers—and the limitations—of modern nation-states. By positioning British domestic history within broader imperial and transnational contexts, *What We Mourn* builds upon scholarship calling for global studies that are not solely bound by national boundaries.[46]

New conceptions of childhood and death did not always result in new emotional regimes that persisted. Particularly in conflicts involving slavery and empire, the more radical messages articulated in moments of collective mourning for children tended to be overlooked, dismissed, or largely forgotten. Even within domestic Britain, childhood and child innocence proved all too malleable and selective foundations for social transformation. At the end of his time with the Spirit of Christmas Present, after visiting "many homes" and "foreign lands," Scrooge discovers two children—Ignorance and Want—hiding under the phantom's robes (fig. 2).[47] Unlike Tiny Tim, they are "wretched, abject, frightful, hideous, miserable." "Where graceful youth should have filled their features out, and touched them with its freshest tints," wrote Dickens, "a stale and shrivelled hand, like that of age, had pinched, and twisted them, and pulled them into shreds." Scrooge, "appalled," literally chokes as he tries to say they are "fine children."[48] In *A Christmas Carol*, it requires a visit from three spirits to redeem the miserly man of business, to transform him from a Malthusian with no sense of the value of a child's life into Tiny Tim's second father. Outside of the precincts of fiction, without the supernatural interventions of Dickens's tale, a real-life Scrooge might also be appalled by the ragged children, but he would just as likely walk away, without a second glance. By bringing attention to public mourning for children—both losses that were recognized and amplified and those regarded as unthinkable and ungrievable—this book explores how collective grief for children shaped major political debates and discourses of the long nineteenth century.

1

"National Grievances"

Petitioning for the Dead and Dying Factory Child

On March 16, 1832, Michael Sadler delivered a three-hour speech in the House of Commons introducing the second reading of the Factories' Regulation or Ten Hours Bill. The Tory MP made the case for government intervention first and foremost by evoking grief for dead and dying children. Arguing that children—and indeed potentially *all* workers—were not able to negotiate their own contracts because of their dependence on employers, Sadler called for Parliament to "protect" them from a "system of cruelty and oppression."[1] "The children of the poor imprisoned in factories," he declared, far from being "free agents," were "literally worked to death."[2] "Premature labour" wrought "premature decay" and "premature death."[3] Blaming the mills for Manchester's higher burial rates for those under forty compared to London and Paris, Sadler demanded, "Where is the man that dares to oppose the effectual regulation of so murderous a system?"[4] Sadler's emotional appeal recalled his earlier poem, "The Factory Girl's Last Day." In it, the daughter whose mother has died and father is unemployed cries out in response to the predawn factory bells: "They killed my little brother,—/ Like him I'll work and die!"[5] Months after Sadler's speech as the debates continued, journals and newspapers sympathetic to factory reform reprinted "The Factory Girl's Last Day" alongside parliamentary evidence of a father mourning the loss of his young daughter from overwork.[6] Public grief for children killed and damaged by factory work, as well as for the past traumas of adult workers, operated at the core of the reform movement; by focusing on the dying child, Sadler and his supporters explored new models of political agency—encompassing working-class voice and action along with awareness of systemic exploitation—that required a new model of governing. For a limited time in the 1830s, grief, mourning, and outrage centered around the figure of the young factory hand suffering early death brought Parliament's attention to the unjust condition of all workers as the dying child came to symbolize larger class and national injustices produced by industrialization.

As Sadler presented the Factories' Regulation Bill in March of 1832, however, not everyone in the House appreciated his public mourning for Britain's dying children, an expression of emotion perhaps considered more suited to poetry and the domestic sphere than Parliament. Sadler recalled that William Marshall, son of the Leeds millowner John Marshall (who watched from under the gallery), "*smiled* while I was describing the misery of a factory child."[7] Sadler had paused in the midst of his monumental speech, observing, "I perceive that I excite the risibility of an honourable gentleman opposite. What there is to smile at in these just representations of infantile sufferings, I am really at a loss to imagine. I will venture however to give him and the House a few more of these amusing facts before I have done with the subject."[8] Elizabeth Gaskell later echoed this moment in *Mary Barton* (1848), a story centered around child death. When in that novel the factory workers eloquently represent their hardships and the hardships of their children, Harry Carson, the millowner's son, performs his version of a smirk by drawing a caricature of the workers—"lank, ragged, dispirited, and famine-stricken"—and passing it around for all the gathered factory owners to laugh.[9] Discovering the drawing, John Barton reaffirms the operatives' demands, declaring, "It makes me more than sad, it makes my heart burn within me, to see that folk can make a jest of striving men," who come to ask "for victuals for the childer, whose little voices are getting too faint and weak to cry aloud wi' hunger."[10] The radicalized Barton concludes, "Now I only know that I would give the last drop of my blood to avenge us on yon chap, who had so little feeling in him as to make game on earnest, suffering men!"[11] By pointing out the smirks and smiles of Liberal millowners, both Sadler and Gaskell explored resistance alongside new political visions ignited by demands that factory workers and their children become cause for national mourning. After concluding his speech, in a letter to his wife, Sadler stressed the power of his appeal to grief for children's premature deaths as a basis for government intervention: "I spoke last night and I believe pretty well"; he noted making "a piece fly" at his opponents. The "country is up," he wrote, and "will not have" children "to be worked 12 hours a day for a cotton lord in the land."[12]

Defenders and detractors of child labor thus presented very different accounts of the economic effects of that labor on standards of living as well as the very nature of the work. Like the Marshalls, most supporters of free trade represented factory children as happy and healthy, certainly better off than many of their working-class counterparts. They opposed, as MP John Hope replied to Sadler, any "interference with free labour" and doubted that "Parliament could protect children as effectually as their parents."[13] However, new ideals of childhood—and the attack on childhood represented by early death—took on new political meaning amid these debates. I am thus not primarily interested here in the much-contested question of whether early industrial labor negatively affected children's health (though I agree with the "pessimists" that it did, while recognizing the biased nature of early committee reports, including Sadler's).[14] Rather, my focus is on how workers and reformers such as Sadler as well as their opponents politicized childhood, along with celebrations of child life and grieving over child death. In the decades following the late eighteenth-century population boom, the proportion of youth comprising the overall population increased, and child labor became even more central to Britain's expanding industrial economy in the 1830s and 1840s.[15] At the same time, the lives and deaths of children moved to the center of political discourse. Michael Sadler, Lord Ashley, Chartist protesters, the young Friedrich Engels, Frances Trollope, Elizabeth Barrett Browning, Elizabeth Gaskell, Charles Dickens, and countless other popular writers brought attention to the dead, dying, or lifeless child.[16] Child laborers did more than provide a sympathetic subject through which to introduce labor reforms, as previous scholars have shown. In the context of suffrage reform surrounding the 1832 Great Reform Act enfranchising men of the new industrial middle classes, a broad political spectrum of reformers came to focus on the working and dying child as a way to explore new potential models of subjectivity, citizenship, and state power.

In the 1830s, many leaders of factory reform used the child worker (often, it should not be forgotten, the "Factory *Girl*") to amplify conditions that affected all workers: the limited nature of liberal concepts of free agency, the radical redefinition of labor as a form of property, and new understandings of the feeling subject. The dead child immediately evoked the political injustices of workers' experiences by symbolizing lives that could have been. Mourning the dead thus underscored the case for how the living should be treated. In the 1830s, labor activists stressed children's ability to feel—physical pain and pleasure along with emotional joy and anguish—as essential aspects of modern childhood, the modern self, and modern political subjectivity. Children's feeling served as a basis for their future knowledge, their religious education, and ultimately their claim as Britons. Correspondingly, their deaths and the annihilation of childlike feeling brought on by industrial labor marked not only a familial loss, but a national one—what Engels eventually termed a "social murder" committed by an "unfeeling bourgeoisie" willing to deny children time that should be "devoted solely to their physical and mental development."[17] Sadler's speeches and poetry, the hundreds of petitions sent to Parliament in the early 1830s demanding factory reform, select committee reports, and even much of the later poetry of Elizabeth Barrett Browning and other popular writers from the 1840s thus cannot be dismissed as mere sentimental sketches of victimized youth. These national grievances—public testimonies of grief for dying children and lost childhoods—became a recognized foundation for demanding British political rights.

This chapter, then, is not another retelling of the campaign for child labor reforms, but rather a history of how childhood came to be defined by feeling in the context of industrialization and how that change shaped politics. My main sources are petitions sent to Parliament in the spring and summer of 1833 by workers on the question of child factory labor. Parliamentary petitions crossed and blurred genres, similar to widely read parliamentary committee reports ("blue books"), social exposés, and industrial fiction.[18] Yet, more than any of these other types of sources, they also provided a more direct voice from the people. Largely overlooked by historians, petitions represent a new source base that can answer new questions. Rather than weighing the evidence for or against improved standards of living caused by industrialization, my focus is on how the recognition of new understandings of childhood, child life, and child death served as arguments for political reform. Through the act of petitioning Parliament, workers across Britain publicly made the case that working-class children's lives were a national concern, and that their deaths were cause for national mourning. They sought, in other words, to make factory children's lives and deaths "grievable," hoping that this public recognition of emotion might serve as a basis for government intervention and their claim to working-class political rights.[19]

The Factory Reform Movement

In many ways, the history of child labor reform, starting with Sadler and the friend who inspired him, the Tory Radical Richard Oastler, is a familiar one, told in histories of industrialization, the campaign for government regulation, and the challenges and limitations of legislative enforcement.[20] Sadler's factory bill stalled in the Commons and was sent to a select committee that he chaired from April to August 1832. The committee report published in August was the first of its kind: In just under seven hundred pages, it printed interviews with over eighty witnesses—mostly mill workers, along with physicians and advocates for reform, including Oastler himself.[21] Newspapers sympathetic to reform began printing selections from the report by early 1833.[22] Supporters of the factory campaign linked it with the abolition of slavery in British colonies that would be passed by Parliament in August that year. Yet critics pointed out Sadler's unbalanced list of witnesses and the failure to have them testify under oath. Sadler had planned to reintroduce a Ten Hours bill in the next session, but with the passage of the 1832 Reform Act his constituency in Yorkshire was abolished, and he lost his campaign to represent Leeds against his longtime rival, the Whig Thomas Babington Macaulay, and the younger John Marshall. Lord Ashley (later seventh earl of Shaftesbury) emerged as the parliamentary leader of the factory movement in January 1833, though his efforts to revive Sadler's Ten Hours Bill faltered against Liberal opposition. Ashley attributed his life's reform work to witnessing as a boy a group of "drunken bearers unsteadily conveying a pauper to his grave" on Harrow Hill in London; he took up the reins of factory reform already attuned to how pauper funerals, mass anonymous graves, and the legalized use of unclaimed corpses from workhouses and hospitals for medical dissection under the 1832 Anatomy Act contributed to what Thomas Laqueur calls the erasure of "the poor from the community of the dead."[23]

Responding to criticisms of bias in the 1832 Sadler Report, Parliament established a Factory Commission for further investigation, despite popular opposition from Sadler and supporters of the Ten Hours movement citing this as another stalling tactic. The Factory Commission—this time dominated by leading Liberals, including Edwin Chadwick, who was appointed along with Thomas Tooke and Thomas Southwood Smith to head the inquiry—published its reports in June and July of 1833.[24] Though less critical than Sadler's report and wary of his earlier evidence citing widespread physical and sexual abuse of young factory workers, the Factory Commission agreed that Parliament should take greater steps to regulate child labor. The passage of the 1833 Factory Act in August fortified the previous Factory Acts of 1802 and 1819, setting and—crucially important—enforcing limitations on child labor in most textile factories, not just cotton mills, through an inspection system. The 1833 Factory Act, which excluded silk factories, banned children under nine from working in textile mills, limited children under thirteen to eight-hour workdays (with a maximum of forty-eight hours per week), and youth over thirteen and under eighteen to twelve hours a day.[25] Other legislation followed, including the 1842 Mines and Collieries Act that outlawed all females and boys under ten from working in underground mines. Eventually passed in 1847, the Factories Act or Ten Hours Act limited women and young textile mill workers under eighteen to ten-hour days.

By the second half of the nineteenth century, even devoted Liberals such as Macaulay accepted limited state regulation of child and female labor in British factories and mines on the grounds that these groups required government protection.[26] During the debates leading to the 1833 Factory Act and 1842 Mines Act, however, industrial work did not necessarily signify child endangerment; drawing on earlier attitudes about childhood and child labor, some experts even testified that factory work promoted children's health and morality. For example, in 1816, James Pattison, a director of the East India Company and owner of a Cheshire silk manufactory, employed over 300 workers, including 12 six-to-seven-year-olds, 23 seven-to-eight-year-olds, 19 eight-to-nine-year-olds, and 129 youth between ten and eighteen.[27] Pattison asserted that their health remained "unexceptionally good"; he claimed that even "very young children" working twelve-and-a-half-hour days "enjoy very excellent health."[28] When asked whether factory work was good for children's morals, he offered a succinct rephrasing of Isaac Watts's hymn "Against Idleness and Mischief": "So far favourable to it, if I may venture to say so, that it keeps them out of mischief; and while they are industriously employed, they are less likely to contract evil habits than if they are idling their time away."[29]

While Pattison was not alone in praising the moral value of industrial employment, the dominant arguments in favor of child factory labor linked it with higher standards of living compared with other forms of work. Siding with owners, for example, the influential Liberal economist Nassau Senior argued against regulation on both economic and moral grounds. In his *Letters on the Factory Act, as It Affects the Cotton*

Manufacture (1837), he warned against any further reduction of the sixty-nine-hour week, claiming that to do so would "destroy profit, or reduce wages to the Irish standard, or raise the price of the commodity."[30] He dismissed the charge that factory work was unhealthy, writing that "the exceeding easiness of cotton-factory labour renders long hours of work practicable."[31] Far from being endangered, Senior claimed that the "factory work-people in the country districts are the plumpest, best clothed, and healthiest looking persons of the labouring class that I have ever seen. The girls, especially, are far more good-looking (and good looks are fair evidence of health and spirits) than the daughters of agricultural labourers. The wages earned per family are more than double those of the South."[32] Senior admitted that factory workers in Manchester appeared "sallow and thinner," but he, like Edwin Chadwick and generations of historians taking the "optimist" position, blamed their condition on poor environmental, housing, and sanitation factors—especially within "Little Ireland," Manchester's worst district and home to thousands of Irish immigrants looking for work.[33]

The most extreme defenders of the factory system pressed beyond economic arguments to suggest that factory work was in no way incompatible with emerging ideals of childhood defined by freedom and play. The Scottish chemist and factory apologist Andrew Ure notoriously trumpeted the benefits of child labor. Like Senior, Ure stressed the relatively higher wages of factory work. Furthermore, in *The Philosophy of Manufactures* (1835), he asserted that the necessities of time discipline and mechanized labor brought on by industrialization benefited rather than harmed children's health. Ure claimed never to have seen during his visits to factories in Manchester and the surrounding districts children beaten or in "ill-humour."[34] He wrote, "They seemed to be always cheerful and alert, taking pleasure in the light play of their muscles,—enjoying the mobility natural to their age. The scene of industry, so far from exciting sad emotions in my mind, was always exhilarating."[35] Rather than being incompatible with new understandings of childhood, the factory, according to Ure, became a site for leisure, amusement, even games. Upon witnessing youthful workers, he proclaimed, "It was delightful to observe the nimbleness with which they pieced the broken ends, as the mule carriage began to recede from the fixed roller-beam, and to see them at leisure, after a few seconds' exercise of their tiny fingers, to amuse themselves in any attitude they chose, till the stretch and winding-on were once more completed. The work of these lively elves seemed to resemble a sport, in which habit gave them a pleasing dexterity."³⁶ In his account, rather than succumbing to exhaustion after a day's labor, child workers—Ure's "lively elves"—"began to skip about any neighbouring play-ground" as soon as they exited the mills; they enjoyed "their little amusements with the same alacrity as boys issuing from a school."³⁷ For Liberals like Ure, child factory workers symbolized the literal livelihood of the working classes shown to prosper from industrialization. Thus, for opponents and supporters of factory reform alike, new ideals of childhood characterized by play, leisure, freedom, and feeling carried political meaning; for both sides of the debate, childhood emerged as an essential foundation for the health of the national community.

The 1833 Parliamentary Petitions

One year after Sadler's speech, in March 1833, a group of over four hundred cotton yarn dressers in Scotland presented the House of Commons with a petition demanding the regulation of child labor in factories.³⁸ The workers noted the rapid increase of industrial production and the subsequent dire health and moral consequences on youth. "These evils," the petitioners claimed, "arise from the anti-Christian, impolitic, and un-*British* system generally practised in our factories, of employing young persons of both sexes promiscuously, at labour more protracted, incessant, and debilitating, than what is allowed to be inflicted on the felons in our houses of correction, or even the slaves of the *West Indies*."³⁹ British industrialization left unchecked, they argued, created generations of children weakened or destroyed, bound to suffer from "a lassitude of body, and recklessness of mind, as inevitably unfit them for receiving useful knowledge, or from profiting by the ordinances of religion."⁴⁰ Denied the "exercises and recreations" required by youth, factory children became "not only the victims of crime, but of disease, decrepitude, and premature death."⁴¹ Thus to preserve "the best interests of their Country," the Scottish factory workers implored Parliament to limit the labor of youth "in such manner as will enable them to obtain that education, and secure that physical strength, as will qualify them for being intelligent and active members of the community, to which indeed, as free-born *Britons*, they are entitled."⁴² Freedom from early death caused by unsafe labor conditions, freedom to pursue an education, even freedom to enjoy childhood recreations, were, according to these Scottish petitioners, rights to be claimed by all Britons.

By highlighting the "disease, decrepitude" and especially the "premature death" of young factory workers, the Scottish petitioners sought to justify new uses of the Constitution and new powers of the government to regulate laissez-faire capitalism. They appealed on behalf of "those whose tender years disable them from judging for themselves, or who want the means of resistance," but aimed for grander reforms for all workers.[43] New ideas of childhood shaped the cotton yarn dressers' arguments. They pronounced youth a period that demanded protection and freedom, while at the same time recognizing children as political subjects. The early death brought on by industrial labor marked a form of national as well as personal tragedy. The "anti-Christian, impolitic, and un-*British* system" of factory labor led Britain to the height of world power, claimed the Scottish protesters, but only by destroying its children and the future interests of the nation.

The Select Committee on Public Petitions—which in 1833 included parliamentary luminaries Sir Robert Peel, Joseph Hume, Daniel O'Connell, and Sir Robert Inglis—reprinted the cotton yarn dressers' statement as a representative example of the types of arguments in the fifteen petitions that they received that week calling for factory regulation.[44] Along with petitions demanding the immediate abolition of slavery, stricter Sabbath observation, repeal of the Union with Ireland, and tax reform, those on factory conditions provided a direct—in many cases the only direct—means for Britons to voice their political views. Petitioning, long prized as the people's most direct form of political participation, a right dating at least to the Magna Carta and reaffirmed by the 1689 Bill of Rights, emerged in the 1830s as a principal tool of popular politics. By the 1830s, disenfranchised groups—including women—signed mass petitions in the thousands to call for the abolition of slavery in British colonies and the end of the so-called apprenticeship system, to protest the New Poor Law of 1834, to demand repeal of the Corn Laws, and to support Chartist claims for working-class male suffrage. As Richard Huzzey, Henry Miller, and Ciara Stewart have shown, petitions are essential sources for understanding nineteenth-century popular political movements, particularly the voices of those Britons and British colonial subjects who continued to be shut out of direct political power after the 1832 Reform Act.[45] "During the course of the long nineteenth century," Miller explains, "petitioning was converted into a mighty instrument for mass politics"; petitions provided "an essential mechanism for representation . . . that did not require elections or the vote."[46] From 1780 to 1918, the people of the United Kingdom sent over one million petitions to the House of Commons; those sent after 1833 contained almost 165 million signatures.[47] (Petitioners also targeted the Lords, the monarchs, and local authorities.) Since the majority of adult men won the right to vote only with the Third Reform Act of 1884, and women (over thirty, along with men twenty-one and over) only in 1918, these petitions, even more than suffrage, defined the nineteenth-century British political nation. Miller argues, moreover, that petitions served as the "drivers of democratisation," by providing forms of representation and collective political action open to all subjects.[48]

Though the nature of individual petitions varied by period, topic, locality, and constituency, they developed certain general formulas establishing a genre of their own. Mostly short texts, they typically began by introducing the petitioners' identity; followed with the list of grievances and specific requests; closed with the conventional line, "And your petitioners will ever pray, &c"; and ended with the list of signatures.[49] Petitions generally recognized hierarchical structures through the nature of their appeals, yet also held potential to challenge those very authorities by asserting the power of subjects' will. Topics ranged from the mundane (complaints about loud dog carts) to the utopian (appeals to reform humanity).[50] Particularly on issues such as factory reform, many replicated melodramatic devices that would become fundamental to the child welfare movement, including a clear delineation of victims and villains, rich and poor, good and evil, as well as a foregrounding of the voices of the disenfranchised.[51] Most crucially, petitions stressed the importance of the writers' self-representation of their own experiences as they appealed to the influence Parliament exerted on individual lives.

Beginning in the first reformed Parliament of 1833, the Select Committee on Public Petitions recorded and printed reports. In its final account for that session, the committee drew attention to the increasingly popular nature of parliamentary petitions. The number of petitions they received was "much greater than in any former Session."[52] Many of these were printed on paper, rather than on more expensive parchment—the earlier practice for petitions to the House of Commons. Petitions were becoming a tool of mass political organization. Paper petitions often repeated passages "apparently sent forth from one common source," rather than drafted independently.[53] Committee members expressed concern that countless signatures on paper petitions were in the same handwriting and warned that interested groups may have paid third parties to gather a fixed number of signatures. They recommended that names be joined by addresses and suggested including "some attestation by another party where names are signed by a mark" (following the practice more common among Scottish petitions).[54] These changes, the committee asserted, would "greatly restore the importance and weight of Petitions, without in any degree interfering with the facility and the just right of the people to approach this House at all times with the representation of their grievances and their wants."[55] The petitions for and against factory regulation presented in the 1833 session exemplify this growing reliance on petitions as a form of popular political voice. Of course, Parliament could—and often did—ignore petitioners, but these documents nonetheless revealed growing public pressure for government factory reform based on emerging ideals of childhood and child death.

The total number of petitions and signatures in 1833 favoring factory regulation far outweighed those against. From February to August, the House of Commons received 143 petitions (with 197,063 signatures) in favor of the Factories' Regulation Bill, and 26 against (with 2,815 signatures).[56] Petitions varied in size: The largest in favor of regulation came from Manchester (organized by Lord Ashley with 30,263 signatures) and Leeds (16,336), but several localities (including Huddersfield, Salford, Halifax, Aberdeen, and Fife) also sent petitions signed by only one person.[57] Unsurprisingly, the bulk of petitions and signatures originated from Britain's industrial centers: the Midlands and North West England along with Glasgow and eastern Scotland. Yet districts throughout Britain from Inverness to Plymouth, Norwich to Cardiff demanded action from Parliament (see map 1). Peter Kirby has argued that most public petitions from industrial districts were *against* regulation, but his study is based on petitions related to the 1842 Mines Bill; the situation was very different in the early 1830s.[58]

The 1833 petitions covered the period from Lord Ashley's attempt to revive a version of Sadler's factory bill to the creation of the Factory Commission and the eventual passage of the 1833 Factory Act. Petitioners against parliamentary regulation voiced arguments later amplified by leading Liberal opponents such as Nassau Senior and Andrew Ure. Writing in favor of the creation of the Factory Commission, they rejected Sadler's report as a one-sided, "unconstitutional" attack filled with "grossly exaggerated statements" of "alleged brutalities."[59] They also opposed what they viewed as the sentimental use of children for regulatory purposes. Master cotton spinners from Chester, for example, feared "the legislation upon this subject has been begun in deception, and is attempted to be carried on under an

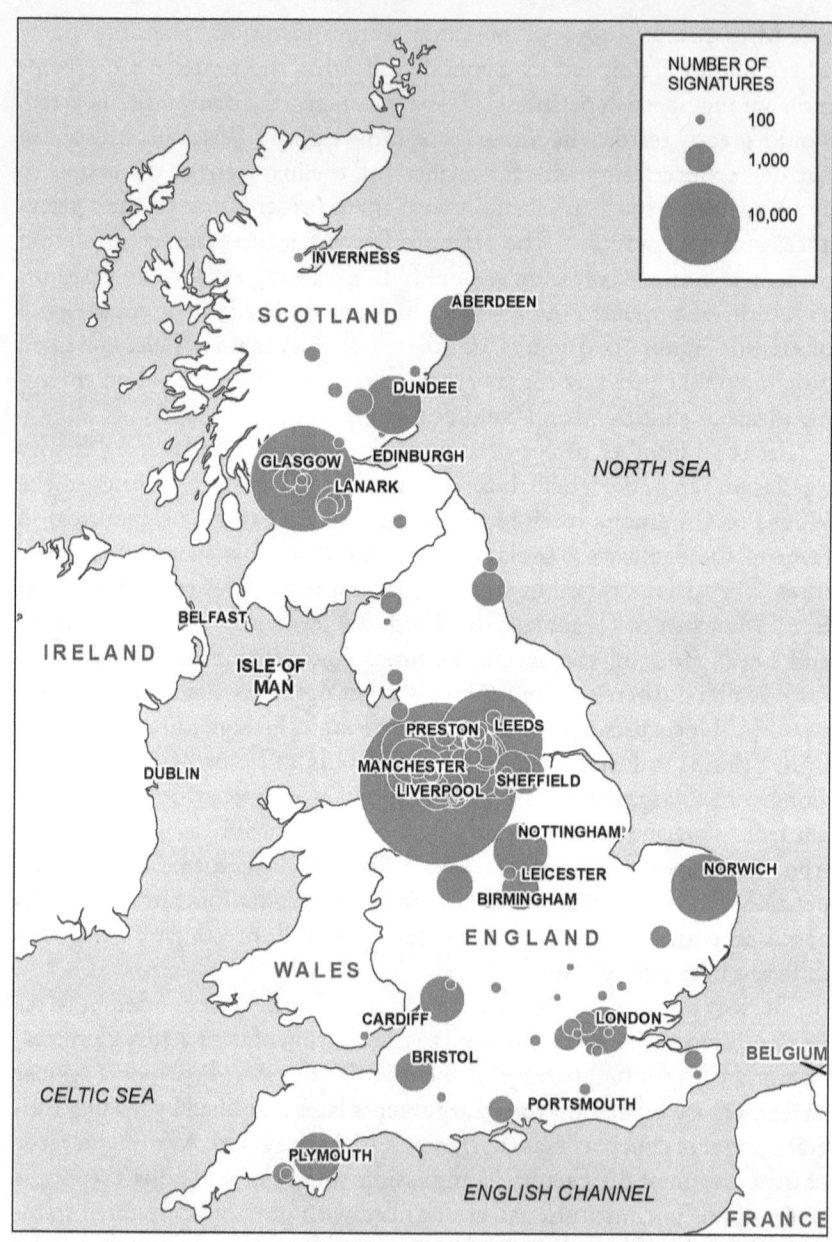

MAP 1. 1833 petitions to the House of Commons in favor of factory regulation. (Neil Curri, Vassar College)

excitement of feelings roused by falsehood and exparte evidence."[60] Limits on weekly hours were unnecessary, these petitioners argued, because employment promoted, rather than harmed, children's health. Woolen manufacturers in Stirling voiced this common refrain: "The work is favourable to health."[61] Likewise in Derby, owners of silk mills attested that girls employed between the ages of nine and thirteen did not suffer from work that they characterized as "very light, easy, perfectly clean, and wholesome."[62] They wrote that, on average, eleven-hour days "are not injurious to the children so employed, but that they enjoy a state of health equal or superior to that which is commonly found amongst the seamers and cheviners of stockings, the menders and tambourers of lace, or any other of the sedentary and domestic occupations usually followed by the children of the working classes in this town or neighbourhood."[63] Another petition signed by eight wool spinners from the border town of Harwick, Scotland, opposed regulation on the grounds that child workers "are not overwrought, that no ill consequence accrue from their light labours, nor are their spirits broken by harsh treatment." Arguing against the proposed bill's fines for industrial injuries, they stressed that "in the very few instances where accidents have occurred, the damage has been owing to the culpable carelessness of the parties hurt."[64]

Petitions in favor of reform painted a very different picture. They generally supported the demands in Sadler's original bill: the reduction of labor to a ten-hour day (with two additional hours for meals), eight-hour limits on Saturdays, and the end of night work.[65] Though they focused on children, they aimed to improve working conditions for all workers. Many opposed the creation of the Factory Commission; they viewed it as a stalling tactic that threatened to overturn Sadler's findings and postpone legislation. In May, for example, delegates from English and Scottish factory districts assembled at Manchester condemned the commission as a blatant attempt by "the haughty oppressor to disguise his system and perpetuate his tyranny."[66] Others scorned the "secret, partial, and unjust proceedings of the Commissioners."[67] They charged Parliament to dismiss the Factory Commission's reports "as unconstitutional, dangerous, and delusive," and to avoid further delay in passing a Ten Hours Bill.[68] Most important, pro-regulation petitioners argued that child deaths in factories neither resulted from individual "carelessness," nor should be treated solely as isolated domestic tragedies according to liberal understandings of free agency. Rather, factory workers' suffering was the natural outcome of a corrupt commercial system that demanded government intervention. Notably, these petitions focused little on the controversial claims of sexual abuse of girls and the beating of youth in factories from Sadler's report and much more on the effects of routine industrial labor.[69] Supporters of reform understood the power of petitions—also called grievances—to amplify workers' literal "crying grievances" in hopes that public mourning might inspire national action.[70]

While historians have critiqued early factory reformers and their supporters for presenting child laborers as simple "victims of avaricious employers," in fact the focus on child suffering and death opened up new avenues of agency and voice for young and adult operatives alike.[71] Certainly some petitions, mirroring the larger debate on reform, referenced the need to "rescue our innocent and defenceless Factory children."[72] Yet overall the petitions recognized the agency of youth as workers and political subjects. Nowhere was this clearer than in the petition signed by 4,332 Manchester mill workers under the age of twenty-one, presented to Parliament by Lord Ashley. These young persons appealed to Parliament by referencing the loss of "all our time and bodily strength" to factories that undermined "our growth ... from our earliest infancy."[73] Industrial labor, they claimed, limited "our constitutional power," "our health and stature," and shortened the "duration of our lives."[74] During the spring and summer of 1833, thousands of youth marched in protests across Lancashire and the West Riding in support of the Ten Hours Bill.[75] Even adult petitioners spoke of their experience as child workers. Petitioners from the New Lanark Cotton Works foregrounded their demands with the knowledge that they "have all of them been employed in Factories from their earliest years."[76] Others emphasized that they wrote "from their own knowledge and experience"; they recounted abuses "we observe, and many of us have experienced"; they detailed conditions they had "long witnessed with sincere regret"; and they testified based on the "evidence" of their "own senses," their "own experience and observation."[77] A group of Glasgow cotton spinners, known for their radicalism, cataloged how "from their own practical experience" the work had ravaged their bodies and souls since a young age, leaving them so "they may be said to exist, but cannot be said to enjoy life."[78] Far from silenced victims, petitioners gave evidence based on their firsthand experience as child workers to supplement the professional witness testimonies of Sadler's report. The language of grief, suffering, and sentiment associated with childhood denied provided the basis for this new discourse. For these workers, personal experience and feeling served as the root of their appeal and argument.

While Liberals identified individual worker carelessness and bad sanitation as the causes of poor health, reformers pronounced the early death of mill workers as a structural national injustice that demanded government action. The pro-regulation petitioners of 1833 returned again and again to the Sadler Committee's medical testimonies from the prior year documenting higher mortality rates among factory workers—deaths that they interpreted in the language of personal as well as national grief and outrage. Along with their own experience, they cited the 1832 Select Committee testimony and written evidence of medical experts (twenty-one English and nineteen Scottish) that ten hours of industrial labor was the maximum that adults could bear, and far too much for children.[79] Petitioners from Ampthill in Bedford County, for example, stressed that the 1832 medical evidence ("so various, so ably stated, so consistent, and so decisive of the present evils of the Factory system"), combined with "the well-attested records of the premature and exuberant mortality of infancy and youth employed in the said Factories," proved that the existing system of child labor was "physically intolerable, injurious to health, and destructive to life itself."[80] Echoing Sadler, the 1833 petitioners asserted that these "premature deaths" demanded public recognition and state action.[81]

The most enraged petitioners went further and leveled charges of murder and infanticide against factory owners, again referencing Sadler and the medical experts from the 1832 report. The physician John Farre had testified before Sadler that in "English factories, every thing [sic] which is valuable in manhood is sacrificed to an inferior advantage in childhood. You purchase your advantage at the price of infanticide; the profit thus gained is death to the child." Farre believed this exchange—industrial profit for infanticide—existed as a system "intended to diminish population" that ultimately endangered the state.[82] Repeating this theme from the 1832 report, Lord Ashley's massive 1833 petition with over thirty thousand signatures likewise condemned the existing system of factory work as "murderous," and concluded by demanding Parliament "put a stop to infanticide, by passing an effective Ten-hours Bill into a Law."[83] A group of Sunday School teachers from the West Riding of Yorkshire also warned that failure to pass the Ten Hours Bill would "bring the displeasure of Divine Providence down upon our trade," since longer hours "grave and skilful [sic] medical men declare to amount to infanticide."[84] Islington residents decried unregulated mill work as "a system of wholesale and yet lingering infanticide, as the most eminent medical men and the ablest physiologists in the Country had previously pronounced it to be."[85] Radical MP John

Fielden, who began working in his father's cotton mill at the age of ten and would go on to join the Chartists and lead the campaign for the 1847 Ten Hours Act, presented the National Political Union petition, from Holborn Hill: "No evidence whatever can justify the toleration of an abuse so crying," they wrote, as forcing youth to work as long as sixteen-hour days; "it is a crime of no ordinary character to endeavour to purchase commercial prosperity with the lives of infants."[86] They denounced the factory manufacture of "slow death," "premature decay," and "infant murder, which in an eastern nation strikes Europeans with horror."[87] The language of murder and infanticide—underscored by reflections on Britain's credibility as a Christian nation and imperial ruler—explicitly reframed millowners' actions as crimes that could no longer be overlooked by the state.[88]

Petitioners' evocation of murder and infanticide not only sought to compel state action in response to individual deaths, but also raised fears about the future reproduction of British culture and civilization. Many petitioners wrote that regulation to a ten-hour day would "ensure comfort and happiness to the children"—qualities they deemed necessary for religious, moral, and civic instruction.[89] They proclaimed new ideals of childhood—innocence, happiness, comfort, protection, and even play—as essential for the creation of upstanding Britons; denied proper childhoods, factory youth would no doubt develop into unruly adults who would undermine the values of the state. Petitioners developed this argument in ways that expressed more or less explicitly the potential threats they themselves posed to future generations. For example, the Glasgow cotton spinners, who wrote that industrial labor from a young age left them unable to "enjoy life," warned that "the whole manufacturing population shall degenerate into the spectral shadows of men and women."[90] Child workers, they argued, "are deprived of all opportunities of acquiring any useful knowledge, in order to the formation of correct and solid principles in after life."[91] Drawing upon Lockean theories, they claimed that child workers' "minds are left an entire blank, ignorance reigns triumphant, and the only education they receive is the vulgar and disgusting slang that too often prevails in all its perfection within the walls of those nurseries of vice and immorality, the Factories."[92] The vicar and clergy from Islington likewise called for the protection of youth "estranged from domestic comfort and controul [sic], deprived of the innocent recreations of childhood, and debarred from all sufficient means of religious culture and the acquisition of useful knowledge."[93] Summing up this common refrain, Newcastle residents expressed their "most heartfelt sorrow" upon the "melancholy consequences" of the factory system: "premature deaths, the early deformity of the human frame, the increase of various and virulent diseases, the engendering of a feeble and sickly race, and the debasement and demoralization of the operative body, by depriving them of time, opportunity, and fitness, to obtain even common and religious education."[94] Not only the deaths of actual children, but also the denial of childhood, newly imagined, promised the moral and intellectual debasement of future generations of Britons.

Petitioners predicted that the factory system's attack on British childhood held dire consequences for the nation. Great Bolton overlookers, carders, and spinners voiced the common concern that factory youth were robbed of comfort and health along with the education that was "indispensable to their spiritual and political welfare."[95] Young petitioners from Manchester similarly wrote that "justice, humanity, sound policy, and the welfare of the State" depended upon factory reform, which would allow them to become "useful members of society."[96] Others stressed that all Britons would suffer if Parliament failed to act. For example, 14,897 Glasgow residents warned of the widespread "present and future ruinous consequences" for "themselves and others" of unregulated factory work that remained "opposed to the precepts of Christianity, the principles of justice and sound policy, destructive to the well-being of society, and obnoxious to the free spirit of the British Constitution."[97] Petitioners thus stressed that factory workers who survived youth embodied a kind of social death for British religious, social, and political values. Simply put, stated Renfrewshire cotton workers, children raised entirely in factories "become useless and ever dangerous members of society," left broken in mind and spirit and "unable, in the case of emergency, to defend their Country against either internal commotion or foreign aggression."[98]

At worst, petitioners forewarned that youth raised in factories would grow into adults who openly turned against the state. A group of 1,237 Owenites developed this argument, centering human rights in childhood and connecting the well-being of youth to that of adults and the nation. They demanded that "human nature should no longer be degraded and abused in the persons of thousands of young children residing and working in Mills and Factories of Great Britain and Ireland."[99] The Owenites reflected on the social and political costs of delay, "imploring your honourable House to consider that society is composed of individuals, and if these individuals are surrounded by demoralizing influences (like those surrounding the poor Factory children) actions of the very worst description must, of necessity, ensue, and consequently society becomes [sic] vicious, unsocial, demoralized, and disorganized."[100] Without reform, they maintained, the people would lose all "confidence and affection" in governors, resulting in anarchy.[101] Petitioners from Staffordshire took up this argument, demanding Parliament pay attention to the "national miseries," "the heart-rending condition" of "the wretched situation of the infant slaves confined in English Cotton Factories."[102] Early death and suffering wrought political rebellion. "The character which avarice and tyranny have thus formed and nurtured," they admonished, "constitutes the basis of a fearful power, which in times of great popular excitement might occasion the most lamentable and destructive consequences": "Society itself may become subject to all the evils of anarchy, as a just retribution of their numerous wrongs."[103]

Yet even as the 1833 petitioners based their predictions of political downfall upon the suffering of children and the fate of future generations, they maintained that child workers were representative of *all workers*—not exceptional. Reformers from Halifax, for instance, warned that "the principles of humanity and justice," as well as "commercial policy," and "the lasting wealth, strength, and happiness of a nation, are incompatible with a system which is not only destructive of the health, the morals, and the social and domestic comforts of *the manufacturing classes in general*, but essentially ruinous to the physical and mental powers of the rising generation."[104] These petitioners highlighted the suffering of young workers, particularly girls, but ultimately concluded that the "evil" of the factory system was *"not confined to any age or sex,"* and that unless owners "are arrested by the strong arm of the Legislature, the community at large must, at no distant period, participate in the fatal results."[105] Other petitions—including those from Bishopsgate and Southwark in London—repeated this language nearly exactly, linking the "happiness of the Nation" to the state of its children along with the manufacturing classes as a whole and warning of the "fatal results" barring legislative reform.[106] The vast majority of pro-regulation petitioners in 1833 sought legislation that would recognize the needs of child workers with the understanding that all workers shared these same demands: limited hours, basic health, domestic comforts, and civic and moral education.

Indeed, the most radical petitioners blurred distinctions separating child and adult workers, while simultaneously drawing upon new ideals of childhood to gain support for all. Along with murder and infanticide, petitioners added theft to their charges against the factory system. Early death and poor health, they argued, deprived children of the only form of property many of them, like their parents, could claim: their own labor. Over one thousand petitioners from Yorkshire, for example, deplored the "lamentable effects produced upon young persons" employed in mills, "by the present unrestricted Factory system, which deprives them of health, of happiness, of domestic comforts, and of that constitutional vigour which often forms their sole property, viz. their power and capacity to labour."[107] Defining labor as a form of property was a recognized rhetorical tactic among radicals—one that the Chartists would take up in their demand for working-class suffrage.[108] This approach emphasized universal injustices, while encouraging intervention on behalf of children. Thus 1833 factory delegates meeting at Manchester decried that "the boasted 'improvements' in machinery have only tended to afford to the wealthy tyrant an irresistible power to grind the operative and his children down to the very dust."[109] They urged Parliament to intervene, arguing that "to refuse or delay the Legislative protection of the property of the poor, which is their labour, during their minority, when the estates of the rich are, and long have been so guarded, would be partial and unjust."[110] Petitioners demanded Parliament act on behalf of children, yet at the same time drew upon language of oppression that questioned how liberal understandings of free agency could apply to any workers, young or adult. Without parliamentary intervention, they claimed, workers of all ages were ground "down to the very dust."

The Factory Act passed in August 1833 largely because of pressure from these now forgotten petitioners. They based their arguments on empathy for the dead and dying factory child, but always underscored the connections between children and adults. Young petitioners asserted their voices as political subjects and workers, knowing—and threatening—that they were destined to become the next generation of Britons. Adult petitioners mourned their own lost childhoods, along with the deaths of child coworkers. The image of the dead and suffering factory child thus served a dual purpose by allowing reformers to make the case for legislative intervention while bringing attention to the generalized suffering of all workers. In July, 795 residents of Johnstone made the point explicitly, writing, "Your Petitioners implore your honourable House to extend the humane feeling now expressed for children, to the hard situation of adults, and for the protection of the life, health, and general comfort of both, to limit the hours of labour for all to ten hours per day."[111] Fully grieving the deaths of factory children required the cultivation of "humane feeling" not only for youth, but also for the lost childhoods and anguish of all workers, along with a reckoning of the national suffering caused by their premature deaths.

Elizabeth Barrett Browning's "The Cry of the Children"

By the 1840s there was an outpouring of poetry and literature featuring industrial child laborers that was informed by the petitioners' campaign of 1833. Like Sadler's "The Factory Girl's Last Day" and John Critchley Prince's "The Death of a Factory Child" (1841), Elizabeth Barrett Browning's "The Cry of the Children," the most popular and successful of these works, is often dismissed as overwrought and sentimental, evoking in modern critics "confusion and even embarrassment."[112] And yet Barrett Browning (then Elizabeth Barrett Barrett) crafted "The Cry of the Children" among the first of her explicitly political poems—a genre many still viewed as unacceptable for women writers.[113] Marjorie Stone traces Barrett Browning's focus on the Corn Laws and agricultural suffering in "The Cry of the Children."[114] While the connections are more contextual than direct, the poem should also be understood in conversation with the 1833 petitions: Similarly to the petitioners, Barrett Browning linked collective mourning for children with the recognition of rights for all of Britain's industrial workers.

Barrett Browning learned of child laborers' testimonies through her writer friend Richard Hengist Horne's work as sub-commissioner for the Royal Commission of Inquiry into Children's Employment, established in 1840 and headed by Lord Ashley. Founded partly in response to the 1838 Huskar Colliery disaster in Silkstone, South Yorkshire, in which eleven girls and fifteen boys ranging in age from seven to seventeen drowned in the mines, the Royal Commission published its first report in 1842.[115] This, in turn, led to the passage of the Mines Act in August 1842 and, together with subsequent reports, increased backing for the 1844 Factory Act and the 1847 Ten Hours Act. Barrett Browning first published "The Cry of the Children" in *Blackwood's Edinburgh Magazine* in August 1843 and included it in her collection *Poems* (1844). Noting Horne's role as compiler of the commission's first report on mines, she wrote to him that the poem "owes its utterance to your exciting causations."[116]

Barrett Browning may have been directly inspired by Horne's report, but her reflections on child death even more closely mirror those of the

1833 pro-regulation petitioners. As in those petitions, Barrett Browning's "The Cry of the Children" brings awareness to the subjectivity and voice of all industrial workers through the grievable lives and deaths of children, girls as well as boys. The poem opens with the assertion that industrial society upends the natural cycles of Romantic childhood: Unlike the "young lambs," the "young birds," the "young fawns," and even the "young flowers," the "young, young children" "are weeping in the playtime of the others."[117] Like the petitioners, Barrett Browning lamented the premature deaths of children, who in her poem repeat, "[W]e die before our time: / Little Alice died last year, her grave is shapen / Like a snowball, in the rime," and "It is good when it happens," "That we die before our time" (stanza 4). The epigraph from *Medea* frames these deaths as murders and infanticides (a theme that, as the next chapter explores, Barrett Browning developed in subsequent poems). Those who survive are left, like the Glasgow cotton spinners, unable to enjoy life, "seeking / Death in life, as best to have" (stanza 5). Barrett Browning also connected the individual deaths of children to the lost promise of Great Britain's future, through its weakened social values and structures. "The old man may weep for his to-morrow," she wrote, "Which is lost in Long Ago" (stanza 2). Much of the poem explores the undermining of Christianity in lives altered by industrial time and mechanization. Drawing directly upon evidence from Horne's report in ways made explicit to readers by *Blackwood's* editorial notes on the poem, Barrett Browning described youth unable to recite the Lord's Prayer: "We know no other words except 'Our Father,'" words repeated simply as "a charm" (stanza 10).[118] Child workers, she claimed, cannot "feel that this cold metallic motion / Is not all the life God fashions or reveals"; unable to envision a Heaven separate from "Dark, wheel-like, turning clouds," they say, "grief has made us unbelieving" (stanzas 8 and 11).

Like the more than four thousand young petitioners from Manchester who demanded parliamentary reform, the children in Barrett Browning's poem are not quiet victims. Rather, as literary critic Peaches Henry argues, they are defiant subjects.[119] Recognition of their words and their pain, Barrett Browning asserted, necessitated national action to restore the "cruel nation" industrial Britain had become to "the country of the free" (stanzas 13 and 1). And although the cries of children represented a more sympathetic subject for Barrett Browning's public, she also, like the petitioners, linked their premature deaths with the anguish and potential revolt of adult workers. The poem concludes with a curse against the murderous factory and millowners who place profit above all else, as well as the nation that supports them, declaring, "But the child's sob in the silence curses deeper / Than the strong man in his wrath" (stanza 13). Empathy and mourning for the child's cries, Barrett Browning proclaimed, were not simply inward-looking distractions, but rather the deepest foundation for political reform.

Contemporary readers readily perceived the structural critique within "The Cry of the Children." Liberal commentators dismissed Barrett Browning's focus on labor conditions, pointing instead to poor sanitation and housing. The *Westminster Review* claimed, for example, that from "Miss Barrett's picture" "it does not yet appear to be understood that misery is to be sought less among the occupations of industry, however repulsive their form, than in the abodes of destitution."[120] Likewise, the free-trade anti–Corn Law outlet *The League* dismissively wrote that "Miss Barrett joins in the mistaken clamour which has been raised against the factory system," stating, "It would be easy to show that the children employed in factories are better off than the children of the same rank in any other department of industry, whether manufacturing or agricultural: they are better fed, better clothed, better educated, more lightly worked, and less dependent on the caprice of masters and employers."[121] The reviewer patronizingly preferred not to "pass heavy censure upon Miss Barrett for having been misled by the factory cry," but generally found fault with the poem's sentimentalism.[122]

Others, however, refused to trivialize and depoliticize her use of sentiment and empathy. Edgar Allan Poe wrote that "The Cry of the Children" "is full of a nervous unflinching energy—a horror sublime in its simplicity."[123] The *English Review* proclaimed the poem was "not to be surpassed for lyrical freedom, and exceeding tenderness, and still more exceeding power," concluding that the poet "is sometimes too weird; rarely too sentimental."[124] Agreeing with the many critics who pointed out the unwieldy rhythm of "The Cry," Barrett Browning recalled that the "first stanza came into my head in a hurricane, & I was obliged to make the other stanzas like it,—*that* is the whole mystery of the iniquity!" "There is a roughness," she emphasized, "my own ear being witness!"[125] British and American reviewers picked up on this "roughness." The poem, wrote *Tait's Edinburgh Magazine*, could not "be read without a choking voice": "The cadence, lingering, broken, and full of wail, is one of the mos[t] perfect adaptations of sound to sense in literature."[126] One reviewer claimed the poem seemed "to be actually written with blood, wrung from the anguished hearts of children"; the result was "a passionate protest against the Mammon-worship of the age, or rather the systematic cruelties to which that worship leads."[127] For another, it was Barrett Browning "herself 'breaking out in a mad moaning'" (quoting a section of the poem describing the dizzying factory "wheels" "droning, turning") through which the children's "awful reality to us, at least, becomes painful."[128]

Elizabeth Barrett Browning envisioned her role as a poet was "to give or rather ... to attempt to give, a voice to a great public suffering."[129] Like the 1833 petitioners, she mourned for child laborers not simply as individuals or as members of families, but as what she termed one of Britain's greatest "national grievances."[130] Their deaths required public mourning, their lives political intervention. Feeling and sentiment for the dying child thus served to inspire parliamentary action. And at this point, in the 1830s and through the early 1840s, public mourning for the dying factory child still held radical potential: Their suffering may have been regarded as more extreme because of their age, but it was nonetheless representative of the larger condition of the industrial working class. "The Cry of the Children" conjoined the "child's sob" with the "strong man in his wrath," just as the 1833 petitions connected workers' premature deaths with threats of anarchy and revolt. In both cases, youth spoke and were represented as political subjects, not mere victims, and public grief gave their voices authority. The focus on child suffering raised larger questions at the core of industrial society about the nature of free agency, the maintenance and reproduction of British power, and the limits of the law and Parliament's authority to regulate industry. As "national grievances," the petitions and Barrett Browning's "The Cry of the Children" presented child death and the lost childhoods of workers not as individual domestic tragedies, but as collective grief. The deaths of child workers and suffering of adults represented an attack on the nation and working people's claims as political subjects. New ideals of childhood extended Lockean claims to the natural rights of life, liberty, and property as fundamental rights of all Britons: the right to health, to leisure and even play, to education, and the right to one's labor as a form of property. Moreover, the focus on childhood, feeling, and sentiment allowed for a much broader spectrum of political actors to enter these debates: women poets such as Barrett Browning, but also young as well as older workers, factory girls as well as boys.

However, the focus on child death to bring attention to workers' "national," "crying grievances" and the iniquities of industrialism did not hold. The 1833 commission marked a shift in sympathy toward Liberal manufacturers based upon distinctions between child and adult workers. As Engels astutely surmised, the 1833 report "comes somewhat nearer the truth than Sadler's," but it "nowhere recognizes the right of the working man to a life worthy of a human being, to independent activity, and opinions of his own. It makes it a reproach to the operatives that in sustaining the Ten Hours' Bill they thought, not of the children only, but of themselves as well."[131] And later, even as Barrett Browning drew inspiration from Horne's report, that document and the debate surrounding the 1842 Mines Act presented a prevailing view of young and female workers as exceptional, rather than as representative of the working class. Instead of focusing on the inhumane working and health conditions that affected miners of all ages, public accounts of the commissioners' report overwhelmingly emphasized moral concerns involving young and female workers. Images of shirtless girls pulling coal carts with chains between their legs and outcry over girls and women "dressed like boys in trousers, crawling on all fours" dominated the press.[132] The resulting legislation excluded all women and girls from working underground in mines, along with boys under ten. Even though women and youth continued to make up a significant portion of the working class, after the 1842 mines report they were increasingly erased from popular accounts of factory and industrial work.[133] At the same time, adult male factory workers more and more based their claims to citizenship upon their role as protectors, rather than cohorts, of children and women.[134] Childhood, a uniquely universal experience, had the potential to unite, but it also all too easily shifted to arguments of exceptionality.

Furthermore, even within the 1833 petitions there were limits to the universal human rights recognized through mourning the dying factory child. As the next chapter explores, Elizabeth Barrett Browning identified industrial exploitation and slavery as two forms of national grievance ravaging Britain and America alike. The 1833 petitioners based their tactics upon and drew support from the abolition movement, but more often than not they appealed to slavery as a foil, rather than as a source of solidarity. Even the Radical John Fielden's petition claimed the life of the British factory worker to be one of "greater endurance and of less comfort" than that of the West Indian slave; the petitioners urged the House of Commons not to delay legislation, "so that Great Britain, whose boast it has been to give freedom to the Negro Slave whenever he sets his foot on her soil, may no longer be reproached with tolerating and fostering a far more immoral encroachment on human rights and happiness, namely, infant Slavery in her manufacturers."[135] National mourning for the deaths of industrial child laborers, their lost childhoods, and the adults they might become marked a potentially radical vision of childhood, one that extended beyond the limits of chronological age and united youth and adults; but the petitioners' radical vision of childhood came with sharp limitations, and ultimately did not persist.

2

"Shrouding My Poor Children"
The Transatlantic Antislavery Campaign

In 1831, a description of what it felt like to be sold by a white West Indian slaver at age twelve appeared in Great Britain: "Oh dear! I cannot bear to think of that day,—it is too much.—It recalls the great grief that filled my heart, and the woeful thoughts that passed to and fro through my mind, whilst listening to the pitiful words of my poor mother, weeping for the loss of her children."[1] Remembering her own childhood, the author described how as her mother dressed her and her siblings in "new osnaburgs"—coarse linen or cotton clothing made to withstand hard labor—in preparation for the marketplace, "she said, in a sorrowful voice, (I shall never forget it!) 'See, I am *shrouding* my poor children; what a task for a mother!'"[2]

The passages are from Mary Prince, who, born into slavery in 1788, fought to survive in Bermuda, Turks Island, and Antigua. In 1828 she was brought to England, where she lived and worked for several weeks at a house on Leigh Street, Bloomsbury, with her enslavers Mr. and Mrs. John Wood, before claiming her freedom. Prince told her life story in *The History of Mary Prince, A West Indian Slave* (1831), the first life account of a Black woman to be published in Britain, a popular tract sold by the antislavery Female Society for Birmingham that reached three editions by the end of the year and rallied support for the 1833 Slave Emancipation Act.[3] Mary Prince's memory of her mother "*shrouding*" her "poor children"—covering them in material as if preparing their bodies for burial as she readied them for violent separation—called attention to the death of children and childhood as fundamental inhumanities of slavery. Grief, loss, and mourning confronted readers as dominant emotions in Prince's

History. She recounted how her mother "mourned over us," how her own "heart was quite broken with grief."[4] Prince's "heart throbbed with grief and terror"; she "mourned and grieved with a young heart for those whom I loved."[5] Yet Prince declared that supporters of slavery acted "without regard to our grief."[6]

Prince, along with other abolitionists, focused on the cruelties suffered specifically by enslaved children in order to gain support for emancipation. Drawing upon the emerging ideal of childhood as a period of innocence requiring protection and domestic care, antislavery activists appealed to a shared sense of grief wrought by the actual deaths of children, along with forms of child suffering caused by slavery that evoked mourning over "lost" or "stolen childhood."[7] This chapter explores how enslaved children's lost or mourned childhood became a major battleground in the fight for abolition. By the late eighteenth and early nineteenth centuries, antislavery activists highlighted the suffering and deaths of children in colonies such as Jamaica, where according to some estimates over half of enslaved infants died in the weeks after birth.[8] Slavery, abolitionists argued, was a particular atrocity against children, who were increasingly understood to require not the rod or the lash, but emotional nurturing and freedom. In contrast to the widespread association of child innocence with whiteness—what Robin Bernstein aptly labels "racial innocence"—that took hold during the second half of the century, early nineteenth-century antislavery activists asserted the essential innocence of all children and proclaimed the denial of modern childhood a fundamental injustice of slavery.[9]

Several overlapping discourses of child death emerged in these antislavery campaigns. Many accounts detailed the actual deaths of enslaved children to stress the complete disregard for the preciousness of child life. Others, like Mary Prince's history, described children's experience of slavery—and particularly their separation from parents—as a kind of figurative death signified primarily by the lack or loss of domestic protections and freedoms that should be extended to all children. Still others presented enslaved people as longing for their own young deaths or the deaths of their children as an escape from slavery. Finally, narratives of enslaved parents, almost always mothers, killing their own children highlighted the idea that slavery was a fate worse than death. Child death in these many forms raised political awareness and sympathy for the abolitionist cause. Descriptions of the suffering and death of unfree children became another example of what Nicole Eustace identifies as an appeal to "emotional sensitivity" as well as the "attendant natural right to liberty" of enslaved people as a basis for political rights.[10] As Hazel Carby has argued, the denial of feelings—particularly grief—among enslaved people was central to the interlocking sexual stereotypes of mistress and slave that upheld the institution of slavery.[11] Establishing enslaved youth's claim to childhood, their ability to feel joy and pain, and positioning them as subjects eliciting shared grief and mourning reinforced their humanity and right to freedom.

And yet, these different discourses imagining the deaths of enslaved children carried very different political meanings. On the one hand, abolitionists' universalizing, liberal arguments for the protection of childhood often promoted narratives of imperial and Christian redemption by envisioning a new future, separate from the past horrors of slavery, carried on by saved or resurrected children. The focus on modern childhood defined above all by innocence allowed many British antislavery campaigners to depoliticize the specific contexts, economies, and structures supporting slavery, and to erase Black resistance. As Bernstein explains, "To be innocent was to be innocent *of* something, to achieve obliviousness"; childhood represented "not merely an absence of knowledge, but an active state of repelling knowledge."[12] Anna Mae Duane elaborates on this point, noting, "The potent image of an innocent child can reduce the complexities of coerced labor to a simple moral equation, in which lawmakers and reformers overlook large economic, social, and legal issues in favor of rescuing individual, appealing children."[13] Focus on innocent children saved in this life or resurrected in the next thus expunged the history of British participation in slavery and the slave trade and drew attention away from the continued violence against the adults these children would become.

On the other hand, however, some abolitionists used accounts of child death to bring attention to the structural foundations and legacies of slavery and to argue for political reforms that would result in true emancipation and equality. Case studies exploring the activism of Elizabeth Barrett Browning—the noted Victorian poet—and Sarah Parker Remond—a freeborn Black abolitionist from Salem, Massachusetts, the first woman to lecture publicly in the United Kingdom against slavery—show how these women protested the death and suffering of children as great injustices of slavery, while at the same time rejecting the more dominant narratives of enslaved children's childhood achieved through limited reforms or heavenly redemption. Through their accounts of infanticide, both women pressed audiences to ask not "How can a society save a child?" but "How does a society come to kill its own?" Both also rejected the modern depoliticizing ideal of child innocence, instead opting to stress the inherent connections between rights for children and adults. All groups politicized childhood and child death, but Barrett Browning and Remond disrupted the links between childhood, innocence, and forgetting as they explained cases of infanticide as calls for remembering past injustices and cause for immediate political transformation.

Within the extensive historiography of slavery, Wilma King was one of the first historians to examine questions of childhood and slavery in her pathbreaking book, *Stolen Childhood: Slave Youth in Nineteenth-Century America* (1995, 2011).[14] More recently, Robin Bernstein has demonstrated how slavery shaped American ideals of childhood, and Anna Mae Duane has called for "child-centered slavery studies."[15] Building on these approaches, this chapter brings attention to how modern ideals of childhood and child death structured the transatlantic British antislavery movement. By the time Prince recorded her memoir in the early 1830s, antislavery campaigners, particularly the growing number of women joining the movement, routinely recognized the suffering and rights of enslaved children in a way that leaders fifty years earlier had not.[16]

The "Inalienable Right of All" to Childhood

The late eighteenth and early nineteenth centuries witnessed major British judicial and legislative challenges to slavery. In the 1772 Somerset case, Lord Justice Mansfield effectively declared slavery illegal on English soil by ruling that James Somerset, who claimed his freedom while living in England, could not be forced back into slavery in Jamaica.[17] More than three decades later in the wake of constant rebellions, the galvanization of the British antislavery movement in the 1780s, and women's first major boycott of slave-produced sugar and textiles in 1791, Parliament abolished the British slave trade in 1807. Slavery continued in British colonies until the Slave Emancipation Act, passed by Parliament in August 1833 and put into effect August 1, 1834.[18] The Emancipation Act granted £20 million to West Indian plantation owners as it claimed to end slavery within most of the British empire, but in fact continued what was to be a system of enforced unpaid "apprenticeship" initially scheduled to last in stages until 1840 in Jamaica and other Caribbean colonies, with the exceptions of Antigua and Bermuda. Children under six years old gained freedom immediately, yet freed children and those born after August 1, 1834, who were left orphaned or neglected by parents could be apprenticed until the age of twenty-one.[19] Older formerly enslaved youth and adults were required to work set terms of six years of forced labor for agricultural workers and four years for domestic servants.[20] Following the Emancipation Act, a revived transatlantic British antislavery movement pushed for the early abandonment of enforced labor in July 1838, after which point British campaigners turned more directly to abolishing slavery in the United States and across the globe.

Before the late eighteenth century, children and childhood tended not to be dominant themes in writings on slavery. Earlier texts that addressed the high mortality rates or mistreatment of enslaved children generally did not emphasize ideals associated with modern childhood: innocence, dependence, and the capacity for joy and domestic affection. Men, not children, remained the primary focus for eighteenth-century British abolitionists. When, for example, in 1783 Olaudah Equiano and Granville Sharp publicized the horrific murder of 132 Africans thrown overboard the *Zong*, a Liverpool slave ship lost on its way to Jamaica, antislavery writers made little distinction between the deaths of the fifty-four children and women taken from the "women's and boys' room" and heaved "through the Cabin Windows" on November 29, 1781, and those of the adult men killed in the days following.[21] In March 1783 an English jury under Mansfield (who ruled in the Somerset case of 1772) decided in favor of the ship owners' request for compensation of lost "property" and ordered insurers to pay £30 for each of the murdered slaves. In May 1783, however, Mansfield reviewed the March case and ruled in favor of a retrial. At the May hearing, the insurers' lawyers, closely advised by Sharp, pressed beyond the limited framework of an insurance claim to accuse the crew and ship owners of murder. Appealing to the Enlightenment rhetoric that would soon be made famous by Thomas Paine, the insurers' lawyer asserted the universal rights of man, proclaiming, "The life of one Man is like the life of another Man whatever the Complexion is, whatever the colour."[22]

The particular experiences of enslaved children remained largely absent from abolitionist texts that underscored the institution's essential inhumanity primarily by asserting the universal human rights shared by enslaved adults—represented most often by adult men. Later accounts of the *Zong* by the formerly enslaved Ottobah Cugoano, who claimed his freedom in London, and Thomas Clarkson described the mass murders with no specific reference to the deaths of women and children, only to those of men.[23] In 1787 Cugoano concluded from the *Zong* killings that British supporters of slavery "either consider them [enslaved persons] as their own property, that they may do with as they please, in life or death;

or that the taking away the life of a black man is of no more account than taking away the life of a beast."[24] That same year, the all-male Abolition Society adopted the Wedgwood cameo medallion of a kneeling enslaved man with the text "Am I not a Man and a Brother?" The image, reproduced on teacups, sugar bowls, hairpins, and other objects became the ubiquitous symbol of the antislavery movement by appealing to Enlightenment ideals as they applied to *adult men*—and, three decades later, to *adult women* with the 1828 version, "Am I not a Woman and a Sister?"[25]

Yet, by the early 1790s, as British women joined abolitionist movements in greater numbers through boycotts and as the proportion of enslaved youth transported from Africa continued to rise, the particular suffering of children under slavery gained attention.[26] British Romantic and Evangelical writers began to focus more intently on the experiences and rights of enslaved children. William Cowper, William Wordsworth, William Blake, Samuel Taylor Coleridge, and others drew attention to slavery through the lens of modern childhood.[27] In 1795 the Evangelical writer Hannah More published *The Sorrows of Yamba; or, the Negro Woman's Lamentation* as part of her Cheap Repository of Moral and Religious Tracts series. More printed several additional versions of the poem, which she reworked from the original by the Scottish poet Eaglesfield Smith.[28] *Sorrows of Yamba* represented the horrors of the Middle Passage from a mother's perspective:

> I in groaning passed the night,
> And did roll my aching head;
> At the break of morning light,
> My poor child was cold and dead.[29]

One of the most widely reprinted antislavery texts of its time, *Sorrows of Yamba* established mothers' mourning for children found "cold and dead" as a main theme of nineteenth-century abolitionist writings.

A further tipping point occurred in 1823 when Thomas Fowell Buxton, vice president of the newly formed Anti-Slavery Society, answered the aging William Wilberforce's call for a revived parliamentary campaign against slavery and presented a motion before the House of Commons for the gradual ending of slavery in British colonies.[30] Buxton had deep connections to the antislavery movement and other reform efforts; he was the brother-in-law of the Quaker prison reformer Elizabeth Fry and father of Charles Buxton, who would later initiate the public inquiry into Governor Edward John Eyre's declaration of martial law and the killing of hundreds of Jamaicans following the 1865 Jamaican Rebellion. Along with banning the flogging of slaves with cart whips and reserving Sunday as a day of rest and religious instruction, Thomas Buxton moved in May of 1823 with the support of the Anti-Slavery Society that all enslaved "children, born after a certain day, ought to be free—free from their birth—never subjected to be bought and sold, and whipped, and brutalized."[31] Buxton argued that enslaving a child from birth was "even a greater crime" than enslaving adult Africans, whose condition he sought to improve gradually.[32] "The public voice is with us," he proclaimed, "and I, for one, will never fail to call upon the public, loudly to express their opinion, till justice has so far prevailed as to pronounce that every child is entitled to liberty."[33] According to this plan, Buxton envisioned that slavery "will never be abolished.... We rather shall leave it gently to decay—slowly, silently almost imperceptibly; to die away and to be forgotten."[34] Children in this formulation represented a break from the past, a blank slate, an innocence linked with forgetting from which could arise a new future supposedly, but never actually, divorced from the decayed remnants of slavery. As was typical of most antislavery reformers, Buxton's appeal to childhood and the liberty of all children did not support social equality. Rather, he envisioned that liberated children would be maintained, educated, and offered religious instruction by the British government, so that "we may raise them into a happy, contented, enlightened, free peasantry."[35] In South Africa and in the calamitous 1841 Niger Expedition, Buxton and his descendants would go on to promote Christian missionary work, commercial agriculture, and trade with Britain as alternatives to slavery in what Elizabeth Elbourne rightly identifies as a rising "conception of humanitarian colonialism that was, at its heart, coercive."[36]

Buxton's 1823 motion, as amended by Foreign Secretary George Canning, passed, leaving the power of execution with colonial legislatures that unsurprisingly rejected Parliament's recommendations.[37] The Anti-Slavery Society's support for ameliorating the conditions of adult slaves and setting an unspecified date for freeing enslaved children sparked critiques from West Indian planters and from abolitionist groups favoring immediate emancipation. After Buxton's effort, however, antislavery campaigners, particularly women, drew even more explicitly on the rhetoric of childhood and stressed the suffering of enslaved women and children. For example, in its first report, the Female Society for Birmingham promised to work for the "melioration of the condition of the unhappy children of *Africa*, till the time shall come, when the lash shall no longer be permitted to fall on the persons of helpless Female Slaves; when our fellow-creatures shall no longer be advertised like beasts for sale, and sold like beasts at a West-India Slave Market; and when every Negro Mother, living under the British dominion, shall press *a free-born infant* to her bosom."[38] Some members of the Female Society independently petitioned Parliament in favor of Buxton's proposal that "every Child born in *every* part of his Majesty's dominions might come into the world the free-born subject of a Monarch," as other British women's groups—including those supporting immediate, not gradual emancipation—stressed the particular injustice of West Indian planters' failure to recognize children's freedom "from the moment of their birth."[39] Through the campaigns for emancipation of British colonial slaves in 1833, the end of the "apprenticeship" system in 1838, and the eventual abolition of slavery in the United States, transatlantic antislavery activists focused their arguments around the ideal of childhood, which they increasingly defined as a right and a marker of shared humanity.

Women's groups began by highlighting the primacy of maternal love for children as a basis for the natural right to liberty and justification for women's involvement in the male-dominated antislavery movement. For example, the 1829 poem "The Negro Mother's Appeal" and accompanying image declared all women's right to keep their children in freedom (fig. 3).[40] The enslaved mother implores the "White Lady, happy, proud, and free" to intervene and prevent the young enslaved child from being taken away and led to the life of hardship and beatings portrayed in the image's background. The separation of mother and child marked a violation of natural laws:

> Though she bears a Mother's name,
> A Mother's rights she may not claim;
> For the white man's will can part
> Her darling from her bursting heart.[41]

The poem demands that white women "plead the cause / Of Nature and her outrag'd laws" by using their "pure, maternal joy" to save the "helpless boy."[42] The accompanying image reinforced the contrast between the two mothers' situations, while asserting their shared natural rights and sympathies. The enslaved mother stands in the doorway, hands in chains in an adaptation of the antislavery movement's newly created "Am I not a Woman and a Sister?" icon. The white woman sits comfortably within

Figure 3. "The Negro Mother's Appeal," *Anti-Slavery Scrapbook* (London: Bagster and Thoms, 1829). (JSTOR Wilson Anti-Slavery Collection)

her home, the table set with tea, while holding her own precious infant on her lap. Transatlantic antislavery campaigners joined Prince in describing children's sale away from parents as a kind of death. "We hear of these unfortunate beings bought and sold in the public market like the beasts with which they are herded," wrote the Ladies' New York City Anti-Slavery Society in a passage later repeated by the Sheffield Association for the Universal Abolition of Slavery; they are "made to suffer a living death by the forcible sundering of all the ties of kindred and affection."[43] Abolitionist songs such as "The Bereaved Mother" and "Gone, Sold and Gone" protested slavery by recounting mothers' grief following the violent separation and sale of children.[44]

The ideal of childhood, along with claims to maternal and family affection, came to serve as a basis for natural rights, most of all liberty. Many writers claimed that enslaved children lacked any experience of ideal childhood: domestic love and protection, innocence, play, joy, and freedom.[45] The American poet and novelist Eliza Lee Cabot Follen, for example, published numerous works contrasting the childhoods of enslaved and free youth. Follen's popular song "Remember the Slave!"—frequently reprinted in British antislavery materials—urged free Christian mothers who lovingly embraced their children, fathers who beamed with paternal pride, and siblings who gathered around the domestic hearth to

> Remember too the poor young Slave,
> Who never felt your joy;
> Who early old, has never known
> The bliss to be a boy.[46]

"Remember the Slave!" defined boyhood in terms of domestic harmony and Christian piety. By appealing to family members in turn—mothers, fathers, brothers, and sisters—to feel the difference and distance between their experiences and those of enslaved children, it inspired action yet also reinforced a salvation narrative. In the end, "Remember the Slave!" suggested that only Christian ministering would "make men free" and enable the boyhood that remained elusive to enslaved youth.[47]

If freedom, love, and joy characterized boyhood, then domestic affection and sexual innocence, along with happiness, defined girlhood. For instance, in their *Appeal to the Christian Women of America* (1836), a text reprinted by several British female abolitionist groups, the Ladies' New York City Anti-Slavery Society reminded Christian daughters of "the mother who watched your helpless infancy, whose unwearied love cherished, and whose counsels guided your riper years" in order to bring attention to "the *slave* whose situation contrasts so strongly with your own." "*Her* infancy," the society claimed, "is without the soothings of tenderness, her childhood without guidance, her maturity without protection or self-respect, existence here is a joyless blank, and futurity dark as vice and ignorance can render it."[48] According to these abolitionist texts, enslaved girls lacked all domestic protection and love; as they aged into their "riper years," they were left especially vulnerable to sexual abuse without a mother's care and guidance. The denial of childhood stripped them of *all* identity, leaving "existence" as a "joyless blank, and futurity dark."

The Boston Female Anti-Slavery Society, the most radical American women's abolitionist group, affirmed the centrality of childhood to the abolitionist cause and human rights in less sentimental terms. In the 1830s the society's African American and white members included Maria Weston Chapman, Lydia Maria Child, and Eunice Davis, along with prominent British abolitionists, such as Harriet Martineau and Anne Erskine Thompson (née Spry), wife of the great antislavery orator George Thompson.[49] The Boston society wrote in an 1839 pamphlet aimed at British and American readers that the "spirit of Slavery, *its life*" resided in the failure to treat enslaved and free children of color as proper children deserving of love and care.[50] Calling for the immediate end of slavery and women's direct political action via petitioning, the writers lamented that the enslaved child was "cast out as a thing of nought," treated with "scorn, reproach, and bitter hate," left to "exclaim with impatient Jonah, 'It is better for me to die than to live.'" "Perchance a cup of sweet is presented to his lips," the pamphlet continued, "but it is quickly dashed therefrom by the hand of one who tauntingly reminds him that such enjoyments belong not to him."[51] The society dedicated itself to the "elevation" of all children by defining the "privileges and blessings" of childhood as "the inalienable right of all."[52]

While white abolitionist writers such as Follen portrayed enslaved children as having little or no understanding of modern childhood, those with direct knowledge of slavery told a more complex history of childhood experienced and then denied. As Wilma King notes, autobiographical accounts by formerly enslaved persons—including Phillis Wheatley's *Poems on Various Subjects* (1773) and Equiano's *Interesting Narrative* (1789)—represent idyllic early childhoods cut short by capture, violence, and suffering under slavery.[53] The importance of claiming a childhood likewise emerged in accounts of those born into slavery. Frederick Douglass, who began his nineteen-month lecture tour of the United Kingdom in 1845, understood the need to state his point directly and with emphasis: "SLAVE-children *are* children, and prove no exceptions to the general rule."[54] In *Narrative of the Life of Frederick Douglass, an American Slave* (1845), *My Bondage and My Freedom* (1855), and *Life and Times of Frederick Douglass* (1881, 1893 revised edition), he described the male enslaved child as embodying the ideal of Romantic boyhood and also detailed how suffering caused by the brutal regime of slavery left children vulnerable and unprotected. Douglass possibly emphasized his own experience of Romantic boyhood in his expanded 1855 memoir partly as a counterpoint to the dominant chorus of transatlantic abolitionist materials, which by the 1830s and 1840s asserted that enslaved youth suffered primarily because slavery fully denied them any experience of ideal childhood. In *My Bondage and My Freedom*, Douglass wrote that he was, for the "first eight years of his life, a spirited, joyous, uproarious, and happy boy"—a "genuine boy," who, like Rousseau's Émile, "runs wild," and, unlike his elite white counterparts, "has no pretty little verses to learn in the nursery."[55] Douglass stressed that, despite enslavers' best efforts, he felt strong familial affection, and that these bonds were part of what defined his childhood. In a key passage, he explained that when his mother, to whom he attributed his "love of knowledge," discovered that he had been denied food, she gifted him a heart-shaped ginger cake and chastised the offender, so that, reflected Douglass, "I learned as I had never learned before, that I was not only a child, but somebody's child."[56]

Yet "my triumph was short," wrote Douglass.[57] His mother, from whom he was taken as an infant, had walked some twelve miles from her plantation to care for Douglass during the night, but she died soon after this visit. From infancy, Douglass had been raised by his beloved grandmother. He remembered his separation from her at about the age of seven as his "first introduction to the realities of slavery."[58] Recalling his mother's death later that same year, Douglass wrote that "*slavery* rises between mother and child, even at the bed of death," as he was denied any knowledge of her illness, deprived the moment of "sacred tenderness, around the death-bed," and left unable to visit her grave, which remained unmarked.[59] In the earliest 1845 telling of his life history most of all, his childhood emerged shaped by the grief of these family separations along with the physical torment of "hunger and cold."[60] By juxtaposing moments of childhood anguish with the overall account of happy boyhood elaborated upon in *My Bondage and My Freedom*, Douglass claimed childhood as a universal state—with no exceptions—and stressed how slavery cruelly refused children freedom, physical comforts, and domestic protection.

While Douglass and Harriet Jacobs, and Equiano and Wheatley before them, recounted childhoods lived and wronged, most white abolitionist accounts presented enslaved youth as fully deprived of childhoods.[61] Where all agreed, however, was that childhood had become a recognized stage of life and, moreover, a universal right—"the inalienable right of all"—long before late nineteenth-century claims about the rights of children championed by the National Society for the Prevention of Cruelty to Children (NSPCC) and other child welfare organizations.[62]

Resurrected Childhood:
"Would Not Death Be Mercy, Compared?"

As childhood took on new meanings, antislavery campaigners cataloged the cruelties of enslaved children, who were not only forcibly stolen from parents and relatives but also beaten, tortured, sexually assaulted, and above all denied care and comfort in their deaths. The pamphlets reprinted by the Leeds Anti-Slavery Society in *Five Hundred Thousand Strokes for Freedom* (1853) sought to rouse readers with accounts of outrages against the very young with titles such as "Murderous Treatment of a Slave Girl," "Murder of an Infant," and "Tender Mercies of Slavery: Treatment of Infants in a Christian (?) Country."[63] Readers learned of a half-starved "girl, about eight years of age," who died following a brutal whipping: The "flesh on the back and limbs was beaten to a jelly—one shoulder-bone was laid bare—there were several cuts, apparently from a club, on the head—and around the neck was the indentation of a cord, by which it was supposed she had been confined to a tree."[64] Such texts freely mixed newspaper and parliamentary reports with fiction that often mirrored experience, as in the account of a dream about an enslaved mother who, when ordered to serve as a wet nurse for her enslaver's son, recalled "my own child was taken from my breast, and soon afterwards died."[65]

Alongside these reports of child separation, torture, and murder, there is another thread within antislavery literature that has received less attention: the often sentimental portrayals of parents, mothers mostly, though sometimes children themselves, mourning a child's impending death or even longing for a child's passing as a merciful escape from slavery. Some actual slave memoirs included death wishes, as when Harriet Jacobs "often prayed for death" to release her and her firstborn child, but these expressions tended to be placed within larger narratives of the fight for freedom.[66] The death wish in these instances served as a survival tactic, a statement of existence, not as an end resolution. White abolitionist materials, however, often imagined childhood death as the natural outcome of slavery and the primary source of comfort, release, and ultimate freedom for children. These transatlantic antislavery materials suggested that without the domestic love, protection, and playful joys of childhood (the very Romantic ideals that Douglass so carefully claimed as his own without overlooking his suffering), enslaved youth had no earthly future; it was in death, rather than in life, that the enslaved child achieved childhood. By reproducing divine childhood as a sort of Christian resolution meant to inspire comfort as well as action, these antislavery narratives suggested that with the intervention of Christian morality and British imperial guidance, the existing social structure could be maintained.

Consider, for example, a woman's handbag from the 1820s, imprinted with the image of an enslaved mother holding her dying infant on one side, and a prose hymn invoking her prayers to God on the other (fig. 4).

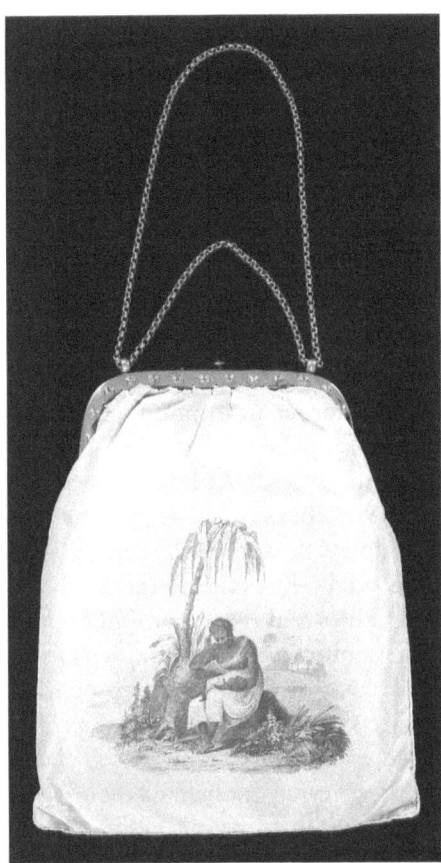

FIGURE 4. Silk abolitionist reticule with image designed by Samuel Lines, produced and sold by the Female Society of Birmingham (ca. 1827). (© Victoria and Albert Museum, London)

The handbag—a prime example of the importance women abolitionists placed on child death and endangerment—was an elite object made from a light blue silk with a silver clasp belonging to the Quaker Rebecca Fox of Tottenham. Commissioned by the Female Society for Birmingham, similar handbags with antislavery texts were given to King George IV and Princess Victoria, along with other aristocrats and the female relatives of leading politicians.[67] The image of woman and child is notably unspecific in historical or geographical context: The mother wears a classical-style dress draped over her shoulder; there are palm trees and a grass thatched hut in the background. The main focus necessarily rests on the mother's grief, presented as timeless and universal, for her child, who lies limply in her arms. The text on the reverse, an extract from a 1781 hymn by Anna Lætitia Barbauld, instructs,

> Negro woman, who sittest pining in
> captivity and weepest over thy sick
> child: though no one seeth thee,
> God seeth thee; though no one pitieth thee,
> God pitieth thee; raise thy voice forlorn
> and abandoned one; call upon him
> from amidst thy bonds for assuredly
>> He will hear thee.[68]

Like the pocket handkerchiefs depicting suffering young slaves that the Boston Female Anti-Slavery Society and other women's groups distributed to "free born, happy" children in order to inspire their "heartfelt *sympathy*" and *"tears,"* the handbag exemplified the growing body of domestic objects imbued with political messages.[69] Although the words suggest that God alone is witness to the mother's pain, the placement of her image on a handbag carried into domestic and public settings—to be displayed, admired, and perhaps debated—links the mother's solitary grief and "voice forlorn" with the sympathies and rising political opposition of women abolitionists. God offers ultimate protection, which extends in the original full hymn by Barbauld from domestic to political realms, from families to villages, from towns to kingdoms and the entire world. Reproduced on a variety of ladies' reticules, sewing bags, plates, and silk doilies, the image and text of the grieving mother and dying child called upon women abolitionists to take immediate action, while reassuring them of their maternal authority based in Christian morality.[70]

During the first half of the nineteenth century, a wide assortment of abolitionist materials popularized representations of child mortality that portrayed enslaved parents not only grieving over dying children, as with the Female Society for Birmingham's handbag, but also praying for the deaths of their children. For example, the poem "A Negro Woman's Lamentation over Her Child" (1829), described an enslaved mother asking God to let her infant die as an escape from the violence of slavery that she imagined as too much for a child to bear. The title borrows from Hannah More's *The Sorrows of Yamba; or, the Negro Woman's Lamentation*, but the emphasis shifts from the mother's longing for her own death to that of her child:

> "But, poor babe! may God prevent it!
> May he take thee shortly home!

>   Not a moment I'd repent it;
>   No!—I pray kind Death to come.
>
>   "Freed from life, thou shalt be blessed;
>   Here thou canst but suffer pain."
>   She said, and wept; her babe caressed;
>   Nor more could say; but wept again.

Ending with a curse on Britain if the country ignored a mother's prayer and delayed in freeing colonial slaves, the poem used the fleeting nature of childhood to press for immediate action.[71] Similarly, the widely reproduced *Appeal to the Christian Women of America* (1836) proclaimed, "As mothers, we feel for her"—the slave mother—"who breathes the bitter prayer as she kisses her unconscious infant, ere she goes forth to hopeless toil, that it may soon die and be at rest beyond the white man's power."[72] Urging women to speak out against slavery, the pamphlet demanded, "What if *man*, not *God*, should claim your first-born, tear him from your arms, bind his tender limbs, and shroud his soul in more than midnight darkness; would not death be mercy, compared with such a doom as this?"[73] Christian death brought by God, rather than man, was understood as merciful salvation from the living death of slavery that would "shroud" the child's "soul." Drawing from this text in their condemnation of the apprenticeship system, the Sheffield Association for the Universal Abolition of Slavery (formerly the Ladies' Anti-Slavery Society of Sheffield) claimed that enslaved "mothers have been known to say, pressing their children to their bosoms, '*We would rather see them die than become apprentices.*'"[74] The 1839 *Annual Report of the Boston Female Anti-Slavery Society* also directed its American and British readers to "think, we pray you, of the slave mother, the innocent gambols of whose child fill her soul with no sweet delight. As she casts her eye forward to his *future lot*, she beholds nought awaiting him, save chains and ignominious servitude. For her boy she breathes no prayer, save that she may lay him in an early grave, where the servant is free from his master."[75] While by far most appeals focused on mothers, fathers were not exempt. Eliza Follen's song "Remember the Slave!" demanded that the public

>   Think of that father's withered heart,
>   The father of a Slave,
>   Who asks a pitying God to give
>   His little son a grave.[76]

These white abolitionist imaginings of prayers for children's early passing suggested that childhood, while incompatible with slavery, could be fulfilled in the afterlife. Christian death brought these children the freedom, joy, and domestic protection withheld in life. In Follen's "The Little Slave's Wish," for example, the boy narrator longs for freedom, a condition that the unsubtle repetition of "little" makes clear should be aligned with childhood. He wishes to be "a little bird," "a little brook," a butterfly, a "wild deer," a "little cloud," yet also a "savage beast" so as to command the power to "shake the forest" with his roar. Thoughts of death ultimately provide freedom denied on earth:

> O, how much better 't is to die,
>   And lie down in the grave,
> Than 't is to be what I am now,—
>   A little negro slave![77]

Another version of Follen's poem published in George Clark's 1845 collection of antislavery songs, *The Liberty Minstrel*, concluded, "My Heavenly Father, let me die, / For then I shall be free."[78] Freedom, like childhood, arrives only in death. Similarly, the American antislavery song from the 1840s, "The Poor Little Slave," reprinted as part of the *Leeds Anti-Slavery Juvenile Series* in 1860, envisioned a solitary enslaved child deprived of parental love, comfort, and sympathy even in mortal sickness. Still, the child held out hope

> That he, at last,
>   When days are past,
> In heaven may have his liberty![79]

Charlotte Elizabeth Tonna, the Evangelical British novelist who also wrote on the suffering of factory children (and the dangers of Roman Catholicism), contributed the song "The Slave and Her Babe" to *The Liberty Minstrel*. Tonna told the story of an enslaved mother willing to suffer lashings for returning from fieldwork in order to care for her baby, who gradually lost the "fulness [sic] from its cheek," the "sparkle from its eye." Upon the babe's death, his mother cries,

> O gentle, loving God, look down!
>   My dying baby see;

> The mercy that from earth is flown,
> Perhaps may dwell with THEE!⁸⁰

Countless abolitionist poems, tracts, and songs like Tonna's imagined enslaved children freed by death, where they joined God and departed loved ones and rejoiced. Antislavery visions of death—specifically Christian death—provided children the liberty, love, and mercy denied in life. Death in this literature marked the moment when enslaved children's *childhood* could be fully realized. This extended even to heavenly play, as in the case of "The Afric's Dream" in which a father remembered his own play in "childhood's careless day," and dreamed of his enslaved son, early dead, who when resurrected likewise "sported in his glee" at last.⁸¹

While these imaginings of formerly enslaved childhood recovered in Christian death reinforced childhood as an inalienable right, they also put off the question of how the rights of childhood might be achieved on earth and what the legacies might be for real children raised under slavery. Visions of divine justice also reinforced British imperial power and racial hierarchies. Moving from empathy to pity in a hymn printed in the 1860 *Leeds Anti-Slavery Juvenile Series*, for example, the "happy English child" sang out thanking God not to have been born a slave, "And wish I were but in the grave, / And all my labour done," but instead placed by God "in this happy land / Where I can hear of Thee."⁸² Rather than, like Douglass, emphasizing the shared natural impulses of childhood, this popular hymn drew upon arguments about the missing childhoods of enslaved children to emphasize difference: the English child's happiness, Christianity, domestic protection, and freedom versus the enslaved child's suffering, pagan beliefs, family separation, and longing for death. The cover illustration for the *Leeds Anti-Slavery Juvenile Series* displayed supplicant adult male and enslaved youth saved from the violence of white male overseers by the angelic, white female figure offering "Liberty to All Men" from above. The overall message emphasized hierarchy and divine intervention more than equal rights and citizenship (fig. 5).⁸³ Built upon the model of the happy *English* child, the ideal of childhood as innocence, a blankness to be filled in and molded, perpetuated narratives of imperial salvation through which liberty was extended to British subjects.

Thus, the antislavery focus on childhood innocence and premature death often prompted abolitionist or ameliorist action, but also fostered a

FIGURE 5. Cover from the Leeds Anti-Slavery Juvenile Series (1860). (JSTOR Wilson Anti-Slavery Collection)

process of forgetting and an avoidance of any fundamental restructuring of the political body that would bring equality or true emancipation. The ideal of divinely resurrected childhood, along with the hierarchical subjectivities it represented, however, was not without its critics. Elizabeth Barrett Browning and Sarah Parker Remond attacked these ideas in their activism as they rejected Buxton's model of a happy free peasantry and instead envisioned a new social order of citizens.

A Curse and a Charge: Elizabeth Barrett Browning and Sarah Parker Remond

The poet Elizabeth Barrett Browning and the abolitionist Sarah Parker Remond both used cases of dying children to gather public support for the antislavery cause. They both also detailed instances of enslaved mothers—one fictional, one real—killing their own children to protect them from the horrors of slavery. Unlike the predominant antislavery texts promising resurrected childhood in the afterlife along with the hope for political resolution, however, Barrett Browning and Remond proclaimed that slavery had created a society completely unable to reproduce itself—in this world or in the next. Their accounts of infanticide called upon the public to reaffirm the preciousness of childhood and the rights of enslaved children, but also to reassess the rights of enslaved and free Black adults. In so doing, both Barrett Browning and Remond eschewed the emphasis on child innocence or unknowingness. Their use of the child was specific and historical, rather than universal and timeless. They understood that children's rights could not be granted in isolation without equal attention to the rights of adults recognized as citizens, rather than imperial subjects.

Barrett Browning was among the most prominent British poets to join the abolitionist cause. Known for her experimental forms and willingness to address political issues, most famously on the condition of women in the novel-poem *Aurora Leigh* (1856), she was both praised upon her death as "one of the foremost poets" of the century and held up as "proof of the impossibility that women can ever attain to the first rank in any imaginative composition."[84] Born in Durham, the eldest of twelve children, she shared in extensive family wealth that came from Jamaican sugar plantations. In a letter to John Ruskin from 1855, she wrote, "I belong to a family of West Indian slaveholders, and if I believed in curses, I should be afraid."[85] Yet several of Barrett Browning's most controversial poems addressed the legacies of slavery and the power of curses: "The Runaway Slave at Pilgrim's Point" (1847), "A Curse for a Nation" (1855)—both originally published in *The Liberty Bell*, an annual fundraising Christmas bazaar giftbook edited by Maria Weston Chapman for the Boston Female Anti-Slavery Society, and included in revised forms in *Poems* (1850) and *Poems Before Congress* (1860), respectively—as well as "Hiram Powers' 'Greek Slave'" (1850) and the posthumously published "An Ode to America."[86]

Barrett Browning wrote "The Runaway Slave at Pilgrim's Point" upon requests in 1845 from Maria Chapman and James Russell Lowell, perhaps along with Eliza Follen, too, on behalf of the American Anti-Slavery Society.[87] The dramatic monologue is told from the perspective of a fugitive slave woman cursing a nation of enslavers and their children at the site of the pilgrims' first landing. The narrator recounts how white men murdered her lover and raped her, and how she then killed and buried her "white-faced" infant son.[88] Literary critics have linked the poem's subject matter to upheavals in Barrett Browning's own life.[89] Surely the poem's themes of slavery, early death, and liberty must have resounded with her experiences: her frequent illness and confinement; her father's refusal to allow her to marry; her three siblings' early deaths, particularly the tragic loss of her closest brother in 1840, which prompted a period of deep depression and prolific writing; her romance with Robert Browning, their elopement in September 1846, and the move from her London sickroom on Wimpole Street to Italy; and, during the period of revisions, the birth of their son in 1849 amid a total of four miscarriages.[90] When Barrett Browning first sent the poem to Lowell in December 1846, she asked that he forgive her late reply and "make allowances for me in remembering that I am only three months married, & in the sudden glare of light & happiness, here in Italy, after my long years of imprisonment in sickness & depression, without so much as the hope of this liberty."[91] And yet, as Sarah Ficke rightly observes, Barrett Browning emphasized the suffering of women in particular without losing sight of "the differences between white female oppression and African slavery."[92] In the same letter to Lowell, she recognized that Britons—including British women—had profited from slavery along with Americans, writing, "I have not forgotten, as an Englishwoman, that we have scarcely done washing our national garments clear of the dust of the very same reproach."[93]

"The Runaway Slave at Pilgrim's Point" was not unique in using accounts of infanticide to underscore the ultimate violence of slavery that pressed a mother to kill her own; Barrett Browning likely drew upon other published examples, fictional and real, of enslaved mothers' infanticide.[94] Her original title for "The Runaway Slave"—"Black and Mad at Pilgrim's Point"—suggests a reference to Wordsworth's "The Mad Mother" (1798). She had also likely read more recent antislavery narratives of infanticide. In 1832, for example, *The Liberator* published "The Slave Mother," a poem included in the "Juvenile Department" and introduced as being based on an 1831 case of infanticide in Kentucky.[95] Unlike antislavery materials exploring a death wish for children, this poem recounted in detail how a mother numbed by trauma took her six-year-old son and two younger daughters to the creek, where she held their heads underwater until they drowned, leaving their cold bodies upon the bank. Although notable for its explicit account of infanticide, particularly for young readers, the poem still reinforced ideals of Christian resurrection and white superiority; the children "Were like the sable night, / But well the wretched mother knew / Their little souls were white."[96] A year before *The Liberty Bell* published Barrett Browning's "The Runaway Slave," the journal included another poem entitled "The Slave Mother." This poem by Maria Lowell, James Russell Lowell's wife, gives no details of actual infanticide, which, if hinted at by the title repeated from *The Liberator*, remains unspoken behind the mother's "exceeding bitter cry" at midnight. Yet in wishing for her daughter's death, the poem's narrator longs to save the "child's pure bloom" from "woman's loathsome doom" and repeatedly prays, "God grant my little helpless one in helplessness may die!"[97] In Lowell's poem and similar works preceding "The Runaway Slave," the dominant account remained one of mothers turning to death, real or imagined, as means to protect the ideal of child purity—particularly for girls threatened by sexual assault and rape. Thus the Boston Female Anti-Slavery Society wrote of witnessing a slave mother "hiding her head in shame at the remembrance of the ignominy to which her womanhood had been subjected," and hearing "the secret prayer arise for death's icy fingers to be laid upon the young brows of her daughters, rather than they should be dishonored by the polluting touch of slavery."[98] Likewise, the Glasgow Ladies' Auxiliary Emancipation Society, which included Angelina Grimké as an honorary member, reported a case of an enslaved mother in the Carolinas killing her children; their captor—also their father, who was preparing to sell the children—discovered the victims slain by their mother, who left them in death "beyond the reach of human wickedness."[99]

Literary scholars, most notably Marjorie Stone and Sarah Ficke, have noted how Barrett Browning both drew upon existing representations of infanticide and raised new tensions unaddressed in the predominantly sentimental works included in *The Liberty Bell* and other antislavery publications.[100] Stone, who has written most extensively on Barrett Browning's abolitionist poetry, emphasizes how in "The Runaway Slave" the poet "departs from convention in representing a slave mother who is also a fugitive and a rebel."[101] Barrett Browning's poem was also unusual for its explicit references to the narrator's rape by multiple white men—causing, as Stone astutely underscores, "'the shame' (not her shame, note)"—and the detailed description of the act of infanticide.[102] More recently, Melissa Valiska Gregory provides a critical overview of Barrett Browning's use of dramatic monologue—a genre for which, Gregory rightfully stresses, "blackface is always waiting in the wings."[103]

What has not yet been fully examined, however, is how thoroughly the poet rejected dominant representations of childhood and child death. In "The Runaway Slave at Pilgrim's Point," Barrett Browning complicated the ideal of childhood as a state of unknowing innocence, even blankness, a site of forgetting and renewal, just as she refused to replicate established narratives of Christian conversion or death and resurrection as the ultimate paths to childhood for enslaved youth. In this regard, Barrett Browning followed Douglass, a frequent contributor to *The Liberty Bell*, whose 1845 *Narrative*, Stone argues, directly influenced Barrett Browning.[104] By doing so, Barrett Browning pushed readers to forgo the "reproductive futurisms"—to use Lee Edelman's term—linked with the unknowing, innocent child, encouraging her public instead to consider the historical contingencies and legacies of slavery, for children and adults alike.[105]

In "The Runaway Slave," Barrett Browning presented an understanding of children and childhood as situated in historical and political contexts, by showing how the violence of racism and slavery formed the life and death of the enslaved woman's child. Born from rape, the narrator's infant is helpless and free from blame, but nonetheless condemned—not by an earlier sense of original sin, but by his heritage marked in the repeated references to his whiteness. Addressing the pilgrim ghosts, the mother declares,

> I am black, you see,—
> And the babe who lay on my bosom so,
> Was far too white, too white for me. (stanza 17)

Rather than describing the child as separate from political conflicts, the poem situates the child as the perpetuator of slavery and racism through a series of associations linking past, present, and future. In the infant's whiteness, for instance, his mother sees the ladies who only yesterday "scorned to pray" beside her at church, and, most maddeningly, "The *master's* look, that used to fall / On my soul like his lash ... or worse!" (stanzas 17 and 21) Furthermore, Barrett Browning called out the deeper roots of American racism by framing the poem as a series of curses against white men and their children, connecting the early pilgrims with their "hunter sons," the enslavers who track down and ultimately murder the fugitive slave mother.[106] As these histories come to life in the look of her infant, she decides to kill the child "to save it from my curse"—a curse that she revokes in the poem's penultimate line—as he struggles against her for "his liberty," "the master-right" (stanzas 21 and 18). Killing her son—the link between past, present, and future—thus disrupts the perpetuation of slavery in that he cannot become the white enslaver. Childhood, for Barrett Browning, is neither apolitical nor ahistorical. The child in "The Runaway Slave" thus cannot offer a vision of heavenly redemption and social renewal, but rather becomes the very site of political conflict.

In relating the child's death, Barrett Browning diverged from established abolitionist patterns by meticulously describing the physicality of infanticide and refusing to reproduce the standard resolution of lost childhood recovered in Christian death. The mother tells the pilgrim souls how she covered her son's face "close and tight" with a handkerchief to obscure his whiteness, how despite the infant's moans and thrashings she "twisted it round in my shawl," until, she says,

> He shivered from head to foot;
> Till after a time, he lay instead
> Too suddenly still and mute. (stanzas 18, 21, 22)

Still addressing the pilgrims, she recounts how "Your fine white angels" "freed the white child's spirit so," but Barrett Browning's description of the child's spiritual salvation refuses to offer consolation through reassurances of resurrected childhood (stanzas 23 and 24). Instead, the slave mother's account of the angels—who, like so many other white figures in the poem, look down upon her with mockery and scorn—underscores the divine as well as earthly violence in this act of salvation. The angels, cries the mother,

> plucked my fruit to make them wine,
> And sucked the soul of that child of mine
> As the humming-bird sucks the soul of the flower.[107]

Far from ensuring an afterlife of domestic protection, carefree play, and liberty, the angels "plucked" and "sucked" the child's soul in a process more evocative of loss, collapse, and suffering than eternal life.

Any consolation that Barrett Browning eventually offered comes not from the white angels, but rather from engagement with the human, physical, and emotional legacies of the violence of racism and slavery channeled through the child's body. While most abolitionist texts end at the moment of the child's death and salvation, "The Runaway Slave" lingers over descriptions of the infant's corpse and burial. The poem's narrator recalls how she "carried the body to and fro," observing, "And it lay on my heart like a stone, as chill."[108] She clutches "the little body," which becomes "My little body," as she makes her escape from "the white man's house" into the forest, so that the child's death marks the beginning of her fugitive status (stanzas 25 and 26). In the forest, by moonlight, she buries the corpse in the blackness of the earth—significantly at a site that she marks and remembers (". . . where? / I know where. Close!"), unlike so many graves of the enslaved.[109] It is this act of burial, followed by union between mother and child through the art of song, that brings measured reconciliation and solace:

> Some comfort, and my heart grew young;
> I sate down smiling there and sung
>   The song I learnt in my maidenhood. (stanza 27)

The particular song, the only one she knows, is important. To offer her dead infant comfort, she sings the song of her murdered lover's name over and over again, the song that she once sang out of love as a girl, the song that she remained unable to sing in life after his murder and her rape. "And thus we two were reconciled, / The white child and black mother, thus," she tells the pilgrims, describing how the "dead child" sang with her from the grave, "To join the souls of both of us."[110] "The Runaway Slave" thus offers reconciliation through art, but only when mediated by attention to the injustices and violence of the past, beginning with the known graves and songs of murdered lovers' names. In the poem's final stanza, the narrator, encircled and killed by the "hunter sons," joins her child "In the death-dark where we may kiss and agree." In the name of her child, she revokes her curse: "White men, I leave you all curse-free / In my broken heart's disdain!" Mother and child are reunited, but, as if directly challenging the scores of abolitionist texts imagining resurrected childhood innocence as the site of restored justice, she remains brokenhearted, tied to the past, her death the result of "liberty's exquisite pain" (stanza 36).

Like Thomas Buxton's parliamentary proposal to free enslaved children while leaving the underlying economic and political structures of slavery intact, most abolitionist accounts of resurrected childhood garnered sympathy for enslaved families and the abolitionist cause, but did little to address the question of how to rebuild a post-emancipation society. By having the narrator of "The Runaway Slave" kill her child, by rejecting the typical account of childhood resurrection, and by stressing that reconciliation must first be dependent upon recognition of past racial violence and injustices, Barrett Browning began to call for transformative politics that no longer reproduced the pilgrims' line of "hunter sons" through the enslaved woman's own would-be-master-child. In examples of personal and political actions, the poem suggests how infanticide might provide a metaphor for such transformation. In the first parts of the poem, the narrator suffers from the scorn of others: church ladies, the white angels, even God and "His white creatures" (stanza 4). However, directly following the description of the child's burial, the fugitive slave mother takes on the powers of rebel warrior, forcing the pilgrim ghosts to flee: "My face is black, but it glares with a scorn / Which they dare not meet by day" (stanza 29). She calls out the hypocrisy of American liberty, pointing to the rope marks scarring her wrists. The shift in perspective that allows her to judge rather than be judged (echoed in the poem's last words, "my broken heart's disdain!") comes with her political call to action for slave rebellion: "lift your hands, / O slaves, and end what I begun! // Whips, curses; these must answer those!"[111] She ultimately revokes her curse, but only after establishing through the act of infanticide that abolition required a reckoning with the past and structural social transformation in order to be successful.

Barrett Browning knew that "The Runaway Slave" pushed the conventions of abolitionist writing, even within the context of the heightened Garrisonian rhetoric of *The Liberty Bell*. Sending the finished poem to Lowell, she claimed to have written it for the sake of both "American honour" and "general mercy & right," anticipating that "perhaps you will think too bitterly & passionately for publication in your country."[112] She also confided to her mentor Mary Russell Mitford, "Nobody will print it, I am certain, because I could not help making it bitter. If they *do* print it, I shall think them more boldly in earnest, than I fancy now."[113] Elsewhere, in a letter to the American writer Cornelius Mathews, Barrett Browning speculated the poem "will never be printed in America, or will, if it should be, bring the writer into a scrape of disfavor. But I did only write conscientiously, you know, in writing at all; and my 'Cry of the Children' was not less written against my own country."[114]

Despite these doubts, Maria Chapman and her sisters praised "The Runaway Slave" as a "distinguished" addition to *The Liberty Bell*.[115] Barrett Browning's critics, however, proved more mixed, responding mainly to the revised version that she included in her *Poems* (1850). In this two-volume collection, Barrett Browning wished to place "The Runaway Slave" next to "The Cry of the Children," she explained to Mitford, in order "to appear impartial as to national grievances."[116] While the *Eclectic Review* hailed Barrett Browning for the "strength of her genius" and quoted large passages from "The Runaway Slave," the *Literary World* published from New York objected in particular to the poem, proclaiming that she would have done better to keep to the "more proper and more truly poetical theme" exhibited in "A Dead Rose."[117] Barrett Browning valued poetry as a means to engage a variety of pressing political debates in addition to slavery: the Corn Laws, child labor, women's rights, and Italian Unification. However, late-nineteenth- and twentieth-century literary critics tended to rebuke or completely overlook her political poems. More renowned as a poet in life than her husband, in death she became primarily known for her love poems as his fame overshadowed hers. "By 1931," notes Marjorie Stone, Barrett Browning's "reputation had sunk so low that Virginia Woolf sardonically described her as relegated to the 'servants' quarters' in the 'mansion of literature.'"[118] Only with the feminist movement of the 1970s did scholars return to *Aurora Leigh* as a major text of its time, and, in the following decades, begin to engage the complexities of "The Runaway Slave at Pilgrim's Point."

Elizabeth Barrett Browning's poetry did, however, find a sympathetic reader in Sarah Parker Remond and other Black abolitionists. Remond, who toured the antislavery lecture circuit in the United Kingdom from 1859 to 1866, had read Barrett Browning's poems and recommended them to the young Charlotte Forten, who lived with Remond's brother in Salem, Massachusetts.[119] Reflecting on "The Runaway Slave at Pilgrim's Point," Forten wrote in her journal, "How powerfully it is written! how earnestly and touchingly does the writer portray the bitter anguish of the poor fugitive as she thinks over all the wrongs and sufferings that she has endured, and of the sin to which tyrants have driven her but which they alone must answer for!"[120] Remond became a naturalized British citizen in 1865, but like Barrett Browning, she eventually moved from London to Florence.[121] In 1887 Frederick Douglass visited Remond in Rome, where she had taken up residence in the mid-1880s. In Florence he also paid his respects to the graves of Barrett Browning and the American abolitionist preacher Theodore Parker "first thing," noting that the "soul of each was devoted to liberty."[122] Although Barrett Browning was almost twenty years older than Remond, they worked in overlapping social circles of reformers dedicated to abolition, women's rights, and Italian Unification, including Maria Weston Chapman, Harriet Martineau, Harriet Beecher Stowe, Clementia Taylor, Frances Power Cobbe, and Fanny Kemble.

Like Barrett Browning, Remond underscored the human destruction of slavery, particularly for women, and the need for a new political foundation in slave and free states through her discussion of rape and infanticide. Unlike the poet, however, Remond drew directly from contemporary events. She presented the actual case of the fugitive slave Margaret Garner, who in 1856 killed her eldest, two-year-old daughter, rather than have her captured and returned to slavery. Similar to the child in "The Runaway Slave," Garner's daughter was described as "nearly white" in complexion.[123] In moving from the abstract to the specific lived experience, Remond's retelling of Garner's infanticide revealed the "ethics of survival"—what Stone, in her discussion of Toni Morrison's 1987 novel *Beloved*, based on Garner's case, defines as "an aesthetic and an ethics complex enough to encompass the appalling contradictions that slavery imposed on people's lives."[124] To a much more detailed extent than Barrett Browning, Remond also outlined the specific political transformation essential to create a world in which a mother would not feel forced to kill her own. Unlike so many contemporary depictions of enslaved children's suffering and death that offered resolution through narratives of childhood reclaimed by way of Christian resurrection or imperial assimilation, Remond explained Garner's infanticide as the outcome of sexual violence and political injustice, linking the suffering of children to the historical denial of personhood. A vital voice in feminist and abolitionist circles, Remond also demonstrated the transatlantic, transnational nature of nineteenth-century debates about human rights and ultimately suggested the limitations of seeking to secure these rights through claims to national or imperial citizenship.

Born in Salem, Massachusetts, in 1826, Remond was the second youngest of eleven children, three of whom died in childhood.[125] Her parents, freeborn members of the Black middle class, were prominent abolitionists; her father, John Remond, came to America from Curaçao as a child, and her mother, Nancy Lenox, was a second-generation free Black American, whose father had fought in the Revolutionary Army.[126] Sarah Remond's brother, Charles Lenox Remond, one of the most widely known antislavery lecturers of the period, traveled as a delegate to the 1840 World Anti-Slavery Convention in London, where he and William Lloyd Garrison objected to the exclusion of female delegates from the conference floor and sat with the women in the balcony.[127] Sarah Remond trained with her brother as a lecturer for the American Anti-Slavery Society. She delivered her first public lectures in 1856 and continued speaking before American and Canadian audiences until she sailed for England on December 29, 1858.[128] Using London as a base for her lecture tours, she studied for two years at Bedford College (the first British higher education college for women, established in 1849) and lived with the college's founder, Elizabeth Jesser Reid, who was also active in the abolition movement and had hosted Harriet Beecher Stowe during her 1853 visit to England.[129] Remond later trained as a nurse at All Saints University College Hospital and resided for a time with Clementia (Mentia) and Peter Taylor (MP for Leicester, 1862–84), whose London residence, Aubrey House, provided a center for radical and feminist politics.[130] Remond joined the Freedmen's Aid Association, founded by Mentia Taylor in 1861, and in 1863 became a founding executive committee member of the Ladies' London Emancipation Society, the first national British women's antislavery organization, whose other board members included Mentia Taylor (as honorary secretary), Frances Power Cobbe, Mary Estlin, Margaret Bright Lucas, Charlotte Manning, Carolyn Ashurst Stansfeld, and Harriet Martineau. In 1866 Remond was one of the 1,499 women who signed the women's suffrage petition presented by John Stuart Mill to Parliament.[131] That August, she left London to travel through Switzerland and Italy, where she eventually settled in Florence, studied medicine at the Santa Maria Nuovo Hospital, and became a practicing physician specializing in obstetrics.[132] After marrying Lazario Pintor in 1877, Remond moved from Florence to Rome. Joined by her two sisters and a close circle of friends and expatriate cohorts, including the African American and Ojibwe sculptor Edmonia Lewis, she qualified as a surgeon and lived in Rome until her death in 1894.[133]

Reflecting on her decision to leave America for England in 1858, Remond wrote that she desired to "visit England, that I might for a time enjoy freedom, and I hoped to serve the anti-slavery cause at the same time."[134] There she joined the campaigns of other freeborn and formerly enslaved Black abolitionists, including Douglass, William Wells Brown, Henry "Box" Brown, William G. Allen, and Ellen and William Craft.[135]

Remond became the first woman to lecture publicly before large audiences for emancipation, although Ellen Craft had written for the cause and offered brief comments when she appeared with her husband and William Wells Brown.[136] After delivering her first lecture at Liverpool's Tuckerman Institute in January 1859, Remond continued her tour throughout the United Kingdom, including visits to Warrington, Dublin and the south of Ireland, London, Bristol, Manchester, Leeds, Edinburgh, and Glasgow.[137] Remond stressed that "she appeared as the agent of no society," "but that in feeling and in principle she was identified with the Ultra-abolitionists of America," the "moral suasion abolitionists," led by Garrison and Wendell Phillips, who argued that ending slavery "could not and ought not to be subordinated to any political schemes or party movements whatever."[138] Donations solicited after her speeches supported various organizations, including the American Anti-Slavery Society and the Boston Female Anti-Slavery Society. She lectured for up to an hour and a half and was typically received with "loud and enthusiastic applause."[139] Reports of Remond's speeches praised her feminine qualities—her "great calmness and self-possession"; her "clear musical voice"; her "pleasing," "remarkably feminine and graceful" appearance; and "her ladylike exterior"—while also noting the rarity of a woman speaking publicly before such crowds.[140] The Liverpool *Daily Post*, for example, reported that the "novelty of a lecture by a lady drew a very large attendance."[141] On January 24, 1859, supporters were turned away from Remond's overcrowded lecture at the Music Hall in Warrington.[142] In November the *Bury Times* wrote that Remond brought "an overflowing audience" with "hundreds of persons seeking in vain to gain admission. The pressure was so great that several persons had to be taken out of the room in a fainting condition."[143] Members of the Mechanics' Institute, "working men and factory operatives," students and abolitionists came to hear Remond speak throughout Yorkshire as she made stops in Leeds, Wortley, Bramley, Hunslet, Barnsley, and Morely.[144] Over two thousand people, with more turned away, attended her Ladies' Emancipation Society lecture at Edinburgh's Brighton Street Chapel as she continued working the lecture circuit in the autumn of 1860.[145] Despite the holiday season and "the almost impassable condition of the streets," some six hundred people assembled at her December Edinburgh lecture, and the crowds continued to come as she spoke at Harwick, Glasgow, Dumfries, Carlisle, and Ulverstone.[146]

Remond, more than any other Black abolitionist speaker touring the United Kingdom in the 1850s and 1860s, brought attention to the particular

FIGURE 6. Sarah Parker Remond, ca. 1865. (Courtesy of Peabody Essex Museum)

suffering of enslaved women and children. In her very first lectures before English audiences, Remond used the case of Margaret Garner's infanticide to illustrate the "horrors of American slavery," establishing a thematic structure for her speeches that she returned to repeatedly through the early 1860s.[147] Speaking at the Warrington Music Hall in January 1859, Remond asked the men and women before her, "Who could give the faintest idea of what the slave mother suffered?"[148] In January 1856, Garner had escaped from northern Kentucky along with her husband, his parents, and the young couple's four children, who ranged in ages from nine months to almost six years old.[149] They reached Cincinnati by traveling across the frozen Ohio River, but were found the next morning by slave catchers at the home of relatives. After armed conflict, during which Garner ultimately used a butcher knife to cut her eldest daughter Mary's throat, the survivors were eventually confined to slavery in Kentucky under the Fugitive

Slave Act of 1850.[150] In her discussion of Garner and in other lectures, Remond, like Barrett Browning, identified the particular suffering of enslaved women from institutionalized rape as well as from the common practice of taking and selling any surviving children. Garner, she stressed at the Warrington Music Hall and before later audiences, "was born a slave, and had suffered in her own person the degradation that a woman could not mention." Describing Garner's tragic flight to Cincinnati, Remond continued:

> There she stood amidst magnificent temples dedicated to God on either hand, but no sympathy or help was afforded her. The slaveholder found her; as he appeared at the door she snatched up a knife and slew her first-born child [sic daughter Mary], but before the poor frenzied creature could proceed further in her dread object, the hand of the tyrant was on her, when she called to the grandmother of the children to kill the others, as she preferred to return them to the bosom of God rather than they should be taken back to American slavery.

"Margaret Garner," asserted Remond, "would rather that her children should suffer death than be left in the hands of such beings as she had been describing."[151] Two years later, before her audience at Chesterfield, Remond declared Garner's infanticide an act of maternal protection. Garner "knew what slavery was, especially to woman," said Remond, "and sooner than her children should become its victims, her very love as a mother compelled her to take their life."[152]

Like Barrett Browning, Remond placed the blame for Garner's infanticide on the tyrannical system of slaveholding upheld for generations by American political institutions, laws, and churches—a conclusion that she reinforced by rejecting to an even greater extent than Barrett Browning the typical narrative of childhood restored in death. In her account of infanticide, Remond offered no lingering thoughts on what peace Garner's daughter might find in God's care, beyond the brief mention of the child returning to "the bosom of God," a biblical phrasing that asserted unity with God while reinforcing Garner's earthly maternal loss. Remond's speeches did not reflect upon domestic union, restored innocence, or justice in the afterlife. Instead, she returned to the still living Margaret Garner and the denial of humanity under slavery. Remond recounted how Garner was "returned to slavery under the Fugitive Slave Law," treated, according to the law, as "chattel!" "She was a thing!" exclaimed Remond. "Yes, every slave below Mason and Dixon's line was a thing!"[153]

Remond framed the account of Garner's rape, her escape, and the tragic death of her daughter so as to link directly the death of this child to structural inequality: the failure of America to grant enslaved people—and free Black men and women—equal rights as fellow humans and American citizens. In her speeches from the winter and spring of 1859, Remond opened by stating that she spoke as "the representative of a race that was stripped of every right and debarred from every privilege—a race which was deprived of the protection of the law, and the glorious influences of religion, and all the strong ties and influences of social life."[154] She explained the effects of the *Dred Scott* Supreme Court decision of 1857, which held that "descendants of the African race, varying in complexion from black to white[,] ... were deprived of every privilege as citizens."[155] Later, in her April 1861 Chesterfield lecture, Remond transitioned directly from Garner's case to reading passages from the slave code "to show with what relentlessness slavery aimed to divest its victims of all human rights," building upon the examples just preceding her account of Garner of enslaved and free Blacks denied their rights under the law, as well equal access to schools, hotels, theaters, and omnibuses.[156] Elsewhere she attacked the unequal treatment of Black Americans in churches, prisons, trades, and businesses.[157] In sum, by framing Garner's infanticide in the context of such all-pervasive violence and discrimination, Remond called for equal rights, citizenship, due process, and social equality. She outlined the depth of work to be done and the legacies of violence, countering Thomas Buxton's vain hope of an earlier generation that saving children in this life or the next might leave slavery "to die away and to be forgotten."

Remond also paired her call for political transformation with a threat and a curse, echoing Barrett Browning. Remond proclaimed that "'liberty or death' was the motto of the American slave"; for her part, Garner was "determined to be free or die in the attempt."[158] Remond reminded her listeners, "There were insurrections taking place constantly on the plantations, and the masters had to go about armed." Although she supported moral persuasion, she believed these rebellions to be justified, stating, "If any class of persons in this world had a right to take their freedom by force it was the slaves."[159] Near the end of her speech, she predicted, "The result of American slavery was this, that the great American republic was destined to be sundered. She thanked God for it. It would be severed, and no power could save it unless a sentiment could be created in the northern mind which would overrule the antagonism of the south."[160]

By appealing to "sentiment" as the antidote to bloodshed, Remond reiterated her belief in human sympathy, which she appealed to most powerfully in the case of Margaret Garner and the death of her child. Like Mary Prince, Remond understood the failure to sympathize with another's grief as a root cause of modern slavery. Sold from her mother, Prince demanded, "Did one of the many by-standers, who were looking at us so carelessly, think of the pain that wrung the hearts of the negro woman and her young ones? No, no! They were not all bad, I dare say, but slavery hardens white people's hearts towards the blacks; and many of them were not slow to make their remarks upon us aloud, without regard to our grief—though their light words fell like cayenne on the fresh wounds of our hearts."[161] Similar to Prince, Remond typically began and ended her lectures with direct appeals for sympathy. And following her third Warrington lecture, women representatives at the Red Lion Hotel offered Remond a gift as "a slight expression of their sympathy and esteem." The women bestowed on Remond a watch, engraved, "Presented to S. P. Remond by Englishwomen, her sisters, in Warrington." Remond acknowledged, "I have been received here as a sister by white women for the first time in my life. I have been removed from the degradation which overhangs all persons of my complexion; and I have felt most deeply that since I have been in Warrington and in England that I have received a sympathy I never was offered before." Remond's understanding of sympathy and sisterhood did not erase differences between Black and white women, but rather served as an occasion to reassert her dedication to women of color. Accepting the watch, she proclaimed, "I receive it as the representative of my race with pleasure. In this spirit I accept it, and I believe I shall be faithful to that race now and for ever."[162]

As childhood took on new meanings at the turn of the nineteenth century, antislavery campaigners came to stress the particular sufferings of enslaved children. They argued that all children, regardless of race, could claim the rights of childhood: domestic love and protection, play, happiness, freedom, innocence. Many white abolitionists suggested that, denied childhood in life, enslaved children might realize childhood in death. Scores of songs, poems, and children's stories imagined enslaved children saved in death and granted childhood by a merciful Christian God. Such accounts raised sympathy for the antislavery cause, but focusing on the ideal of resurrected childhood suggested that the political body founded on slavery, too, might be salvaged. In these accounts of childhood granted through death, the ideal of childhood allowed antislavery reformers to avoid questions about the continued inequalities facing enslaved and free Black adults. Childhood thus served as a basis for establishing shared human rights, but also as an impetus for forgetting injustices past and present.

Unlike most antislavery narratives, however, the deaths of children recounted by Barrett Browning and Remond were unequivocally violent deaths—not simply longed-for deaths that brought divine justice through restored childhood, but deaths described in physical detail before their audiences, deaths that rejected the depoliticized, ahistorical use of childhood innocence. Their accounts, while grounded in Christian morality, evaded divine or imperial resolutions. Barrett Browning and Remond linked their appreciation of child life with the human rights of citizenship. Thus, their histories of infanticide underscored the need to name past injustices and fully grant equal rights to adults, as well as children, in order to enact true emancipation. Perhaps unsurprisingly, Barrett Browning's and Remond's more complex appeals to the preciousness of child life and their more radical visions of social justice were for a long time forgotten. Like Mary Prince, who disappeared from the historical record after 1833, and Barrett Browning, remembered for a period primarily for her love poems, Remond has only recently begun to enter into histories of the abolition movement.

Remond valued the "sisterhood" and rights she experienced in England enough to become a naturalized British citizen in 1865.[163] British citizenship offered Remond legal recognition and civil liberties. Her British status provided a stark contrast to the American Embassy's earlier denial of her U.S. citizenship in November 1859, along with her access to a U.S. passport and visa for travel from Britain to France; the U.S. official who rejected her visa application argued that under the *Dred Scott* decision she could not claim the rights of an American citizen because of her race.[164] However, despite the relative freedom Remond experienced in the United Kingdom, she left England in August 1866 for Italy after publicly denouncing the rising tide of British imperial racism that she witnessed during the Civil War and in the aftermath of the 1865 Jamaican Rebellion.[165] Remond reminded readers of the London *Daily News* that Governor Eyre's brutal, indiscriminate violence against Jamaicans—including the killing of over four hundred people, mass floggings, and property destruction—directly contradicted the fundamental ideal upheld in the 1772 Somerset case: that all people, regardless of color, should claim equal protection of the law. From Florence, she highlighted the dangers of "slavery in the past and its hateful remnants in the present" as she condemned

Eyre's defender Thomas Carlyle, "the literary leader of public opinion," for inciting "a feeling of hatred towards the coloured race ... in the minds of many Englishmen."[166] But Remond's protest remained a minority voice even as John Stuart Mill and others debated Eyre's actions in Parliament and called for him to be charged with murder.[167]

Before leaving for Italy, Remond joined her hosts Peter and Mentia Taylor in a discussion with other prominent social reformers, including Frances Power Cobbe and Mary Carpenter, on the question, "What *is* the great cause of the age?" "Parliamentary Reform?" "Teetotalism?" "Women's Suffrage?" "The conversion of the world to Theism?" "Why! The Industrial Schools Bill *of course!*" Only Remond singled out for continued urgency the "Abolition of Slavery."[168] Nonetheless, as a woman of many countries, she sought to maintain her ties to Britain. Later, from Italy, where Remond established her career as an obstetrician and built the social networks of a global citizen, she petitioned every six months to keep her British citizenship—a request that the British Home Office finally declined in December 1868, underscoring the tenuous claims of citizenship and the limits of the nation, particularly the imperial nation, as a foundation for human rights.[169]

3

"Suppressed Grief"

Mourning the Death of British Children and the Memory of the 1857 Indian Rebellion

KATHERINE BARTRUM, a twenty-three-year-old woman from Somerset, had been living in India for less than a year with her husband, Robert, an assistant surgeon, when the Indian Rebellion began in May of 1857.[1] In June, Bartrum and her infant son joined other British women and children in leaving the military station at Gonda for the Residency buildings in Lucknow. She remained there during what became known as the siege of Lucknow. In the following months, she suffered the death of her husband in combat and nursed her son through cholera. When the siege ended in November 1857, Bartrum traveled with other British survivors to Calcutta, where her son, Bobbie, died days before she set sail alone for England. For Bartrum and many other British participants in the Great Rebellion, the deaths of family members, particularly children, revealed not only the violence at the heart of empire but also the ultimate instability of British domestic life and identity within the imperial context. During the worst moments of the conflict, the frequency of child death and the inability to mourn these deaths suggested a collapse of the domestic sphere as an idealized place of protection and training for elite British children being raised to become the next generation of imperial rulers.

Like many other Britons in India, Katherine Bartrum sought, and sometimes struggled, to experience the deaths of her husband and son according to British, middle-class understandings of death. In the relative safety of Calcutta following her escape from Lucknow, Bartrum recorded her attempts to mourn her son's death in line with British practices in her memoir, letters, and an 1858 published account. With the aid of her companion, Emmie Polehampton, the "Florence Nightingale of Lucknow" and widow of the Lucknow chaplain, Bartrum reconstructed the elaborate rituals of the Christian "good death."[2] Polehampton's own firstborn infant had died just months before the rebellion began, and she orchestrated Bartrum's mourning in ways that mirrored her own, creating community and support through the child's last moments. Polehampton had been among the first to recognize the severity of Bobbie's illness as the women made plans to travel from Calcutta to England.[3] When Bobbie died just over one week later, it was Polehampton who came in the middle of the night and directed Bartrum to lay her struggling child on her lap. Bartrum recalled, "He was gasping for breath, when I turned away my head, for I *could* not see my child die. She [Polehampton] said, 'Look, how bright his eyes are growing!' and 'now his eyes grew bright and brighter still, too bright for ours to look upon' . . . and *so* 'the Lord called the child.'"[4] Polehampton, who months before had begged her husband to let her keep her dead child's corpse close to her for just a few hours longer, washed and dressed the infant and laid his body next to his mother on her bed. In the morning, the two women arranged roses and orange blossoms around the child and, at midday, they had a photographer take his picture—just as Polehampton and her husband had done for their own infant.[5] The postmortem daguerreotype was tinted "to take off the pallor of the effect," and it showed Bobbie "as if he were smiling in sleep."[6] The child was now, according to his mother, "no longer babe but angel."[7] That evening, the doctor came to fasten down the coffin lid, and the two ladies rode in the mourning coach along with the coffin to the burial ground, where they were joined by other survivors from Lucknow for the funeral and placement of the inscribed tombstone.[8]

The next day, Katherine Bartrum set sail for England, recalling in the final passages of her personal and later published memoirs how, on leaving Calcutta, she "bade farewell to the land, where all I loved best, had found a resting place."[9] By ending her memoir with this statement, Bartrum connected the deaths of her child and husband with leaving India and linked her ultimate personal loss with the larger imperial upheaval.[10] Even before Bobbie's death, she had written to her father, "I long to bid farewell to India, the only spot in it which possesses any interest for me is the grave of my Husband," a site that, to her great consternation, was neither known nor marked.[11] Upon her son's death, she declared, "I am stripped of all, I am empty & desolate, all is gone now."[12]

For Britons in India, mourning rituals held multiple meanings. The practices surrounding grief and death served as methods of identifying and connecting the British and European community abroad as well as recognizing Christian salvation. In his classic work *The Hour of Our Death* (1981), Philippe Ariès identifies the late eighteenth century as a period of transition for Western death and mourning practices marked by the rise of the "beautiful death," in which death brought suffering yet also offered peace and happiness to the dying and reunion with departed loved ones.[13] Burial in overcrowded, unsanitary urban churchyards declined as cemeteries reconfigured into peaceful sites for walking and reflection moved from the center of towns to the outskirts, and individually marked tombstones increasingly replaced anonymous or mass graves. The new cemeteries, modeled after Paris's Père Lachaise, which opened in 1804, resembled garden settings where, according to George Mosse, "death supposedly lost its sting as it became part of an enchanting landscape."[14] The deathbed also emerged as an appropriate setting primarily for the immediate family, not the larger public. More recently, scholars such as Pat Jalland and Drew Gilpin Faust have elaborated on the nineteenth-century ideal of the Christian good death during which, writes Faust, "the deceased had been conscious of his fate, had demonstrated willingness to accept it, had shown signs of belief in God and in his own salvation, and had left messages and instructive exhortations for those who should have been at his side."[15] While young children and infants remained unable to articulate such overt statements of salvation, descriptions of child death in this tradition often noted a change in the child's eyes, a turning toward God, as in the case of Bartrum's son, which must be witnessed and acknowledged by the present adults, as well as a final look of peace or contented sleep.

Child death amid the Indian Rebellion of 1857, however, proved a different matter. Similar to the Crimean War, which Lara Kriegel marks as "a transition point in the maintenance of death" between the mass battlefield graves of the Napoleonic Wars and the Imperial War Graves Commission's individual markers of the Great War, the conditions of death far from home during the Indian Rebellion often made such manifestations of the good death impossible.[16] This chapter traces change over time in British representations of child death during the Indian Rebellion, drawing on a variety of different "texts": letters, diaries, memoirs, published accounts, and press reviews, along with visual sources such as cartoons, historical illustrations and paintings, public memorials, and even a fifty-three-foot painted panoramic scroll documenting the main sites of conflict. Private letters were often later published and personal memoirs reviewed by the press alongside published works. Together these sources reveal the blurred boundaries between private and public, individual and collective memory, personal and collective grief. The varied source base and ability to track one source, a letter or diary, for example, through several manifestations—the original entry, the published form, and then reviews—illuminates how individual expressions of grief took shape in the public discourse and collective memory of 1857.

During the initial months of the conflict and in the earliest published British accounts, the deaths of children became war stories—embellished and often symbolic—for the British public, and what under normal circumstances would have been inappropriate material for public discourse served as a powerful, emotive rallying point for British militarism. The diaries and memoirs written during the siege of Lucknow and published and circulated among British readers in 1858 and the following years, however, portrayed child death as more complicated. The focus shifted from vengeance to grief, and it became clear that survivors could not always mourn children's deaths in a manner that reinforced British values and Christian traditions. The inability to grieve and commemorate the good deaths of children revealed tensions inherent in the domestic ideals justifying British imperialism. When proper burial and mourning rituals for children could not be carried out, the British sense of national community frayed, and doubts about the cost of empire emerged. Images and narratives of the violent deaths of children grew to be so destabilizing that they had to be suppressed. Ultimately, the deaths of children were either represented as good deaths or erased from the public memory of the rebellion, leaving unrecognized the traces of unmoored, hopeless grief recorded during the fighting. Later British memorials built during the mid-1860s and following decades typically represented the deaths of British women, a much more stable symbol than children, obscuring the accounts of child death that had initially been so prevalent. This process demonstrates the ways in which the experience of grief was a form of remembering those who died as well as the ties that bound the dead to the living, a process that, as Judith Butler has argued elsewhere, potentially "furnishes a sense of political community."[17] The elements of grief for dead children that served national purposes entered into the collective memory of the rebellion, while those that did not remained forgotten or left unarticulated without language for expression.

Militaristic Representations of Child Death

During the first months of the rebellion, the deaths of British children were typically represented to the British public in the same way as the deaths of British women; both representations reinforced understandings of the conflict as a mutiny against legitimate authority in need of immediate suppression. The rebellion ended with the brutal subjugation of Indians by the British forces and the transfer of power from the East India Company to the British Crown in 1858. Noting the overwhelming focus on the deaths of British women as a call for vengeance, many scholars stress that the conflict marked a major shift in British models of empire as the metropole turned away from the liberal imperial reformist rhetoric promoted by Thomas Macaulay and John Stuart Mill in the early nineteenth century and openly espoused violence as the means to uphold racial hierarchies.[18] British forces responded to the uprising with a wholesale attack on Indian communities, burning entire villages and staging public hangings that were photographed and displayed back in Britain as spectacular demonstrations of British power.[19] Before his death, Bartrum's husband, Robert, described how soldiers routinely shot or hanged Indian prisoners. "At first I loathed the idea," he wrote to his mother in England, "but now I have become so callous to it, that I feel a pleasure in seeing those creatures revenged upon."[20] In the following decades, the British colonial government retreated from highly symbolic forms of religious and cultural intervention that sparked widespread resistance. As the British strengthened ties with the Indian elite, however, government and private initiatives constructed even greater racial distinctions between Indian and British populations through census reports, health reform, anthropological projects, public exhibitions, museum displays, and intensified segregation within urban spaces.[21]

Perhaps no aspect of the conflict was more important in shaping British responses than narratives about British women being attacked by Indian men. At the Cawnpore (hereafter Kanpur) massacres of June 27 and July 15, 1857, forces under Nana Sahib of Bithur opened fire on the formerly besieged Europeans who were promised safe passage to Allahabad, and then Nana Sahib ordered the approximately two hundred surviving European women and children retained as hostages at the Bibighar or "House of the

Ladies" to be killed, leaving their bodies in a well. Appealing to the ideal of virtuous British womanhood, the British public and government used accounts of the Kanpur massacres to justify the violent retaliation of the British army against rebel forces and Indian communities. For many Britons, British womanhood came to symbolize the values associated with the British "civilizing mission": Christianity, chivalry, and self-sacrifice, as well as a belief in racial superiority.[22] The British public understood attacks on British women and children as attacks on British domesticity and imperial authority, and in the years following the rebellion, ruling the home continued to serve as a model for ruling the empire.[23]

Britons fighting in India and those remaining in Britain circulated gruesome reports of Indians killing British women and children to rally military support against an enemy portrayed as brutal and uncivilized. "Cawnpore! Cawnpore!" became a common battle cry as British-led forces charged against rebel soldiers, and some of the earliest published images of the rebellion to reach Britain focused on child death to present the conflict as an attack on the British home and family.[24] In October 1857 at the height of the crisis, *Punch* printed a cartoon showing Queen Victoria holding a dead infant, the child's eyes peacefully closed, surrounded by barefoot children and grieving women in mourning attire kneeling in prayer, thereby bringing the issue of child death and the rebellion directly to the British domestic public. The caption from *Henry V*, "O God of Battles! Steel My Soldiers' Hearts!," defended British soldiers' brutality against Indians in the name of protecting children (fig. 7). The cartoon thus linked child death in the imperial context to Britain's history, culture, and national interests, represented in this case by the monarch herself as mother.

Such depictions of child death drew sharp, antagonistic distinctions between Britons and Indians. In the November 1857 cartoon "Too 'Civil' by Half," *Punch* critiqued Governor-General Charles Canning's supposed leniency toward rebel soldiers, represented in this case by the sneering sepoy shown holding a sword covered with the blood of two small, dead British children as he cowers under the ready bayonet of a British soldier (fig. 8). Canning sought to distinguish between Indians who participated in the rebellion and those who did not in meting out punishments, but the reference to the death of British children in this image served to reinforce understandings of the conflict as a battle of all Indians against all Britons. Most popular of all was John Tenniel's response to the Kanpur Massacre published in *Punch* (August 22, 1857), "The British Lion's

FIGURE 7. "O God of Battles! Steel My Soldiers' Hearts!" Queen Victoria shown mourning children killed in the Indian Rebellion and calling for vengeance. *Punch*, October 10, 1857. (Courtesy of Vassar College Library)

Vengeance on the Bengal Tiger" (fig. 9). By depicting the British lion as leaping in attack toward the Bengal tiger preparing to devour a naked European woman and child, Tenniel conflated fears of murder and rape and asserted that British military actions were in response to an attack on British women and children. This image was widely reproduced, displayed in British parlors, and even referenced as a recruiting tool to sway young men to enlist for India.[25]

As was the case with the *Punch* cartoons, illustrations in one of the first histories of the rebellion, Charles Ball's *History of the Indian Mutiny* (1858), used the deaths of British children along with those of women to promote a sense of British victimization, Christian righteousness, and racial superiority.[26] More starkly Orientalist than much of the text itself, Ball's widely reproduced steel engravings created exaggerated racial distinctions between white Britons and dark rebel soldiers.[27] Brutal portrayals of Indians killing naked white women and children, such as the "Massacre of English Officers and Their Wives at Jhansi," which shows

FIGURE 8. "Too 'Civil' by Half: The Governor-General Defending the Poor Sepoy." *Punch*'s reference to child death as a means to condemn Governor-General Charles Canning's Clemency Resolution of July 31, 1857, which sought to check indiscriminate British military force against all Indians. *Punch*, November 7, 1857. (Courtesy of Vassar College Library)

an Indian soldier holding an upside-down, naked British child soon to be killed by another's sword, literally foregrounded child death, thus constructing a narrative of the rebellion that seemed to justify British retaliation (fig. 10). An unclothed male child on the left lies in nearly the exact same position as the fallen British soldier on the right. The conflation of child and adult soldier suggests that Britain's domestic interests were aligned with its military power and that Britain's future imperial supremacy was also at stake. Other historical illustrations in Ball's account memorialized British families in India as heroic and, in many cases,

FIGURE 9. "The British Lion's Vengeance on the Bengal Tiger," John Tenniel, *Punch*, August 22, 1857.

FIGURE 10. "Massacre of English Officers and Their Wives at Jhansi," in Charles Ball, *The History of the Indian Mutiny*, volume 1 (London, 1858). (Courtesy of Vassar College Library)

FIGURE 11. "Massacre at Cawnpore," in Charles Ball, *The History of the Indian Mutiny*, volume 1 (London, 1858). (Courtesy of Vassar College Library)

solemnly secure in their Christian faith. The "Massacre at Cawnpore," for example, contrasted the chaos and violence of the rebel soldiers with the illuminated British family grouped below the church steeple: the mother who holds her two young children until the end, the father who stands resigned to his fate with his head in prayer (fig. 11).

Thus, during the rebellion and in the immediate aftermath, public mourning for British children who died served much the same purpose as mourning for British women. Dead children became a rallying point for British military mobilization and symbols of British innocence, Christian sacrifice, racial difference, and moral superiority. The tortured child's body was the ultimate sign of uncivilized warfare and British martyrdom, creating the boundaries of community by drawing on a standard set of visual formats reaching back at least to Foxe's *Book of Martyrs* (1563).[28] In one of the most extreme examples of such uses of British childhood, Harriet Tytler, wife of Captain Robert Tytler and the only elite British woman present during the battle to reclaim Delhi, demonstrated that children, like women, could readily embody the values of British imperialism. She famously named her child born during the siege "Stanley Delhi-Force" (having rejected the name "Battlefield Tytler" as too extreme) and claimed that on his birth the soldiers declared, "We shall have victory now that this baby has come to avenge the deaths of the murdered children."[29] Such references to child death presented the imperial conflict as an attack on the British domestic sphere, but the overwhelming message was one of vengeance rather than grief or loss for the dead.

Childhood, Domesticity, and the Siege of Lucknow

By the mid-nineteenth century, childhood was rooted in the domestic sphere, and both childhood and domesticity emerged as key sites where British identity at home and abroad was taught, debated, and evaluated. Middle-class Britons increasingly situated the child as the source of adult accomplishments and values, reinterpreted childhood as a distinct time of innocence best suited for education rather than work, and pursued a wide array of protective reforms exemplified by the child labor laws of the 1830s and 1840s.[30] It was within the revered bourgeois home (as well as in institutionally re-created "homes" for working-class children whose own domestic settings state and philanthropic reformers deemed lacking) that children learned about religion, came to understand their class status through interactions with servants, developed a sense of their gender roles, and ideally began to realize what it meant to be British. Reformers recognized the political significance of child socialization in imperial contexts as well. Philanthropists hailed institutions such as the Free Church of Scotland orphanage in Calcutta as "a well-cultured garden" in the midst of "moral waste," and domestic guides instructed mothers to talk with children only in English, for "religious and moral instruction" could not be conveyed "in the native tongue."[31] Actual child-rearing practices among the British in India often challenged such cultural distinctions, highlighting instead existing forms of cultural plurality, hybridity, and contestation. Many British children in India, for example, primarily spoke Indian languages rather than English, interacted more often with Indian servants than with their European parents, were themselves the offspring of racially mixed unions, or otherwise came to be understood as racially distinct from the adult British population.[32] And yet the ideals of British childhood and domesticity remained central to the project of empire.

The presence of a significant group of British women at Lucknow, who, unlike the women of Kanpur, survived to write about their experiences, temporarily complicated such uses of children and the domestic sphere as symbols of empire. Over the course of five months, from June through November 1857, between two and three thousand British, European, and Indian soldiers and civilians and their family members were besieged in the buildings surrounding the Lucknow Residency, an area covering thirty-three acres.[33] On September 25, 1857, General James Outram's troops joined General Henry Havelock's forces from Kanpur to lead an unsuccessful relief of Lucknow, adding approximately one thousand reinforcements and new supplies to the Residency compound. It was not until November 17 that Sir Colin Campbell led the successful relief of Lucknow and arranged for the travel of the Residency survivors to Calcutta by way of the Secundrabagh (a garden palace where only days before Campbell's troops had killed nearly two thousand Indian soldiers), Kanpur, and Allahabad. From Calcutta many, like Katherine Bartrum and Emmie Polehampton, departed for England. It was during the evacuation of the Residency survivors from Lucknow to Calcutta that the lasting narratives focused on the chivalrous relief of Lucknow, the overwhelmingly violent suppression of Indian rebels, and the heroism of British women took hold.[34]

Yet even as the Lucknow survivors' journey to Calcutta reinforced the emphasis on the Kanpur massacre and the heroic relief of Lucknow, survivors' accounts detailing the conditions of the siege and its aftermath presented a view of British domesticity and civilization as internally fractured, weakened, and at times even questioned. Certainly, most of the public reports of the siege focused on the relief, which provided the first material for the British press and was even the subject of the melodramatic playwright Dion Boucicault's *Jessie Brown; or, The Relief of Lucknow: A Drama, in Three Acts* (1858). Yet soon these accounts were joined by the outpouring of published memoirs, letters, and diaries written by survivors of the siege. Like the British captive of the 1842 First Anglo-Afghan War who observed "our party were seized with a scribbling mania" driven by those "who had the most retentive memories, or fertile inventions," those at Lucknow knew that the British press eagerly awaited their reports.[35] In 1858 alone, the year of Charles Ball's *History of the Indian Mutiny*, survivors published over ten accounts of the Lucknow siege, and others circulated their memoirs and letters privately, with the press in some cases reviewing these writings as well.[36]

Many memoirs were accounts written by women of the upper classes, such as Bartrum, Polehampton, and others connected to key officials within the Residency buildings. Georgina Harris had settled in Lucknow where her husband served as the head army chaplain only a few weeks before the rebellion began. The preface to her diary, likely the first published narrative of the siege written by a woman, noted, "As no *lady's* diary has hitherto been given to the public, the friends of the writer have thought that it might interest others, beyond the family circle, to communicate additional information on a subject in which the British nation feels so deep an interest."[37] Lady Julia Inglis, wife of the Lucknow brigadier, wrote one of the other better-known reports of the siege by a woman. She first circulated her private papers in 1858, when they were reviewed alongside published works, and later published *The Siege of Lucknow: A Diary* in 1892, when it would be praised by *The Times* for bringing world attention to the conditions of the siege along with the more familiar details of the relief.[38] Reviewers also took note of Bartrum's account, published in the immediate aftermath of events as *A Widow's Reminiscence of the Siege of Lucknow* (1858), as well as Polehampton's letters and diary, published as *A Memoir, Letters, and Diary* (1858) along with the writings of her husband, Henry Polehampton, the Lucknow chaplain who died during the siege.[39] One of the most widely reviewed reports written by a woman was *Day by Day at Lucknow: A Journal of the Siege* (1858), written by Adelaide Case, widow of Colonel William Case, who died in the battle of Chinhat.[40]

British press reviews of women's accounts of the Lucknow siege alternately valorized these women for their domestic strength or mocked them for domestic frivolity in the midst of war, but in all cases presented a vision of the British private domestic sphere as fundamentally able to withstand political upheaval. Reviewers routinely commented on the "womanly" and "feminine" perspectives of female authors, most of whom were gentlewomen.[41] Often such references served to bring attention to women's skills of caring for the living, nursing the sick, and preparing the dead within the Residency. Reviewers marveled at how women during the rebellion continued to mark the days of domestic importance—"birthdays, wedding-days, death-days, and household anniversaries."[42] Reinterpreting women's Lucknow accounts for the larger British public, reviewers suggested that this continuation of domestic routines helped participants survive the destruction of war. One writer for *The Critic*, for example, positively remarked how Adelaide Case opened a passage with a description of a wartime "horror"—an amputation conducted without chloroform—and ended this short section of her diary with a vision "proper to her [role] as a woman and a mother" of "peaceful, hopeful expectation": the marking of a child's fourth birthday.[43] By the late nineteenth century, elite women survivors of Lucknow were widely recognized for their distinctly feminine contribution to upholding British imperial values. One reviewer of Inglis's diary wrote for *The Academy* in 1892, "Many versions of the heroic defense of Lucknow have been given to the world since then—versions military and versions domestic—so that all mankind may be said to have enjoyed the opportunity of studying the audacity of the men, the patience of the women, the whole grand display of virtues which, in excusable pride, we call 'British.'"[44]

In addition to praising women for their domestic virtues, however, the British press sometimes also ridiculed women writers for their domestic frivolity associated with children, displacing onto these women larger concerns about the sustainability of British customs and traditions within the empire during a time of conflict. Some reviewers expressed disdain for female survivors who retreated into domestic activities and a feminine perspective as a means to create moments free from, or, oblivious to, the ravages of war. Directly after quoting Harris's shock and fear following the massacre at Delhi, the reviewer for *The Athenaeum* wrote, "Still, in the intervals, the lady ascends to the roof of a lofty building to appreciate the scenery around Lucknow, or enters into family merriment to play with a child." The reviewer went on to detail in patronizing tones Harris's earnest concern for the fate of her dog "poor Bustle," and then contrasted Harris's experience of the initial uprising at Lucknow with the trifling style of her own text: "In the midst of this half-melancholy, half-lightsome prattle, comes the roar of cannon, with slaughter and alarm, and the words burn on the paper, 'Oh, mother! Mother! How dreadful it is! We have just heard there is a rising in the city.'"[45] Using the cries of a child to relay the violence of the situation, the reviewer accentuated Harris's supposed lack of understanding and her reliance on domestic comforts in the midst of war.

In the most explicit critique of the Lucknow women's domestic perspectives, *The Rambler* began its review of Case's *Day by Day at Lucknow* by noting, "This journal is interesting from its very dullness. The mere notification of the succession of facts by one who has no power of describing them, still less of reasoning upon them, gives an idea of that weary time which a less wearisome style could not give."[46] Ignoring Case's descriptions of mine explosions, shelling, and the death of her husband, *The Rambler* presented her memoir as "the aptest symbol of the vacant suffering which the ladies" experienced during the siege by focusing almost entirely on Case's distress on having to leave behind her crockery and other personal belongings when officers ordered the evacuation of the Residency.

The reviewer silenced Case's pain and reduced her suffering, and that of the other female survivors, to a domestic farce in which "they found moving as great a dislocation of comfort as if they had been comfortable where they were."[47] Thus, the domestic could be used to represent the resilience of British imperial values, but it also became a means through which to express doubts related to the project of replicating British culture and traditions within the empire by deflecting concerns onto unreasonable women. Nonetheless, reviewers asserted that the feminized British domestic realm, whether praised as a source of national strength or mocked as ridiculous, could withstand even the most hostile imperial settings.

The Lucknow accounts written during the siege, however, were themselves quite different. Survivors expressed deep distress over how the conflict overturned British domestic life, provoked tensions within the British community, prevented the fulfillment of British cultural practices, and even raised serious doubts about British policies in India. Harris described a dinner conversation where someone, perhaps the commander Sir Henry Lawrence (the name is marked out in her text), "thinks the tribulation we are now in is a just punishment to our nation for the grasping spirit in which we have governed India; the unjust appropriation of Oude being a finishing stroke to a long course of selfish seeking our own benefit and aggrandisement."[48] The strains of the siege unleashed doubts about the British imperial project and also revealed internal divisions within the British community as class tensions surfaced over sleeping arrangements, food distribution, and accusations of profiteering within the Residency compound.[49] Reviewers may have stressed British nationalism as supported by women's continuation of their domestic roles, but the British women writing about the siege were clear that they were entering a military setting that made traditional domestic relations and spaces impossible. Maria Germon recalled, "When we drove up to the Residency everything looked so warlike—guns pointed in all directions, barricades and European troops everywhere—such a scene of bustle and confusion."[50] Soon women's diaries documented a preoccupation with the more immediate dangers of war, such as battle plans, constant shelling, nursing the wounded, and the organization of women's night watches.[51]

From the very first days of the siege, British civilians encamped in the Residency emphasized the lack of proper domestic spaces—especially the overcrowding and commingling of children and adults, servants and employers—to describe the disruptions of war. It was "a perfect barrack," "just like a rabbit warren," wrote Germon. "At last Miss Nepean offered me a corner in one room—but the perfect babel it was with the number of children and the heat being fearful up to then and no *punkah* going, it was enough to drive one wild." Germon stressed how far the Residency was from the ideal middle-class home by focusing on the lack of servants to operate the punkah, or ceiling fan; the lack of privacy; and the constant proximity to children. That evening "two Padres tried to have prayers but we could scarcely hear anything from the babel of tongues and the sound of the screams of so many children—it was perfect misery."[52] "The noise of the children in this house is something dreadful," wrote Case, "and there is not one hole or corner where one can enjoy an instant's privacy."[53] In his memoir of the siege, L. E. Ruutz Rees similarly recalled, "All privacy was destroyed, and the houses within the Residency compound resembled small barrack rooms rather than the apartments of respectable families."[54]

Furthermore, the siege disrupted imperial hierarchies among British women and Indian servants primarily established and maintained in domestic settings. As more and more Indian civilians fled the Residency, British women identified the lack of deference they received from remaining Indian servants and their own new roles as "the maid-of-all-work," washerwoman, cook, or nurse as the most immediate outcomes of political rebellion.[55] During the siege, elite British women dedicated themselves to physical labors previously foreign to their class status without losing sight of how the rebellion challenged imperial hierarchies maintained within the home. In a letter to her father written during the evacuation, Bartrum surmised, "India is no place for Englishwomen now & *never* will be as it has been, the natives have lost their fear & therefore their respect for Europeans."[56]

The siege context at Lucknow prompted internal domestic conflicts among Britons and frequent speculation about suicide and self-destruction of the besieged community. A dispute supposedly started by two wives arguing about the placement of a curtain ended with the sergeant major of the Seventh Cavalry shooting and killing the riding master of the same regiment.[57] Several suicides caused great distress along with theological debates about whether self-annihilation would be appropriate if the rebels captured the Residency.[58] Some women even began to carry laudanum and prussic acid with them for this purpose, and Julia Inglis remarked how she and her husband, the brigadier in charge of the garrison after Sir Henry Lawrence died, discussed how to make arrangements for women and children as well as the sick and wounded in the case of a successful attack. She wrote, "At one time he talked of blowing us up at the last minute, but

I have since heard this would have been impracticable. It was strange how calmly we talked on these subjects."[59] Far from ensuring imperial futurity, the spaces, hierarchies, and very constructions of British domesticity and childhood faced annihilation during the monthslong siege.

Child Death and Suppressed Grief at Lucknow

The death of children during the months of siege was by far the most pervasive and devastating of such disorders to British domesticity. The press reports and reviewers' retelling of survivors' accounts from Lucknow tended to focus on select instances of child death that might be described with pathos, but the original survivors' accounts stressed the overwhelming yet commonplace experience of child death along with great distress over the inability to mark these deaths according to British practice.

The exact number of women and children who died during the Lucknow siege is difficult to determine. While nearly half of the besieged population consisted of native Indian troops and Indian noncombatants—a fact often omitted from the British public memory of Lucknow—the available records of civilian deaths are usually limited to Britons of the middle and upper classes. One British painted memorial scroll created to commemorate the major events and sites of the rebellion includes a picture of the Lucknow churchyard with a caption stating that in addition to the uncounted soldiers' wives and children who died, seven out of the sixty-eight British ladies present died along with twenty-three of their sixty-six children.[60] As an appendix to his account of the siege, L. E. Ruutz Rees included a more complete list of the families of British officers and nonmilitary men present at Lucknow. According to his estimate, which still does not take into account the families of British soldiers or Indians, eighteen out of 232 women and fifty-eight out of 271 children died during the siege and evacuation. In addition, approximately fifty boys from the Martinière College took shelter in the Residency, of whom "a few" died or were wounded.[61] Since these populations had access to superior accommodations, food supplies, and medical attention, it is reasonable to assume that child death rates among the families of European enlisted soldiers, Indian troops, and servants would have been significantly higher. What is striking in all the available estimates is that children died at much higher rates than women.

The context of these child deaths caused a breakdown of British mourning practices specifically used in the colonial context to preserve

British values. Child death, always a tragedy, became even more difficult within the siege setting. It became impossible to interpret and memorialize child deaths according to the ideal of the Christian good death recalled in Bartrum's description of her son's final moments. Like adults, children during the rebellion often died alone, without forewarning, awareness, any clear connection to God, or communal commemoration. Overwhelmed by the sheer number of deaths and unable to follow conventional mourning patterns for children and other family members, survivors of the siege suffered from "suppressed grief"—illness resulting from grief put off by the immediate demands of survival or left unarticulated and unseen. Indeed, Adelaide Case's doctor used the term "suppressed grief" to describe her illness following her husband's death, and many women experiencing child death demonstrated similar characteristics. Inglis noted that Case's health improved once she arrived in Calcutta after the siege ended, stressing how important it had been for Case to secure proper mourning dress including a widow's cap.[62] During the months of the siege, British survivors expressed remorse and guilt over their inability to prevent or properly mourn the deaths of family members. Most of all, child death underscored that Britons were powerless to protect their own, that they were unable to maintain their cultural practices in a foreign land, and, for some, that the sacrifice for Britain's imperial mission proved too great.

Fulfilling typical mourning patterns was difficult in part because most of the children who died during the siege experienced deaths that could not conform to nineteenth-century domesticated ideals of childhood or death. Living in makeshift, overcrowded barracks, parents regretted that children lacked the domestic and religious supports to ease their final moments. The means of child death—typically by shell fire or disease—were often sudden and violent. In the early weeks of the siege, Bartrum first witnessed the carnage of the conflict when she saw a child killed as she held her own infant in her arms. She recalled in her diary, "I was dreadfully shocked this morning as I was standing at the window, watching a little girl playing in the court-yard, a round shot [cannonball] struck her in the head, & dashed out her brains. I had never seen anyone killed before, & it was a horrid shock, so much so, that I fell down in a faint on the floor. I can never think of that poor little girl without a shudder."[63] Bartrum was surely familiar with other violent deaths by this point, but in describing the death of this girl she stressed how the act disrupted her middle-class vision of playful childhood nourished in safe domestic spaces—gardens and courtyards. Bartrum framed her shock in terms of a reaction not only to witnessing horrific bloodshed but also to the disordering of domestic and public, child and adult, play and warfare.

The horrific courtyard death described by Bartrum and others of this kind completely overturned the modern notion of protected, innocent childhood. As the siege continued, such deaths became a more common occurrence. In language often much starker than Bartrum's, diarists recorded how "one child was killed and another wounded by the bursting of a shell,"[64] how "a boy . . . was killed by a chance ball,"[65] and how "poor Mrs. Eldridge's idiot daughter had her leg taken off by a round shot, and died in great agony."[66] In a rare reference to the death of an Indian child, Colina Brydon noted that "Gungoo," her servant, "lost her youngest but one girl. She had been wounded in the foot but had recovered. Internal worms killed her."[67] Many injuries resulted from the Residency members' own shells, not those of rebel soldiers. On an evening in September, Case wrote that "one of our own shells burst, and pieces came back into the ladies' square, killing one child and wounding another, and also wounding two poor sweepers."[68] Similarly, Inglis wrote that she and her baby barely missed being hit by "a fragment from one of our own shells, which often recoiled and fell inside our entrenchments."[69] As in most wars, these cases of injury and death from friendly fire did not feature prominently in the British public memory of the Indian Rebellion.

Along with shelling, children suffered from general malnutrition as women and men struggled with the most basic of domestic duties: providing food for children. By July, many in the compound showed signs of scurvy. Captain Birch noted that it was a common illness, reporting that "scurvy took the form of loose teeth, swollen heads, and boils, and gained the name of 'garrison disease.'"[70] Infants and children of all but the wealthiest lacked fresh milk. Bartrum declared that milk "is more precious than gold" for the care of her infant, and she was lucky to receive daily supplies from other ladies.[71] Other women of the Residency were not as fortunate. Case wrote, "A great many children are suffering dreadfully from want of proper nourishment; it is so very difficult to procure milk." She went on to detail how a widow who had already endured the deaths of three children came to Julia Inglis to request goat milk for her dying baby. The infant had been born on the first day of the attack during which the woman's husband was killed, resulting in her inability to nurse from "grief and fretting."[72] Inglis, who managed to bring several milk goats with her into the Residency, refused the request, claiming, "It went to my heart to refuse her; but at this time I had only just enough for my own children, and baby could not have lived without it."[73] Inglis hoped the woman would understand her decision to let another child die so that hers might have milk, but Case remarked that the woman's request for "nourishment for her child," a need shared by many, "made an impression on me I shall not easily forget."[74] Those women who could nurse their own infants expressed notable thanks, acknowledging how malnutrition, stress, and grief made many within the compound unable to do so.[75] Another mother sat sewing when she witnessed the decapitation of her ten-year-old daughter by a cannonball that crashed through the wall. The woman was subsequently powerless to nurse her infant, who eventually starved to death.[76]

As more and more Indian servants left the Residency complex, infants also experienced the loss of wet nurses. When Mrs. Clark gave birth prematurely, she was unable to nurse, and Bartrum and the other ladies who assisted her through delivery could find no one in the Residency to serve as a wet nurse. The mother soon died, followed by her baby girl three days later.[77] Describing another case, Georgina Harris, wife of the head chaplain, wrote, "All the children are very bad; the want of fresh air and exercise, and the loss of their accustomed food, have made them all ill. Little Herbert D[ashwood]'s wet-nurse is in such a bad humour, and always threatening to run away, and declaring her milk is gone, so we have been trying to wean the poor child."[78] Like many other infants in the Residency, Herbert ate arrowroot and sago mixed with small amounts of milk or water as substitutes—a concoction that the child disliked and may have caused him to experience diarrhea that then developed into dysentery.[79] Nearly two weeks after weaning the infant, and days before his death, Harris lamented, "I fear little Herbert cannot recover: he seems to be sinking. It makes one's heart ache to look at his little suffering face. He is so weak he scarcely ever cries, and when he does, it is such a little feeble wail it is pitiable to hear."[80]

Given these conditions, children became even more susceptible to infectious diseases, resulting in multiple and sudden child deaths that further disrupted customary mourning rituals. In mid-August, a period of widespread disease in the Residency complex, Colina Brydon regretted that "so many little children are suffering and sinking."[81] Dr. Gilbert Hadow wrote, "You saw the little things drooping and dying from day to day," stressing, "This was the saddest part of all."[82] A typical diary entry from this time recorded that "Mrs. Hersham's and Mrs. Kendal's babies died. It is sad the number of children who are dying: they get diarrhoea, for which there seems no cure."[83] Smallpox and cholera, a notably quick and violent illness, were the most deadly diseases to infect Residency members. Cholera first appeared in mid-June, and by June 25 there were at least one hundred cases and forty deaths from the disease, though there was never a full-blown epidemic.[84]

As child deaths became more common, diary entries recorded them in plain wording. Julia Inglis wrote, "A child of Mrs. Radcliffe's died to-day from cholera after a few hours' illness," and, on the following day, "One of Mrs. Martin's children died to-day, and another one was not expected to live."[85] In contrast to the usually elaborate descriptions of child death and the rituals that accompanied children's last moments in middle-class Victorian culture, most diarists began to mark deaths in the form of lists with little or no additional commentary: "Poor Mrs. Watson and Mrs. Soppitt each lost their only child of cholera during the day,"[86] "Mrs. Strangway's eldest child died of cholera,"[87] "Mrs. B[oileau]'s baby died in the early morning,"[88] "Mrs. Dashwood's baby died last night."[89] While technically serving as records of the conditions and time of death, such diary entries also demonstrate how war interrupted and changed the process of mourning. The blunt, list-like records of deaths suggest both the frequency of child death and a form of "suppressed grief," highlighting the extreme difficulty of survivors to write about and bear witness to these deaths in familiar ways.

Even as individuals did their best to come together to offer support through the mourning process, customary communal rituals became increasingly difficult to maintain. When the baby of a woman sharing her living quarters with Bartrum died, Bartrum described how she "helped the poor mother wash it & dress it, & prepare it for its last resting place."[90] However, in another case, a mother's inability to witness her child at the exact moment of death caused great anguish. Harris wrote, "Poor little Ina Boileau died in the night; she was so very ill all yesterday, we knew she could not live; her poor mother, who had been watching her all night, had fallen asleep quite exhausted, and when she awoke she found the poor child quite cold in her arms; her cry of anguish awoke us all; poor creature! she is distracted, and reproaches herself with having gone to sleep; but of course she could not help it, and she would not allow any one else to watch with her."[91] This was no Christian good death affirming community and peaceful childhood; exhausted and without the presence of others to support her, the mother witnessed neither the child's end of suffering nor her acceptance by God.

After death, the mourning practices associated with burial presented further challenges and distress. Britons had long used burial to symbolize differences between Christians and Hindus, who typically practiced cremation.[92] In order to limit the spread of infectious diseases in the extremely overcrowded Residency buildings, the bodies of the dead were promptly removed from relatives. Grieving parents had little opportunity to hold and sit with the bodies of dead children, which were taken to the makeshift hospital or "dead-house" to be buried that night.[93] Generally unable to secure coffins—much less gravestones—for their offspring, parents searched the Residency buildings for suitable boxes in which to place children's bodies.[94] Even small boxes were difficult to obtain, and it became the general rule for dead children as well as adults to be sewn into any available material—their bedding, a tablecloth, or sacks—before burial.[95] When the Cowper baby died, Inglis described how "the nurse sewed it up in some cloth, and Mr. Cowper carried it to the deadhouse—a sad office for a father, but we could hardly grieve for the little one who had been born in such troublous times."[96]

From the "dead-house," bodies of the dead could not be put to rest in a peaceful cemetery, ideally a place for future visits and memorialization. In order to avoid sniper fire, burials took place during the night in the churchyard, which had not previously been used as a cemetery, but soon became "filled with heaps of the corpses" from the garrison.[97] Since the beginning of the siege, it had been difficult to find servants willing to dig graves—work that was restricted by caste as well as onerous and dangerous because the churchyard was an easy target. Eventually, it became the general practice to bury all individuals who died each day in a common grave site rather than in separate graves.[98] Denied proper burials and funerals, which according to Thomas Laqueur had come by the nineteenth century "to be regarded as the bare necessities of civilization," the dead from the Residency faced death like paupers, in mass, undifferentiated graves.[99] By August, the smell of the churchyard was so noxious "owing to the shallowness of the graves" that even the chaplain James Harris did not accompany the dead to their burial but rather read the funeral service "over the dead in the hospital porch," a difficult decision made only after considering his role as the sole surviving chaplain and placing his "duties to the living before the dead."[100] After the brigadier ordered that graves be dug at a greater depth and covered with charcoal, Harris attempted a return to his graveside duties, but the smells and experience immediately incapacitated him so that he "vomited about two hours incessantly."[101]

The nighttime burials (a time of burial associated with suicides in the nineteenth century) made survivors keenly aware of the limitations on rituals aimed at reaffirming connections among Europeans. Mourners bemoaned the lack of participation by Europeans in the funeral service. In July, Case wrote of "some little child which had just died. We saw it carried past in the dark to its last resting place. We saw no Europeans with it, poor little thing!"[102] Lamenting the fate of children buried without a proper service, Case later recorded in early September that "five babies had been buried during the night."[103] Before and after the rebellion, British cemeteries in India served as sites testifying to British imperial power—sacred, usually segregated spaces in which Britons memorialized their dead and maintained a connection with them through frequent visitation.[104] The siege, however, revealed the futility of such efforts, if only for a brief moment, as Europeans could not even join together as a community to mark the burial of their dead. Only Emmie Polehampton insisted on fulfilling conventional mourning practices and her role as a chaplain's wife when her husband died by securing a gravestone for him and regularly visiting his grave site against orders.[105] For the vast majority of Lucknow survivors, the Residency cemetery came to symbolize the isolation of Britons in a foreign land as well as their inability to care for their own. After her daughter Ina died without witnesses, Mrs. Boileau continued to struggle with the stark contrast between the realities of wartime death and her expectations. A sergeant managed to make her a small coffin in which she personally arranged her daughter's body. But the final burial provided no solace, and the cemetery proved unable to absorb the sting of death within its walls or offer hope of resurrection and eternal peace. Boileau wrote, "At twelve o'clock she [Ina] was carried away to that wretched mournful churchyard.... Oh, God Almighty comfort me."[106] By January 1858, less than two months after the evacuation, reports surfaced that the British burial ground at Lucknow had been desecrated, the church razed and replaced with a bazaar.[107]

Child Death and the Public Memorials of 1857

As Indrani Sen has demonstrated, grief over the death of a child could potentially reveal deep connections among Indians and Europeans. After experiencing the death of her son in the early 1800s, the Evangelical children's author Mary Martha Sherwood—who popularized fictional scenes of children tainted by original sin facing Christian good deaths in her bestselling series *The Fairchild Family* (1818, 1842, 1847)—recalled the shared grief she experienced with her child's ayah, whom Sherwood had seen "unfeignedly weeping for her boy." Sherwood wrote, "There are moments of intense feeling, in which all distinction of nations, colours, and castes disappears, and in their place there only remains between two human beings one abiding sense of common nature. . . . The scene of that weeping woman has power . . . to cause my tears to flow afresh."[108] It was unlikely, as Sherwood suggested, that grief erased the hierarchical relationship of employer and servant, yet the women's shared mourning connected, rather than polarized, Indians and Europeans.

However, after the relief of Lucknow, the British public and press immediately set about making visible only those forms of grief that fit national purposes by reestablishing conventional mourning patterns that unified Britons and reinforcing accounts that minimized the frequency and violence of child death. One of the very first priorities for relief workers along with securing food and basic provisions was to distribute proper mourning attire to women survivors as they traveled from Lucknow to Calcutta.[109] The widow's black dress or mourning cap instantly identified her as someone who had sacrificed for Britain, while providing established outlets for expressing grief. As the British press represented survivors' accounts to the public, reviewers generally omitted or downplayed the regular instances of child death without hope or purpose and instead gave greater attention to the rare cases in which survivors described the death of a child during the siege in the conventional terms of a Christian good death, thereby reaffirming British communal and Christian values. "Anywhere else it would be profanity to enter into these mysteries of family sorrow," wrote a reviewer for *The Athenaeum* when reflecting on the death of a child, "but every throb of the English heart at Lucknow belongs to history."[110] These testimonies of child death no longer belonged to individual families but rather became public. However, the account that entered history was a glorified version of death, in this case of the infant Herbert Dashwood, who died soon after he was weaned from the Indian wet nurse who had nourished him. Omitting this essential context, multiple reviewers quoted the unusually detailed description of Herbert's death from Harris's diary, reassuring the British public that the dead child "looked so sweet and happy; the painful look of suffering quite gone, and a lovely smile on his dear little baby face."[111] Reviewers said nothing of Herbert's dependence on his Indian wet nurse and remained silent on the many examples of child death during the siege that did not conform to this model of the good death. The "sweet and happy" death of the Dashwood child reasserted the imperial good death—and British resurgence—even in the most war-torn of imperial settings.

The controversy over Joseph Noel Paton's painting *In Memoriam* confirmed that the public increasingly had little tolerance even for highly stylized narratives of child death during the rebellion.[112] Paton's original version of the painting exhibited at the Royal Academy in May 1858 displayed British women, children, and an Indian ayah at Kanpur waiting in a cellar as Indian sepoys descended the steps with bayonets in hand. The central British woman painted in the classical tradition held a Bible. According to reviewers for *The Times*, her manner conveyed "Christian resignation" and "Christian fearlessness even in the very shadow of death"—values reinforced by the sleeping, peaceful young child at her knees.[113] However, another reviewer saw "terror, anguish, despair on every face," concluding, "The subject is too revolting for further description.... The picture is one which ought not to have been hung."[114] Responding to the public outcry over the painting, Paton eventually shifted the setting from Kanpur to Lucknow, and painted over the advancing sepoys with a group of Highland soldiers leading the relief, thereby turning a scene of death into one of rescue.

In the years following 1858, the initial construction and subsequent meanings associated with public memorials of the rebellion revealed a deep anxiety about the place of child death in the public memory of this war. In contrast to survivors' accounts and the images of children's dead bodies splayed across the pages of *Punch* during the height of the conflict, later memorials tended to erase child death, focusing instead primarily on the deaths of British women. In the most notable example, the memorial at the well of Kanpur where European women and children had been killed, the deaths of children were too painful to represent in any embodied visual form. An initial architectural plan for the memorial "proposed a sculpture consisting of dead children lying at the feet of an English woman leaning against a cross pierced with a sword."[115] But Viceroy and Lady Canning, who commissioned the memorial paid for by the residents of Kanpur, rejected this proposal as too horrific. The final version completed in 1865 was by Baron Carlo Marochetti, who had also designed the Crimean War memorial at Scutari. It displayed an "Angel of the Resurrection" above the well and became widely known as "the Ladies' Monument" (fig. 12).[116] Even though nearly twice as many children as women had been killed at Kanpur, in the long term their deaths could not be represented in their own right, but were rather used to reinforce messages of British women's self-sacrifice and resilience. According to Stephen Heathorn, the Kanpur monuments, a main attraction for Britons in India, became "significant symbolic sites of memory for the raj as a whole." The regulation of the site reinforced racial

"SUPPRESSED GRIEF" 97

FIGURE 12. Photograph of the memorial at Kanpur. The handwritten caption notes, "Marble figure 'Angel of the Resurrection' Sculptured by [Carlo] '*Marochetti*' from designs drawn by Lady Canning. It stands over 'the Well' at Cawnpore which contained a great company of Christian people massacred in the Great Mutiny of 1857." From the Memorial Volume of Photographs, Newscuttings, Letters and Souvenirs, Relating to Charlotte Elizabeth Canning (1817–61), Wife of Earl Canning (1812–62), Governor-General of India, 1856–62, British Library, Asian and African Studies. (© British Library Board MSS Eur. D661)

exclusion by forbidding all Indians from visiting the memorial well, and in this context the angel statue signified the ideals of British rule: "sacrifice, duty, fortitude and above all, the ultimate triumph over those who had threatened properly constituted authority and order."[117] Standing in for the nation, the silenced women of Kanpur, not children, served to represent an empire founded on the civilizing mission.

At Lucknow as well, memorials to 1857 reinforced narratives of British fortitude and heroism. When Julia Inglis made her diary available to the larger public in the 1890s, one reviewer wrote, "The charming undulating grounds shown to visitors of to-day as 'The Residency' at Lucknow can afford but little notion of the space wherein more than a thousand

Europeans, male and female, cooped up with a crowd of servants and sepoys, defended their lives for fifteen weeks."[118] After noting the discrepancy between the existing memorials and the experience of the siege, however, the reviewer went on to reinforce the message of British bravery and heroism, making only one brief mention of the "innocent children" and no mention of their circumstances or deaths. Lucknow, like Kanpur and Delhi, emerged as a major site for Britons following "mutiny tours."[119] Photographers obligingly documented the ruins of the Residency buildings, vigilantly preserved by the Archaeological Survey of India, and tourists routinely purchased copies for their memorial scrapbooks.[120] The dominant narratives of the Lucknow siege that surfaced highlighted the valor of the military men and the service of women such as Emmie Polehampton, recognized as a "ministering angel" for her aid to the suffering, but had little if anything to say about the children who died.[121]

Predictably, the memorials to 1857 created a history and memory of the rebellion that reinforced the foundations of the British imperial project. Erasing the magnitude, violence, and hopelessness of child death in wartime proved an essential feature of this history. Whereas the deaths of British women served to strengthen British ideals of a beneficent empire based on the civilizing mission, the deaths of British children ultimately raised questions about the sustainability of British rule in India. Rather than signifying a transfer of female domestic values to the imperial context, the deaths of children from starvation, malnutrition, disease, and shell fire accentuated how, particularly at times of conflict, it became impossible to fulfill conventional British domestic ideals. Beyond the obvious destruction of a new generation of Britons in India, child death revealed the difficulty of maintaining British cultural traditions and hierarchies in the colonies. Typically cared for by Indian servants and, during the siege, put to rest by Indians rather than Europeans, in their deaths just as in their lives British children complicated understandings of a unified British community pitted against Indian rebels. Ultimately, however, as the Lucknow survivors' accounts reached the British public, any doubts about the stability of the British domestic sphere within the empire were either displaced onto "vacant" women writers like Adelaide Case, presented as more concerned with crockery than victory, or forgotten altogether. As more British women settled in India after 1858, an ever more rigid Anglo-Indian colonial domesticity and sexual morality took hold, banishing concubinage and cross-racial intimacies from public view and reinforcing the lines of urban segregation.[122]

The political context of the Indian Rebellion shaped how Britons grieved child death, and grief, in turn, ultimately served to strengthen British imperialism. Without access to communal British mourning rituals, including the witnessing of a child's death and salvation, the preparation of the body, the funeral and burial service, and the marking of the grave for future visitation, survivors initially struggled to articulate and perform their grief. They pointed to their inability to mourn for children who died during war as a means to highlight the incongruity between an idealized childhood in safe, "British" domestic spaces and extreme wartime violence. These accounts suggested, in fact, that children should never have been present in such circumstances. The initial reports from Lucknow marked a "cultural trauma," and like many mid-Victorian literary and historical representations of "the Mutiny," they contained what Christopher Herbert identifies as a "sometimes dizzying rhetorical instability" and "incurable self-contradiction" about such fundamental questions as the excessiveness of British force, the law, race, and religion—contradictions ultimately overshadowed by repeated cries for vengeance and rising imperialist propaganda following the 1865 Jamaican Rebellion and late Victorian colonization of Africa.[123] The swift reclamation of British grieving rituals beginning with the distribution of mourning attire as survivors made their way from Lucknow to Calcutta and the retelling of child wartime casualties as beautiful deaths surely allowed many survivors to express their sorrow more openly, providing them with comfort and solace. However, such nationalistic expressions of grief also left much unspoken and unremembered: the anguish of violent child death, the struggle for resources divided unequally among the besieged population, the awareness that Indian as well as British children were dying and that Britons were dependent on Indians for survival, and the utter loss of oneself that can come with grief for another (Bartrum's sense that she was "stripped of all," "empty & desolate")—in sum, the collapse of an idealized British domestic sphere as a foundation of empire. The forms of national mourning and memory that eventually dominated public accounts reaffirmed the ties that bound all Britons along with the distinct subject positions that had been eroded during the conflict: military men and domestic women, British colonizers and Indian subjects, nurturing adults and innocent, protected children.

4

"A Loud and Bitter Cry"

The Mourned and Unmourned in Late Nineteenth-Century Urban Public Health Debates

In her 1871 pamphlet, *Women and Doctors: or Medical Despotism in England*, Mary Catherine Hume-Rothery condemned what she viewed as the dangerous collaboration between the medical profession and the state. Hume-Rothery, daughter of the Radical MP Joseph Hume, was a supporter of women's suffrage and equality. She emerged as a leader in the campaigns against compulsory smallpox vaccination and the Contagious Diseases (CD) Acts that imposed state regulation of prostitution.[1] Claiming that "doctors are the popes of the nineteenth century in England," she railed against a host of modern compulsory public health measures: not only the Vaccination Acts (1853, 1861, 1867, 1871) and CD Acts (1864, 1866, 1869), but also various Habitual Drunkards bills. She decried proposals that death certificates be granted by only qualified (male) medical practitioners or health officers, denounced plans for the registration and burial of stillborn children, and opposed local laws requiring the notification of infectious diseases.[2] Such laws, and the medical boards of health that enforced them, she argued, acted against the "true principles of self-government, and of civil and religious liberty."[3] "An Englishman's house is no longer his own," she declared, asserting that "no such despotism ever existed in this free (?) country as is now wielded by the so-called State medical authorities."[4] Hume-Rothery stressed the particular oppression of women by the CD Acts in public spaces and, in the privacy of homes, physician rooms, and hospitals, women's vulnerability to rape and sexual assault by male medical authorities, who left victims "stifling their secret horror and loathing as treason against the all-trusted medical dictator."[5] Her jarring text drew upon personal, political, and spiritual registers as she connected these "secret horrors" to the new powers of the modern medical state, which she understood as infringing upon bodily integrity and violating individual rights. She associated public health with rape, state-licensed prostitution, tyrannical government mandates, and restrictions on the mourning of the dead. Such oppressive structures, she argued, acted against "free trade in medicine," creating a system in which Englishwomen "dare no longer call their bodies or their babes their own."[6]

Throughout *Women and Doctors*, child death served as the ultimate signifier of male medical authorities' and the state's overreach, while public grief for dead children gave voice to political resistance. Hume-Rothery blamed the death of Princess Charlotte and her infant in 1817 on the male obstetrician Sir Richard Croft (who later committed suicide), and indeed presented the death of her own firstborn son as the result of having relied on a male physician, rather than a midwife.[7] Petitioning Parliament, she opposed reforms intended to sideline female midwives, writing, "The unnatural and revolting practice of Man-midwifery is the cause of immeasurable mischiefs, of countless deaths of mothers and babes."[8] She warned of cases of "death from vaccination" and "from the unwarranted and premature use of instruments in childbirth."[9] Under the Vaccination Acts, she protested, "parents are fined and imprisoned for refusing to submit their children to what they regard, and justly regard, as the deadly risk of receiving into their infant veins corrupt matter."[10] In response to such increasing local and national state efforts to regulate public health, she correctly predicted widespread popular resistance embodied by the "justice-loving, and child-loving heart of John Bull."[11]

By the 1870s and 1880s, the child's dead body had become a contested site in debates over the responsibilities and limits of state public health initiatives. A new politics of childhood emerged, in which medical reformers and their opponents mobilized celebrations of child life and grief over child death for political purposes. While in the 1830s Michael Sadler's references to dying factory children could still spark smirks among his fellow parliamentarians, by the century's end, scenes of young British corpses and dying children evoking the need for government intervention were ubiquitous and hard to dismiss. Building upon the 1870 (England and Wales) and 1872 (Scotland) National Education Acts, local and national governments extended their reach over youth and the domestic sphere.

These efforts resulted in a series of laws that expanded the influence of the state, including the Infant Life Protection Acts (1872, 1897) curtailing "baby farming" and infanticide; the Criminal Law Amendment Act (1885) raising the age of consent for girls from thirteen to sixteen; and the Children's Acts (1889, 1908), which extended definitions of child abuse and neglect, increasing state powers to claim custody from parents. Supporting these reforms were new philanthropic organizations, such as the Society for the Preservation of Infant Life, founded in 1870, and the National Society for the Prevention of Cruelty to Children, established in 1889. Although the state remained a "messy, fractured entity," it defined its role more and more as a protector of infant and child life.[12] The state intervened not only in questions of child labor, but also in education, childcare, sexuality, nourishment, medical treatment, and disease prevention. Yet even as government officials justified their actions through this new politics of childhood, their opponents similarly weaponized child death and mourning. For Hume-Rothery and her anti-vaccinationist supporters who pitted parents against "medical despots," the dead child came to represent the suffering caused by an interventionist state that disregarded the rights of "child-loving" Britons. Thus, by the last decades of the nineteenth century, mourning the British child's dead body held particular importance in debates over the role of the state and the rights of citizens, inspiring both demands for, and popular opposition to, greater state intervention in public health.

Through these public health debates, fears of infant mortality and the treatment of young corpses outlined communal values negotiating the boundaries of state power. As Thomas Laqueur contends in *The Work of the Dead*, "the dead make social worlds," the "corpse demands the attention of the living."[13] Over centuries and across the globe, Laqueur argues, the treatment of the dead is an expression of community values and the very nature of humanity. In late nineteenth-century Britain, regulating who could register a death, who could prepare a body for burial, who could grieve a child's passing in public became means of granting and denying political voice. This chapter explores the politicization of child death and mourning through case studies of three of the most influential nineteenth-century public health reforms: the Reverend Andrew Mearns's *Bitter Cry of Outcast London* (1883) and urban housing reform, Josephine Butler's leadership against the Contagious Diseases Acts (repealed in 1886), and the protest movement against compulsory smallpox vaccination (effectively ended in 1907). In each of these campaigns, public mourning for dead children—no doubt sincere and deeply felt—emerged as a dominant discourse laid claim to by all sorts of opposing groups. Appeals to the preciousness of child life and the mourning of child death served as recognized strategies for those seeking political legitimacy: local and state officials working to redefine the role of the state as well as women and working-class men, including those newly granted suffrage and those who continued to be disenfranchised under the Reform Acts of 1867 and 1884. Communal responses to the figure of the child corpse could justify new state powers, new political voices, new conceptions of rights.

Behind the debates over late-Victorian public health reforms was an emerging and highly contested "emotional regime," William Reddy's term for the "normative order for emotions" that is essential to "any stable political regime."[14] This emotional order prioritized expressions valuing child life along with fears of child harm as a means to bolster state authority. The state, as Antoinette Burton argues, is not in this sense an established "forged" entity, but rather "something *always* in the process of *becoming*," "an historically pliable ideal always being performed through repetitive and ritualized acts, but never fully achieved."[15] Among these "repetitive and ritualized acts" were communal displays of grief for children. Such moments highlighted developing understandings of the modern medical state and the fraught relationship between public health reforms serving the common good and individual rights. Most of all, new agents avowed their bereavement and love for children as a foundational claim to political rights and representation within the nation.

The Bitter Cry of Outcast London (1883)

To make the case for state public health reforms, the Congregationalist minister Andrew Mearns's *Bitter Cry of Outcast London* (1883) lamented child death in London's worst working-class neighborhoods. Drawing on the works of earlier journalists and health reformers such as Edwin Chadwick and William Farr, Mearns used his wildly successful short pamphlet to educate a broad audience on the conditions and case studies of working-class housing that before had mainly been limited to the reports of medical officers of health.[16] *The Bitter Cry* prompted the creation of the Royal Commission on the Housing of the Working Classes (1884–85) and resulted in legislation, such as the Housing Act of 1885, that transformed London's urban landscape. The new laws empowered London's central authority, the Metropolitan Board of Works, to build and manage affordable rentals for the working classes.[17] First published in October 1883 as a penny pamphlet by the London Congregational Union, *The Bitter Cry* became a national sensation after the editor William T. Stead publicized the work through leading articles, editorials, and response letters from readers in the *Pall Mall Gazette*. *The Bitter Cry* scandalized audiences with its account of sexual immorality involving children. "Incest is common," wrote Mearns, in overcrowded homes.[18] Scholars have focused on how this first reference to incest in so public a forum transformed working-class housing into a national issue.[19] Yet working-class responses to child death—and the implied necessity of local government intervention—were an equally important and even more thoroughly documented aspect of *The Bitter Cry*'s argument.

The Bitter Cry became a national sensation in the 1880s, but Mearns drew upon decades of earlier public health campaigns. The identification of cities as death traps and the subsequent call for public health measures gained momentum in the 1830s with workers' efforts to document higher mortality rates in factory towns—a theme taken up by industrial novelists and critics of the 1840s and 1850s. Many of these accounts featured the deaths of children. For example, in *The Condition of the Working Class in England* (published in German in 1845 and first translated into English in 1886), Friedrich Engels stressed the particular danger cities posed to youth. "Nowhere," he decried, "are so many children run over, nowhere are so many killed by falling, drowning, or burning, as in the great cities and towns of England."[20] Those who survived early childhood, asserted Engels, remained more likely to die early from the "life-long traces" stamped upon young digestive organs and bodies damaged by unfit food and improper clothing, reliance on child-soothing spirits and opiates, exposure to disease and urban filth, and the eventual burdens of industrial labor.[21] By the 1850s and 1860s, cholera (the "best of all sanitary reformers," according to *The Times*) and other diseases propelled municipal governments to improve urban conditions by providing clean water and sewage systems.[22] In his famous Crystal Palace campaign speech of 1872, Benjamin Disraeli celebrated the public health policies, including urban sanitation and housing reform, that contributed to his victory over William Gladstone as prime minister in 1874. "Well, it may be the 'policy of sewage' to a Liberal member of Parliament," declared Disraeli. "But to one of the labouring multitude of England, who has found fever always to be one of the inmates of his household—who has, year after year, seen stricken down the children of his loins, on whose sympathy and material support he has looked with hope and confidence, it is not a 'policy of sewage,' but a question of life and death."²³ Conservatives and socialists alike featured the figure of the dead child in their rhetoric.

Infant and child death rates surfaced as major issues of national and imperial alarm by the late nineteenth century.²⁴ New methods of statistical analysis brought new knowledge of mortality patterns as census results, parliamentary committees, and extensive publications by the Royal Statistical Society (founded in 1834 and granted a royal charter in 1887) supplied additional data. The 1874 Births and Deaths Registration Act made compulsory the civil registration of all births and deaths in England and Wales, a practice initiated in 1837 under the newly created General Register Office.²⁵ According to Edward Higgs, whereas the registration of births and deaths began "for the purpose of determining the lines of descent that affected property rights," by the 1870s the protection of infant life proved a motivating force behind the 1874 legislation requiring registration.²⁶ During the last decades of the century, the General Register Office's numbers revealed an intractably high infant mortality rate (the deaths of children under one year old), which remained elevated and actually rose at the century's end even as national death rates for older children and adults steadily fell. Child mortality was highest in impoverished metropolitan neighborhoods. In Liverpool, for example, the 1899 infant death rate was 136 per one thousand live births in upper-class districts and 274 in working-class areas, but the poorest streets in this group experienced an infant mortality rate of 509.²⁷ In this context, representations of child death and particular concern about the care of children's dead bodies became common themes in public health debates. Urban reformers mobilized representations of dead children alongside stubborn infant mortality rates to call for state action against overcrowding and poor sanitation, environmental pollution and infectious diseases.²⁸

Mearns based his study of London housing not only on the work of earlier medical reformers, but also on the journalistic tradition of urban travel literature, in some cases taking material directly from George Sims's previously published exposé on urban housing, *How the Poor Live* (1883).²⁹ Like the architect George Godwin and other writers in the genre before him, Sims introduced elite readers to his "book of travel" by situating impoverished London within the context of Britain's rapidly expanding empire. He promised to take readers "into a dark continent that is within easy walking distance of the General Post Office," in hopes that "the wild races who inhabit it will, I trust, gain public sympathy as easily as those savage tribes for whose benefit the Missionary Societies never cease to appeal for funds."[30] Along with details of dilapidated and diseased interiors, Sims reprinted reports of children's dead bodies kept in overcrowded homes in order to argue for magistrates' increased powers to remove corpses and regulate burial practices.[31] By the 1880s, most working-class families buried kin within four days after death,[32] but Sims featured extreme cases: the body of a child kept by parents in Spitalfields for fifteen days after the child's death, the "dead body of a child which had died of scarlet fever" that "lay exposed on a table in one corner of the room," and another child from Spitalfields "whose body was retained for nine days."[33] He concluded that it was "an appalling fact that the poor have grown so used to discomfort and horrors that they do not look upon a corpse in the room they live, and eat, and sleep in as anything very objectionable!"[34] In Sims's account, dead children were everywhere.

Even more than Sims's exposé, *The Bitter Cry of Outcast London* brought attention to child corpses in working-class homes and neighborhoods. Mearns acknowledged the influence of *How the Poor Live* on his own work and directly incorporated one spectacular case from Sims in *The Bitter Cry* involving the body of a deceased baby kept for days within the home of the infant's parents and two siblings. The incident, also widely reported in newspaper inquest columns, occurred on Wych Street (an area demolished by the London County Council in 1901) in Central London. Mearns wrote that the "infant was the second child who had died, poisoned by the foul atmosphere; and this dead baby was cut open in the one room where its parents and brothers and sisters lived, ate and slept, *because the parish had no mortuary and no room in which post-mortems could be performed!*"[35] The alleged lack of care for the infant's body—culminating in its dissection within the domestic setting—signaled the failure of government along with parents. The original account by Sims quoted the newspaper inquest report in which jury members declared "that there being no mortuary was a disgrace to the local authority" and "that the circumstances surrounding the case they had investigated were a disgrace to this enlightened age."[36] In *The Bitter Cry*, Mearns paired the case with other examples of childhood suffering: "eight destitute children" orphaned and on their way to the workhouse, and "a neglected, ragged, bare-legged little baby girl of four" left alone for most of the day by her militiaman father and drunken mother "in charge of the infant that we see crawling about the floor." Mearns suggested that his readers could "see" and feel what working-class families could not. "The child-misery that one beholds is the most heart-rending and appalling element in these discoveries," Mearns concluded, noting that "from the beginning of their lives they are utterly neglected."[37] The infant corpse heartlessly dissected within the family's living area thus represented much more generalized examples of child neglect and domestic collapse (hunger, poverty, sexual abuse, lack of parental oversight) associated with overcrowding as the need to protect childhood emerged as a main argument for urban reform. But more than this, Mearns claimed to document a lack of feeling, a lack of mourning for, or even acknowledgment of, working-class children by their families.

The Bitter Cry was littered with other examples of child corpses that, according to Mearns, remained unnoticed, unrecognized, and unmourned. In addition to the case of the Wych Street children "poisoned by the foul atmosphere" of their home, Mearns described finding within "these rotten and reeking tenements" "seven people living in one underground kitchen and a little dead child lying in the same room." In another case, a "poor widow" resided with "her three children, and a child who had been dead thirteen days."[38] Nothing separated the living from the dead in these brief case histories. Any details of what happened to children's corpses focused on their inhumane treatment. In addition to the Wych Street dissection, The Bitter Cry told of how in Bermondsey there "were recently found the bodies of nine infants, which had been deposited in a large box at the foot of some stairs in an undertaker's shop."[39] In a singular case recording parental anguish, readers learned a "mother's death was caused by witnessing one of her children being run over."[40] Death pervaded these London neighborhoods, according to Mearns, where the only shelter for the poor was "a living tomb."[41] Even the very air was contaminated by "the putrefying carcases of dead cats or birds, or viler abominations still."[42] And yet, like the "half-drunken Irishwoman" who presented "a putrid turkey, utterly unfit for human food, which she tells us she is going to cook for dinner," Mearns implied that most inhabitants of London's slums had yet fully to distinguish the living from the dead, much less properly grieve these deaths.[43]

By repeating shocking examples of neglected childhood and neglected child corpses throughout his short exposé, Mearns thus not only brought new attention to the interiors of working-class homes as Anthony Wohl has shown, but also suggested society's failure to recognize and cultivate the very interiority and preciousness of modern childhood among the working classes.[44] Quoting Dickens's *Dombey and Son* (1846–48), Mearns claimed that the slums "bred 'infancy that knows no innocence.'"[45] Like his predecessors, he suggested that working-class families failed to appreciate emerging understandings of childhood that separated work from domestic spaces, and even failed to notice or mourn in any way the deaths of their own children. For Mearns and his supporters, hearing the "bitter cry" of the London poor depended on sympathy and recognition originating from the middle classes and the larger public. In this model of urban reform, the child's sense of self and interiority (identified by Carolyn Steedman as a fundamental aspect of modern childhood) remained to be expressed and mourned by reformers such as Mearns and his readers.[46]

For Mearns, however much he insisted on the factual basis of his report, it was this appeal to emotion, the ability to make readers feel anguish and pain on behalf of children, that shaped his approach and goals. His "recital of plain facts," wrote Mearns, "must be to every Christian heart a loud and bitter cry."[47] Sims likewise prefaced *How the Poor Live* with a direct appeal to his readers' sympathies. "If an occasional lightness of treatment seems to the reader out of harmony with so grave a subject," he wrote, "I pray that he will remember the work was undertaken to enlist the sympathies of a class not generally given to the study of 'low life.'"[48] Writing three decades before Mearns, George Godwin also referenced the emotional turmoil that he anticipated readers might feel as well as his own suffering as he examined London's housing problem. "Some of our readers will perhaps say to us," he reflected, "'Your statements are too truthful, too minute, and they give us pain.' We regret to be forced to give pain: what we have seen and what we have written have caused more grief to ourselves than to our readers."[49] Likewise, Mearns recounted the "feeling" caused by such cases of "heart-breaking misery" that left witnesses "oppressed in spirit and absorbed in painful thought," disoriented and unbound, unsure "whither they are going."[50] Grief stripped away false securities, while enabling new possibilities.

The Bitter Cry demanded public action. Mearns called for Christian churches to do more to help the poor than "superficial and inadequate district visitation" and "indiscriminate distribution of material charities."[51] His solution required nondenominational collaboration among Christians, but also most crucially state intervention. He declared, "Without State interference nothing effectual can be accomplished upon any large scale."[52] The Artisans' Dwellings Act of 1875 had only resulted in greater overcrowding by demolishing the worst areas and raising rents. According to Mearns, the "state must make short work of this iniquitous traffic, and secure for the poorest the rights of citizenship; the right to live in something better than fever dens; the right to live as something better than the uncleanest of brute beasts."[53] By mourning child deaths, Mearns reclaimed the working classes from their outcast status. *The Bitter Cry of Outcast London* based the right of all citizens to decent housing on the inherent interiority and humanity of all, especially working-class children, whose innocence, suffering, and death called for national recognition and mourning. And yet, *The Bitter Cry*'s visionary ideal of the right to good housing gained support through the erasure and silencing of other forms of mourning—that of working-class mothers and fathers, neighbors and communities that lay at the heart of their very claims to citizenship. By claiming that children in London's most impoverished neighborhoods remained "unmourned," Mearns erased working-class grief.

Josephine Butler's Public Mourning and the Contagious Diseases Acts

Josephine Butler (1828–1906), the leader of the campaign to repeal the CD Acts, witnessed the death of her only daughter, Evangeline, then five years old, after the child fell over the stair banister onto the marble floor some forty feet below as she rushed to greet her parents. In the months that followed, Butler steadily turned her spiritual and emotional energies of grief toward public philanthropic work. Recalling this period in her life, she wrote:

> Music, art, reading, all failed as resources to alleviate or to interest. I became possessed with an irresistible desire to go forth and find some pain keener than my own, to meet with people more unhappy than myself (for I knew there were thousands of such). I did not exaggerate my own trial. I only knew that my heart ached night and day, and that the only solace possible would seem to be to find other hearts which ached night and day, and with more reason than mine. I had no clear idea beyond that, no plan for helping others; my sole wish was to plunge into the heart of some human misery, and to say (as I now knew I could) to afflicted people, "I understand: I too have suffered."[54]

Following Eva's death in the summer of 1864, Butler, her husband, and their three sons moved from Cheltenham to Liverpool in January 1866. Here she immersed herself in social work with women workhouse inmates, prostitutes, and "friendless girls." She quickly emerged as a supporter of women's suffrage and education, and as the national leader for the campaign against the CD Acts.

Rather than detailing the specific goals of her work in these areas (topics that have already received substantial scholarly attention), my focus is on how the death of her daughter and her bereavement shaped Butler's public persona and activism.[55] A devout Anglican, she emphasized that spirituality required worldly action. Although Butler always remained a controversial figure, she in part legitimated her public prominence not only through such references to women's spirituality, but also through her personal grief as a mother who lost her only daughter. Observers frequently remarked on Butler's "sadness" and spirituality to describe her allure and to justify her public presence. She built a cross-class alliance of women by seeking out other forms of suffering that resonated with her own. As the death of children gained new prominence during the nineteenth century, Butler drew upon her maternal mourning to elicit empathy and claim a place for women in the urban public sphere. As a libertarian, she challenged the CD Acts and other public health policies that she deemed violated individual rights. At the same time, she rejected liberal notions of political rights as limited to property-owning male citizens. For Butler, the campaign against the CD Acts revealed an understanding of rights based upon bodily integrity as well as the human ability of feeling citizens to suffer and grieve and empathize.

FIGURE 13. George Frederic Watts's portrait of Josephine Butler in widow's cap and mourning dress was part of his Hall of Fame collection of the nation's great figures (the only painting of a woman in this series). Butler remarked that the portrait captured the sorrows and suffering of her past. *Josephine Butler* by George Frederic Watts, 1895, oil on canvas. (© National Portrait Gallery, London)

More than any other issue besides slavery, the state regulation of prostitution (legal in the United Kingdom) instituted in the CD Acts galvanized the feminist movement, bringing together women and men from the working and middle classes and reinforcing their commitment to women's suffrage as the ultimate means to guarantee women's constitutional rights. Both the antislavery movement and the campaign to repeal the CD Acts (a crusade also referred to as "abolition" by Butler) provided women with the experience of public speaking and political organizing for a just and righteous cause. Opponents of the CD Acts combined religious and moral rhetoric with the language of political rights to demand women's full liberties as citizens. Like many other feminist reformers active in the 1870s and 1880s, the repealers directly challenged sexual and legal double standards for men and women.

Initially passed as military provisions, the CD Acts at first received little debate and discussion even though they marked an extreme restriction of women's rights. After a government study of the military found soldiers suffering from remarkably high rates of venereal disease, Parliament passed the first CD Act of 1864 to regulate sex workers in select ports and garrison towns in southern England and Ireland. The subsequent acts extended regulation to eighteen ports and military districts in the United Kingdom. The CD Acts empowered plainclothes policemen in these areas to detain any women suspected of prostitution and force them to undergo regular fortnightly medical examinations to check for disease. A woman who refused to submit voluntarily to the examination had to present her case before the local magistrate to prove she was not a prostitute. If, as often happened, the court rejected her statement and she still refused the exam, she could be sent to prison. When doctors diagnosed the detained woman as having a sexually transmitted infection, she could be forcibly hospitalized for months. Furthermore, the CD Acts required women identified as prostitutes to register as such. As Judith Walkowitz has shown, many working women turned to sex work periodically in times of economic crisis rather than as a full-time profession, but by publicly identifying these women as prostitutes, the CD Acts contributed to their isolation as an outcast group.[56]

Florence Nightingale condemned the acts early on, but widespread public opposition began only in 1869 and lasted through the suspension of the CD Acts in 1883 and their eventual repeal in 1886. By 1867 doctors and sanitary reformers proposed an extension of the legislation to the north of England (where opposition to the Vaccination Acts was strongest), suggesting that they envisioned the CD Acts as a model of new state powers for all of the United Kingdom rather than simply reforms limited to ports and garrisons. Some prominent women supported regulation, including the physician Elizabeth Garrett Anderson, the only female member of the British Medical Association for nineteen years after her admission in 1873. In 1869, however, opponents of the CD Acts formed the National Association for the Repeal of the Contagious Diseases Acts—a group that excluded women from its first meeting and thus prompted Butler and Elizabeth Wolstenholme Elmy to create the Ladies' National Association for the Repeal of the Contagious Diseases Acts (LNA). Both organizations worked to gain support through petitioning, holding large public meetings, forming local branch associations, and lobbying members of Parliament and the electorate. They wrote pamphlets and circulated information through their official journal, *The Shield*. British women had previously drawn upon their domestic authority and knowledge to take political stands against slavery, the New Poor Law of 1834, the Corn Laws, and in other campaigns. Yet, for many, the movement to repeal the CD Acts marked a new level of public activism and leadership. As Walkowitz remarks, the "campaign brought thousands of respectable women, the 'shrieking sisterhood,' into the political arena for the first time."[57]

The health of military men motivated initial support for the CD Acts, but medical experts also justified unprecedented encroachments upon women's rights through appeals to improve infant mortality rates. As early as 1846, the physician William Acton observed that adults with syphilis experienced very low mortality rates, but "that syphilis is particularly fatal during the first year of age."[58] A French study from 1885 estimated that congenital syphilis resulted in the deaths of 68 percent of infants born to parents with the illness, leading the British Royal Statistical Society to conclude that "apart from any question of abstract morality, the benefit of stamping out syphilis for the saving of infant life is obvious."[59] Protecting child life and innocence soon emerged as dominant themes on both sides of the debate. An advocate for repeal noted that those "who oppose the Acts are charged with heartless disregard for the innocent and unborn, who suffer miserably for the sins of their husbands and their parents." The medical statistics on syphilis and infant mortality were exaggerated, the author argued, stressing that the "protection of innocent women and children is an after-thought, and the shallowest of pretences" for laws that "violate the moral feelings of the country."[60] Feelings gained traction as political argument. Within this context, Josephine Butler's public mourning over her daughter's tragic death held political power. It allowed her to oppose the CD Acts in the name of women's rights while unquestionably valuing child life.

Almost all assessments of Josephine Butler's life emphasize the link between Eva's death and Butler's emergence as one of the century's greatest feminist reformers. Stead, whose "Maiden Tribute of Modern Babylon" (1885) was largely inspired by Butler's work, characterized Eva's death as the turning point in Butler's life. Reflecting on this tragedy, he wrote, "Such was the call which first roused Josephine Butler to action."[61] Comparing Butler to "the great mediaeval saints" (even suggesting that she might be "the reincarnation of St. Catherine of Siena or St. Theresa"), he praised Butler for "that divine quality of the soul which manifests itself in deeds of moral heroism."[62] Stead stressed Butler's Evangelical approach to religion, her fundamental belief that spirituality inspired and even necessitated worldly action—what Helen Mathers has called an "'active experience' of Christ."[63] Yet he also associated Butler's accomplishments with personal suffering. Those who worked closely with her, Stead claimed, could "appreciate the agony of soul, the long martyrdom of passionate pity, through which she, our leader, passed unshrinking and undismayed."[64] In this passage from Stead's 1907 memorial in the *Review of Reviews*, he made no direct reference to Eva's death, but rather a generalized allusion to Butler's "agony" and "martyrdom," thereby conflating the experience of her daughter's death with the public attacks she suffered as leader of the campaign to repeal the CD Acts.

Butler's obituary in *The Times* devoted greater attention to her early interest in questions of sexual double standards and prostitution, but, like Stead, positioned Eva's death as the moment when Butler began to engage these issues in the public sphere. Focusing on the domestic nature of her early married life at Oxford in the 1850s, where her husband, George, took a position as a university examiner, *The Times* wrote that Josephine Butler "proved a most capable and sympathetic helpmate to her husband, drawing maps for his lectures, or puzzling out old Chaucers in the Bodleian."[65] Even so, the *Times* obituary retold the well-known anecdote of how, at Oxford, "her indignation was first aroused against 'certain accepted theories in society,'" such as "'that a moral lapse in a woman was immensely worse than in a man,' and that the social evil was to be passed over in silence."[66] Frustrated by the "society of celibates, with little or no leaven of family life,"[67] Butler, according to *The Times*, began her work with women by taking in a servant from Newgate prison, "a young betrayed mother who had been sentenced for the murder of her infant."[68]

The *Times* stressed, however, that it was after the family moved from Oxford to Cheltenham and then, after Eva's death, to Liverpool that Butler fully dedicated herself to reform work and the previously fraught boundaries between domestic and public spaces receded. Citing Butler's own words that her daughter's death impelled her to "go forth and find some pain keener than my own," *The Times* proceeded to list the urban public spaces where Butler applied her sympathetic energies: "the hospital," the "oakum-picking sheds of the Liverpool workhouse," and "the quays." Shared suffering blurred the distinctions between home and city. "Into the garrets of their house the Butlers 'crowded as many as possible of the most friendless girls who were anxious to make a fresh start.'" In 1866, *The Times* wrote, they founded a "House of Rest for such cases—which long afterwards became a municipal institution—and also an industrial home for healthy and active but friendless girls."[69]

Butler's public and shared mourning thus became an essential part of her identity as a public speaker and reform leader. She was selected to represent the repeal movement because of her status as an elite married woman and mother, but also because of her grief following Eva's death. "She bore the marks of a sad and terrible consecration," wrote Canon Henry Scott Holland. "She had a magnetic influence over the spirit, and she laid on us the compulsion of a call to the service of the broken and wounded."[70] Similarly, two of Butler's coworkers in the repeal campaign underscored the effects of Butler's sorrow as she took her position to deliver a speech in Bristol in 1870. "As she moved to the table she raised her eyes with such a look of inexpressible sadness, as if the weight of the world's sin & sorrows rested on her innocent head," remarked one of the women from the audience; a "woman Christ to save us from our despair was the involuntary thought that came into my head & has never left it."[71] After Butler's death, the *Review of Reviews* concluded the list of qualities that allowed her to lead a "nation to revolt" by stressing her "mother's tenderness enlarged by sorrow and sympathy to enfold a world of suffering and sin."[72] Likewise, on Butler's death, the Reverend Thomas Phillips declared, "She went out into the streets saying to other people's daughters—'Come home with me—I had a daughter once.' That henceforward was to be the distinguishing characteristic of her work. Others went to save souls, and others to rescue women: but her mission was to save daughters and be a mother to the lost."[73] Butler's power to move audiences—bringing grown men to tears and inspiring vitriol from brothel owners and their supporters—stemmed from many factors, including her beauty, her feminine demeanor and elite background, and her religious spirit.⁷⁴ But, as these testimonies demonstrate, her ability to connect with others through her grief over Eva's tragic death remained an essential element of her public persona.

In her own writings, Butler emphasized that her turn toward public reform work stemmed from her intensified religious commitment to worldly action and the need to communicate her personal grief following Eva's death. Butler published an early account of Eva's death, a letter written from the house in Cheltenham in August 1864, in her book recounting life with her husband, *Recollections of George Butler* (1892).⁷⁵ In the published letter, Butler conveyed the violence of her daughter's death—"the shock of the suddenness of that agonising death"—"the fall, the sudden cry, and then the silence." "It was pitiful to see her," wrote Butler, "helpless in her father's arms, her little drooping head resting on his shoulder, and her beautiful golden hair, all stained with blood, falling over his arm."⁷⁶ Butler contrasted the violence of this death with the "sweet life" of her daughter, who "never gave us a moment of anxiety, her life was one flowing stream of mirth and fun and abounding love."⁷⁷ While recognizing the potential of what seemed to be "a most cruel accident" to undo her belief in God, Butler survived with an even greater faith.⁷⁸ She reaffirmed God's presence in her accounts of Eva's last moments, drawing upon Evangelical models of the good death, particularly the child's dying recognition of God as witnessed and acknowledged by adults.⁷⁹ Butler explicitly noted the moment when Eva met God: "Her face, as she lay in death, wore a look of sweet, calm surprise, as if she said, 'Now I see God.' We stood in awe before her. She seemed to rebuke our grief in her rapt and holy sleep."⁸⁰ Toward the end of her life, Butler recalled this moment in a letter to her eldest son, George, stressing Eva's transformation: "I wish you could have seen her look then. You know what a merry face she generally had. But now the merry look had changed for one of the most deep and holy *wonder*, grave and solemn."⁸¹ For herself and her husband, Butler observed, "This sorrow seemed to give in a measure a new direction to our lives and interests."⁸² She later told a friend, "What a piercing sorrow it was to lose my sweet Eva, and what an inspiration, in a certain way, the memory of her was to me."⁸³ For Butler, her daughter became a model of Christian action. "She was always showing her love in active ways," recalled Butler. "We used to imagine what it would be when she grew up, developing into acts of mercy and kindness."⁸⁴

The Butlers' move to Liverpool in 1866 provided ample opportunities. In contrast to "the academic, intellectual character of Oxford" and "the quiet educational and social conditions at Cheltenham," Liverpool was a global shipping port, the former center of the trade of enslaved people, characterized by "great wealth" and "abject poverty," "perpetual movement," and "the clash of interests in its midst."[85] It was here that Butler sought out "other hearts which ached night and day," recognizing, "It was not difficult to find misery in Liverpool."[86] She experienced her fullest expression of unrestrained sorrow not within the privacy of her home, where she was left alone as her "husband and sons began their regular life at the College," or even earlier, still at Cheltenham, when she comforted herself and her bereaved husband in his study: "I kneeled beside him, and, shaking myself out of my own stupor of grief," wrote Butler, "I spoke 'comfortably' to him, and forced myself to talk cheerfully, even joyfully, of the happiness of our child."[87] Instead, Butler wrote of expressing her most intense anguish publicly within the oakum sheds of the Liverpool workhouse along with some two hundred women and girls. The sound of kneeling and praying together with these women, Butler described, "was a strange sound, that united wail—continuous, pitiful, strong—like a great sigh or murmur of vague desire and hope, issuing from the heart of despair, piercing the gloom and murky atmosphere of that vaulted room, and reaching to the heart of God."[88]

In her philanthropy and campaign against the CD Acts, Butler gave voice to her maternal grief, loss, and suffering as the basis for empathy and reform. Her speeches, writings, and even her carte de visite, a photograph of the Scottish sculptor Alexander Munro's bust showing her in mourning soon after Eva's death, told how grief inspired and legitimated her public presence (figs. 14 and 15).[89] Butler's work in Liverpool began when a Quaker friend advised, "God hath taken to Himself her whom thou lovedst; but there are many forlorn young hearts who need that mother's love flowing from thine. Go to — Street, No. —, and knock." She obeyed, and found a refuge with some "forty lost girls" in need of "a mother's love." According to Stead, "Light had broken in upon her darkness, and a great love and compassion for the lost daughters of other mothers entered into the wounded heart of this bereaved mother; and Mrs. Butler's destiny was fixed. She rose and went out, and began her ministry."[90] In her first publication against the CD Acts, written anonymously in 1870 under the pseudonym "an English Mother," Butler described bonding with a "poor repentant girl" by tending her bedside, stroking her hair, and kissing her forehead with "a pure love."[91] Butler developed these themes in "The Dark Side of English Life: Illustrated in a Series of True Stories," in which she

FIGURE 14. Sepia studio portrait of commemorative marble bust of Evangeline Butler by Alexander Munro. (Northumberland Archives ZBU/E/3/A/11/13)

FIGURE 15. Josephine Butler's carte de visite, a signed photograph of the sculpture of her by Alexander Munro. (Courtesy of the University of Liverpool Library, JB 2/1/6)

recounted the suffering of young sex workers and "abandoned women"—"Marion," "Katie," "Margaret," "Emma," and "Laura"—detailing the care she offered them through their dying days as they achieved union with God.[92] "Marion" lived with the Butlers for three months before her death. During this time, she studied the Scriptures with an intellect that rivaled George Butler's students at Oxford. Her "long death struggle" lasted twelve hours. She lost sight, then speech, soaked in perspiration from moving "her arms like a swimmer, as if she felt herself sinking in deep waters."[93] Before death she welcomed God and offered forgiveness to her abusers. Motherhood, as Walkowitz observes, served as a "political device" for Butler, allowing her to circumvent patriarchal authority, to claim political legitimacy and assert maternal oversight over women and girls.[94] She strove to cross class divides by appealing to maternal grief, while reminding readers through vivid accounts of the young women's repentance and good deaths that God was on their side.

Butler's maternal grief also resonated as she spoke directly to men who had sinned to bring them to her cause. With the opening passages of *The Hour Before the Dawn: An Appeal to Men* (1876), she characterized her writing as "the language of one who mourns for sin." She identified herself as "a fellow-sinner, a fellow-sufferer; for not in vain have I sat in darkness and in the shadow of death." Butler pleaded, "Do not reject my invitation and message of hope, for the language I speak is no rhetoric; every word is wrung out of a heart which has been exercised by no common suffering."[95] She placed her own personal anguish as the foundation of her empathy with other women and recognized the power that such shared suffering gave her to build a movement, appealing to men as well as to women. Toward the end of her life, Butler reflected on the success of the movement against the CD Acts. Drawing upon the example of Christ as well as her own personal history, she concluded that all successful social movements were based upon suffering: "In order to produce a movement of a vital, spiritual nature *someone must suffer*, someone must go through sore travail of soul before a living movement, outwardly visible, can be born."[96]

Feelings of grief and suffering also lay at the heart of Butler's understanding of citizenship and her condemnation of a patriarchal state that failed to recognize women. In her account of "Margaret," Butler provided a shockingly sympathetic take on infanticide, evoking Elizabeth Barrett Browning's "The Runaway Slave at Pilgrim's Point" and Sarah Parker Remond's antislavery lectures. In Butler's telling, Margaret, abandoned by the lover who refused to meet her eye, took the life of their infant. Bringing the child to the wood, she demanded in her madness, "Will ye die at once, now, my bonny, in your mammy's breast, or will ye linger long in your wasting weakness, and let me fetch in the police and the registrar of deaths to see that you have died after the lawful fashion—as a virtuous woman's bairn may die—of hunger?" Conflating her lover's abandonment with that of state officials prepared to witness a child die from hunger, Margaret "wrapped the wee limbs in her shawl, tighter, tighter, tighter, and the baby's breath was gone," just as the mother in "The Runaway Slave at Pilgrim's Point" "covered" her infant's "face in close and tight."[97] Modern policemen and state bureaucrats replaced pilgrim fathers. But, like Barrett Browning, Butler also concluded by asking, "Was Margaret the real murderer of that child?" What, she imagined, would happen if "the murdered infants, now hidden beneath the soil of England, were to rise to-day, and, spectre-like, stand face to face, not with their mothers, but with their *fathers?*"[98] This "infant army of spectres"—a militant visual incantation of maternal grief—would reveal before God, Butler declared (again with reference to Barrett Browning), the devastating loss of a political system founded upon the practice of "Women weeping out of sight, / Because men made the laws."[99]

For Butler, women's claims to suffrage and equal treatment under the law, including freedom from persecution of the CD Acts, thus rested not upon liberal notions of male property ownership, but upon human rights established in part through the ability to feel pain and sorrow, as well as hope and joy, and to recognize these emotions in others. To this end, the tactics of the repeal movement emphasized the physical harm and emotional anguish of enforced medical exams, what Butler and others termed "instrumental rape."[100] In the words of Hume-Rothery, the CD Acts set "police spies" against women, who were "legally violated by infernal steel and glass instruments, in the hands of male hirelings."[101] Repealers stressed that in the name of public health, the acts treated women as "chattel" rather than as human beings who feel pain and share a fundamental right to bodily autonomy. On the question of women's suffrage, Butler wrote in 1892 that men "do not know that at the bottom of that desire, underneath many other good motives, there lies a bitterness of woe which is the most powerful stimulus towards the desire for representation in the Legislature."[102] Following the repeal of the CD Acts, she anticipated some "new terrible injustice" that might bring "women to utter once more the bitter cry to which none of our legislators could pretend to be deaf." "But have we not," she proclaimed, demanding the vote, "as it is, sufficient trouble, and misery, and degradation among our own sex to make us utter even now the bitter cry—a cry however at the same time of hope, courage and confidence?"[103] Recognizing pain, above all grief and the loss of potential life it evoked, remained at the core of her argument for political rights and citizenship. The social world Butler envisioned, notes Elaine Hadley, was based on neither marketplace "private individualism" nor socialism, but rather on "a collective moral sense."[104]

The implicit and explicit use of the language of grief by Butler and her supporters marked a shift in the emotional regime similar to *The Bitter Cry of Outcast London*. Mourning, specifically mourning for children, paired in ways expected and unexpected with claims to interiority, bodily integrity, and the rights of citizenship. For Butler, grief identified her appreciation of child life, born and unborn, allowing her to refute charges that those women who opposed the CD Acts cared little for infant life. Eva's early death also resonated in the lives of women with futures cut short by poverty. Where Mearns professed to represent the unmourned, Butler voiced her own bitter cry. Maternal grief served as a source of empathy and legitimacy to connect her with the suffering of working-class women. Through her maternal grief, she gained power and authority to speak in public of things previously unspeakable for a woman: sex work, sexual assault, and government persecution of women. For the men and women of the anti-vaccinationist movement, public mourning and representations of children's corpses took even greater prominence as a basis for claims to citizenship and, in turn, sparked intense criticism.

Anti-Vaccinationist Funeral Processions as Political Protest

On March 23, 1885, anti-vaccinationists organized a giant international demonstration at Leicester. Protesters gathered from Great Britain and Ireland, Belgium, France, Germany, Switzerland, and even America. *The Times* reported over 20,000 marchers; other sources estimated as many as 100,000 people attended the event.[105] Demonstrators incorporated public displays of grief and mourning for children allegedly harmed by smallpox vaccination. Marchers created a storied procession to exhibit their criticisms of the Vaccination Acts: Along with displays of "furniture seized for blood-money," a model of Holloway prison, a horse and cow representing the sources of vaccination, and an effigy of Edward Jenner hanged from a gallows and scaffold, there was "a well-appointed hearse, with a child's coffin inscribed, 'Another victim of vaccination.'"[106] The *Daily News* reported

Figure 16. A life-sized float at the 1885 Leicester rally against compulsory vaccination reproduced this familiar image portraying the death of infants at the hands of doctors and the state. "Vaccination Act for Jenner-ation of Disease," *Police Illustrated News* (1886).

that "a real coffin for a child, covered with wreaths," was carried on a "carriage bier, and followed by mourners."[107] Banners highlighted women's grief with statements such as "Rachels are weeping for their children all over the land" and "The mothers of England demand repeal."[108] Women rode in wagons declaring to fight "against experimental butchery upon their defenceless little ones."[109] One life-size float reproduced an image familiar in the anti-vaccination press: "a skeleton vaccinating an infant in its mother's lap, while a policeman grips her uplifted hand—the mother's face being full of agony and the babe's face of infantine unconsciousness—while the skeleton and the officer of the law are grinning with horrid expressiveness" (fig. 16).[110] The day's events concluded with a burning of the Vaccination Acts to the tune of "Rule Britannia."

During the last decades of the nineteenth century, anti-vaccinationist demonstrators like those at the Leicester rally organized funeral processions to oppose what they viewed as the "medical tyranny" of the state, embodied in the Vaccination Acts. Drawing upon radical funeral traditions, anti-vaccinationists claimed public spaces as theirs in which to mourn and assert their communal rights of citizenship. They demanded Parliament hear their protests by distributing black-bannered handbills and publishing postmortem photographs of children.[111] Other radical groups, notably trade unionists, Chartists, and later suffragettes, employed funeral processions as a form of political protest.[112] But never before had there been such a direct political use of funeral traditions featuring child death. The anti-vaccinationists' actions demonstrate how emotions tied to childhood emerged as crucial markers of political legitimacy by the late nineteenth century. Public mobilization of grief for dead children (real and imagined) served to condemn state policies while affirming working-class and women's political rights. At the same time, the explicitly political expressions of mourning sparked controversy and ultimately reinforced widespread representations of the anti-vaccinationists' marginality and even inhumanity. The political and public expressions of mourning for children proved so new that they created a backlash from critics, who not only lambasted the anti-vaccinationists' medical arguments, but also decried their open displays of emotion as vulgar and inauthentic.

Despite the medical miracle of smallpox vaccination, which replaced earlier, more dangerous inoculation practices and saved millions of lives, anti-vaccination grew into one of the most popular movements of the nineteenth century. Nadja Durbach argues that opposition arose against state vaccination policies largely because of the class-based nature of the legislation, in addition to continued medical and religious resistance to the use of the cowpox vaccine developed by Edward Jenner in the 1790s.[113] The 1853 Vaccination Act required the vaccination of all infants within three months of birth in England and Wales, six months in Scotland. Popular resistance increased significantly after the 1867 act enforced compulsory vaccination more rigorously by appointing public vaccination officers and increasing penalties for noncompliance. By this time, private doctors who served wealthier clients generally preferred using calf lymph for the vaccine matter, while public vaccinators relied mostly on arm-to-arm vaccination.[114] Opponents of this method objected to the possible transmission of blood diseases, including erysipelas and in extremely rare cases syphilis, and to the widespread practice of harvesting vaccine lymph supplies directly from the cowpox pustules of recently vaccinated children primarily from the working class. Fear proved a main driving force behind the movement, since the actual threat of dying from diseases transmitted by arm-to-arm vaccination remained very low.

Yet political inequalities also fueled opposition to compulsory vaccination as adults objected to what they took as insufficient regard for the lives of working-class children as well as to the use of class-based methods of enforcing the law. Parents who refused to vaccinate their children could be fined up to twenty shillings, a punishment that, after 1867, could be imposed repeatedly until the child reached the age of fourteen. And after the 1871 Vaccination Act, guardians could also be fined twenty shillings for failing to return children to the public vaccinator for lymph extraction to fill national reserves—a process viewed by many as evidence of a vampiric state extracting the life force from working-class children. Parents unable to afford fines as well as court costs risked having their household goods seized and sold at public auctions; if fines remained unpaid, parents were liable to be sentenced to up to two weeks imprisonment. Durbach details the growth of the anti-vaccination movement, so that in Leicester, the center of protest, some factories closed for the 1885 anti-vaccinationist demonstration.[115] The government eventually created a clause for conscientious objection to vaccination in 1898, which in 1907 could be granted by a simple oath before a local magistrate or justice of the peace, thereby effectively undoing compulsory vaccination in Britain.[116] Victorian journalists and writers often characterized anti-vaccinationists as a fringe movement, but Durbach underscores their deep ties with other working-class groups, particularly the labor movement, Protestant dissenters, and women's rights campaigners.[117] Many women like Hume-Rothery who opposed compulsory vaccination also served as leaders of the women's movement; these included activists such as Frances Power Cobbe, Josephine Butler, Elizabeth Wolstenholme Elmy, Ursula Bright, Millicent Garret Fawcett, and the working-class suffragist Jessie Craigen.[118]

Leading up to the Leicester international rally, in the midst of the *Bitter Cry* controversy, the debates over the Third Reform Bill, the growing women's suffrage movement, and the campaign against the CD Acts, anti-vaccinationists experimented with funeral cortèges as political protests. In London, late in the afternoon of August 5, 1884, just hours after Lord Salisbury brought petitions to the House of Lords demanding the repeal of compulsory vaccination laws, the "House of Commons was assailed ... by an extraordinary procession of petitioners."[119] A brass band playing the "Dead March" from Handel's *Saul* (first performed at the King's Theatre in 1739 and by this time regularly used in state funerals) led the demonstration. Following the band was a group of six women wearing mourning dress, each holding a baby in her arms, riding aloft a carriage and pair, the typical sort of passenger carriage used for funerals. While it was not unusual for working-class women to join funeral processions, the mere presence of these female mourners challenged earlier strictures against the attendance of upper- and middle-class women.[120] As late as 1870, *Cassell's Household Guide* cautioned elite women not to follow the example of the poor by allowing women at funeral services, where they too often "interrupt and destroy the solemnity of the ceremony with their sobs."[121] It was more accepted for middle-class women to attend services and processions by the last decades of the century, but only if they kept their grief contained—exactly what the anti-vaccinationists refused to do. The women protesters sang along with the band as they distributed handbills embellished with black mourning borders. The leaflets explained that the demonstrators came before the House of Commons in response to "the child of a couple living in Peckham [who] had been vaccinated, and three weeks later died of erysipelas."[122] Banners stated the case more forcefully: "Murdered by Compulsory Vaccination."[123] Demanding the repeal of the Vaccination Acts, the protesters ended their circular with "an appeal to the working women of South London to join in this demand of the Legislature." Several of the regional newspapers that reported on the procession alongside updates of General Gordon and the siege of Khartoum spitefully suggested that "the appeal seemed to have fallen on deaf ears, the working women being probably otherwise engaged."[124] The anti-vaccinationists did not go completely unheard, however, for that evening the group of women demonstrators interviewed the Liberal MP for Stockport Charles Hopwood "in the outer hall of the House of Commons."[125]

By publicly bringing women's grief for children through the streets of London and into the House of Commons (albeit restricted to the "outer hall"), the protesters sought to gain recognition and place blame on the state for harming children. The strategic use of a funeral procession drew attention to the deaths of children that anti-vaccinationists claimed went unrecognized by the government. The use of widely shared visual and musical mourning customs may have raised sympathy for grieving parents. But protesters also hoped the appeal to emotion would highlight what they claimed the government overlooked: the supposedly deadly effects of the Vaccination Acts on individual working-class children and the inequalities embedded in state public health legislation.

The use of funeral processions to personify anti-vaccinationist protest reflected the movement's established rhetoric that working children were "Murdered by Compulsory Vaccination." In 1879 the London Society for the Abolition of Compulsory Vaccination cited a parliamentary report from the previous year to conclude that "25,000 children are slaughtered annually by diseases inoculated into the system by vaccination," and that "a far greater number are injured and maimed for life by the same unwholesome rite."[126] Mary Hume-Rothery used similar rhetoric in her pamphlet *150 Reasons for Disobeying the Vaccination Law, by Persons Prosecuted Under It* (1878), which reproduced statements taken mostly from police court reports. The case of Charles Washington Nye of Chatham, imprisoned eight times for disobeying the Vaccination Acts, opened the document by proclaiming that "he lost two children, murdered by vaccination at one time."[127] Subsequent entries reported cases of children "injured," "damaged," "ruined," "poisoned," "killed," and "murdered." James Button, a farmer from Norfolk, declared, "I cannot suffer my children to be vaccinated until I can allow my conscience to brand me as a murderer."[128]

Along with pamphleting, anti-vaccinationists used music to spread their melodramatic message of an all-powerful medical state threatening the lives of children. In the fall of 1884, the *Vaccination Inquirer* declared that the music halls of South London supported their cause with nightly performances of "As the Wind Blows." The lyrics told a tale of dying infants, mercenary doctors, corrupt state officials, and grieving mothers:

> Do you see yonder building?—a doctor's, no doubt,
> For a carriage and pair's at the door.
> Hundreds of women will pass in and out,
> With babes in their arms by the score.
>
> There at the table, with airs like a prince,
> A doctor sits day after day,
> Tainting poor children with poisonous lymph,
> While quietly he pockets the pay.
>
> Forced vaccination some thousands has slain,
> Or sent to their premature graves.
> Babes may be poisoned, yet still you exclaim,
> "Britons shall never be slaves!"[129]

By February 1885 the *Vaccination Inquirer* printed lyrics for a "Vaccination-Funeral Ode" to be sung to the tune of "Hark the Herald Angels Sing":

> They have slain our bonny boys;
> Festered o'er their infant joys.
> Swine that rend us from our pearls,
> They have slain our little girls.—
> Vaccination, skin and bone,
> Laughs upon his gory throne.[130]

Using familiar hymns and tunes for new purposes, demonstrators transformed the popular Christmas carol into an eight-verse testimony portraying wholesome children in gruesome danger. In the anti-vaccinationist formulation, the medical state threatened, rather than protected, innocent children; it was the "swine" that killed "bonny boys" and "little girls," destroying "infant joys," all the while mocking the people as a despotic tyrant from "upon his gory throne."

Anti-vaccinationists thus reinforced notions of childhood innocence, but (unlike Mearns) they did so within the populist framework of classic liberalism stressing individual rights and liberties.[131] The class-based nature of the Vaccination Acts encouraged anti-vaccinationists to overlook the vast number of lives saved through medical advancement and instead focus on the threat to personal rights and bodily autonomy. According to Jessie Craigen, who organized several London marches, even if one accepted the medical benefits of vaccination (which she did not), the death of the Peckham infant mourned in the August 1884 funeral procession resulted from the state's putting the lives of working-class children at greater risk for the benefit of public health. Craigen wrote, "Each citizen has an equal right with all others to protection for life and health, and the State has no right to force destruction, or the rule of destruction, on any, even for the supposed benefit of all."[132] And while many anti-vaccinators expressed support for antislavery movements, their repetition of "Britons never will be slaves!" from "Rule Britannia" positioned their rights as British citizens in contrast to colonial subjects. Later, in 1898, Lord Salisbury declared compulsory vaccination acceptable for imperial subjects, but not for English citizens. "It is idle to tell me that the people [anti-vaccinationists] are wrong or that they are deceived; as long as they have feelings they will resist," he proclaimed. "They are Englishmen, and it is no use to quote to me the precedents of India and Ceylon to show the way in which their prejudices can be overcome."[133]

The funeral processions of the mid-1880s took these messages and tactics to the streets. Their highly emotional demonstrations epitomized, like Butler's campaign, what Elaine Hadley identifies as a late-Victorian melodramatic mode characterized by "an inclusivity more populist than paternalist and a sentiment more shrill than stately," and "most often associated, especially by its critics, with women."[134] On Saturday, December 20, 1884, anti-vaccinationists held another more elaborate protest in the form of a London funeral procession that this time crossed from the East End to the West End. The march, led by Craigen, followed the death of a child for whom anti-vaccinationists contested the physician's officially recorded cause of death. "An infant killed by vaccination in Hackney was certified by the medical attendant as having died of scarlet-fever and whooping cough," reported the *Vaccination Inquirer*, "although there were no signs of eruptive fever, nor did the mother ever hear the child cough."[135] Local officials denied demands for an inquest. Opposed by the law and by medical authorities, Craigen "took the matter up"; she appealed to shared forms of grief and mourning to bring the anti-vaccinationist cause—and specifically the testimonies of working women and mothers—before the public.[136] The procession "passed through the principal streets, attracting great attention," bringing the subjective world of emotion and feeling into public display as a core political message of the movement representing working families, including thousands who still remained disenfranchised just weeks after the Third Reform Act gained royal assent.[137]

The December 1884 procession followed what by then had become a familiar pattern. The *Sheffield Daily Telegraph* identified the Anti-Vaccination Society's tactics as a form of "street realism" that homed in on the group's "claim that the enforcement of the law of vaccination is a direct source of infant mortality" and "embodied it into a series of demonstration funerals."[138] First came the band riding in an open brake carriage as they played the "Dead March." Next to the driver, a woman supported a large placard with the message reading, "To the memory of a child killed by Act of Parliament."[139] An open hearse drawn by two horses followed the band. It carried a child's small white coffin encircled with wreaths. At the rear filed "a number of mourning coaches filled with women in black," along with "a banner inscribed, 'In memory of 1,000 children who have died this year through vaccination.'"[140] Countering the law and medical authorities, anti-vaccinationists gave a central place to child sufferers and the women who mourned them, including the otherwise unheeded Hackney mother who had never heard her child cough, but remained unable to overturn the official cause of death. The understanding of these protests as a form of realism—representations of the real with an emphasis on ordinary experience as well as on people as individuals with psychological depth—legitimated and "embodied" the truths and witnesses that anti-vaccinators claimed the state ignored.

The majority of newspapers responded, however, by challenging the very feelings, emotions, and experiences that anti-vaccination protesters sought to reveal and uphold as legitimate sources of popular political authority. In an article titled "What Are We Coming To!," *The Globe*, one of London's oldest evening papers and a strong critic of the anti-vaccinationists, declared the procession to be an "outrage," a "hideous spectacle" of "revolting character."[141] By this point associated with a more conservative readership, *The Globe* decried the inauthenticity of emotion in what it understood to be a moment of lowbrow melodramatic theatricality, rather than what the *Sheffield Daily Telegraph* had termed "street realism." According to *The Globe*, the protest amounted to "a mock funeral procession" that presented "caricatures of a most solemn and most saddening religious ceremonial." Rather than conveying sincere grief, the women of the mourning carriages made "pretence to be overcome with woe." The article concluded, "It would be a waste of time and trouble to appeal to the feelings of people who get up such shameful exhibitions as this shocking burlesque. They cannot have any feelings, or they would not so flagrantly violate the most elementary principles of public decorum."[142] *The Globe*'s insistence that mourning for children should remain private, and that such public, explicitly political referencing of grief must necessarily be inauthentic, highlighted the newness and controversial nature of the anti-vaccinationists' tactics. They sought to give voice and visual representation to what they understood as the otherwise ignored bereavement of parents whose children died following politically mandated vaccination. But critics of the movement asserted that the anti-vaccinationists' grief, like their claims to scientific knowledge, was staged and irrational—a false vulgarization, a "burlesque" caricaturing sincere emotion and undermining legitimate political authority.

It was particularly the public display of emotion for political purposes and the bringing of working-class protests and female mourners into the thoroughfares of London's West End that riled the newspaper. The author appealed to Parliament as "the custodians of the law" to prevent such demonstrations in the future in order to "uphold public decency." Otherwise, *The Globe* claimed, "West-end streets will soon be utterly unfit for persons of any refinement or feeling to walk or drive through."[143] Parliament and the law were to regulate public spaces and public emotions. Regional papers echoed *The Globe*'s condemnation of the anti-vaccinationists and their tactics. *Berrow's Worcester Journal* declared that the "burlesque recently enacted by them in the West-end streets of London was as disgraceful as it was scandalous." The newspaper singled out the women's "mock grief" as "really disgusting" and supported *The Globe* in arguing that such a "revolting sight" should have been "instantly stopped by the police authorities." "The vaccination alarmists might at least be content with their private 'public' meetings," wrote *Berrow's Worcester Journal*, "without outraging the feelings of the English people by ridiculing the most solemn of our religious rites."[144] Gauging the "feelings of the English people," of course, cannot simply be done by a review of press reports. The *Sheffield Daily Telegraph*, one of the country's leading papers that expressed greater support of the anti-vaccinationist cause, underscored the mixed crowd response to the demonstration. A bystander who condemned the procession as a "'ghastly blasphemous parody' was at once set upon by half a dozen women, which showed that the anti-vaccinationists had their sympathizers distributed freely abroad amongst the crowd."[145] Such disputes in the streets and in the press over whether the funeral cortège from East to West London was a meaningful act of street realism or a burlesque parody suggest that much more was at stake than the standards of public emotion. Though misguided in their grasp of science, by openly and publicly mourning the Hackney child, anti-vaccinationists asserted the grievability of this individual child's death as a means to demand political recognition and challenge the powers of the state: the medical officials issuing death certificates, the police, and Parliament.

Three months later, in March 1885, the international protest at Leicester enacted these local London tactics on a grand scale. However, here another contingent of marchers joined the bands, the effigy of Jenner, and the child's coffin followed by mourners and banners testifying to mothers' grief: a group of five to ten thousand unvaccinated children. One wagon filled with youth bore the anti-vaccinationist motto "They that are whole need not a physician," words attributed to Jesus in all three synoptic Gospels.[146] The *Vaccination Inquirer* heralded the "infantile law-breakers"; it was in their "honour the day was devoted, looking so fresh, and wholesome, and free from blemish, that many and many a warm heart must have cursed the horrid tyranny which threatened them." These children, with "bright, happy faces," joined in "waving their own tiny bannerets and cheering with delight," as "mothers at upper windows clasping their infants" looked on.[147] The children's contingent put the new nineteenth-century ideal of childhood on display in the flesh. The innocence, happiness, and health of child marchers embodied English liberty, just as expressions of mourning for premature child death exposed state tyranny. As one eyewitness recalled, "Leicester, Monday, 23rd of March, 1885, will be a golden date on the page of memory, a birthday of liberty. It should be known as the Children's Day."[148] The successful undoing of compulsory vaccination following the 1907 act rested not upon scientific arguments, but on the conscientious objection of parents who testified to the sincerity of their beliefs and the sanctity of their children. By the early twentieth century, both the new ideal of happy, unblemished childhood, full of sovereign potential, and public expressions of grieving following child death would become lasting components of political culture.

Andrew Mearns, Josephine Butler, Mary Hume-Rothery, and the anti-vaccinationists all foregrounded child life and death, albeit in very different ways, to gain a public voice as they set out to define the limits and responsibilities of the modern medical state. By the 1870s and 1880s, child death carried unprecedented weight in public health debates as the child's corpse emerged as a symbol and actual site of contested state power. On the one hand, Mearns's account of London neighborhoods overflowing with unmourned children's bodies, left in boxes and alleyways, appealed to grief as a basis for state action and a foundation for the fundamental right to decent housing. Similarly, references to infant mortality and congenital syphilis served as an argument in favor of state regulation of prostitution under the CD Acts. On the other hand, Butler and the anti-vaccinationists reaffirmed their grief for the loss of child life as they warned of an overreaching state that infringed upon the individual rights of women and the working classes in the name of public health. For all of these groups, in a period when child and infant mortality remained horrifically high, notions of child innocence and mourning for child death heralded a new politics of childhood that shaped negotiations between state power and individual rights.

During the last decades of the nineteenth century, expressions of public, shared mourning for children marked a substantial shift in the emotional regime. And, though not uncontested, this change proved long-standing.

Children's lives were celebrated in the Leicester marchers' "Children's Day," their deaths mourned in public protests before Parliament, in the streets, and in the press. Love and grief for children as future citizens presented new ideals of rights based on universal claims to feeling and human interiority, rather than upon class, gender, or property ownership. Voicing and acknowledging the deaths and bitter cries of those previously outcast became a means to reimagine the social body. Reformers such as Mearns shocked readers with accounts of unmourned child deaths to assert new rights, including the right to housing for all. But women and the working classes, the groups most excluded from traditional politics and most affected by the structural inequalities inherent in public health legislation, relied most heavily on this new democratic emotional regime. They appealed to grief and emotion as a means to gain political legitimacy and voice. Through these expressions of mourning for child death, they asserted that their individual lives mattered.

5

"A Life of Her Own"

Women, Maternity, and the Politics of Grief

"For masterpieces are not single and solitary births," argued Virginia Woolf in *A Room of One's Own* (1929), "they are the outcome of many years of thinking in common, of thinking by the body of the people, so that the experience of the mass is behind the single voice."¹ Woolf wrote in praise of the eighteenth-century author Aphra Behn and the great female novelists to follow, but her words also echoed her relationship with a text that she helped bring into print a decade and a half earlier: *Maternity: Letters from Working Women* (1915), a collection of 160 letters selected from 386 Women's Co-operative Guild member survey respondents. *Maternity* provided the first widely publicized account by working women of their experiences with pregnancy, childbirth, abortion, miscarriage, stillbirth, and child death. When Margaret Llewelyn Davies shared the full collection of letters with Virginia and Leonard Woolf, Virginia asked her friend, "My dear Margaret, whats [sic] the use of my writing novels? You've got the whole thing at your fingers ends—and it will be envy not boredom that alienates my affections."² Eventually published in 1915, the guild members' accounts of maternal struggle and child death fueled wartime nationalism along with eugenicist fears of population decline and "race suicide." At the same time, however, the collective grief of working women reinforced a growing sense of their own voice and rights. In her introduction to the selected letters, Davies, a pacifist, envisioned a society in which "woman has the means and the leisure to live a life of her own without which she is unfit to give life to her children."³

Anticipating Woolf's demand for a fixed income and a room of one's own, Davies both echoed and repositioned eugenicist rhetoric: Without "a life of her own," the working woman remained "unfit" to raise the next generation. Through their collective, public accounts of maternal grief, working women demanded their social and political rights first as a necessary foundation for future generations.

Founded in 1883, the Women's Co-operative Guild developed within the British cooperative movement. It served to give women a voice within the movement's campaigns in support of greater educational opportunities, cooperative trade, unions, internationalism, and universal adult suffrage. By the time *Maternity* was published in 1915, the guild had some 32,000 members and over 600 local branches in England.[4] Margaret Llewelyn Davies (whose aunt Emily Davies founded Girton, the first residential British women's college) served as the guild's general secretary from 1889 until her retirement in 1921. She orchestrated major campaigns aligned with socialist and feminist goals, including women's suffrage, a minimum wage and equal pay for women, improved housing, and divorce law reform, the last of which brought the Women's Co-operative Guild into conflict with male cooperative officials, resulting in the suspension of the Central Co-operative Board annual grant of £400 from 1914 to 1918.[5] Beginning in 1906, the guild's attention turned to infant welfare.[6] Guild members succeeded in including a 30s. maternity grant in Lloyd George's 1911 Insurance Act—a benefit that became the wife's property when the act was amended in 1913, marking, according to Davies, "the first public recognition of the mother's position in the home."[7] "After 1913," notes Susan Pedersen, "a man could collect the maternity benefit only if he had a signed authorization from his wife."[8] Alongside these victories, Davies arranged for the collection and publication of *Maternity: Letters from Working Women* to demonstrate the need for a much more extensive national system of free universal maternity care: municipal maternity centers and state-funded benefits to cover fees for midwives, doctors, and home helpers in the weeks before and after birth.[9]

Focusing on the Women's Co-operative Guild member accounts of the deaths of their children, this chapter explores how *Maternity: Letters from Working Women* created a public commemoration of maternal grief as a foundation for women's rights. As Regenia Gagnier concludes in *Subjectivities: A History of Self-Representation in Britain* (1991), the letters trace an evolution through which "the Guildswomen transform themselves from subjective isolation within their bodies to subjects with claims upon the

State."[10] While Gagnier explores women's physical hardships and labor, I argue that grief, particularly grief over the loss of child life (innocent lives unlived and unrealized), also served as a principal emotional marker of these working-class women's interiority and subjectivity, providing justification for their claims to their yet unmet rights of citizenship. Many of the women who responded to the guild drew parallels between the isolation and suffering of working women and the extinguished lives of children who died young, stillborn infants, and miscarriages. Working women's emotional responses to child death avoided the sensationalism, pity, and melodrama of so many Victorian exposés. The guildswomen's mourning for their lost children became a public outcry voiced in their own words, not projected by the middle classes as Andrew Mearns and other nineteenth-century reformers had done in texts such as *The Bitter Cry of Outcast London* (1883). *Maternity: Letters from Working Women* presented mourning the loss of child life as a foundation for women's recognition as citizens and their political goals, including the guild's demands for municipally run national maternity care centers and women's suffrage. As a collective text written by the Women's Co-operative Guild, *Maternity* presented a model of citizenship that connected working-class women's shared physical and emotional struggle with the more abstract language of human rights.[11] At the core of this process, providing both moral and political legitimacy to their claims, lay public commemoration and grief for children who had died.

Collecting and Publishing the Letters

By the late nineteenth century, politicians and professionals presented infant mortality as an issue of national concern. Although average death rates improved significantly after 1870, infant mortality for children under one year failed to decrease at the same rate and even worsened for a period in the 1890s, amounting to one-quarter of all national deaths at the end of Victoria's reign.[12] Overall death rates for children under five declined by roughly a third between the 1870s and early 1900s, but remained alarmingly high. As Ellen Ross shows, a study of London's impoverished mothers served by the General Lying-In Hospital between 1877 and 1882 found that only about one-fifth of the women had not lost any children, and a horrific 62 percent suffered the deaths of two or more.[13] There were improvements by the early 1900s, but conditions continued to vary widely by locality. In 1910 London, the infant mortality rate in more affluent

Hampstead was 60 deaths under one year per thousand live births compared with 146 per thousand for Shoreditch in the East End, and within wards far greater disparities often persisted.[14]

Political attention to child mortality increased alongside Britain's expanding empire and concerns over the strength of its military. The poor physical state of recruits volunteering for the South African War of 1899–1902 sparked a series of social exposés, leading to the creation of the parliamentary Inter-Departmental Committee on Physical Deterioration. The committee's 1904 report dismissed the more extreme fears of physical "deterioration," but highlighted infant mortality as a major cause for national alarm. Most contemporary studies—as now classic histories by Anna Davin, Carol Dyhouse, Ellen Ross, and others have noted—continued to link infant mortality with the isolated actions of mothers, citing either working-class women's child-rearing ignorance or their industrial labor (particularly in the northern factory districts, where infant mortality rates tended to be highest) as primary causes.[15] Key reforms, like the 1906 state provisions for school meals, sought to address the "child citizen" outside the confines of the family unit, or, as with the 1908 Children Act, expanded nineteenth-century definitions of child neglect and abuse to allow for greater state regulation of child-rearing without addressing underlying structural inequalities.[16] Medical and government reformers remained hesitant to tackle child mortality in ways that fundamentally reworked understandings of the family and the state. Assistance typically took the form of mothers' clinics, health visitors, and other kinds of aid modeled on the sort of charity distained by most guildswomen, who viewed such efforts as demeaning.

By the 1910s, however, a number of middle and working-class activists rejected the idea that women's factory work or poor parenting skills were to blame for child mortality, shifting the focus instead to women's lack of political rights and economic equality. The Fabian Women's Group, created in 1908 by the suffragist and socialist Maude Pember Reeves and the anarchist Charlotte Wilson, anticipated many of the Women's Cooperative Guild's arguments in *Round About a Pound a Week* (1913), first published by Reeves the previous year as a Fabian Tract.[17] Ross hails the book as "a defense of the intelligence and industry of working-class women so often maligned by infant welfare officials."[18] Reeves based her study on a survey of forty-two working-class families in North Lambeth, London, struggling to care for young infants on the subsistence wage of a pound a week. The continuation of horrific infant and child mortality rates into the twentieth century demanded state action, according to Reeves. In the families she surveyed, nearly one out of every ten children was stillborn or died soon after birth, and, of those surviving, more than one-fifth died before reaching adulthood.[19] Reeves stressed that one hundred years earlier, before state limitations on child labor and national education, working-class children would have been economic assets for families. By the early twentieth century, however, the state claimed oversight over the welfare of children without providing the means for their survival, holding parents accountable and even sending them to prison if found guilty of neglect. Shifting perspective to working mothers, Reeves described how an "extraordinarily tidy, clean woman," "an excellent manager," was "horrified and bewildered at the entrance of police officers into her home" for an inquest after the death of her son at seven months from bronchitis; the "disgrace" never left her, and surely added to the pain of burying her infant in a "common grave with seven other coffins of all sizes."[20] This "masculine State," Reeves claimed, "representing only male voters, and, until lately, chiefly those of the richer classes, has been crude and unwise in its relations with all parents guilty of the crime of poverty."[21] In *Round About a Pound a Week*, Reeves presented her plan to complete the century-long project of state protection of child life: a legal minimum wage, family endowments, universal school medical clinics (expanding on the 1906 model of state-funded school meals), local baby clinics, guaranteed affordable housing, and provisions for burial as "a free and honourable public service."[22]

Davies and the Women's Co-operative Guild took up many of these same demands, likewise seeking to combine socialism with feminism by foregrounding child mortality. Like Reeves, Davies began with a survey of working mothers. In 1911 she asked Women's Co-operative Guild members to detail their experiences of childbirth, focusing on whether, under the existing National Sick Insurance provisions, they were able to "secure the doctoring, nursing, and nourishing necessary for the health of both mother and child."[23] From the beginning, as Linda Gordon argues, the respondents were "experienced activists working for a political purpose": They spoke about private matters of marriage, sex, pregnancy, abortion, and child death "not as a form of complaint or self-indulgence, but in a carefully strategized political cause."[24] Davies shared the initial survey responses with members of Lloyd George's administration to win the 30s. maternity benefit in 1911, and then used the firsthand accounts to argue for a much more extensive system of National Care of Maternity. By May 1914 she referenced the "conclusive evidence" offered by then "over 200 Guild members, who, in the interests of motherhood, described their own experiences."[25] The following May, Davies reported having received some four hundred responses.[26]

In the spring of 1915, Davies struggled to find a publisher for *Maternity*. Virginia Woolf had tried to find an outlet for the "amazing" letters, sending them in February 1915 to her half-brother Gerald Duckworth in hopes that his press would print the collection "with lots of photographs."[27] Duckworth declined, however, and by May 1915 Davies had formed an agreement with the publisher of *Round About a Pound a Week*, George Bell and Sons, to print a selection of the guild letters along with several photographs "in similar style" to Reeves's defense of working families.[28] Later in 1915, Bell and Sons published *Married Women's Work*, a study by the Women's Industrial Council edited and introduced by the novelist, suffragist, and Fabian socialist Clementina Black, also a strong advocate for a minimum wage for women. Like Reeves and Davies, Black claimed that women's employment should not be blamed for child mortality; rather, she wrote, the "only general conclusions derivable from statistics of infantile mortality are that poverty and density of population are unfavourable to the health and survival of babies."[29] That same year Bell and Sons also published *Women in Modern Industry* by Barbara Hutchins. One of the first women's labor historians, Hutchins had conducted the interviews with working-class women from Yorkshire for Black's book. In *Women in Modern Industry*, she offered an expansive account of "the evolution of the woman wage-earner" and "her gradual achievement of economic individuality and independence" before and after industrialization and into the initial months of the First World War.[30] *Maternity: Letters from Working Women* thus joined a handful of influential studies arguing for increased state benefits for working women by appealing to rising wartime nationalism while paradoxically holding onto a feminist and socialist vision of human rights and cooperation.

For the survey, Davies contacted about 600 married officials of the Women's Co-operative Guild—the organization that she believed "might justly claim to speak with greater authority than any other body for the voteless and voiceless millions of married working-women of England."[31] She asked the women to reflect on their pregnancies and respond to five questions:

1. How many children have you had?
2. How soon after each other were they born?
3. Did any die under five years old, and if so, at what ages and from what causes?
4. Were any still-born, and if so how many?
5. Have you had any miscarriages, and if so how many?[32]

Although Davies desired a qualitative rather than a statistically precise survey, she knew the numbers told a chilling story. Of the 386 responses received providing details of 400 women's cases, 348 women were mothers who gave complete numerical responses. Of these, 42.4 percent (148) had experienced stillbirths or miscarriages, many more than once.[33] One-quarter of the women—24.7 percent (86)—"lost children in the first year of life."[34] Davies emphasized the particular dangers during pregnancy and childbirth and within infants' first twelve months, though the women also reported on the deaths of older children. She sent a follow-up letter requesting information from respondents about family wages and the occupations of their husbands, which were listed in an appendix to highlight the range of working-class families affected by poverty. Colliery and railway operatives represented the largest groups. Most husbands worked as laborers or artisans, but some held clerical or semiprofessional positions, including an engineer, a policeman, a postal employee, a shopkeeper, and a teacher.[35] Overall, Davies concluded that "at least two-thirds" of working women from these families experienced "conditions of maternity which are not normal and healthy."[36]

The published version of *Maternity: Letters from Working Women* framed the firsthand accounts to make the case for parliamentary reform. The Liberal MP and president of the Local Government Board Herbert Samuel, sponsor of the 1908 Children Act, provided a short preface, followed by Davies's introduction. Leaving no doubt about what actions to take, the book concluded by summarizing the Women's Co-operative Guild's National Scheme. The plan prioritized a pregnancy and maternity benefit, distributed in weekly payments of £3 10s. (in addition to the 30s. already granted under national insurance), along with state-funded support services: an increase in the number of health visitors in order to implement the 1915 Notification of Births (Extension) Act requiring the registration of all births and stillbirths; greater government coordination with midwives and nurses; local maternity and infant centers that, Davies stressed, should make a point to employ women doctors; maternity hospitals and homes; milk depots; paid home helpers in the weeks before and after childbirth; and the creation of a Ministry of Health with a Maternity and Infant Life Department. At all levels, the guild demanded greater representation by working-class women as government officials. True "democratic government," Davies argued, required "a partnership between the women who are themselves concerned, the medical profession, and the State."[37] Unlike the late-nineteenth-century libertarians who called for the reduction of state powers (including Josephine Butler in her campaign against the Contagious Diseases Acts and other leaders of the anti-vaccination movement), the guild sought to address the many inequalities facing women by amplifying their voices within an ever more expansive vision of the state.

The Letters

The letters from women comprised the bulk of the book. Without the originals, it is impossible to know why Davies, perhaps with input from Woolf, selected the 160 that she did for inclusion.[38] Davies claimed to publish the letters "exactly as written by the women," except for changes in spelling, punctuation, and the omission of names, places, and "a few medical details."[39] The letters appear in numbered order, each introduced by only a summary heading (many taken from extracted quotations) in all capitals, such as "I AM A RUINED WOMAN," "INFLAMMATION," "KEPT ALL TO MYSELF," "MANY MISCARRIAGES," "AN INDOMITABLE WILL," "A HEALTHY MILL-WORKER," "I THINK A LOT," "SUFFERING AND HARD WORK," "I OVERDID MYSELF," and "HUSBAND WHO WAS A NURSE AND MOTHER."[40] At the conclusion of most letters, the only commentary, in italics, is a summary of the family's wages, the total number of children born, and any stillbirths or miscarriages. Thus, just as the parliamentary campaign in support of the guild's national maternity reforms frame the book's opening and closing, each letter is framed by the subject heading and summary details linking women's suffering and child mortality to poor wages, along with insufficient medical care, bad housing, and above all else the need for women's national representation as equal partners.

Many of the women wrote of miscarriages, stillbirths, and the deaths of children with what may appear to be little emotion, but the effect of their collective writing becomes a form of public commemoration and mourning. Entry after entry identified child death as shared experiences.

"I have had a delicate husband for fifteen years," wrote one woman, "and I have had nine children, seven born in nine years. I have only one now; some of the others have died from weakness from birth."[41] "I have had six, one dead," added another in what became a common refrain.[42] "In the first place," replied another writer, "I have had eight children; seven is now living."[43] "I have had nine children; eight are living."[44] A mother of seven lamented, "It is my three last babies I have buried."[45] "My baby only lived seven months," stated one respondent.[46] "As you will see (from my having lost six children in succession before I reared one)," began a letter, "I was very unfortunate in my early married life, and at one time thought I was not going to rear any children."[47] Responding to Davies's survey questions, the women identified miscarriages and stillbirths along with child death. A mother of three surviving children disclosed, "Besides two still-born children, I have had two miscarriages."[48] One of several writers who supported family limitation recounted an extreme case of multiple deaths: "A cousin (a beautiful girl) had seven children in about seven years; the first five died in birth, the sixth lived, and the seventh died and the mother also. What a wasted life!"[49] While not all of the letter writers had experienced the death of a child, many had, and many more than one. The collective presentation of these working women's histories transformed their personal losses into cause for national mourning and reform.

As they documented shared experiences of child death, letter writers gave evidence supporting the guild's claims that the mother's physical health and malnutrition directly affected infant welfare. As one mother simply stated, in order to feed her family, "I was obliged to go without."[50] The women clearly identified the effects of their own deprivation on the next generation. One writer testified that her "past struggle" with hunger and poverty caused by her husband's intermittent employment "left its mark on the physique of my children. One has since died of heart disease, aged ten years; another of phthisis, sixteen years; my youngest has swollen glands."[51] Another woman who suffered multiple miscarriages explained, "My two first were lost from malnutrition because I could not retain my food."[52] The author of "MOTHER LAST," who took in boarders to make ends meet, also struggled with her health following a miscarriage. "I have had seven children," she chronicled, "one died at birth, one at one year old, and five are living."[53] Like many of the women, she explained that any available food went first to her husband and then to her surviving children. "OUT OF BED ON THE THIRD DAY" similarly described how a new mother fainted as she got up to prepare gruel for herself after childbirth. The mother of nine, who at the time that she wrote had only one surviving child, testified, "I can say truthfully my children have died from my worrying how to make two ends meet and also insufficient food." Reinforcing the guild's campaign to increase state supplements paid directly to mothers, she recognized the inequality of reserving food for husbands, yet also understood how the labor market reinforced patriarchalism within the home, clarifying that "we must give our husbands sufficient food or we should have them home and not able to work; therefore we have to go without to make ends meet."[54] Letter after letter identified the basic lack of food and resources, not maternal neglect, as the main cause of infant mortality. "No one but mothers who have gone through the ordeal of pregnancy half starved," wrote one woman, "to finally bring a child into the world to live a living death for nine months, can understand what it means."[55]

Almost all of the respondents also felt the strains of domestic labor, sometimes made worse by additional paid work, and identified its effects on their pregnancies, their surviving children, and their own bodies. Physically demanding labor—washing, ironing, sewing, cleaning, cooking, baking, caring for sick family members—resulted in miscarriages or stillbirths and prevented future pregnancies.[56] "I feel sure my first baby was still-born through hard work and lifting," stated an advocate for state maternity homes.[57] Another identified her drudgery during pregnancy as the reason that all three of her girls "suffer with their insides" and a "dear boy was born ruptured." She worked eleven-hour shifts at a screw factory until two or three weeks before childbirth, and then turned to caring for lodgers and took in washing, working "up till an hour or so before baby was born."[58] A mother of seven who had survived three stillbirths and four miscarriages stressed the strains of caring for living children: "I lost a sweet little girl, aged four years and eight months." The child, she wrote, "was ill a fortnight, and I nursed her night and day. I was so done up with attending her and the grief, that I had a dreadful miscarriage which nearly cost me my life. I had to work very hard to do everything for my little family, and after that I never had any more children to live. I either miscarried, or they were still-born."[59] Another writer likewise recounted how she "dragged about in misery and in great pain" after a "shock" from lifting a washing tub that led to her child's stillbirth.[60] "Now," she wrote, "if there had been such a thing as a Maternity Centre where I could have sent for someone, or could have attended without that feeling of expense, I could have been relieved of all that suffering."[61] Many stressed the long-term health consequences of inadequate maternal care. A woman whose mother died at the age of fifty-two after having thirteen children (ten who survived into adulthood) wondered whether women's early deaths at a time "when they should be having the best of their lives" resulted from the "lack and care and rest during the times they are having their babies."[62] This, too, was a common refrain. "Care and rest would have cured me," claimed a mother of five, "but I was too proud for charity, and no other help was available. You may say mine is an isolated case," she stressed. "It is not."[63]

Along with paid employment and housework, the physical toll of husbands' sexual demands and the close spacing of pregnancies became, for many women, another form of domestic labor and a reminder of women's inequality within marriage. A mother of seven recorded that her older husband "had not a bit of control over his passions" and expected her "to do what he had been in the habit of paying women to do." Over the course of three years, she "had three children and one miscarriage," leaving her "very weak and suffering from very bad legs." Still, she stressed, "I had to work very hard all the time I was pregnant. My next child only lived a few hours."[64] Other women identified husbands' unwanted sexual demands as yet another cause of physical and emotional suffering. "I became an easy prey to sexual intercourse," is how a mother of four explained her state of exhaustion and grief, following the death of an infant daughter.[65] One woman wrote of earning extra income sewing, while doing all the "housework, washing, baking" and making her family's clothes. But the greatest injury came from her husband's failure to realize "that the wife's body belongs to herself." "Pain of body and mind," she insisted, came from "the father's ignorance and interference," and left "its mark in many ways on the child."[66] Foregrounding the health of children provided women with a means to assert their own bodily integrity. "Fathers ought to control their bodies for the sake of the mother and child," insisted the author of "AGAINST LARGE FAMILIES," referencing "several instances where a mother's life has become intolerable through the husband's lack of control."[67] Even as many respondents recognized the kindness and support of loving husbands, they advocated for more education on women's reproductive health alongside greater control over their own bodies by asserting their needs, their voices, their rights. And although they often appealed to child welfare as a means to legitimate these demands, they also spoke of their own claims to subjectivity. According to a mother of seven, "We must let the men know we are human beings with ideals, and aspire to something higher than to be mere objects on which they can satisfy themselves."[68]

Faced with these conditions, many women detailed efforts to limit their fertility, reflecting the overall national decline in average family size after 1870.[69] They called for better, more public instruction on reproductive health of the kind offered through the guild along with what one letter referred to as "mechanical prevention of family."[70] Some made agreements with husbands to restrict family size, though such partnerships proved exceptional. After giving birth to her sixth child, followed by a miscarriage, the author of "UTTERLY OVERDONE" simply "went on strike."[71] Many spoke of "preventatives"—most often drugs aimed at inhibiting conception and inducing miscarriages and abortions (often with little distinction). Under the 1803 Ellenborough Act, providers of abortions could be prosecuted, but it was not until the greater commercialization of procedures in the 1840s and 1850s that trials became more common, leading to a strengthening of punishments against women seeking abortions under the 1861 Offences Against the Person Act.[72] By the late nineteenth century, doctors expressed particular concern over married women's use of abortifacients, portraying their attempts to limit family size as selfish and undeserving of any sympathy otherwise offered to the "unmarried ignorant girl in her first pregnancy trying to conceal her shame."[73] Given the legal and medical context, the pervasive references to preventatives in *Maternity* are striking.

In more or less explicit terms, the letters document the widespread use of abortion among working-class women—practices that, if not always encouraged, at least received understanding and sympathy in the letters, unlike in the medical literature. "I confess without shame that when well-meaning friends said: 'You cannot afford another baby; take this drug,' I took their strong concoctions to purge me of the little life that might be mine," wrote a woman for whom motherhood had "ceased to be a crown of glory" and had "become a fearsome thing to be shunned and feared."[74] Recognizing working-class women's reliance on abortifacients, she argued, "Race suicide, if you will, is the policy of the mothers of the future. Who shall blame us?"[75] More obliquely, a mother who had already experienced the death of a child and three stillbirths described how she "fell downstairs" when six months pregnant, an accident that, she recalled, "killed the child." She wrote, "Perhaps it seems wicked to you, but I was glad, because it left my hands free for a time to look after the other two."[76] Even when writers warned against taking drugs and other dangerous measures, they did so with understanding that working women resorted to such options out of necessity. As Davies wrote in the introduction, public opinion remained divided on such preventatives (though the Women's Co-operative Guild would campaign more directly for women's access to birth control after the war). She emphasized "the evil which results from the use of drugs to procure abortion" on the health of women and children. However, directly addressing those who shamed married women for resorting to such methods, she stressed that the root "cause of the evil lies in the conditions which produce it," not in married women's selfishness: "Where maternity is only followed by an addition to the daily life of suffering, want, overwork, and poverty, people will continue to adopt even the most dangerous, uncertain, and disastrous methods of avoiding it."[77]

Indeed, in response to Davies's questionnaire about pregnancies, child mortality, stillbirths, and miscarriages, the lack of access to proper medical care emerged as a main theme in *Maternity*. Women expressed reluctance to call on doctors, whose fees could leave working families in debt for months. Many writers also emphasized their want of funds to hire a day servant or nurse to help in the weeks before and after childbirth and the toll this took on their health and on the health of their children. "I for one think," wrote one respondent, "that if I had a little help from someone I should have had my children by my side to-day."[78] The letters told of countless physical hardships, most often silently endured, associated with childbearing: nausea, vomiting, constipation, hemorrhoids, headaches, toothaches, leg cramps, varicose veins, sleeplessness, baldness, jaundice, fainting, anemia, incontinence, kidney infections, heart disease, uterine prolapse, puerperal sepsis, eczema transmitted from doctors, and more. A woman who nearly bled to death from a miscarriage declared, "I am a ruined woman through having children."[79]

In other cases, writers used the guild's forum on child mortality to provide glimpses of cruel and insensitive treatment by doctors. One woman described, "I have had the doctor's arm in my body, and felt his fingers tearing the afterbirth from my side." ("I hope," she concluded, "I have not tired you with my letter."[80]) A mill worker suffering from years of hard labor explained that doctors had to use instruments to deliver all of her children, and she "lost two from injury at birth."[81] Another woman explained she "had a very bad time at the birth with instruments," leaving her without "strength enough to drag through day after day."[82] Such invasive procedures may have proved necessary, but more often women testified of medical neglect. An inexperienced doctor left "a poor little baby boy with a very large swollen head dreadfully cut, and a young mother dreadfully cut also."[83] Another woman blamed her "long illness" on "the doctor hurrying the birth, instead of giving nature a chance," and being "rough in handling me."[84] The author of "OH, THE HORRORS WE SUFFER!" simply stated, the "doctors who attended me never told me anything concerning my babies or myself."[85] Working-class women, however, proved well aware of the disastrous effects of such disregard. One mother wrote, "As a result of inattention by the doctor attending me I was badly torn during the birth."[86] Another asserted, "I might say that I have had two children. The first one was still-born, but it was owing to the doctor not paying proper attention to me."[87] He dismissed the woman's claims that she was in advanced labor, assured her that "he would not be needed until the morning after," and refused to return again when called. "Consequently," she lamented, "the child was suffocated in the birth." When her husband went to tell the doctor of the child's death, "he said he was very glad, as he wanted his rest."[88] (For her second birth, the woman sent for a different doctor, but found he was drunk when she needed him.) Such accounts of medical neglect and mistreatment—placed, as they were, alongside rarer cases of doctors' sensitive, qualified care—rallied support for universal maternal welfare as a fundamental right deserved by all.[89]

The accounts of child death in *Maternity* are not "good" or "beautiful" deaths. The letters rather show what Ellen Ross and Julie-Marie Strange have argued elsewhere: how important physical bodily responses and silence could be for working-class women's mourning.[90] The communal mourning in *Maternity* revealed the worldly, rather than the spiritual, causes and effects of child death. There is no sense of death as heavenly sleep, no release from suffering, no reunion with God, no signs of salvation, no peace—in other words, the letters convey little sense of childhood reclaimed in the afterlife. To be sure, the survey questions and letter format prompted a certain type of response focused on material conditions. Furthermore, by the late nineteenth century, more secular approaches were replacing the "good death." But, even so, the near total omission of the language of heavenly salvation and childhood reclaimed is significant. (In an exceptional case mentioning God, a mother wrote of her three-year-old's death from diphtheria: "It was a happy release to me, as he was an epileptic, and I thanked God, much as I loved him, that he was taken from this life, where even sound people have a difficulty to exist."[91] Yet even here, the mother stressed *her* release, rather than the child's.) The women writers did not use euphemisms. They did not talk of their children "passing away" or "breathing their last breath" or "departing from this earth"—all phrasings that suggest a transition from physical to spiritual realms or at least some other destination.

Instead, in remarkably similar language, the women wrote in terms of stark divisions between the living and the dead: So many of their children were living, so many were dead. They most often used the words "died" or "dead." "My first child (a boy) died when he was eight months old," wrote a mother of three, recalling how when she became ill "he had to be taken from the breast, no food agreed with him, convulsions set in, and my loved one died."[92] The women spoke in terms of "having" and no longer having living children. "I have had seven children, and three have died," declared a woman who welcomed making her experiences "a public question."[93] When they turned to other language, it was primarily the language of loss: "I lost a little girl"; "I have lost two of my four babies, and had a miscarriage"; "I had two children, lost one, and lost my husband by consumption."[94] A miner's wife recounted how, after nineteen years of marriage, three of her children died: "I lost my baby first, a grand little girl of two," then "I lost a fine lad of fourteen in the fever hospital," and, two years later, "we lost a girl of twelve from tubercular disease of the kidneys from cow's milk."[95] A mother who struggled with malnourishment beginning with her first pregnancy wrote, "We had a little girl, which we had always longed for, only to lose it as soon as it came into the world, for I have no strength in my inside."[96] These losses, deeply felt, underscored the physicality of death and the material resources needed to sustain life along with the ties between mother and child.

Although starkly worded, the women's descriptions also revealed their sense of injustice over the specific loss of child life. So many of the accounts repeated the use of "only" in chronicling children's brief lives before death: "My baby only lived seven months"; "My next child only lived a few hours"; "He only lived twelve hours"; "He only lived four days."[97] Women writers often provided the exact length of time children lived in years, months, sometimes hours. This phrasing emphasized a particular kind of life—a child's life—cut short. The loss that mothers experienced was not understood as inevitable or unavoidable. The cumulative effect of these letters was not only a shared expression of grief and mourning, but also a public outcry against the injustice of child lives lost—and also of women's lives "done up" through grief, overwork, hunger, and "violent sickness."[98] Reenforcing this public recognition of grief over lives lost, one of the photographs—titled "Fifteen Children, Four Living, Father an

FIGURE 17. "Fifteen Children, Four Living, Father an Iron-Moulder." Photograph from original edition of *Maternity: Letters from Working Women* (London: George Bell and Sons, 1915).

Iron-Moulder"—published in the original 1915 edition lined the four surviving siblings along a crumbling Liverpool building under their mother's eye, leaving gaps, rents in the wall, visually marking lives unlived (fig. 17). By responding to the guild's survey, working-class women decided to make their grief public in an effort to correct, as one woman protested, "agony [that] ought never to have been, with proper attention."[99]

Overcome by grief, the physical and emotional loss—or "waste" as some women put it—of mother and child blurred together. The letters recounted layers of loss connecting mother and child: the central loss of child life; mothers' loss of weight, milk, wages, rest, and control over their own bodies; and their loss of faith, spirit, and reason, along with fears of their own loss of life. Reflecting on the death of her infant, her multiple stillbirths, and a miscarriage, a woman testified, "When I look back to my early married life I could cry for the girl who endured so much for life that was wasted."[100] In the letter titled "A HALF-STARVED PREGNANCY," another author described the death of her second child as an experience that "is only one example of what thousands of married working women have to endure."[101] Her husband, a railway worker, earned just over £1 a week for 72 hours of labor. To save for the doctor's fees, she, like many other respondents, took in laundry work and "had to do without common necessaries," while caring for her husband during periods of illness and their three-year-old child.[102] Supporting the guild's primary claim that the survival of infants depended upon the health of mothers, she linked her physical deprivations directly to her second child's death, explaining that "when my baby was born I nearly lost my life, the doctor said through want of nourishment." She continued, "When I got up after ten days my life was a perfect burden to me. I lost my milk and ultimately lost my baby. My interest in life seemed lost."[103] The collective waste of lives from material deprivation blurred between mother and child: The mother's milk and child's death and mother's loss of interest in life intertwined to reveal a sense of shared human vulnerability and dependence, both physical and emotional.

Through their grief and recollections of lives undone, the collective women's voices in *Maternity* revealed the inadequacies of liberal individualism: They questioned liberalism's solutions—family, home, work, and charity—and, moreover, they questioned the limited nature of the rational liberal individual self. Again and again, they showed lives destroyed through hard labor. The domestic hearth and workplace offered little solace. One woman complained of streets where factories blocked all light from kitchens and polluted neighborhoods with the "continual grinding of machinery." Her critique of industrial capitalism connected women wage workers with mothers and children. She wrote, "Knowing that it is mostly women and girls who are working in these factories gives you the feeling that their bodies are going round with the machinery. The mother wonders what she has to live for; if there is another baby coming she hopes it will be dead when it is born. The result is she begins to take drugs." "All this tells on the woman physically and mentally," she concluded, asking, "Can you wonder at women turning to drink?"[104] Temporary relief from the "grinding" of women's bodies by machinery or reproduction too often took self-destructive forms: drink and harmful abortifacients.

Similarly, the author of "A HALF-STARVED PREGNANCY" found little comfort within liberal frameworks. When her child was born, she wrote, "I had to depend on my neighbours for what help they could give during labour and the lying-in period. They did their best, but from the second day I had to have my other child with me, undress him and see to all his wants, and was often left six hours without a bite of food, the fire out and no light, the time January, and snow had lain on the ground two weeks." Alone and with only intermittent help from neighbors, she struggled with hunger, darkness, and cold, while caring for her older child. After the infant's death, when she confessed her "interest in life seemed lost," she felt "nervous and hysterical." Grief prompted an unraveling of the rational self, and the city spaces outside her home offered no relief. She wrote, "When I walked along the streets I felt that the houses were falling on me, so I took to staying at home, which of course added to the trouble."[105] The limited networks of family and neighbors were not enough. And, unlike late nineteenth-century New Women who turned to the public sphere for affirmation, this woman felt crushed by the city itself. She demanded, "Can we any longer wonder why so many married working women are in the lunatic asylums to-day? Can we wonder that so many women take drugs, hoping to get rid of the expected child?"[106] "I think," proclaimed the last entry in the collection, "if it had not been for the Women's Guild I should have been in the asylum."[107] The letters challenged notions of self-help and hard work, the core ideals of nineteenth-century liberal individualism, critiquing the paths such ideals perpetuated for working women—alcoholism, self-harm, the asylum—as structural outcomes rather than individual failures.

Instead, through their writing and the efforts of the guild, women and their supporters reclaimed a new kind of collective subjectivity and articulated a new vision of the state. "It was the Women's Co-operative Guild which saved me from despair," wrote the author of "A HALF-STARVED PREGNANCY."[108] Her solution, echoed in so many of the other letters Davies selected, was a national community in which women's voices, women's work, and women's grief were recognized, a state modeled on the Women's Co-operative Guild, which appealed to female interiority—emotional and intellectual—along with recognition of women's domestic labor and bodily integrity as a basis for rights and suffrage. The letters spoke directly to the guild's proposal for state-funded maternity care, narrating an arc from unmoored grief and isolation to collective action. "If only the State would do something that would give *all* working mothers the assurance that during pregnancy, where needed, means would be provided whereby they could get an all-important rest before confinement, and that proper attention should be provided during and after so long as necessary," wrote the author of "A HALF-STARVED PREGNANCY." She believed, "It would make all the difference between a safe and speedy confinement, a better offspring, therefore a better asset of the State, and a broken-down motherhood, and a race of future parents who start in life very often with a constitution enfeebled through the mother having to undergo privation, as well as the mental and physical strain that childbirth entails."[109] By detailing their maternal struggles and grief, writers claimed their right to nourishment, medical care, and rest, along with paid domestic labor, education, and ultimately suffrage.

Like the author of "A HALF-STARVED PREGNANCY," several writers emphasized the health of future Britons, adopting eugenicist rhetoric promoting national and racial strength. One claimed, "The child is the asset of the nation, and the mother the backbone. Therefore, I think the nation should help to feed and keep that mother, and so help to strengthen the nation by her giving birth to strong boys and girls."[110] According to "A WRECK AT THIRTY," "Our children are a valuable asset to the nation, and the health of the woman who is doing her duty in rearing the future race should have a claim upon the national purse."[111] But for the most part the guild writers did not understand their role as simply "nursemaids" of the state. As Ellen Ross has argued more generally of working-class women of this generation, they "incorporated the Infant Welfare movement's definitions of motherhood into a new sense of their own rights in relation to husbands and even to children."[112] This came across in the guildswomen's demands for women's bodily autonomy, for state-supported health care, and even for educational opportunities. "I'd like to develop mentally," stated a mother of five, "but I must stifle that part of my nature."[113] The fight to ensure that women—not husbands or landlords—directly received maternity payments marked a key moment in restructuring women's role as workers and citizens in their own right, but it was not enough.

Whereas the liberal state and liberal individualism based on male property ownership erased women, the guild's collective vision of the state brought attention to women's subjectivity. The very act of writing—beginning with each woman's decision to respond to the guild's survey, making her private grief public—as well as the collective publication of the letters, envisioned a state that represented women, as Davies and her collaborator Virginia Woolf well understood. "It is the first time," Herbert Samuel proclaimed in his preface, "that the facts have been stated, not by medical men or social students, but by the sufferers themselves, in their own words."[114] While Herbert also appealed to pronatalist arguments, he opened by emphasizing women's direct claims on the state: "Woman," he wrote, quoting Kant, "is an end in herself, and not merely a means to an end."[115] The respondents underscored the importance of documenting working women's experiences, in many cases for the first time, in their own voices. A mother who blamed the death of her infant daughter on the effects of her own hard labor as a girl asserted, "It is high time that something was done by the Government to lessen the sufferings of mothers, which has always been hidden as something not to be talked about."[116] Often working women internalized this social erasure of their suffering. A woman who struggled without doctors noted, "Of course, I thought we must put up with it, and they would only laugh at me."[117] Some writers were tentative. One woman concluded, "I do hope you will not feel that this letter is morbid, and that I delight in writing horrors, for I do not, and had you not asked for information I should never have written this all down."[118] Another closed, "I do hope I have not done wrong in relating so much of my past, and that it may be of some use in the furthering of our scheme."[119] Others expressed a sense of relief, even joy at the prospect: "I feel so glad you have given me this opportunity to just say something on the subject."[120] Taken together, the autobiographical letters with their subheadings and "I" statements pronounced the collective subjectivity and claims of working women, alongside their losses caused by material want.

Maternity: Letters from Working Women thus gave expression to the political elements of grief that, once revealed, formed new understandings of the individual and the state. This often began with the raw expression of loss, of lives undone, upon the death of a child. Such grief revealed *"the tie"* that comprises identity; as Judith Butler explains, "I think I have lost 'you' only to discover that 'I' have gone missing as well."[121] "One does not always stay intact," Butler observes, in grief, as in desire.[122] But along with this loss of self, the women's accounts of grief in *Maternity* also created space for a social transformation supported by the guild's proposals. In *Precarious Life*, Butler also describes how grief can deliver such a community, by bringing attention to how "we might struggle for autonomy in many spheres," while remaining conscious of "the demands that are imposed upon us by living in a world of beings who are, by definition, physically dependent on one another, physically vulnerable to one another."[123] Through mourning, in other words, "something about who we are is revealed, something that delineates the ties we have to others, that shows us that these ties constitute what we are, ties or bonds that compose us."[124] By writing their own histories of grief, working women imagined a new kind of political community linking their lives, their subjectivities, with the state. "I say," concluded the author of "AN AWFUL STRUGGLE," "God speed co-operation, the greatest blessing possible for the people."[125]

Public Reactions

Public response to the letters was mixed. George Bell and Sons distributed the first edition of *Maternity* in September 1915.[126] Later that month, Virginia Woolf asked Davies, "Did you see your very warm review in the Times?" "Your Guild I find quoted everywhere."[127] By May 1916 the widely reviewed book was in its third edition with over two thousand copies sold.[128] Most reviews focused on how improvements in maternity care could benefit the future health of the nation at a time of war. The pacifist Davies eventually advocated for greater access to safe methods of birth control (an interest she shared with a number of letter writers in *Maternity*), but she also understood the practical advantages of arguing for women's rights by promoting pronatalist policies. The guild insisted that the war made the question of child life "more obviously imperative," adding, "It was clear that the Guild's great contribution to the problems of the war would be its scheme for the care of the mothers of the race."[129] Published reviews echoed this nationalist, pronatalist rhetoric, calling for the state to intervene, as the *British Medical Journal* advised, "in order that there may be in the future strong and healthy men and women to carry on its imperial tasks."[130]

Other responses, however, included pronatalist arguments about the future health of the nation while also stressing the need to acknowledge publicly working-class women's suffering and mourn the deaths of their children. Before addressing fears of "race suicide," the Fabian socialist *New Statesman* described *Maternity* as "a grim and terrible record of long-drawn out human anguish; of suffering and the fateful heritage of suffering, for the most part quite unnecessary in a civilized community; of a national neglect made possible only by the silent patience with which women endure social injustice, and by the heedlessness of our governing classes to the personal hardships of what seems to them almost a different race."[131] Similarly, the Women's Social and Political Union's *Votes for Women* began its review by criticizing "people who grow sentimental about motherhood." "As a rule, they do not mean motherhood; they mean maternity. It is the replenishing of the race they have in mind, not the glory of the mother or the happiness of the child." *Votes for Women* decried "the daily murder of motherhood that goes on in this country (and in every country where men will persist in trying to rule alone)," summing up "the prevailing note" of *Maternity* as "one of unutterable pain and suffering."[132] Drawing upon *Maternity* along with other books on infant mortality—including Clementina

Black's edited interviews, *Married Women's Work*—another article in *Votes for Women* painted a gruesome picture "of modern 'civilisation'" in which domestic child deaths mirrored those of soldiers in the war. "In such a picture," proclaimed the organ of militant suffragettes, "we should see the hope and promise of motherhood turned to bitterness, disease and loss; we should see the pleasant land of England strewn with corpses like a battlefield; and only in the spirit which desires liberty and equality should we see any chance of salvation from these innumerable and intolerable ills."[133] Dead children's bodies, like corpses on a battlefield, called out for burial and public mourning, along with satisfaction of women's claims upon the state. The Women's Social and Political Union (WSPU) demanded the vote for mothers who, also like soldiers, "risk their lives," who "not merely in the heroisms and sufferings of childbirth but in the patient industrial and domestic labour of years, *give their lives* for the country and the country's children—*the mothers have no direct or open power at all.*" The WSPU concluded, "Maternity will never be handled as a national health problem till women have the vote."[134]

Alongside the press reviews, the Women's Co-operative Guild coordinated a series of political campaigns amplifying women's testimonies in *Maternity*. Davies initially used the gathered testimonies to help convince Lloyd George's government to make the maternity insurance benefit the sole property of women. Later, guildswomen and their children staged a protest, seeking far more extensive reforms than the 30s. maternity benefit. Davies and her life partner, Guild Assistant Secretary Lilian Harris, later recalled that it "was a new thing one day when a lot of mothers and babies invaded Whitehall." They insisted before Local Government Board President Herbert Samuel that "during the war, maternity was more important than ever."[135] Throughout the war years, the guild's internal "hints to speakers" advised lecturers to draw material directly from *Maternity*.[136] They came to argue that the national 30s. maternity insurance benefit proved a "failure," because it gave only minimal aid to select married women and treated pregnancy as an "illness."[137]

The guild campaigned instead for the much more extensive National Maternity Scheme. In May 1917, for example, representatives spoke before Lord Rhondda, then president of the Local Government Board and soon-to-be Minister of Food Control implementing wartime rations. The Welsh industrialist and statesman, himself the fifteenth of seventeen children of whom only five survived, had recently returned to politics after escaping the sinking of the *Lusitania* along with his only child, the militant suffragette Margaret Haig Thomas.[138] Supportive of the guildswomen's demand for a national Ministry of Health (which would be established in 1919), Rhondda listened to their proposal for universal, free maternal care. Adding to the letters from *Maternity*, working-class women recounted their experiences. A Welshwoman told "Lord Rhondda of what went on in his coalfields."[139] Another representative spoke of a newborn's dead body kept in a drawer as there "was nowhere else to put it."[140] Elizabeth Layton, a midwife from London, described a case of unsupervised children who accidently set their house on fire, causing injuries to their mother, the loss of her milk, and the death of the baby.[141] (In 1931 Layton published her life account in the Women's Co-operative Guild's *Life as We Have Known It*, edited by Davies with an introduction by Virginia Woolf.) Though the feminist-socialist campaign for family allowances ultimately faced resistance from within the British labor movement that remained committed to the male "family wage" in the interwar period, the 1918 Maternity and Child Welfare Act met many of the guild's demands for locally funded maternity centers, nurseries, paid midwives and health visitors, and food for mothers and children, marking, according to Deborah Dwork, "the establishment of the modern welfare system," a foundation for the National Health Service created in 1948.[142] Protection of child life—and collective grief over child death—prompted a far-reaching revision of the role of the state.

Gradually, the guild's primary focus on infant mortality shifted to other issues: opposition to conscription (passed in 1916) and DORA 40D (the expanded powers of the state under the Defence of the Realm Act allowing for the arrest of women accused of transmitting venereal diseases to servicemen), alongside support for the cooperative movement's longtime goals of internationalism, anti-militarism, and anti-capitalism.[143] The demand for universal women's suffrage also gained steady attention during this period. The Women's Co-operative Guild annual reports show the expansion of their aims. The bulk of the 1914–15 report concerned the guild's national maternity scheme. When the issue of women's suffrage arose, it stood as a means to support these reforms.[144] Notably, however, by the early 1920s, the guild's annual reports began listing its national maternity proposals under the overall rubric of "Women Citizenship Questions."[145] This marked a change in emphasis, though not a change in belief. As members of the guild, they had long advocated that "the right to vote" for all, "married and single, rich and poor," "should be based on humanity and not on property."[146]

The foregrounding of women's grief over miscarriages, stillbirths, and the deaths of their children as a basis for recognition and the rights of citizenship in *Maternity: Letters from Working Women* demonstrates a reworking of the "emotional frontier" surrounding childhood and death.[147] By bringing attention to the deaths of children, particularly at a time of war, the guild marked the limitations of public mourning practices and, at the same time, pressed for a restructuring of who was represented, who was recognized as having rights within the wider political community. What is striking about *Maternity: Letters from Working Women* is that in this case working-class women were telling their own stories of suffering and mourning, survival and collaboration, for the first time in such a public forum. Their letters testified that rather than lacking grief (as so many Victorian texts and even later histories had suggested), it was the larger British community that had thus far failed to recognize working-class women's grief and suffering. *Maternity* created the very published document that served as a public, national commemoration of dead children. Working-class women spoke for themselves, though no doubt mediated by Davies, bringing attention to their own subjectivity, selfhood, and claims to citizenship, based in large part on their emotional experiences of grieving the deaths of their children—deaths that they defined in terms of private loss and as the outcome of structural injustices: poor wages, unemployment, endless domestic labor, lack of medical support, insufficient education, inequality within marriage, and the withholding of women's suffrage.

The focus on child death fed concerns about Britain's future along with fears of "race suicide." Davies and the guild appealed to nationalism and pronatalism to promote their cause, and no doubt the war allowed *Maternity* to have the relatively broad readership that it did. At the same time, through these accounts of mourning, the guild brought attention to the lives and agency of working-class women. The letters argued for maternal care as a means to improve national health. But the guildswomen also knew too well that motherhood was "no crown of glory." With sympathy for women driven to asylums and self-harm, they proposed reproductive "strikes," birth control, and abortions as sensible options for women seeking the best care for their families. Their testimonies help us to understand not only how women's subjectivities and citizenship were tied to reproduction, but also, in the words of Carolyn Steedman, how "by refusing to mother," women "have refused to reproduce themselves or the circumstances of their exile."[148] No future was possible, the collection stressed, without first providing the working woman with "a life of her own."

Davies and Harris argued that before the women's cooperative movement, the nation "felt no responsibility" for the working woman's welfare. "Without money of her own," they claimed, "with no right even to her housekeeping savings, with no adequate protection against a husband's possibly cruelty, with no legal position as a mother, with the conditions of maternity totally neglected, she had existed apart, voiceless and unseen."[149] But by answering Davies's questionnaire, the authors of *Maternity* wrote their histories into the national story; they also showed how the state's interest in child mortality could not be divided from the material conditions of their lives as working-class women—their labor, their food, their husbands, and even their experiences with drunken doctors who ignored their pain. For themselves, guildswomen emphasized that the guild revealed "how our lives are linked together," and how "it has brought us out."[150] For women who "feel sometimes that we are not living but just existing somehow," it "opened up a new life."[151] Such expressions of interiority went hand in hand with the guildswomen's demand for political self-representation and a new vision of the state—based on communal ties rather than on liberal individualism—advanced through the platform of public mourning for the lives, child and adult, they had lost.

Conclusion

By the early twentieth century, mourning for children had become a frequent centerpiece of global human rights campaigns. Even as child mortality rates improved, the dead child's body reproduced in photographs, in government reports, and in charity appeals came to serve as the "dominant signifier of death," a reminder of the inequalities that persisted worldwide.¹ Images of dead and mutilated children traversed the globe bringing attention to the horrors of King Leopold II's reign over the Congo Free State (1885–1908) and the effects of the British wartime naval blockade on German and Austrian civilians.² In the aftermath of the First World War, the League of Nations passed the Geneva Declaration of the Rights of the Child (1924), followed by the United Nations General Assembly's adoption of the Declaration of the Rights of the Child (1959) guaranteeing happiness, affection, love, protection, and play, along with education, nourishment, housing, and medical care. Into the twenty-first century, international humanitarian movements continue to cultivate shared grief for children as a means to raise awareness about genocide and famine, poverty and forced displacement, border conflicts and mass shootings. Nineteenth-century understandings of child innocence and child death shape our appeals to universal human rights, to this day amplifying both the strengths and the weaknesses of political movements founded on modern childhood.

Scholars such as Lynn Hunt and Jenny Martinez have argued that modern notions of human rights emerged from the contexts of the American and French revolutions and the abolition of the transatlantic slave trade, but the case studies presented here underscore the importance of constructs of childhood in that process.³ Rousseau, whom Hunt identifies as initially popularizing the concept of human rights in the eighteenth century, published *The Social Contract* in 1762, the same year as

157

Émile; his formulations of rights and childhood were coeval.⁴ The ideal of universal innocence—in theory extending beyond all barriers of race, class, or gender—made the child a prime vehicle for articulating claims to human rights. Unevenly across the long nineteenth century, mourning for child death took on new meanings as it became ever more common to understand young death as "premature" rather than the work of God's will. Just as Hunt argues that "new kinds of feelings" (namely new forms of empathy fostered through novels) "created a new social context" in which people understood human rights to be "self-evident," new understandings of childhood and grief created a world in which mourning for children might become politicized and democratized as a means of securing, expanding, and redefining those rights in practice.⁵

But as the image of the innocent, suffering, dying child emerged as a wildly successful subject for fundraising and organizing in the nineteenth century, it also set the stage for the erasure and forgetting of social and political particulars. The framework of child innocence often served to depoliticize events. By the twentieth century, the trope of the dying child became more and more emptied of radical meaning. For example, in 1919 the sisters Dorothy Buxton and Eglantyne Jebb founded the Save the Children Fund, an international charity appealing to "a vision of global childhood," a clear sequel to the antislavery campaigns of their predecessors.⁶ (Dorothy married Charles Roden Buxton, great-grandson of the abolitionist Thomas Fowell Buxton, in 1904.) As Emily Baughan astutely recounts, power shifted early on between the sisters, moving from Buxton, who "saw humanitarian action as a gateway to radical politics," to Jebb, whose organization ultimately demonstrated how humanitarianism often serves as "a means of reimagining the imperial past."⁷ Soon ex-colonial officials, including Lord Lugard, former governor-general of Nigeria, dominated the charity's leadership, which afforded negligible representation for Africans and the parents of children purportedly in need of saving. Recognition of child death and communal grief thus provided a basis for universal humanity and rights. At the same time, however, modern ideals of childhood based on innocence—a lack of knowledge, a lack of experience, even a lack of context, economic or otherwise—also contributed to the continuation of imperial and other hierarchies. Focusing on childhood often meant ignoring troublesome particularities.

Tracing the origins of the ideal of childhood innocence to its roots in the long nineteenth century underscores how it has always been a selective trope, never universal. Some child lives—most notably, the factory child—became grievable, while others—enslaved youth and British children killed in imperial conflict—were soon forgotten, as collective grief for these children disrupted narratives of British imperial strength and benevolence. Public accounts of British child deaths in the 1857 Indian Rebellion ultimately reinforced the ties between empire, domesticity, and childhood, leaving unanswered the fundamental question of "what, politically, might be made of grief besides a cry for war."[8] Still other deaths, such as the thousands of Indian children killed and forcibly displaced, many of them traveling across the globe to Trinidad and other Caribbean colonies to replace enslaved labor in the years following the Indian Rebellion, remained largely invisible to the British public.[9]

And yet, while uneven and selective, collective public grief for suffering and dead children helped give voice to a broader range of political actors than ever before. The idea that a child's early death stemmed from worldly injustice, rather than divine intervention, brought those without suffrage or equal protection under the law into political debates and public spaces in new ways. Grief offered a mode of expression and a platform, especially for those shut out of formal politics, allowing protesters to envision new roles for the state and new conceptualizations of rights. Many were women, who refused any longer to keep their "sobbing out of sight / Because men made the laws."[10] But men, too, advanced political arguments for better futures based on lost child lives. Petitioners called for government protections of child and adult workers. Aristocratic women carried reticules displaying an enslaved mother mourning her child's impending death, and Sarah Parker Remond toured the United Kingdom speaking out against slavery by appealing to the devasting case of Margaret Garner's desperate act of infanticide. Working-class Londoners marched alongside child coffins to protest compulsory vaccination, and Josephine Butler likewise gained voice and authority as a mother in mourning objecting to what she viewed as the dangerously oppressive powers and authority of the state. Meanwhile Andrew Mearns appealed to grief for dead children to make the case that access to good housing should be a fundamental right of all citizens—an appeal that the women writing on behalf of the Women's Co-operative Guild expanded to include basic health care, food, and equality within marriage along with suffrage. Carrying their own and others' private grief into the public sphere with petitions and marches, public lectures and poetry allowed some of the most marginalized people to assert the value of their lives and their claim to rights. Their political beliefs ranged from Liberal to Tory, libertarian to socialist. Some sought greater government interventions, while others demanded an end to the medical "tyranny" of the state. But they all understood child death as a subject necessitating the government's attention. They democratized and politicized their grief by appealing to the preciousness of child life and the tragedy of premature child death as they engaged the state both within and beyond the walls of Parliament.

The most radical of these campaigners proved most likely to question distinctions between children and adults even as they raised support by alluding to modern ideals of childhood and child death. They drew upon the language of grief and childhood, newly conceived as the foundation of individual and social identity, to press larger questions of subjectivity and rights. The 1833 petitioners demanded factory regulation by emphasizing the connections between child and adult workers, notably their shared suffering, political agency, and human rights, including the right to "happiness." Sarah Parker Remond and Elizabeth Barrett Browning rejected modern constructions of child innocence as a depoliticized state of forgetting in their valuing of Black life, adult and child alike, as a necessary requirement of a just world. And the Women's Co-operative Guild recounted child death after child death to argue for the essential meaning of working-class women's lives, including their health and constitutional rights. Childhood, for these reformers, presented a means toward transformative politics, rather than being an end in itself. Even these groups, however, struggled with how to enact such transformative visions while working from within the British imperial state: they saw their demands for the improvement of adult workers as well as children pushed aside, co-opted into paternalistic solutions, or, like Remond, lost faith in the British imperial nation-state altogether.

By bringing attention to the political meanings of collective acts of mourning, *What We Mourn* underscores how public grief over child death is tied to visions of the state, its powers, and its limits. At times, shared grief for children provided a framework for structural, even militant revolutionary reforms that questioned the futurity of the state as it existed. Some of the more radical 1833 petitioners decried the "murder" and "infanticide" of industrial capitalism and the factory system, citing the harm it caused adults as well as children and threatening violent revolt if Parliament failed to act. Remond related the details of Garner's case in part to justify the armed resistance of enslaved people. While speaking metaphorically, Josephine Butler imagined an "infant army of spectres" confronting a state that failed to grant women equal rights and suffrage.

And even the pacifist Women's Co-operative Guild prompted militant suffragettes to recognize what others did not—how the country was filled with corpses of women and children like any battlefield on the Western Front. Yet while many used collective grief to raise support for structural reforms, more often than not the rhetoric of modern childhood promoted piecemeal solutions based on exceptionalism and age-based protections. Together these histories reveal the limitations of popular political movements founded on grief for the lost lives of children alone. An infant army of spectres may have haunted Great Britain in the long nineteenth century, but lasting changes that addressed more widely shared social and economic inequities proved harder to achieve.

NOTES

Introduction

1. *The Good Little Boy* (London: Religious Tract Society, n.d.), 4. The Religious Tract Society, founded in 1799, expanded its list of inexpensive tracts specifically aimed at child readers in the 1810s and 1820s. See William Jones, *The Jubilee Memorial of the Religious Tract Society: Containing a Record of Its Origin, Proceedings, and Results, A.D. 1799 to A.D. 1849* (London: Religious Tract Society, 1850), 123–27. Mary Martha Sherwood, author of the wildly popular *The History of the Fairchild Family* (1818), which contained similar accounts of child death, also published Religious Tract Society pamphlets.
2. *Good Little Boy*, 1.
3. *Good Little Boy*, 2.
4. *Good Little Boy*, 4.
5. *Good Little Boy*, 4.
6. Charles Dickens, *A Christmas Carol* [1843] (London: Penguin Books, 1984), 71.
7. Dickens, *Christmas Carol*, 84.
8. Dickens, *Christmas Carol*, 137.
9. Dickens, *Christmas Carol*, 11. Among the many scholarly works analyzing the anticipated death of Tiny Tim and for a critique of the reproductive futurism inherent in Scrooge's transformation, see Lee Edelman, *No Future: Queer Theory and the Death Drive* (Durham, NC: Duke University Press, 2004), 33–66.
10. Charles Darwin, "Charles Darwin's Memorial of Anne Elizabeth Darwin," April 30, 1851, *Darwin Correspondence Project* (University of Cambridge), https://www.darwinproject.ac.uk/people/about-darwin/family-life/death-anne-elizabeth-darwin. See Randal Keynes, *Annie's Box: Charles Darwin, His Daughter and Human Evolution* (London: Fourth Estate, 2001).
11. William Wordsworth, "We Are Seven," in *Selected Poems and Prefaces*, ed. Jack Stillinger (Boston: Houghton Mifflin, 1965), 50, line 37.
12. "Charles Dickens," *British Medical Journal* 1, no. 494 (June 18, 1870): 636; "Little Emily," *The Aldine* 5, no. 9 (September 1872): 178. On Victorian literary representations of child death, see Laurence Lerner, *Angels and Absences: Child Deaths in the Nineteenth Century* (Nashville: Vanderbilt University Press, 1997).

13. Peter Razzell and Christine Spence, "The History of Infant, Child and Adult Mortality in London, 1550–1850," *The London Journal* 32, no. 3 (November 2007): 288.
14. Jonas Hanway, as quoted in Helen Berry, *Orphans of Empire: The Fate of London's Foundlings* (Oxford: Oxford University Press, 2019), 101.
15. Alysa Levene, *Childcare, Health and Mortality in the London Foundling Hospital, 1741–1800: "Left to the Mercy of the World"* (Manchester: Manchester University Press, 2007), 49.
16. The literature detailing the effects of industrialization and urbanization on standards of living and mortality during this period is extensive. For an overview, see Romola Davenport, "Urbanization and Mortality in Britain, c. 1800–50," *Economic History Review* 73, no. 2 (2020): 455–85; Simon Szreter and Graham Mooney, "Urbanization, Mortality, and the Standard of Living Debate: New Estimates of the Expectation of Life at Birth in Nineteenth-Century Cities," *Economic History Review* 51, no. 1 (February 1998): 84–112; Robert Woods, *The Demography of Victorian England and Wales* (Cambridge: Cambridge University Press, 2000), 360–80.
17. B. R. Mitchell, *British Historical Statistics* (Cambridge: Cambridge University Press, 1988), 57–58. After the Famine years, infant mortality for Ireland was lower, with approximately one out of every ten children under the age of one dying.
18. F. B. Smith, *The People's Health, 1830–1910* (New York: Holmes and Meier, 1979), 68–69.
19. José Harris, *Private Lives, Public Spirit: A Social History of Britain, 1870–1914* (Oxford: Oxford University Press, 1993), 54, as quoted in Pat Jalland, *Death in the Victorian Family* (Oxford: Oxford University Press, 1996), 124.
20. M. Jeanne Peterson, *Family, Love, and Work in the Lives of Victorian Gentlewomen* (Bloomington: Indiana University Press, 1989), 108–15; Jalland, *Death in the Victorian Family*, 119–42; see also Lerner, *Angels and Absences*, 14–17; William Benham, ed., *Catharine and Craufurd Tait, Wife and Son of Archibald Campbell, Archbishop of Canterbury: A Memoir* (London: Macmillan, 1882).
21. Ellen Ross, *Love and Toil: Motherhood in Outcast London, 1870–1918* (Oxford: Oxford University Press, 1993), 189–94; Julie-Marie Strange, *Death, Grief and Poverty in Britain, 1870–1914* (Cambridge: Cambridge University Press, 2005), 230–62, 261 quotation. Also see David Vincent, "Love and Death and the Nineteenth-Century Working Class," *Social History* 5, no. 2 (May 1980): 223–47; Anthony Wohl, *Endangered Lives: Public Health in Victorian Britain* (Cambridge, MA: Harvard University Press, 1983), 41–42.
22. Linda Pollock, Robert Woods, and Anthony Fletcher are among those historians who challenge the earlier views of Philippe Ariès, *Centuries of Childhood: A Social History of Family Life*, trans. Robert Baldick (New York: Alfred A. Knopf, 1962), and Lawrence Stone, *The Family, Sex and Marriage*

in England (New York: Harper and Row, 1977), that high child mortality rates prevented premodern parents from attaching deep bonds of affection to children or from mourning their deaths. See Linda Pollock, *Forgotten Children: Parent-Child Relations from 1500 to 1900* (Cambridge: Cambridge University Press, 1983); Robert Woods, *Children Remembered: Responses to Untimely Death in the Past* (Liverpool: Liverpool University Press, 2006); Anthony Fletcher, *Growing Up in England: The Experience of Childhood, 1600–1914* (New Haven, CT: Yale University Press, 2008), 81–93.

23. Leonore Davidoff offers an important exception in her chapter on sibling death in *Thicker Than Water: Siblings and Their Relations, 1780–1920* (Oxford: Oxford University Press, 2012), 308–34.
24. Isaac Watts, "Solemn Thoughts of God and Death," in *Divine Songs* (London: M. Lawrence, 1715), 15.
25. Watts, "Praise to God for Learning to Read," in *Divine Songs*, 12.
26. Hugh Cunningham, *Children and Childhood in Western Society Since 1500* (London: Longman, 1995); Harry Hendrick, *Children, Childhood and English Society, 1880–1990* (Cambridge: Cambridge University Press, 1997).
27. *The Emile of Jean Jacques Rousseau*, trans. and ed. by William Boyd (New York: Teachers College Press, 1956; 1762), 40.
28. *Emile of Jean Jacques Rousseau*, 33.
29. Henry Edward and Benjamin Waugh, "The Child of the English Savage," *Contemporary Review* 49 (1886): 688.
30. Henry Edward Waugh and Benjamin Waugh, "Child of the English Savage," 688.
31. See Holly Brewer, *By Birth or Consent: Children, Law, and the Anglo-American Revolution in Authority* (Chapel Hill: University of North Carolina Press, 2005); contributions by Laura Lovett, Steven Mintz, Stephen Lassonde, Leslie Paris, and Mary Jo Maynes in the forum entitled "Age: A Useful Category of Historical Analysis," *Journal of the History of Childhood and Youth* 1, no. 1 (Winter 2008): 89–124; and the roundtable essays by Corinne Field and Nicholas Syrett, Pat Thane, Bianca Premo, Ishita Pande, Corrie Decker, Sayaka Chatani, and Ashwini Tambe published in "Chronological Age: A Useful Category of Historical Analysis," *American Historical Review* 125, no. 2 (April 2020): 371–459.
32. Brewer, *By Birth or Consent*, 1.
33. Jane Humphries, *Childhood and Child Labour in the British Industrial Revolution* (Cambridge: Cambridge University Press, 2010), 39; E. A. Wrigley and R. S. Schofield, *The Population History of England, 1541–1871: A Reconstruction* (Cambridge: Cambridge University Press, 1981), 217.
34. Sarah Maza, "The Kids Aren't All Right: Historians and the Problem of Childhood," *American Historical Review* 125, no. 4 (October 2020): 1281, 1284, emphasis in original.

35. Jalland, *Death in the Victorian Family*, 26ff.
36. Thomas de Quincey as quoted in David McAllister, *Imagining the Dead in British Literature and Culture, 1790–1848* (Cham, Switzerland: Palgrave Macmillan, 2018), 5. Also see Judith Flanders, *Rites of Passage: Death and Mourning in Victorian Britain* (London: Picador, 2024), 3.
37. Thomas Laqueur, *The Work of the Dead: A Cultural History of Mortal Remains* (Princeton, NJ: Princeton University Press, 2015), 14.
38. Laqueur, *Work of the Dead*, 212, 93.
39. See William Reddy, *The Navigation of Feeling: A Framework for the History of Emotions* (Cambridge: Cambridge University Press, 2001). For other introductions to the rich scholarship on the history of emotions, see, for example, Rachel Ablow, "Introduction: Victorian Emotions," *Victorian Studies* 50, no. 3 (Spring 2008): 375–77; Tanya Agathocleous, *Disaffected: Emotion, Sedition, and Colonial Law in the Anglosphere* (Ithaca, NY: Cornell University Press, 2021); Rob Boddice, *The History of Emotions* (Manchester: Manchester University Press, 2018); Jamie Bronstein, *The Happiness of the British Working Class* (Stanford, CA: Stanford University Press, 2023); Thomas Dixon, *Weeping Britannia: Portrait of a Nation in Tears* (Oxford: Oxford University Press, 2015); Jane Lydon, *Imperial Emotions: The Politics of Empathy Across the British Empire* (Cambridge: Cambridge University Press, 2020); Stephanie Olsen, "The History of Childhood and the Emotional Turn," *History Compass* (August 25, 2017), https://doi.org/10.1111/hic3.12410; Barbara Rosenwein, *Emotional Communities in the Early Middle Ages* (Ithaca, NY: Cornell University Press, 2006); Susan J. Matt and Peter N. Stearns, eds., *Doing Emotions History* (Urbana: University of Illinois Press, 2014); Lucy Noakes, *Dying for the Nation: Death, Grief and Bereavement in Second World War Britain* (Manchester: Manchester University Press, 2020); Jan Plamper, *The History of Emotions: An Introduction* (Oxford: Oxford University Press, 2012); Carol and Peter Stearns, "Emotionology: Clarifying the History of Emotions and Emotional Standards," *American Historical Review* 90, no. 4 (October 1985): 813–36.
40. Judith Butler, *Precarious Life: The Powers of Mourning and Violence* (London: Verso, 2004), 38.
41. Butler, *Precarious Life*, xiv.
42. Sara Ahmed, *The Cultural Politics of Emotion*, 2nd ed. (New York: Routledge, 2015), 191, emphasis in original.
43. Among the many works on Victorian death and mourning practices, see Gillian Avery and Kimberley Reynolds, eds., *Representations of Childhood Death* (Houndmills, Basingstoke, Hampshire: Macmillan Press, 2000); David Cannadine, "War and Death, Grief and Mourning in Modern Britain," in *Mirrors of Mortality: Studies in the Social History of Death*, ed. Joachim Whaley (New York: St. Martin's Press, 1981), 187–242; James

Curl, *The Victorian Celebration of Death* (Devon: David and Charles, 1972); Flanders, *Rites of Passage*; Jalland, *Death and the Victorian Family*; Strange, *Death, Grief and Poverty in Britain*; Gerhard Joseph and Herbert Tucker, "Passing On: Death," in *A New Companion to Victorian Literature and Culture.* ed. Herbert Tucker (Chichester: Wiley-Blackwell, 2014); Laqueur, *Work of the Dead*; Deborah Lutz, *Relics of Death in Victorian Literature and Culture* (Cambridge: Cambridge University Press, 2015); McAllister, *Imagining the Dead*; John Morley, *Death, Heaven and the Victorians* (London: Studio Vista, 1971); Ruth Richardson, *Death, Dissection and the Destitute*, 2nd ed. (Chicago: University of Chicago Press, 2000); Esther Schor, *Bearing the Dead: The British Culture of Mourning from the Enlightenment to Victoria* (Princeton, NJ: Princeton University Press, 1994); Terri Sabatos, "Images of Death and Domesticity in Victorian Britain," PhD diss., Indiana University, 2001; Andrew Smith, *Gothic Death, 1740–1914: A Literary History* (Manchester: Manchester University Press, 2016); Lou Taylor, *Mourning Dress: A Costume and Social History* (London: George Allen and Unwin, 1983); Michael Wheeler, *Death and the Future Life in Victorian Literature and Theology* (Cambridge: Cambridge University Press, 1990); John Wolffe, *Great Deaths: Grieving, Religion, and Nationhood in Victorian and Edwardian Britain* (Oxford: Oxford University Press, 2000).

44. Laqueur, *Work of the Dead*, 17.
45. Strange, *Death, Grief and Poverty in Britain*, 100.
46. See for example Ellen Boucher, *Empire's Children: Child Emigration, Welfare, and the Decline of the British World, 1869–1967* (Cambridge: Cambridge University Press, 2014); Jennifer DeVere Brody, *Impossible Purities: Blackness, Femininity, and Victorian Culture* (Durham, NC: Duke University Press, 1998); Antoinette Burton, "Who Needs the Nation?: Interrogating 'British' History," *Journal of Historical Sociology* 10, no. 3 (1997): 227–48; Ronjaunee Chatterjee, Alicia Christoff, and Amy Wong, "Undisciplining Victorian Studies," *Victorian Studies* 62, no. 3 (2020): 369–91; David Pomfret, *Youth and Empire: Trans-Colonial Childhoods in British and French Asia* (Stanford, CA: Stanford University Press, 2015).
47. Dickens, *Christmas Carol*, 99.
48. Dickens, *Christmas Carol*, 100–101.

1. "National Grievances"

1. Michael Sadler, "Factories' Regulation Bill," *Hansard Parliamentary Debates*, House of Commons, vol. 11, March 16, 1832, col. 340–49, 360, quotation at 345.
2. Sadler, "Factories' Regulation Bill," 349, 360.
3. Sadler, "Factories' Regulation Bill," 354, 378, 388.

4. Sadler, "Factories' Regulation Bill," 372.
5. Michael Sadler, "The Factory Girl's Last Day," reprinted in J. T. Ward, *The Factory System*, vol. 2 (New York: Barnes and Noble, 1970), 44.
6. See "The Factory Girl's Last Day," *The Ware Patriot* 57 (n.d.): 660; "The Factory Girl's Last Day," *The Religious Intelligencer* 18, issue 11 (August 10, 1833): 176; "The Factory Girl's Last Day," *The Weekly True Sun* 9 (April 7, 1833); "The Factory Girl's Last Day," *Workingman's Advocate* 4, issue 43 (June 8, 1833): 1.
7. Michael Sadler, March 17, 1832, LSE Coll. Misc. 62 1 7, as quoted in Simon Harratt, "Sadler, Michael Thomas (1780–1835)," *The History of Parliament: The House of Commons, 1820–1832*, ed. D. R. Fisher, 2009, https://www.historyofparliamentonline.org/volume/1820-1832/member/sadler-michael-1780-1835, emphasis in original.
8. Michael Thomas Sadler, *Speech of Michael Thomas Sadler, Esq. in the House of Commons, Friday, March 16, 1832, on Moving the Second Reading of the Factories' Regulation Bill*, 3rd ed. (London: Seeley and Sons, Hatchard and Son, 1832), 27; Robert Benton Seeley, *Memoirs of the Life and Writings of Michael Thomas Sadler, Esq. M.P. F.R.S. &c.* (London: R. B. Seeley and W. Burnside, 1842), 373; Alfred (Samuel Kydd), *The History of the Factory Movement from the Year 1802, to the Enactment of the Ten Hours' Bill in 1847*, vol. 1 (London: Simpkin, Marshall, 1857), 182; Charles Wing, *Evils of the Factory System Demonstrated by Parliamentary Evidence* (London: Saunders and Otley, 1837), 272. *Hansard*'s reports a slightly different account of this moment, citing Sadler as saying, "But, Sir, some may be tempted to suspect the accuracy of certain of the foregoing statements, from their improbable character. It may be thought almost impossible that children should be assembled thus early, and dismissed thus late, and still kept through the whole period in a state of active exertion. I will attempt to explain these facts" (*Hansard Parliamentary Debates*, House of Commons, vol. 11, March 16, 1832, 366).
9. Elizabeth Gaskell, *Mary Barton*, ed. Macdonald Daly (London: Penguin, 1996), 184. Thanks to Susan Zlotnick for reminding me of this scene.
10. Gaskell, *Mary Barton*, 187.
11. Gaskell, *Mary Barton*, 188.
12. Sadler, as quoted in Harratt, "Sadler, Michael Thomas (1780–1835)."
13. John T. Hope, "Factories' Regulation Bill," *Hansard Parliamentary Debates*, House of Commons, vol. 11, March 16, 1832, 386, 393.
14. Sadler's report and the subsequent studies of the Factory Commission have long served as principal evidence in debates over the effects of early industrialization on British standards of living. Highly disputed at the time, these documents remain so among historians. Debates on the standard of living question are among the most rife and contested in British history. On the one hand, the "optimists" highlight industrialization's eventual positive

effects on wages and associate any initial increases in death rates primarily with environmental and sanitary conditions. Peter Kirby, for one, argues that "excessive infant and child illness and mortality recorded in industrial towns resulted overwhelmingly from environmental, rather than occupational causes" (*Child Labour in Britain, 1750–1870* [Basingstoke: Palgrave Macmillan, 2003], 15; for more in-depth development of this argument, see Peter Kirby, *Child Workers and Industrial Health in Britain, 1780–1850* [Woodbridge, Suffolk: Boydell Press, 2013]). The "pessimists," on the other hand, blame the conditions of industrial labor for higher death rates, while also raising concerns about changes in living standards that cannot easily be monetized, such as loss of worker independence, increased time regulation, and environmental devastation. See, for example, J. L. and Barbara Hammond, *The Town Labourer, 1760–1832: The New Civilization* (London: Longmans, Green, 1919), and E. P. Thompson, *The Making of the English Working Class* (New York: Pantheon Books, 1963). For a review of this literature with particular attention to infant mortality rates, see Melanie Reynolds, *Infant Mortality and Working-Class Child Care, 1850–1899* (New York: Palgrave Macmillan, 2016), 4–5.

15. Nigel Goose and Katrina Honeyman, introduction to *Childhood and Child Labour in Industrial England: Diversity and Agency, 1750–1914*, ed. Nigel Goose and Katrina Honeyman (Surrey, UK: Ashgate, 2013), 4–5. On the contributions of child workers to industrialization, see also Katrina Honeyman, *Child Workers in England, 1780–1820: Parish Apprentices and the Making of the Early Industrial Labour Force* (Burlington, VT: Ashgate, 2007), and Jane Humphries, *Childhood and Child Labour in the British Industrial Revolution* (Cambridge: Cambridge University Press, 2010).

16. On Chartist demands for political rights linked to images of dying children, see Lisa Surridge, "Working-Class Masculinities in *Mary Barton*," *Victorian Literature and Culture* 28, no. 2 (2000): 331–43.

17. Friedrich Engels, *The Condition of the Working Class in England*, ed. Victor Kiernan (New York: Penguin Books, 1987), 128, 138, 172.

18. Many scholars have explored this mixing of genres. See, for example, Alysa Levene and Jean Webb, "Depictions of the 'Ideal Child' in Nineteenth-Century British Literature and Legislature," *Journal of the History of Childhood and Youth* 12, no. 1 (Winter 2019): 26–44; Mary Poovey, *Making a Social Body: British Cultural Formation, 1830–1864* (Chicago: University of Chicago Press, 1995).

19. Judith Butler, Precarious *Life: The Powers of Mourning and Violence* (London: Verso, 2004), xiv.

20. See, for example, Robert Gray, *The Factory Question and Industrial England* (Cambridge: Cambridge University Press, 1996); Honeyman, *Child Workers in England*; Kirby, *Child Labour in Britain* and *Child Workers and Industrial*

Health; Clark Nardinelli, *Child Labour and the Industrial Revolution* (Bloomington: Indiana University Press, 1990); Marjatta Rahikainen, *Centuries of Child Labour: European Experiences from the Seventeenth to the Twentieth Century* (Aldershot, UK: Ashgate Publishing, 2004); J. T. Ward, *The Factory Movement, 1830–1855* (London: Macmillan; New York: St. Martin's Press, 1962). For a novel quantitative analysis of working-class autobiographical accounts of boys' labor, see Humphries, *Childhood and Child Labour*.

21. *Report from the Committee on the Bill to Regulate the Labour of Children in the Mills and Factories of the United Kingdom* (August 8, 1832).
22. See, for example, "The Factory Bill," *The Standard*, January 12, 1833.
23. Thomas Laqueur, *Work of the Dead: A Cultural History of Mortal Remains* (Princeton, NJ: Princeton University Press, 2015), 314, 317. On the Anatomy Act and similar commodification of enslaved people's bodies in North America, see Ruth Richardson, *Death, Dissection and the Destitute*, 2nd ed. (Chicago: University of Chicago, 2000), and Daina Ramey Berry, *The Price for Their Pound of Flesh: The Value of the Enslaved, from Womb to Grave, in the Building of a Nation* (Boston: Beacon Press, 2017).
24. Factories Inquiry Commission, *First Report of the Central Board of His Majesty's Commissioners Appointed to Collect Information in the Manufacturing Districts, as to the Employment of Children in Factories, and as to the Propriety and Means of Curtailing the Hours of their Labour* (House of Commons, June 28, 1833); Factories Inquiry Commission, *Second Report of the Central Board of His Majesty's Commissioners Appointed to Collect Information in the Manufacturing Districts, as to the Employment of Children in Factories* (House of Commons, July 15, 1833).
25. Factory Act 1833 (3 & 4 Will. IV) c. 103; "In the House of Lords Last Night, The Factories' Regulation Bill," *The Times*, August 27, 1833.
26. For Macaulay's defense of limited child labor legislation, see his speech of May 22, 1846, reprinted in J. T. Ward, ed., *The Factory System*, vol. 2: *The Factory System and Society* (New York: Barnes and Noble, 1970), 172–80.
27. Ward, *Factory System*, 2: 68.
28. James Pattison, testimony before Sir Robert Peel's Committee of 1816, reprinted in Ward, *Factory System*, 2: 68, 69.
29. Pattison, testimony before Sir Robert Peel's Committee of 1816, reprinted in Ward, *Factory System*, 2: 69.
30. Nassau W. Senior, *Letters on the Factory Act, as It Affects the Cotton Manufacture, Addressed to the Right Honourable the President of the Board of Trade* (1837), reprinted in Ward, *Factory System*, 2: 150.
31. Senior, *Letters on the Factory Act*, reprinted in Ward, *Factory System*, 2: 149, emphasis in original.
32. Senior, *Letters on the Factory Act*, reprinted in Ward, *Factory System*, 2: 151–52.

33. Senior, *Letters on the Factory Act*, reprinted in Ward, *Factory System*, 2: 152.
34. Andrew Ure, *The Philosophy of Manufactures* (1835), reprinted in Ward, *Factory System*, 2: 156.
35. Ure, *Philosophy of Manufactures*, reprinted in Ward, *Factory System*, 2: 156.
36. Ure, *Philosophy of Manufactures*, reprinted in Ward, *Factory System*, 2: 156.
37. Ure, *Philosophy of Manufactures*, reprinted in Ward, *Factory System*, 2: 156. Donald Cardwell notes, "Ure's comments on social conditions were sometimes patently absurd. He once claimed that workers in cotton mills were less liable to cholera than the rest of the population and that working at a temperature of 150 °F was not harmful. Such ills as afflicted the workers were due to their inordinate taste for bacon." See Donald Cardwell, "Ure, Andrew (1778–1857)," *Oxford Dictionary of National Biography* (Oxford University Press, online ed., 2004), https://doi.org/10.1093/ref:odnb/28013.
38. House of Commons, *Fourth Report from the Select Committee on Public Petitions* (March 12, 1833), 79, Center for Research Libraries (CRL). The Cotton Yarn Dressers of Scotland's petition included 416 signatures.
39. *Fourth Report from the Select Committee on Public Petitions*, 86, CRL, emphasis in original.
40. *Fourth Report from the Select Committee on Public Petitions*, 86, CRL.
41. *Fourth Report from the Select Committee on Public Petitions*, 86, CRL.
42. *Fourth Report from the Select Committee on Public Petitions*, 86, CRL, emphasis in original.
43. *Fourth Report from the Select Committee on Public Petitions*, 86, CRL.
44. *Fourth Report from the Select Committee on Public Petitions*, 79, CRL.
45. Richard Huzzey, Henry Miller, and Ciara Stewart, "Petitioning and the Politics of Nation, Gender, and Empire," conference panel, North American Conference on British Studies, Providence, RI, 2018; Richard Huzzey and Henry Miller, "Petitions, Parliament and Political Culture: Petitioning the House of Commons, 1780–1918," *Past and Present* 248, no. 1 (2020): 123–164; Henry Miller, *A Nation of Petitioners: Petitions and Petitioning in the United Kingdom, 1780–1918* (Cambridge: Cambridge University Press, 2023). For scholarship on earlier English petitions, see Thomas W. Smith and Helen Killick, eds., *Petitions and Strategies of Persuasion in the Middle Ages: The English Crown and the Church, c. 1200–c. 1550* (Woodbridge: York Medieval Press, 2018). On the use of petitions by free people of color in British antislavery campaigns, see Ramesh Mallipeddi, "Political Rights and the Printed Word," in "The End of Print: A Roundtable," special issue, *Journal of British Studies* (March 4, 2025), https://doi.org/10.1017/jbr.2024.187. I have accessed the 1833 petitions from the Center for Research Libraries microfiche collection, rather than using the ProQuest collection, *Public Petitions to Parliament, 1833–1918*.
46. Miller, *Nation of Petitioners*, 276.

47. Miller, *Nation of Petitioners*, 27.
48. Miller, *Nation of Petitioners*, 278.
49. Miller, *Nation of Petitioners*, 2.
50. Miller, *Nation of Petitioners*, 51.
51. On the child welfare movement and nineteenth-century uses of the melodramatic mode more generally, see Lydia Murdoch, *Imagined Orphans: Poor Families, Child Welfare, and Contested Citizenship in London* (New Brunswick, NJ: Rutgers University Press, 2006), 12–42; Peter Brooks, *The Melodramatic Imagination: Balzac, Henry James, Melodrama, and the Mode of Excess* (New Haven, CT: Yale University Press, 1976); Elaine Hadley, *Melodramatic Tactics: Theatricalized Dissent in the English Marketplace, 1800–1885* (Stanford, CA: Stanford University Press, 1995); Patrick Joyce, *Democratic Subjects: The Self and the Social in Nineteenth-Century England* (Cambridge: Cambridge University Press, 1994), 176–90; Rohan McWilliam, "Melodrama and the Historians," *Radical History Review* 78 (2000): 57–84; Judith Walkowitz, *City of Dreadful Delight: Narratives of Sexual Danger in Late-Victorian London* (Chicago: University of Chicago Press, 1992).
52. *Forty-Second Report from the Select Committee on Public Petitions* (August 29, 1833), 1657, CRL.
53. *Forty-Second Report from the Select Committee on Public Petitions*, 1657, CRL.
54. *Forty-Second Report from the Select Committee on Public Petitions*, 1657, CRL.
55. *Forty-Second Report from the Select Committee on Public Petitions*, 1657, CRL.
56. *Forty-Second Report from the Select Committee on Public Petitions*, 1654, CRL; *Forty-First Report from the Select Committee on Public Petitions: August 7–13, 1833* (August 28, 1833), 1601, CRL.
57. "Petition of the Inhabitants of the Borough of Leeds," *Eighth Report from the Select Committee on Public Petitions* (March 26, 1833), 240, CRL; "Petition of the Inhabitants of the Borough of Manchester," *Thirty-Fourth Report from the Select Committee on Public Petitions* (July 10, 1833), 1326, CRL.
58. Kirby, *Child Labour in Britain*, 103.
59. "Petition of the Master Flax Spinners of Dundee," *Twenty-Fourth Report from the Select Committee on Public Petitions* (June 5, 1833), 978, CRL; "Petition of the Operatives Working in Various Mills in Rochdale," *Eleventh Report from the Select Committee on Public Petitions* (April 19, 1833), 387, CRL; "Petition from Mr. George William Wood [Lancaster]," *Tenth Report from the Select Committee on Public Petitions* (April 2, 1833), 318, CRL.
60. "Petition of the Master Cotton Spinners and Manufacturers of Hyde," *Eleventh Report from the Select Committee on Public Petitions* (April 19, 1833), 387, CRL.
61. "Petition of the Subscribers, Woollen Manufacturers Stirling," *Twentieth Report from the Select Committee on Public Petitions* (May 23, 1833), 791, CRL.

62. "Petition of the Owners and Occupiers of Silk Mills and Factories ... in the Borough of Derby," *Fortieth Report from the Select Committee on Public Petitions* (August 16, 1833), 1582–83, quotation at 1583, CRL.
63. "Petition of the Owners and Occupiers of Silk Mills and Factories ... in the Borough of Derby," *Fortieth Report from the Select Committee on Public Petitions* (August 16, 1833), 1582–83, quotation at 1583, CRL.
64. "Petition of Woollen Yarn Spinners, of Harwick, in Roxburghshire," *Thirty-Seventh Report from the Select Committee on Public Petitions* (July 26, 1833), 1447–48, quotation at 1448, CRL.
65. See, for example, "Petition of the Operative Cotton Spinners ... in the County of Renfrew," *Twenty-First Report from the Select Committee on Public Petitions* (May 23, 1833), 831, CRL.
66. "Petition of the Delegates from the Factory Districts of England and Scotland," *Twenty-Third Report from the Select Committee on Public Petitions* (May 31, 1833), 932, CRL.
67. "Petition of the Members of the Short Time Committee, established at Bradford, in Yorkshire," *Thirty-Third Report from the Select Committee on Public Petitions* (July 5, 1833), 1288, CRL.
68. "Petition of the Overlookers of Mills and Factories in and Near Bradford, Yorkshire," *Thirty-Third Report from the Select Committee on Public Petitions* (July 5, 1833), 1288–89, quotation at 1288, CRL.
69. For petitions highlighting concerns of sexual abuse of female workers, see the same language repeated in "Petition of Inhabitants of the Chapelry of Rastrick, Halifax," *Thirty-Fourth Report from the Select Committee on Public Petitions* (July 10, 1833), 1329, CRL; "Petition of Friends of the Society for Improving the Condition of Factory Children," *Thirty-Eighth Report from the Select Committee on Public Petitions* (August 5, 1833), 1492, CRL.
70. "Petition of the Operative Cotton Spinners ... in the County of Renfrew," *Twenty-First Report from the Select Committee on Public Petitions* (May 23, 1833), 831, CRL.
71. Kirby, *Child Workers and Industrial Health*, 2. For an excellent collection featuring essays exploring child labor and agency, see Goose and Honeyman, eds., *Childhood and Child Labour*, especially Kathryn Gleadle's "'We Will Have It': Children and Protest in the Ten Hours Movement," 215–30.
72. "Petition of Mule Spinners, Employed in Cotton Factories in Manchester," *Eleventh Report from the Select Committee on Public Petitions* (April 19, 1833), 386, CRL.
73. "Petition of the Children and Young Persons ... Employed in Mills and Factories in Manchester," *Thirty-Fourth Report from the Select Committee on Public Petitions* (July 10, 1833), 1328, CRL.
74. "Petition of the Children and Young Persons," *Thirty-Fourth Report from the Select Committee on Public Petitions*, 1328, CRL.

75. Gleadle, "'We Will Have It': Children and Protest in the Ten Hours Movement," 215.
76. "Petition of Operatives of New Lanark Cotton Works," *Sixth Report from the Select Committee on Public Petitions* (March 19, 1833), 149, CRL.
77. "Petition of the Operative Cotton Spinners ... in Johnstone (County Renfrew)," *Twenty-First Report from the Select Committee on Public Petitions* (May 23, 1833), 831, CRL; "Petition of the Undersigned Inhabitants of the City of Glasgow," *Thirty-First Report from the Select Committee on Public Petitions* (June 28, 1833), 1223, CRL; "Petition of the Undersigned Overlookers, Carders, Spinners ... in Great Bolton (County Lancaster)," *Thirty-First Report from the Select Committee on Public Petitions* (June 28, 1833), 1222, CRL; "Petition of the Inhabitants of the Borough of Manchester," *Thirty-Fourth Report from the Select Committee on Public Petitions* (July 10, 1833), 1326, CRL.
78. "Petition of Operative Cotton Spinners of Glasgow," *Sixth Report from the Select Committee on Public Petitions* (March 19, 1833), 147–48, CRL.
79. See *Report from the Committee on the Bill to Regulate the Labour of Children in the Mills and Factories of the United Kingdom*, "Appendix: Comparative Table of the Duration of Life," 608–12. This point is repeated in many of the petitions. See, for example, "Two Petitions of Gentry, Clergy, Medical Men, and Tradesmen of the Township of Little Bolton" and "Petition of Inhabitants of the Borough of Bradford, in Yorkshire," *Second Report from the Select Committee on Public Petitions: February 26–March 1, 1833*, (n.d.), 65, CRL; "Petition of Operative Cotton Spinners and Others of Chorley," *Sixth Report from the Select Committee on Public Petitions* (March 19, 1833), 149, CRL; "Petition of the Electors of the Borough of Manchester," *Seventh Report from the Select Committee on Public Petitions* (March 22, 1833), 197, CRL; "Petition of Mule Spinners, employed in Cotton Factories in Manchester," *Eleventh Report from the Select Committee on Public Petitions* (April 19, 1833), 386, CRL; "Petition of the Undersigned Overlookers, Carders, Spinners, and Others, Employed in Cotton Mills in Great Bolton," "Petition of Mule Spinners, employed in Cotton Factories in Manchester," *Thirty-First Report from the Select Committee on Public Petitions* (June 28, 1833), 1222–23, CRL; "Petition of the Undersigned Spinners, Carders, Overlookers, and Others, Employed in Cotton Mills, in the Townships of Tyldesley cum Shackerley and Atherton," *Thirty-Fourth Report from the Select Committee on Public Petitions* (July 10, 1833), 1324, CRL.
80. "Petition of the Inhabitants of Ampthill," *Twenty-Fifth Report from the Select Committee on Public Petitions* (June 7, 1833), 1022, CRL.
81. See "Petition of Cotton Yarn Dressers of Scotland," *Fourth Report from the Select Committee on Public Petitions* (March 12, 1833), 86, CRL; "Petition of the Master, Wardens, Searchers, Assistants, and Commonality of the Corporation of Cutlers in Hallamshire," *Fourteenth Report from the Select*

Committee on Public Petitions (April 29, 1833), 567, CRL; "Petition of the Magistrates, Clergy, Medical Gentlemen, and Others, Resident in Stockport," *Thirty-Fourth Report from the Select Committee on Public Petitions* (July 10, 1833), 1327, CRL.

82. John Farre, August 7, 1832, *Report from the Committee on the Bill to Regulate the Labour of Children in the Mills and Factories of the United Kingdom*, 600. See also 601.

83. "Petition of the Inhabitants of the Borough of Manchester," *Thirty-Fourth Report from the Select Committee on Public Petitions* (July 10, 1833), 1326, CRL.

84. "Petition of Sunday School Teachers of North Byerley and Bowling, in the West Riding of York," *Sixth Report from the Select Committee on Public Petitions* (March 19, 1833), 150, CRL.

85. "Petition of the Undersigned Inhabitants of the Parish of Islington, in the County of Middlesex," *Thirteenth Report from the Select Committee on Public Petitions* (April 23, 1833), 492, CRL.

86. "Petition of the Undersigned Persons, Being Members of the Council of a Society Calling Itself the National Political Union . . . Holborn Hill," *Thirty-Fourth Report from the Select Committee on Public Petitions* (July 10, 1833), 1325, CRL.

87. "Petition of the Undersigned Persons . . . Holborn Hill," 1325, CRL.

88. On discourses of infanticide and empire, see Daniel Grey, "Creating the 'Problem Hindu': *Sati*, Thuggee and Female Infanticide in India, 1800–60," *Gender and History* 25, no. 3 (November 2013): 498–510, and "'It Is Impossible to Judge the Extent to Which the Crime is Prevalent': Infanticide and the Law in India, 1870–1926," *Women's History Review* 30, no. 6 (2021): 1028–46.

89. "Petition of the Magistrates and Councillors of the Royal Burgh of Cupar, in the County of Fife," *Thirty-Ninth Report from the Select Committee on Public Petitions* (August 12, 1833), 1543, CRL.

90. "Petition of Operative Cotton Spinners of Glasgow," *Sixth Report from the Select Committee on Public Petitions* (March 19, 1833), 148, CRL.

91. "Petition of Operative Cotton Spinners of Glasgow," 148, CRL.

92. "Petition of Operative Cotton Spinners of Glasgow," 148, CRL.

93. "Petition of the Vicar and Clergy of the Parish of St. Mary, Islington, in the County of Middlesex," *Thirteenth Report from the Select Committee on Public Petitions* (April 23, 1833), 492, CRL.

94. "Petition of the Undersigned Inhabitants of the Town and County of Newcastle-upon-Tyne," *Thirty-Third Report from the Select Committee on Public Petitions* (July 5, 1833), 1287–88, CRL.

95. "Petition of the Undersigned Overlookers, Carders, Spinners, and Others, Employed in Cotton Mills in Great Bolton," *Thirty-First Report from the*

Select Committee on Public Petitions (June 28, 1833), 1223, CRL. This language is repeated in other petitions.
96. "Petition of the Children and Young Persons, Under Twenty-One Years of Age, Employed in Mills and Factories in Manchester," *Thirty-Fourth Report from the Select Committee on Public Petitions* (July 10, 1833), 1328, CRL.
97. "Petition of the Undersigned Inhabitants of the City of Glasgow," *Thirty-First Report from the Select Committee on Public Petitions* (June 28, 1833), 1223, CRL.
98. "Petition of the Operative Cotton Spinners, and Others Employed in Cotton Factories in Johnstone (County Renfrew)," *Twenty-First Report from the Select Committee on Public Petitions* (May 23, 1833), 831, CRL.
99. "Petition of the Undersigned Disciples, Advocates, and Friends of the 'Social and Rational System of Society,' as Developed and Propagated by Robert Owen, Late of New Lanark," *Twelfth Report from the Select Committee on Public Petitions* (April 19, 1833), 442, CRL.
100. "Petition of the Undersigned Disciples, Advocates, and Friends of the 'Social and Rational System of Society,' as Developed and Propagated by Robert Owen, Late of New Lanark," *Twelfth Report from the Select Committee on Public Petitions* (April 19, 1833), 442, CRL.
101. "Petition of the Undersigned Disciples, Advocates, and Friends of the 'Social and Rational System of Society,' as Developed and Propagated by Robert Owen, Late of New Lanark," *Twelfth Report from the Select Committee on Public Petitions* (April 19, 1833), 443, CRL.
102. "Petition of the Undersigned Inhabitants of the Borough and Foreign of Walsall, in the County of Stafford," *Thirteenth Report from the Select Committee on Public Petitions* (April 23, 1833), 491, CRL.
103. "Petition of the Undersigned Inhabitants of the Borough and Foreign of Walsall," 491–92, CRL.
104. "Petition of the Undersigned Inhabitants of the Chapelry of Rastrick, in the Parish of Halifax (York)," *Thirty-Fourth Report from the Select Committee on Public Petitions* (July 10, 1833), 1329, CRL, emphasis added.
105. "Petition of the Undersigned Inhabitants of the Chapelry of Rastrick," 1329, CRL, emphasis added.
106. See, for example, "Petition of the Undersigned Friends of the Society for Improving the Condition of Factory Children . . . City of London Tavern, Bishopsgate Street," and "Petition of the Undersigned Inhabitants of Peckham," *Thirty-Eighth Report from the Select Committee on Public Petitions* (August 5, 1833), 1491–93, CRL.
107. "Petition of the Undersigned Inhabitants of the Township of Horton, in the County of York," *Twelfth Report from the Select Committee on Public Petitions* (April 19, 1833), 443, CRL. For a similar argument, see "Petition of the Undersigned Friends of the Society for Improving the Condition of Factory

Children ... City of London Tavern, Bishopsgate Street," *Thirty-Eighth Report from the Select Committee on Public Petitions* (August 5, 1833), 1492, CRL.
108. Gareth Stedman-Jones, *Languages of Class* (Cambridge: Cambridge University Press, 1983); Joan Wallach Scott, *Gender and the Politics of History* (New York: Columbia University Press, 1988).
109. "Petition of the Delegates from the Factory Districts of England and Scotland," *Twenty-Third Report from the Select Committee on Public Petitions* (May 31, 1833), 931, CRL.
110. "Petition of the Delegates from the Factory Districts of England and Scotland," 932, CRL.
111. "Petition of the Inhabitants of the Town of Johnstone," *Thirty-Fourth Report from the Select Committee on Public Petitions* (July 10, 1833), 1328, CRL.
112. Peaches Henry, "The Sentimental Artistry of Barrett Browning's 'The Cry of the Children,'" *Victorian Poetry* 49, no. 4 (Winter 2011): 535. As Henry notes, literary scholars of Barrett Browning's work long dismissed her sentimental poetry. For scholarship arguing for the potential of sentimental literature to inspire political reform, along with Henry, see June Howard, "What Is Sentimentality?" *American Literary History* 11, no. 1 (Spring 1999): 63–81; Fred Kaplan, *Sacred Tears: Sentimentality in Victorian Literature* (Princeton, NJ: Princeton University Press, 1987); Karen Sánchez-Eppler, *Touching Liberty: Abolition, Feminism, and the Politics of the Body* (Berkeley: University of California Press, 1993); Robert C. Solomon, *In Defense of Sentimentality* (New York: Oxford University Press, 2004); Jane Tompkins, *Sensational Designs: The Cultural Work of American Fiction, 1790–1860* (New York: Oxford University Press, 1985).
113. Barrett Browning identified herself as a "sort of fossil republican," rather than a supporter of any particular political party. Elizabeth Barrett Browning, letter to John Kenyon, February 8, 1845, in Philip Kelley and Scott Lewis, eds., *The Brownings' Correspondence*, vol. 10 (Winfield, KS: Wedgestone Press, 1992), letter 1832, 60.
114. Marjorie Stone, "Witness Narratives and Working-Class Suffering: 'The Cry of the Children,' *Corn Law Rhymes*, and Elizabeth Barrett Browning's Unpublished Hunger Ballad," *Victorian Studies* 62, no. 4 (Summer 2020): 616–43.
115. "Devastating Storm," *The Times*, July 7, 1838; Children's Employment Commission, *First Report of the Commissioners on the Employment of Children (Mines)* (London: HMSO, 1842), Witness no. 101, 248–49.
116. Letter from Elizabeth Barrett Browning to Richard Hengist Horne, August 7, 1843, in Philip Kelley and Ronald Hudson, eds., *The Brownings' Correspondence*, vol. 7 (Winfield, KS: Wedgestone Press, 1989), letter 1349, 274.
117. Elizabeth Barrett Browning, "The Cry of the Children," Poems, in *The Complete Works of Elizabeth Barrett Browning*, vol. 3, ed. Charlotte Porter and

Helen Clarke (New York: Thomas Y. Crowell, 1900), stanza 1, 53. Unless otherwise noted, all subsequent quotations from Barrett Browning's poetry are to this edition with the stanza number referenced in the text.
118. See editorial note to "The Cry of the Children," *Blackwood's Edinburgh Magazine* 54 (August 1843): 261–62; Henry, "Sentimental Artistry," 550.
119. Henry, "Sentimental Artistry," 545. Marjorie Stone also explores how Barrett Browning, through "an act of empathetic imagining," recognizes working children as subjects demanding their rights, in "Witness Narratives," 633–34.
120. *The Westminster Review* (December 1844), in Philip Kelley and Scott Lewis, eds., *The Brownings' Correspondence*, vol. 9 (Winfield, KS: Wedgestone Press, 1991), 375.
121. *The League*, December 7, 1844, in Kelley and Lewis, *Brownings' Correspondence*, 9: 379.
122. *The League*, December 7, 1844, in Kelley and Lewis, *Brownings' Correspondence*, 9: 379.
123. Edgar Allan Poe, *The Broadway Journal*, January 4, 1845, in Kelley and Lewis, *Brownings' Correspondence*,10: 352.
124. Archer Thompson Gurney, *The English Review*, December 1850, in Philip Kelley, Scott Lewis, and Edward Hagan, eds., *The Brownings' Correspondence*, vol. 16 (Winfield, KS: Wedgestone Press, 2007), 329.
125. Letter from Elizabeth Barrett Browning to Hugh Stuart Boyd, September 18, 1843, in Kelley and Hudson, *Brownings' Correspondence*, letter 1381, 7: 331, emphasis in original.
126. *Tait's Edinburgh Magazine*, November 1844, in Kelley and Lewis, *Brownings' Correspondence*, 9: 365.
127. Charles Peterson, *Peterson's Magazine*, December 1855, in Philip Kelley, Scott Lewis, Edward Hagan, Joseph Phelan, and Rhian Williams, eds., *The Brownings' Correspondence*, vol. 22 (Winfield, KS: Wegestone Press, 2015), 278–79.
128. *Tait's Edinburgh Magazine*, January 1856, in Kelley et al., *Brownings' Correspondence*, 22: 289; "The Cry of the Children," stanza 7.
129. Elizabeth Barrett Browning, letter to Mary Russell Mitford, February 8, 1845, in Kelley and Lewis, *Brownings' Correspondence*, letter 1833, 10: 62.
130. Elizabeth Barrett Browning, letter to Mary Russell Mitford, September 24, 1850, in Kelley, Lewis, and Hagan, *Browning's Correspondence*, letter 2881, 16: 200.
131. Engels, *Condition of the Working Class in England*, 187.
132. Children's Employment Commission, *First Report of the Commissioners (Mines)* (London: HMSO, 1842), Parliamentary Papers, 24, 76.
133. Patricia Johnson, *Hidden Hands: Working-Class Women and Victorian Social-Problem Fiction* (Athens: Ohio University Press, 2001).

134. See Gray, *Factory Question and Industrial England*; Anna Clark, *The Struggle for the Breeches: Gender and the Making of the British Working Class* (Berkeley: University of California Press, 1995).
135. "Petition of the Undersigned Persons, Being Members of the Council of a Society Calling Itself the National Political Union . . . Holborn Hill," *Thirty-Fourth Report from the Select Committee on Public Petitions* (July 10, 1833), 1325–26, CRL.

2. "Shrouding My Poor Children"

1. Mary Prince, *The History of Mary Prince: A West Indian Slave* (London: Penguin Books, 2004), ed. Sara Salih, 10.
2. Prince, *History of Mary Prince*, ed. Salih, 10, emphasis in original.
3. The *History* is a complicated text, transcribed by the writer Susanna Strickland, sister of the historian and novelist Agnes Strickland, and commissioned and edited by the Scottish poet Thomas Pringle, who had recently returned to England from South Africa and was serving as the secretary of the Anti-Slavery Society. Much of the scholarship on Prince concentrates on her voice and agency in the *History*, along with the ensuing libel cases concerning omitted details deemed too indecent for antislavery readers of Prince's relationship with a man before her marriage in Antigua to the freeman Daniel James. See Mary Prince, *The History of Mary Prince: A West Indian Slave* (Ann Arbor: University of Michigan Press, 1997), ed. Moira Ferguson; Prince, *History of Mary Prince*, ed. Salih.
4. Prince, *History of Mary Prince*, ed. Salih, 12.
5. Prince, *History of Mary Prince*, ed. Salih, 11, 13. See also especially 10, 18, 22.
6. Prince, *History of Mary Prince*, ed. Salih, 11.
7. The term "stolen childhood" is a reference to Wilma King's foundational history of enslaved children in the United States, *Stolen Childhood: Slave Youth in Nineteenth-Century America*, 2nd ed. (Bloomington: Indiana University Press, 2011). For more recent work on child slavery in the U.S., see Anna Mae Duane, ed., *Child Slavery Before and After Emancipation: An Argument for Child-Centered Slavery Studies* (New York: Cambridge University Press, 2017).
8. Sasha Turner, *Contested Bodies: Pregnancy, Childrearing, and Slavery in Jamaica* (Philadelphia: University of Pennsylvania Press, 2017), 152; Sasha Turner, "The Nameless and the Forgotten: Maternal Grief, Sacred Protection, and the Archive of Slavery," *Slavery and Abolition* 38, no. 2 (2017): 232, 235.
9. Robin Bernstein, *Racial Innocence: Performing American Childhood from Slavery to Civil Rights* (New York: New York University Press, 2011). For a

discussion of how abolitionists, such as Frederick Douglass, countered the association of childhood and child innocence with whiteness, see 55–63.

10. Nicole Eustace, "Emotion and Political Change," in *Doing Emotions History*, ed. Susan J. Matt and Peter N. Stearns (Urbana: University of Illinois Press, 2014), 167. On abolitionists' linking of affect and political rights, also see Elizabeth B. Clark, "'The Sacred Rights of the Weak': Pain, Sympathy, and the Culture of Individual Rights in Antebellum America," *Journal of American History* 82, no. 2 (September 1995): 463–93, especially 474, 486–87. Nicole Eustace and Sarah Knott provide important models examining the emotional arguments supporting the American Revolution. See Nicole Eustace, *Passion Is the Gale: Emotion, Power and the Coming of the American Revolution* (Chapel Hill: University of North Carolina Press, 2008), and Sarah Knott, *Sensibility and the American Revolution* (Chapel Hill: University of North Carolina Press, 2009).

11. Hazel Carby, "Slave and Mistress: Ideologies of Womanhood under Slavery," in *Reconstructing Womanhood: The Emergency of the Afro-American Woman Novelist* (New York: Oxford University Press, 1987), 28.

12. Bernstein, *Racial Innocence*, 6, emphasis in original. The art historian Anne Higonnet likewise argues that "Romantic childhood as a subject deflects knowing because it was constructed to be the denial of knowledge. Romantic childhood was a state of not-knowing." See Anne Higonnet, "What Do You Want to Know About Children?," in *Picturing Children: Constructions of Childhood Between Rousseau and Freud*, ed. Marilyn R. Brown (Burlington, VT: Ashgate, 2002), 204. For Higonnet's more extensive critique of Romantic childhood innocence, see *Pictures of Innocence: The History and Crisis of Ideal Childhood* (New York: Thames and Hudson, 1998). Henry Louis Gates Jr. describes this more general process of forgetting African history and enslavement in "History the Slaveholders Wanted Us to Forget," *New York Times*, February 5, 2017.

13. Anna Mae Duane, introduction to *Child Slavery Before and After Emancipation: An Argument for Child-Centered Slavery Studies*, ed. Anna Mae Duane (New York: Cambridge University Press, 2017), 16.

14. Wilma King, *Stolen Childhood: Slave Youth in Nineteenth-Century America*, 2nd ed. (Bloomington: Indiana University Press, 2011). Also see Corinne Field, *The Struggle for Equal Adulthood: Gender, Race, Age, and the Fight for Citizenship in the Antebellum America* (Chapel Hill: University of North Carolina Press, 2014); Catherine Jones, *Intimate Reconstructions: Children in Postemancipation Virginia* (Charlottesville: University of Virginia Press, 2015); Wilma King, "'Suffer with Them till Death': Slave Women and Their Children in Nineteenth-Century America," in *More Than Chattel: Black Women and Slavery in the Americas*, ed. David Barry Gaspar and Darlene Clark Hine, 147–68 (Bloomington: Indiana University Press, 1996);

Katherine Paugh, *The Politics of Reproduction: Race, Medicine, and Fertility in the Age of Abolition* (Oxford: Oxford University Press, 2017); Marie Jenkins Schwartz, *Born in Bondage: Growing Up Enslaved in the Antebellum South* (Cambridge, MA: Harvard University Press, 2000); Turner, *Contested Bodies*; Turner, "The Nameless and the Forgotten"; Colleen Vasconcellos, *Slavery, Abolition, and Childhood in Jamaica, 1788–1838* (Athens: University of Georgia Press, 2015).

15. Bernstein, *Racial Innocence*; Duane, *Child Slavery Before and After Emancipation*.

16. On women in British antislavery movements, see Elizabeth J. Clapp and Julie Roy Jeffrey, eds., *Women, Dissent, and Anti-Slavery in Britain and America, 1790–1865* (Oxford: Oxford University Press, 2011); Moira Ferguson, *Subject to Others: British Women Writers and Colonial Slavery, 1670–1834* (New York: Routledge, 1992); Clare Midgley, *Women Against Slavery: The British Campaigns, 1780–1870* (London: Routledge, 1992); Clare Midgley, *Feminism and Empire: Women Activists in Imperial Britain, 1790–1865* (London: Routledge, 2007); Kathryn Kish Sklar and James Brewer Stewart, eds., *Women's Rights and Transatlantic Antislavery in the Era of Emancipation* (New Haven, CT: Yale University Press, 2007).

17. Following the Somerset case, the former slave Joseph Knight claimed his freedom in Scotland, and the Scottish Court of Sessions eventually ruled in his favor in 1778.

18. The August 24, 1833, Slave Emancipation Act excluded territories ruled by the East India Company and the islands of Ceylon and Saint Helena until 1843, when Parliament removed these exceptions.

19. The enforced labor of freed children through the "death, poverty, or neglect of their parents" was a major point of antislavery protest. See, for example, *Petition to Her Majesty, Queen Victoria, from the Ladies of Glasgow and Its Vicinity, Adopted at the Public Meeting Held in the Rev. David King's Chapel, 1st August, 1837* (Glasgow: Glasgow Chronicle, 1837), 1, JSTOR Wilson Anti-Slavery Collection.

20. Keith McClelland, "Redefining the West India Interest: Politics and the Legacies of Slave-Ownership," in *Legacies of British Slave-Ownership: Colonial Slavery and the Formation of Victorian Britain*, ed. Catherine Hall, Nicholas Draper, Keith McClelland, Katie Donington, and Rachel Lang (Cambridge: Cambridge University Press, 2014), 139. The "apprenticeship" system required both groups to work 75 percent of their time for former slaveholders for no payment, unless they worked overtime.

21. On the *Zong* murders, the court cases involving the Liverpool owners' subsequent insurance claim, and the antislavery responses, see James Walvin, *The Zong: A Massacre, the Law and the End of Slavery* (New Haven, CT: Yale University Press, 2011), quotation of evidence from James Kelsall, 156.

22. Mr. Pigot, as quoted in Walvin, *The Zong*, 147. Although Mansfield decided in favor of a retrial, there is no record of one.
23. Thomas Clarkson, *An Essay on the Slavery and Commerce of the Human Species, Particularly the African, Translated from a Latin Dissertation Which Was Honoured with the First Prize in the University of Cambridge in the Year 1785*, 2nd ed. (London: J. Phillips, 1788), 98–99; Ottobah Cugoano, *Thoughts and Sentiments on the Evil of Slavery* [1787] (London: Dawsons of Pall Mall, 1969); Walvin, *The Zong*, 175. Also see Thomas Fowell Buxton's much later account, which, quoting the *Memoirs of Granville Sharp* (1820), makes no reference to the gender or age of the Africans killed by the *Zong* crew: *The African Slave Trade* (London: J. Murray, 1839), 104–6.
24. Cugoano, *Thoughts and Sentiments*, 111.
25. Midgley, *Women Against Slavery*, 97–98.
26. Wilma King surveys literature detailing the growing proportion of enslaved children transported from Africa. She notes, citing Audra Diptee, that "from 1786 to 1792, 27 percent of the Africans transported from West Central Africa were children." This proportion increased significantly after the British and U.S. abolition of the slave trade in 1807 and 1808. By "the second quarter of the nineteenth century, more than 60 percent of the Africans transported to the New World were boys and girls." See Wilma King, *Stolen Childhood*, 3.
27. Debbie Lee, *Slavery and the Romantic Imagination* (Philadelphia: University of Pennsylvania Press, 2002).
28. [Hannah More] Cheap Repository, *The Sorrows of Yamba; or, the Negro Woman's Lament* (London: J. Marshall, 1795). On the authorship of "The Sorrows of Yamba," see Alan Richardson, "'The Sorrows of Yamba,' by Eaglesfield Smith and Hannah More: Authorship, Ideology, and the Fractures of Antislavery Discourse," *Romanticism on the Net* 28 (November 2002), http://id.erudit.org/iderudit/007209ar. For comparisons with Eaglesfield's poem, see E. S. J., "The Sorrows of Yamba," *Universal Magazine of Knowledge and Pleasure* 101 (July 1797): 43–44.
29. *The Sorrows of Yamba; or, the Negro Woman's Lamentation*, 5, stanza 12.
30. *Hansard Parliamentary Debates*, House of Commons (May 15, 1823), col. 257–360, see especially col. 273. See Olwyn Mary Blouet, "Buxton, Sir Thomas Fowell, First Baronet (1786–1845)," *Oxford Dictionary of National Biography* (Oxford University Press, online ed., 2010), https://doi.org/10.1093/ref:odnb/4247; Catherine Hall, "Anti-Slavery Society (*act*. 1823–1833)," *Oxford Dictionary of National Biography*, https://doi.org/10.1093/ref:odnb/96359.
31. Thomas Fowell Buxton, *Hansard Parliamentary Debates*, House of Commons (May 15, 1823), col. 263.

32. Thomas Fowell Buxton, *Hansard Parliamentary Debates*, House of Commons (May 15, 1823), col. 269.
33. Thomas Fowell Buxton, *Hansard Parliamentary Debates*, House of Commons (May 15, 1823), col. 270.
34. Thomas Fowell Buxton, *Hansard Parliamentary Debates*, House of Commons (May 15, 1823), col. 266. Buxton cites New York, New Jersey, Philadelphia, Ceylon, Bencoolen, St. Helena, and Columbia as having successfully taken a similar gradualist approach to ending slavery. See cols. 266–68.
35. Thomas Fowell Buxton, *Hansard Parliamentary Debates*, House of Commons (May 15, 1823), col. 274.
36. Elizabeth Elbourne, *Empire, Kinship and Violence: Family Histories, Indigenous Rights and the Making of Settler Colonialism, 1770–1842* (Cambridge: Cambridge University Press, 2022), 307–71, quotation 374.
37. See George Canning's amendment, *Hansard Parliamentary Debates*, House of Commons (May 15, 1823), cols. 285–86. On the question of freeing enslaved children, he assented "that the progeny of slaves must not be eternally slaves," but refused to offer any timeline for this reform. See cols. 359–60.
38. *The First Report of the Female Society, for Birmingham, West-Bromwich, Wednesbury, Walsall, and Their Respective Neighbourhoods, for the Relief of British Negro Slaves* (Birmingham: Richard Peart, 1826), 15–16, emphasis in original, JSTOR Wilson Anti-Slavery Collection. Also see *Ladies Society for the Relief of Negro Slaves, Founding Meeting Held West-Bromwich, 8th April 1825*, as quoted in Midgley, *Women Against Slavery*, 44.
39. *The First Report of the Female Society, for Birmingham, West-Bromwich, Wednesbury, Walsall, and Their Respective Neighbourhoods*, 11, emphasis in original; *The Fourth Annual Report, of the Ladies' Association, for Salisbury, Calne, Melksham, Devizes, &c. in Aid of the Cause of Negro Emancipation* (Calne: T. P. Baily, 1829), 10, JSTOR Wilson Anti-Slavery collection.
40. "The Negro Mother's Appeal," *Anti-Slavery Scrap Book* (London: Bagster and Thoms, 1829), n.p., JSTOR Wilson Anti-Slavery Collection. Clare Midgley identifies the Peckham Ladies' African and Anti-Slavery Society as the probable producer of this book of collected poems (*Women Against Slavery*, 232, n. 29).
41. "Negro Mother's Appeal," n.p., lines 9–12.
42. "Negro Mother's Appeal," n.p., lines 27–28, 33, 34.
43. Ladies' N.Y. City Anti-Slavery Society, *Appeal to the Christian Women of America* (New York: William S. Dorr, 1836), 2. The Sheffield Association for the Universal Abolition of Slavery (formerly the Ladies' Anti-Slavery Society of Sheffield) repeated this quotation in *An Appeal to the Christian Women of Sheffield, from the Association for the Universal Abolition of*

Slavery (Sheffield: R. Leader, 1837), 7. On the resistance and vital domestic bonds within enslaved communities, see, for example, Wilma King, "'Suffer with Them till Death': Slave Women and Their Children in Nineteenth-Century America," in *More Than Chattel: Black Women and Slavery in the Americas*, ed. David Barry Gaspar and Darlene Clark Hine, 147–68 (Bloomington: Indiana University Press, 1996).

44. "Gone, Sold and Gone," words by John Greenleaf Whittier, music by George W. Clark; "The Bereaved Mother," words by Jessie Hutchinson, in George W. Clark, *The Liberty Minstrel* (New York: Leavitt and Alden, 1845), 5–7, 46–47. Antislavery songs in particular focused on the separations of enslaved parents and children. In Clark's collection, see, for example, "What Means That Sad and Dismal Look?," 8–9; "The Bereaved Father," 10–11; "Slave Girl Mourning Her Father," 12–13; "Negro Boy Sold for a Watch," 16–17; "Song of the Coffle Gang," 22–23; "Brothers Be Brave for the Pining Slave," 26–28; "Domestic Bliss," 34; "The Blind Slave Boy," 37–39; "My Child Is Gone," 43; "Sleep On My Child," 49; "Christian Mother," 131; "The Slave's Lamentation," 168–169. Also see *Five Hundred Thousand Strokes for Freedom: A Series of Anti-Slavery Tracts, of Which Half a Million Are New First Issued by the Friends of the Negro* (London: W. and F. Cash, 1853), "The Farewell of a Virginian Slave-Mother to Her Daughter Sold into Southern Bondage," no. 10; "Sale and Separation of a Family," no. 41; "Negro Boy Sold for a Watch," no. 25; "Parting of a Slave-Mother and Her Son," no. 74; also see "Auctioneering Advertisements," no. 15; "Slave Auction in a Southern City," no. 16; "Sale of Aged Negroes," no. 17; "The Blind Slave Boy," no. 26; "Scene on Board a Steam-Boat at Wilmington," no. 27; "The Gentlemen Farmers of Virginia Attending Their Cattle-Market," no. 48; "Slave-Auction in Virginia," no. 49; "Auction of a Young Woman, with Reflections," no. 51; "Tender Mercies of the Domestic Institution," no. 53; "Sale of Slaves in Virginia," no. 64; "The Virginia Slave Crop," no. 65; "Voices from Slavery," no. 66; "Blasting Influence of Slavery on the Social Circle," no. 68; "The Slave-Trade in Columbia," no. 70; "A Few Words on Abstinence from Slave Produce," no. 73; "Intellect and Capabilities of the Negro Race," no. 79. Antislavery societies also regularly published extracts of advertisements for the sale of slave children. See, for example, "We wish to present the friends of the poor African, with a recent advertisement of the Sale of a Negro Child [extracts from supplement to the *Royal Jamaica Gazette*]," August 1, 1827 (Soho: Howlett and Brimmer, 1827).
45. Debora C. De Rosa, *Domestic Abolitionism and Juvenile Literature, 1830–1865* (Albany: State University of New York Press, 2003), see especially 43–50.
46. "Remember the Slave!" (n.p., 1830), lines 21–24, JSTOR Wilson Anti-Slavery Collection. Other British abolitionist publications reproduced

this poem. See, for example, *Three Years' Female Anti-Slavery Effort, in Britain and America: Being A Report of the Proceedings of the Glasgow Ladies' Auxiliary Emancipation Society, Since Its Formation in January, 1834* (Glasgow: Aird and Russell, 1837), 64, JSTOR Wilson Anti-Slavery Collection. Follen republished the song in *Hymns, Songs, and Fables for Young People*, rev. ed. (1831; Boston: William Crosby and H. P. Nichols, 1848), 50–52.

47. "Remember the Slave!," line 26. For a similar comparison of a child's experience of domestic safety and Christian piety in contrast to the "poor slaves," see "A Child's Evening Hymn," in *Leeds Anti-Slavery Juvenile Series* (Leeds Anti-Slavery Association, 1860), JSTOR Wilson Anti-Slavery Collection.
48. Ladies' New York City Anti-Slavery Society, *Appeal to the Christian Women of America* (New York: William S. Dorr, 1836), 9, emphasis in original. Selections of the *Appeal to the Christian Women of America* were reprinted in *An Appeal to the Christian Women of Sheffield* (1837) and *Three Years' Female Anti-Slavery Effort* (1837).
49. On the Boston Female Anti-Slavery Society, see Debra Gold Hansen, *Strained Sisterhood: Gender and Class in the Boston Female Anti-Slavery Society* (1993); Jean Fagan Yellin and John C. Van Horne, *The Abolitionist Sisterhood: Women's Political Culture in Antebellum America* (Ithaca, NY: Cornell University Press, 1994).
50. *Sixth Annual Report of the Boston Female Anti-Slavery Society* (Boston: Dow and Jackson, 1839), 5, emphasis in original. The report was aimed at a transatlantic female audience; it included correspondence with British antislavery leaders, such as Elizabeth Pease and E. Waterhouse of the Sheffield Association for the Entire Abolition of Slavery, as well as an Address of the Boston Female Anti-Slavery Society to the Women of Great Britain.
51. *Sixth Annual Report of the Boston Female Anti-Slavery Society*, 5.
52. *Sixth Annual Report of the Boston Female Anti-Slavery Society*, 5.
53. King, *Stolen Childhood*, 6–9, 28–29. (Also see Bernstein, *Racial Innocence*, 43, for a discussion of Blake's abolitionist poetry stressing childhood of enslaved. Bernstein describes a change in the U.S. around the mid-nineteenth century as "writers began to polarize black and white childhood.")
54. Frederick Douglass, *My Bondage and My Freedom* (1855), reprinted in *Frederick Douglass: Autobiographies*, edited by Henry Louis Gates Jr. (New York: Library of America, 1994), 143, emphasis in original. On Douglass's tour of the United Kingdom and his role as leader of the international abolitionist movement, see R. J. M. Blackett, *Building an Antislavery Wall: Black Americans in the Atlantic Abolitionist Movement, 1830–1860* (Baton Rouge: Louisiana State University Press, 1983), 79–117.
55. Douglass, *My Bondage and My Freedom*, 145, 144. On Douglass and the ideal of Romantic boyhood, see Bernstein, *Racial Innocence*, 60–63.

56. Frederick Douglass, *Life and Times of Frederick Douglass* (1893 edition), reprinted in *Frederick Douglass: Autobiographies*, ed. Henry Louis Gates Jr. (New York: Library of America, 1994), 484. For a slightly alternative description of this scene, see *My Bondage and My Freedom*, 155.
57. Douglass, *My Bondage and My Freedom*, 155; *Life and Times*, 484.
58. Douglass, *My Bondage and My Freedom*, 150, quotation; *Life and Times*, 481.
59. Douglass, *My Bondage and My Freedom*, 155, quotation, emphasis in original, 157; *Narrative of the Life of Frederick Douglass, An American Slave* (1845), reprinted in *Frederick Douglass: Autobiographies*, edited by Henry Louis Gates Jr. (New York: Library of America, 1994), 16; *Life and Times*, 484.
60. Douglass, *Narrative of the Life*, 33.
61. Harriet Jacobs, *Incidents in the Life of a Slave Girl* (Boston: For the author, 1861), 11, 15.
62. The NSPCC was founded in 1889, following the creation of the Liverpool (1883) and London (1884) branches.
63. *Five Hundred Thousand Strokes for Freedom*, "Murderous Treatment of a Slave Girl," no. 39; "Murder of an Infant," no. 42; "Tender Mercies of Slavery: Treatment of Infants in a Christian (?) Country," no. 60.
64. *St. Louis Republican* article reprinted in "Murderous Treatment of a Slave Girl," *Five Hundred Thousand Strokes for Freedom*.
65. "Paradise of Negro Slaves: A Dream, by Dr. [Benjamin] Rush," no. 30, *Five Hundred Thousand Strokes for Freedom*, 3. This pamphlet was original published in 1798.
66. Harriet Jacobs, as quoted in Wilma King, *Stolen Childhood*, 52. Also see Sarah H. Ficke, "Crafting Social Criticism: Infanticide in 'The Runaway Slave at Pilgrim's Point' and *Aurora Leigh*," *Victorian Poetry* 51, no. 2 (Summer 2013): 254–55.
67. "Artifact: Silk Handbag from the 1820s Made to Support the Anti-Slavery Movement," *The Abolition Project*, http://abolition.e2bn.org/source_37.html, in the Collection of The Library of the Religious Society of Friends. See silk reticule printed in black with steel frame and chain, designed by Samuel Lines, made by the Female Society for Birmingham, Birmingham, ca. 1827, Victoria and Albert Museum, T.20–1951, http://collections.vam.ac.uk/item/O68954/reticule-lines-samuel/.
68. "Artifact: Silk Handbag from the 1820s Made to Support the Anti-Slavery Movement," *The Abolition Project*, http://abolition.e2bn.org/source_37.html, in the Collection of The Library of the Religious Society of Friends. The text is an extract from Anna Lætitia Barbauld, *Hymns in Prose for Children* (London: J. Johnson, 1781), hymn 8, 53–63. The single verse was often reproduced without attribution. See, for example, ["Prayer About a Negro Slave"], n.t., n.p., 1840, one-page printed verse for distribution, JSTOR Wilson Anti-Slavery Collection.

69. Letter from Melissa Ammidon, of the Boston Female Anti-Slavery Society, to the Lowell Female Anti-Slavery Society, July 14, 1835, as quoted in De Rosa, *Domestic Abolitionism and Juvenile Literature*, 40, emphasis in original. Robin Bernstein provides an astute discussion of the meanings and scripted uses of handkerchiefs and other "Tomitudes"—the "items of material culture representing [Harriet Beecher] Stowe's characters," "from dolls and card games to statuary and embroidery to jam jars and tobacco tins"—in *Racial Innocence*, quotation at 9.
70. For other examples of objects with the imprinted image and text, see *Negro Woman who sittest pining in captivity and weepest over thy sick child*, silk doily with transfer, ca. 1830s–1850s, The Davis Museum at Wellesley College, Museum purchase, Erna Bottigheimer Sands (Class of 1929) Art Acquisition Fund, Object No.: 2008.182; Purse 82.137.2, owned by Elizabeth Margaret Chandler, Daughters of the American Revolution, https://collections.dar.org/mDetail.aspx?rID=82.137.2&db=objects&dir=DARCOLL; silk reticule printed in black with steel frame and chain, designed by Samuel Lines, made by Female Society for Birmingham, Birmingham, ca. 1827, Victoria and Albert Museum, T.20–1951; and a similar design with an overseer holding a whip next to the mother and infant: printed silk reticule bag, designed by Samuel Lines, made by Female Society for Birmingham, Birmingham, ca. 1825, Victoria and Albert Museum, T.227–1966.
71. Children's Friend, "A Negro Woman's Lamentation Over Her Child," *Anti-Slavery Scrap Book*, n.p., quotation lines 25–32; see lines 33–36.
72. Ladies' New York City Anti-Slavery Society, *Appeal to the Christian Women of America* (New York: William S. Dorr, 1836), 5. The pamphlet, which echoes Angelina Grimké's *Appeal to the Christian Women of the South* (1836), was excerpted in *An Appeal to the Christian Women of Sheffield* (1837).
73. Ladies' New York City Anti-Slavery Society, *Appeal to the Christian Women of America*, 10–11.
74. *An Appeal to the Christian Women of Sheffield*, 5, emphasis in original.
75. *Sixth Annual Report of the Boston Female Anti-Slavery Society*, 20–21.
76. "Remember the Slave!," lines 13–16.
77. Follen, "The Little Slave's Wish," in *Hymns, Songs, Fables, for Young People*, 69–71, lines 1, 5, 9, 13, 17, 21, 23, 33–36. For a discussion of this song and Follen's revised version, see De Rosa, *Domestic Abolitionism and Juvenile Literature*, 47–48.
78. Eliza Lee Follen, "The Slave Boy's Wish," in Clark, *Liberty Minstrel*, 9. A version very close to this is also printed in the *Leeds Anti-Slavery Juvenile Series* (1860), JSTOR Wilson Anti-Slavery Collection.
79. "The Poor Little Slave," from *The Chartered Oak*, lines 18–20, in the *Leeds Anti-Slavery Juvenile Series* (1860), JSTOR Wilson Anti-Slavery Collection;

and in Clark, *Liberty Minstrel,* 45. Also see "Little Benny," in the *Leeds Anti-Slavery Juvenile Series* (1860), for another example of an enslaved boy's death wish after being sold as a seven-year-old from his mother.
80. Charlotte Elizabeth, "The Slave and Her Babe," in Clark, *Liberty Minstrel,* 13.
81. "The Afric's Dream," words by Miss Chandler, in Clark, *Liberty Minstrel,* 20–21, lines 10, 19. Also see "The Little Slave Girl," 138–39.
82. "I thank the goodness and the grace," quotations lines 4, 11–12, 19–20, *Leeds Anti-Slavery Juvenile Series* (Leeds: Leeds Anti-Slavery Association, 1860), JSTOR Wilson Anti-Slavery Collection. This hymn appears in multiple issues. Also see "Hymn for Children" in this collection.
83. "I thank the goodness and the grace" and facing cover illustration, *Leeds Anti-Slavery Juvenile Series,* no. 8 (Leeds: Leeds Anti-Slavery Association, 1860), JSTOR Wilson Anti-Slavery Collection.
84. *British Quarterly Review* 34 (October 1861) and *Edinburgh Review* 114 (October 1861), as quoted in Marjorie Stone, "Browning [née Moulton Barrett], Elizabeth Barrett (1806–1861)," *Oxford Dictionary of National Biography* (Oxford University Press, online ed., 2008), https://doi.org/10.1093/ref:odnb/3711.
85. Frederic G. Kenyon, ed., *The Letters of Elizabeth Barrett Browning,* vol. 2 (New York: Macmillan, 1897), 220, as quoted in Marjorie Stone, "Cursing as One of the Fine Arts: Elizabeth Barrett Browning's Political Poems," in *Critical Essays on Elizabeth Barrett Browning,* ed. Sandra Donaldson, 184–201 (New York: G. K. Hall, 1999.
86. "The Runaway Slave at Pilgrim's Point" and "A Curse for a Nation" were originally published in *The Liberty Bell* in December 1847 and 1855, respectively, although these publications were dated for the coming years. See Andrew Stauffer, "Elizabeth Barrett Browning's (Re)visions of Slavery," *English Language Notes* 34, no. 4 (June 1997): 30.
87. Letter from Eizabeth Barrett Browning to Cornelius Mathews, mid-January 1847, in Philip Kelley and Scott Lewis, eds., *The Brownings' Correspondence,* vol. 14 (Winfield, KS: Wedgestone Press, 1998), letter 2648, 99. Marjorie Stone suggests that Eliza Follen may have also asked Barrett Browning to write the poem for *The Liberty Bell,* because both Follen and Chapman signed the 1844 and 1845 issues sent to Barrett Browning. See "Elizabeth Barrett Browning and the Garrisonians: 'The Runaway Slave at Pilgrim's Point,' the Boston Female Anti-Slavery Society, and Abolitionist Discourse in the *Liberty Bell,*" in *Victorian Women Poets: Essays and Studies,* ed. Alison Chapman, vol. 56 (Cambridge: D. S. Brewer, 2003), 42. The first known reference to "The Runaway Slave" in Barrett Browning's letters is in a letter to Mary Russell Mitford, December 1, 1845, in Philip Kelley and Scott Lewis, eds., *The Brownings' Correspondence,* vol. 11 (Winfield, KS: Wedgestone Press, 1993), letter 2122, 213.

88. Elizabeth Barrett Browning, "The Runaway Slave at Pilgrim's Point," in *The Complete Works of Elizabeth Barrett Browning*, vol. 3, ed. Charlotte Porter and Helen Clarke (New York: Thomas Y. Crowell, 1900), 165, stanza 19. Unless otherwise noted, citations of the poem are from this version, originally published in *Poems* (1850).
89. For a concise summary of these arguments, see Melissa Schaub, "The Margins of the Dramatic Monologue: Teaching Elizabeth Barrett Browning's 'The Runaway Slave at Pilgrim's Point,'" *Victorian Poetry* 49, no. 4 (Winter 2011): 558–59; and Stone, "Elizabeth Barrett Browning and the Garrisonians," 37–38.
90. Elizabeth Barrett Barrett's sister Mary died at the age of three. Her brother Samuel died on February 17, 1840, from fever while in Jamaica, and her closest brother, Edward (whom she called "Bro"), drowned in a sailing accident on July 11, 1840. Elizabeth Barrett Browning had four miscarriages between March 1847 and July 1850. See Stone, "Browning [née Moulton Barrett], Elizabeth Barrett (1806–1861)," *Oxford Dictionary of National Biography*; and Marjorie Stone, "Between Ethics and Anguish: Feminist Ethics, Feminist Aesthetics, and Representations of Infanticide in 'The Runaway Slave at Pilgrim's Point' and *Beloved*," in *Between Ethics and Aesthetics: Crossing the Boundaries*, ed. Dorota Glowacka and Stephen Boos (Albany: State University of New York Press, 2002), 140.
91. Elizabeth Barrett Browning to James Russell Lowell, December 17, 1846, Baylor University Armstrong Browning Library, Digital Collection; published (in part), Kelley and Lewis, *Brownings' Correspondence*, letter 2644, 14: 86–87.
92. Ficke, "Crafting Social Criticism," 250.
93. Elizabeth Barrett Browning to James Russell Lowell, December 17, 1846, Baylor University Armstrong Browning Library, Digital Collection; published (in part), Kelley and Lewis, *Brownings' Correspondence*, letter 2644, 14: 86–87.
94. On Barrett Browning's treatment of infanticide in the context of other submissions to *The Liberty Bell*, see Ficke, "Crafting Social Criticism"; Stone, "Elizabeth Barrett Browning and the Garrisonians," 33–55. For a discussion of the 1846 case of Nelly, a fourteen-year-old enslaved mother indicted for infanticide, see Wilma King, "'Mad' Enough to Kill: Enslaved Women, Murder, and Southern Courts," *Journal of African American History* 92, no. 1 (Winter 2007): 37–56.
95. "The Slave Mother," *The Liberator* 2, issue 3 (January 21, 1832): 11. For a report of the original case, see "Slavery Record: Annual View of Slavery," *The Liberator* 1, issue 52 (December 24, 1831): 206.
96. "The Slave Mother," *The Liberator* 2, issue 3 (January 21, 1832): 11, lines 54–56. Garrison reprinted this poem in *Juvenile Poems, for the Use of Free*

American Children of Every Complexion (1835). See De Rosa, *Domestic Abolitionism and Juvenile Literature*, 61–62, 158 n. 28.

97. Maria Lowell, "The Slave Mother," *The Liberty Bell* (Boston, MA: Anti-Slavery Fair, 1846), 250–52, quotations lines 7–8, 38, 39–40, 47–48. Stone also links this poem with Francis Harper's "The Slave Mother, a Tale of the Ohio" (1874) and Toni Morrison's *Beloved* (1987). See "Elizabeth Barrett Browning and the Garrisonians," 53.
98. *Sixth Annual Report of the Boston Female Anti-Slavery Society*, 19.
99. C. Stuart, "Anecdotes of American Slavery," in *Three Years' Female Anti-Slavery Effort*, 61.
100. Ficke, "Crafting Social Criticism"; Stone, "Elizabeth Barrett Browning and the Garrisonians," 33–55; Stone, "Between Ethics and Anguish," 140–46. Long dismissed by literary critics, "The Runaway Slave" has received more attention in recent decades. In addition to the above articles, see, for example, Elizabeth Battles, "Slavery Through the Eyes of a Mother: *The Runaway Slave at Pilgrim's Point*," *Studies in Browning and His Circle* 19 (1991); Sarah Brophy, "Elizabeth Barrett Browning's 'The Runaway Slave at Pilgrim's Point' and the Politics of Interpretation," *Victorian Poetry* 36, no. 3 (Fall 1998): 273–88; John MacNeill Miller, "Slavish Poses: Elizabeth Barrett Browning and the Aesthetics of Abolition," *Victorian Poetry* 52, no. 4 (Winter 2014): 637–59; Ann Parry, "Sexual Exploitation and Freedom: Religion, Race, and Gender in Elizabeth Barrett Browning's 'The Runaway Slave at Pilgrim's Point,'" *Studies in Browning and His Circle* 16 (1988): 114–26; Schaub, "Margins of the Dramatic Monologue"; Stauffer, "Elizabeth Barrett Browning's (Re)visions of Slavery"; Stone, "Cursing as One of the Fine Arts"; Charlotte Sussman, *Consuming Anxieties: Consumer Protest, Gender, and British Slavery, 1713–1833* (Stanford, CA: Stanford University Press, 2000), 197–205.
101. Stone, "Elizabeth Barrett Browning and the Garrisonians," 50–54, quotation at 51.
102. Stone, "Elizabeth Barrett Browning and the Garrisonians," 50–54, quotation at 53. Barrett Browning added the description of rape in stanza 15 after the Wellesley draft that is the primary focus of Stone's analysis.
103. Melissa Valiska Gregory, "Race and the Dramatic Monologue," *Victorian Studies* 62, no. 2 (Winter 2020): 217.
104. On the influence of Douglass's *Narrative* on Barrett Browning, see Stone, "Elizabeth Barrett Browning and the Garrisonians," 49; "Between Ethics and Anguish," 145.
105. Lee Edelman, *No Future: Queer Theory and the Death Drive* (Durham, NC: Duke University Press, 2004), 3.
106. Stanza 30. The second stanza reinforces this connection between pilgrims and slave owners: "O pilgrims, I have gasped and run / All night long from the whips of one / Who in your names works sin and woe!"

107. Stanza 23. Note how these lines suggest a reversal of John 10:28: "And I give unto them eternal life; and they shall never perish, neither shall any *man* pluck them out of my hand" (King James Bible).
108. Stanza 24. Ficke also stresses Barrett Browning's emphasis on the enslaved child's physicality, though this point leads her to different conclusions. See "Crafting Social Criticism," 257.
109. Stanza 20. The account of the child's burial also suggests the mother's geographical displacement, as his body is described as being "between the roots of the mango."
110. Stanza 28. For a nuanced analysis of this section of the poem as an example of "artistic freedom and emotional generosity" bringing the potential of interracial reconciliation, see Sussman, *Consuming Anxieties*, 204.
111. Stanzas 33 and 34. For a discussion of the ways in which Barrett Browning transforms the typical judgment function of the dramatic monologue by encouraging readers to "condemn only slavery, not the slave," see Schaub, "Margins of the Dramatic Monologue," 566.
112. Elizabeth Barrett Browning to James Russell Lowell, December 17, 1846, Baylor University Armstrong Browning Library, Digital Collection; published (in part), Kelley and Lewis, *Brownings' Correspondence*, letter 2644, 14: 86–87.
113. Letter from Elizabeth Barrett Browning to Mary Russell Mitford, February 8, 1847, *Brownings' Correspondence*, letter 2654, 14: 117, emphasis in original.
114. Letter from Elizabeth Barrett Browning to Cornelius Mathews, mid-January 1847, *Brownings' Correspondence*, letter 2648, 14: 99.
115. Stone, "Elizabeth Barrett Browning and the Garrisonians," 54.
116. Letter from Elizabeth Barrett Browning to Mary Russell Mitford, September 24, 1850, in Philip Kelley, Scott Lewis, and Edward Hagan, eds., *The Brownings' Correspondence*, vol. 16 (Winfield, KS: Wedgestone Press, 2007), letter 2881, 200.
117. Reviews of Elizabeth Barrett Browning's *Poems* (1850) in *The Eclectic Review* (March 1851): 295–303, reprinted in Philip Kelley, Scott Lewis, and Edward Hagan, eds., *The Brownings' Correspondence*, vol. 17 (Winfield, KS: Wedgestone Press, 2010), 290; *The Literary World* (February 1, 1851), 85–86, reprinted in *Brownings' Correspondence*, 17: 289.
118. Stone, "Browning [*née* Moulton Barrett], Elizabeth Barrett," *Oxford Dictionary of National Biography*.
119. On June 10, 1854, Charlotte Forten recorded in her diary that Sarah Remond "had a volume of Mrs. Browning's poems, from which I read 'Prometheus Bound' and 'Casa Guidi Windows'" (Charlotte L. Forten, *The Journal of Charlotte L. Forten*, with an introduction and notes by Ray Allen Billington [New York: The Dryden Press], 1953), 38. Also see Sibyl

Ventress Brownlee, "Out of the Abundance of the Heart: Sarah Ann Parker Remond's Quest for Freedom," PhD diss., University of Massachusetts Amherst, 1997, 106.

120. *Journal of Charlotte L. Forten*, 36. For Forten's March 8, 1857, description of reading *Aurora Leigh*, see 82.

121. Naturalisation Papers: Remond, Sarah Parker, from the United States of America. Certificate 4809 issued September 11, 1865, The National Archives (TNA) HO 1/123/4809.

122. Douglass, *Life and Times*, 1015; William S. McFeely, *Frederick Douglass* (New York: W. W. Norton, 1991), 328–29.

123. "Anti-Slavery Tracts No. 15," in Wilbur H. Siebert Underground Railroad Collection: The Underground Railroad in Ohio: Hamilton County series 4, vol. 7, box 56, as quoted in Nikki Taylor, *Driven Toward Madness: The Fugitive Slave Margaret Garner and Tragedy on the Ohio* (Athens: Ohio University Press, 2016), 145, n. 25; see also 99.

124. Stone, "Between Ethics and Anguish," 153.

125. Remond wrote that she was one of ten siblings (*Our Exemplars*, 276), but Sirpa Salenius notes that Salem City Hall birth records document eleven children born to Remond's parents, Nancy Lenox and John Remond (*An Abolitionist Abroad*, 26). Remond's brief autobiographical statement was first printed in *Our Exemplars, Poor and Rich; or, Biographical Sketches of Men and Women Who Have, by an Extraordinary Use of the Opportunities, Benefited Their Fellow Creatures*, ed. Matthew Davenport Hill, with an introduction by Lord Brougham (London: Cassell, Petter, and Galpin, 1861), 276–86. A shortened version of this piece was reprinted in the *English Woman's Journal* 7, issue 40 (June 1, 1861): 269–75. The most extensive published historical account of Remond is Sirpa Salenius, *An Abolitionist Abroad: Sarah Parker Remond in Cosmopolitan Europe* (Amherst: University of Massachusetts Press, 2016). For other histories of Remond, see Celeste-Marie Bernier and Hannah-Rose Murray, eds., *Nineteenth-Century African American Speeches in Britain and Ireland* (Edinburgh: University of Edinburgh Press, 2024); Brownlee, "Out of the Abundance of the Heart"; Willi Coleman, "'Like Hot Lead to Pour on the Americans . . .': Sarah Parker Remond—From Salem, Mass., to the British Isles," in *Women's Rights and Transatlantic Antislavery in the Era of Emancipation*, ed. Kathryn Kish Sklar and James Brewer Stewart (New Haven, CT: Yale University Press, 2007), 173–88; Willi Coleman, "Remond, Sarah Parker (1826–1894)," *Oxford Dictionary of National Biography* (Oxford: Oxford University Press, online ed., 2022), https://doi.org/10.1093/ref:odnb/100414; Elizabeth Crawford, "Remond, Sarah Parker," *The Women's Suffrage Movement: A Reference Guide, 1866–1928* (London: Routledge, 1999), 594–95; Audrey A. Fisch, "'Negrophillism' and Nationalism: The Spectacle of the African-American Abolitionist," *American Slaves*

in Victorian England: Abolitionist Politics in Popular Literature and Culture (Cambridge: Cambridge University Press, 2000), 69–90; Midgley, *Feminism and Empire*, 144–46; Midgley, *Women Against Slavery*; Carla L. Peterson, "'Whatever Concerns Them, as a Race, Concerns Me': The Oratorical Careers of Frances Ellen Watkins Harper and Sarah Parker Remond," in *"Doers of the Word": African American Women Speakers and Writers in the North, 1830–1880* (New York: Oxford University Press, 1995), 119–45; Dorothy B. Porter, "Sarah Parker Remond, Abolitionist and Physician," *Journal of Negro History* 20, no. 3 (July 1935): 287–93; Sirpa Salenius, "Interracial Networks of Transatlantic Activism: Sarah Parker Remond Reassessing Black Womanhood," in *Connecting Women: National and International Networks During the Long Nineteenth Century*, ed. Barton Hacker et al. (Washington, DC: Smithsonian Scholarly Press, 2021), 47–61; Dorothy Sterling, "Women with a Special Mission," in *We Are Your Sisters: Black Women in the Nineteenth Century* (New York: W. W. Norton, 1984), 175–80; Shirley J. Yee, *Black Women Abolitionists: A Study in Activism, 1828–1860* (Knoxville: University of Tennessee Press, 1992); Teresa Zackodnik, "'White Slaves' and Tragic Mulattas: The Antislavery Appeals of Ellen Craft and Sarah Parker Remond," in *The Mulatta and the Politics of Race* (Jackson: University Press of Mississippi, 2004), 42–74.

126. Coleman, "'Like Hot Lead,'" 173–74.
127. Angela Davis, *Women, Race and Class* (New York: Vintage Books, 1983), 48.
128. Remond dates the beginning of her first lecture tour through New York in 1857 ("Sarah P. Remond," in Hill, *Our Exemplars*, 285). Coleman notes that Remond began delivering public lectures in late 1856 ("'Like Hot Lead to Pour on the Americans,'" 177). On the connections between Reid, Stowe, and Remond, see Salenius, *Abolitionist Abroad*, 98.
129. Register for years 1859–1860 and 1860–1861, Bedford College Register Michaelmas 1849–Easter Term 1871, Archives, Royal Holloway, University of London [RHUL], BC AR201/1/1; Miss Remond, Register of Students Courses, 1856–1872, Session 1859–1860, no. 12, p. 31, RHUL, BC AR202/1/1.
130. Remond lived with the Taylors from December 1861 until October 1864. See Salenius, *Abolitionist Abroad*, 115.
131. Mentia Taylor was on the organizing committee for the women's suffrage petition, and the final signatures were collated at Aubrey House. See Elizabeth Crawford, "Taylor [*née* Doughty], Clementia (1810–1908)," *Oxford Dictionary of National Biography* (Oxford University Press, online ed., 2004), https://doi.org/10.1093/ref:odnb/45468; Crawford, "Remond, Sarah Parker," 594–95.
132. Most biographies of Remond describe her as a general physician, but Salenius specifies her work as an obstetrician. See Salenius, *Abolitionist Abroad*, 7.

133. Salenius, *Abolitionist Abroad*, 194–95.
134. "Sarah P. Remond," in Hill, *Our Exemplars*, 286.
135. For a list of black abolitionists in the British Isles, 1830–65, see C. Peter Ripley, ed., *The Black Abolitionist Papers*, vol. 1: *The British Isles, 1830–1865* (Chapel Hill: University of North Carolina Press, 1985), 571–73. Also see R. J. M. Blackett, *Building an Antislavery Wall: Black Americans in the Atlantic Abolitionist Movement, 1830–1860* (Ithaca, NY: Cornell University Press, 1989); Bernier and Murray, *Nineteenth-Century African American Speeches*.
136. On U.K. lectures by the Crafts and Brown, see Blackett, *Building an Antislavery Wall*, 124–126; Salenius, *Abolitionist Abroad*, 89; Ilyon Woo, *Master Slave Husband Wife: An Epic Journey from Slavery to Freedom* (New York: Simon and Schuster, 2023).
137. Brownlee, "Out of the Abundance of the Heart," 127–35; "Miss Sarah P. Remond in Ireland," *The Anti-Slavery Advocate* 2, no. 29 (May 1859): 232; "Miss Remond in Scotland," *The Anti-Slavery Advocate* 2, no. 50 (February 1861): 399.
138. "Speech by Sarah P. Remond Delivered at the Athenaeum, Manchester, England, 14 September 1859," *Manchester Weekly Times*, September 17, 1859, reprinted in Ripley, *Black Abolitionist Papers*, 1: 457; "Slavery in America," *Derbyshire Courier*, April 13, 1861.
139. "A Lady Lecturer on Slavery," *Reading Mercury, Oxford Gazette, Newbury Herald and Berks County Paper*, etc., March 26, 1859.
140. "Slavery in America," *Derbyshire Courier*, April 13, 1861; "Miss Remond's Anti-Slavery Lecture," *Freeman's Journal and Daily Commercial Advertiser* (Dublin), March 15, 1859; "Miss Remond in Bristol," *The Anti-Slavery Advocate* 2, no. 33 (September 1859): 267.
141. *Daily Post* (Liverpool), as reprinted in *The Liberator*, February 18, 1859.
142. Ripley, *Black Abolitionist Papers*, 1: 435.
143. "Miss Remond at Bury," *The Anti-Slavery Advocate* 2, no. 35 (November 1859): 283. [Article reprinted from *The Bury Times*.]
144. "Miss Remond in Yorkshire," *The Anti-Slavery Advocate* 2, no. 38 (February 1860): 306.
145. "Lecture by a Lady of Colour on American Slavery," *The Morning Chronicle*, October 8, 1860; "Miss Remond in Edinburgh," *The Anti-Slavery Advocate* 2, no. 47 (November 1860): 377–78.
146. "Miss Remond in Scotland," *The Anti-Slavery Advocate* 2, no. 50 (February 1861): 399.
147. "Speech by Sarah P. Remond Delivered at the Music Hall, Warrington, England, 24 January 1859," *Warrington Times*, January 29, 1859, reprinted in Ripley, *Black Abolitionist Papers*, 1: 437. For later reports of Remond's speeches that follow this pattern with similar phrasing, see, for example, "Lecture on American Slavery," *Waterford Mail*, April 9, 1859, and "Slavery

in America," *Derbyshire Courier*, April 13, 1861. Based on newspaper reports, Brownlee notes that Remond did not include details of Garner's case before London audiences. However, it is likely that some newspapers were hesitant to reprint details of Remond's account of Garner's rape and infanticide and instead used more coded descriptions. Describing Remond's lecture in Southwark, for example, the *Morning Star* noted her speech was "distinguished by much pathos, and replete with statements of a deeply affecting character, more particularly descriptive of the degraded, brutalized, and defenceless condition of the enslaved women of America, on whose behalf the speaker made a powerful and touching appeal." Reprinted in "Our Metropolitan Correspondence: London, 22nd July, 1859," *The Anti-Slavery Advocate* 2, no. 32 (August 1859): 255; Brownlee, "Out of the Abundance of the Heart," 130.

148. "Speech by Sarah P. Remond Delivered at the Music Hall," 437.
149. Taylor, *Driven Toward Madness*, 7, 39. On Margaret Garner and her legacy, also see Mark Reinhardt, *Who Speaks for Margaret Garner?* (Minneapolis: University of Minnesota Press, 2010), and Steven Weisenburger, *Modern Medea: A Family Story of Slavery and Child-Murder from the Old South* (New York: Hill and Wang, 1998).
150. Ohio officials then issued a warrant for the Garners' arrest to have them tried for murder in that state. This prompted the Garners' slaveholders to send the family away on March 7, 1856, to New Orleans for sale to avoid extradition. On the way, the Garners' steamship collided with another ship, resulting in the drowning of the couple's youngest daughter, Cilla. After being returned to Kentucky and surreptitiously sent south again to New Orleans for sale, Margaret Garner and her husband, Robert, were separated from their two boys. Margaret Garner died from typhoid in 1858. See Taylor, *Driven Toward Madness*, 86–87, 126.
151. "Speech by Sarah P. Remond Delivered at the Music Hall," 437.
152. "Slavery in America," *Derbyshire Courier*, April 13, 1861.
153. "Speech by Sarah P. Remond Delivered at the Music Hall," 438. In a speech in Manchester (September 14, 1859), she likewise stated, "The slaves are essentially *things*, with no rights, political, social, domestic, or religious: the absolute victims of all but irresponsible power." See "Speech by Sarah P. Remond Delivered at the Athenaeum," 457–58.
154. "Speech by Sarah P. Remond Delivered at the Music Hall," 435.
155. "Speech by Sarah P. Remond Delivered at the Music Hall," 436.
156. "Slavery in America," *Derbyshire Courier*, April 13, 1861. She raises these same points in other lectures, but without always reading directly from the slave code.
157. "Speech by Sarah P. Remond Delivered at the Music Hall," 439; "Lecture on American Slavery," *Waterford Mail*, April 9, 1859; "Speech by Sarah P.

Remond Delivered at the Athenaeum," 459. Remond expanded upon her personal experiences of discrimination in her autobiographical account published in Hill, *Our Exemplars* and "A Colored Lady Lecturer," *English Woman's Journal*, June 1, 1861.
158. "Speech by Sarah P. Remond Delivered at the Music Hall," 438, 437.
159. "Speech by Sarah P. Remond Delivered at the Music Hall," 439.
160. "Speech by Sarah P. Remond Delivered at the Music Hall," 440.
161. Prince, *History of Mary Prince*, ed. Salih, 11.
162. "Speech by Sarah P. Remond, Delivered at the Red Lion Hotel, Warrington, England, 2 February 1859," *Warrington Times*, February 5, 1859, reprinted in Ripley, *Black Abolitionist Papers*, 1: 446.
163. Naturalisation Papers: Remond, Sarah Parker, from the United States of America. Certificate 4809 issued 11 September 1865, The National Archives (TNA) HO 1/123/4809.
164. Remond traveled from America to Britain using a U.S. passport signed by Secretary of State Lewis Cass. The American Embassy's subsequent rejection of her visa application and right to a U.S. passport sparked widespread condemnation in the British press in late 1859 and January 1860. See Elizabeth Stordeur Pryor, *Colored Travelers: Mobility and the Fight for Citizenship Before the Civil War* (Chapel Hill: University of North Carolina Press, 2016), 106–7; Salenius, *Abolitionist Abroad*, 105–11.
165. See "Sarah P. Remond to Editor, London *Daily News*, 7 November 1865," reprinted in Ripley, *Black Abolitionist Papers*, 1: 568–69; Sarah P. Remond, "Negro Character," *The Liberator*, December 22, 1865, reprint of November 1865 letter to London *Daily News*; Sarah P. Remond, "Colonization," *The Freed-Man* (February 1, 1866): 162–63; "Letter from Sarah P. Remond," *National Anti-Slavery Standard*, November 3, 1866.
166. Sarah Parker Remond, "The Negro Race in America," *Daily News* (September 22, 1866).
167. On Charles Buxton's and John Stuart Mill's leadership of the Jamaica Committee and the efforts to hold Eyre accountable, see Bernard Semmel, *The Governor Eyre Controversy* (London: MacGibbon and Kee, 1962).
168. Frances Power Cobbe, *Life of Frances Power Cobbe as Told by Herself* (London: Swan Sonnenschein, 1904), 283, emphasis in original; Midgley, *Women Against Slavery*, 196.
169. Naturalisation Papers: Remond, Sarah Parker, from the United States of America. Certificate 4809 issued 11 September 1865, The National Archives (TNA) HO 1/123/4809. Remond's naturalization papers, granted in 1865, noted that "it is her intention to continue to reside permanently within the United Kingdom. That the Grounds upon which your Memorialist seeks to obtain the rights and capacities of a natural born British subject are as follows; She has to all intents and purposes adopted England as

her Country and is desirous of being able to obtain and hold real or leasehold property in this Country where many of her most intimate friends reside. The strong prejudice against persons of African descent which is entertained by a large proportion of the Inhabitants of the United States and the social disabilities under which such persons consequently suffer have determined your Memorialist under no circumstances to return to reside in America." Remond's revolutionary advocacy for equality and rights that extended beyond the nation-state was reinforced by her friendship with Giuseppe Mazzini, a close cohort of Mentia and Peter Taylor. On Remond's support for Italian unification and time in Italy, see Salenius, *Abolitionist Abroad*, 121–96.

3. "Suppressed Grief"

1. Jane Robinson, *Angels of Albion: Women of the Indian Mutiny* (London: Penguin Books, 1996), 161. I have used the term "Indian Rebellion" rather than "Sepoy Mutiny" to underscore that the conflict was not merely sparked by protests within the army against the use of Enfield rifle bullets greased with fat from cows and pigs but rather a more popular anticolonial political movement. See Biswamoy Pati, ed., *The Great Rebellion of 1857 in India: Exploring Transgressions, Contests and Diversities* (London: Routledge, 2010). For other examples of the extensive literature on the 1857 Rebellion, see Gautam Bhadra, "Four Rebels of Eighteen-Fifty-Seven," in *Selected Subaltern Studies*, ed. Ranajit Guha and Gayatri Chakravorty Spivak (Oxford: Oxford University Press, 1988), 129–75; Gautam Chakravarty, *The Indian Mutiny and the British Imagination* (Cambridge: Cambridge University Press, 2005); Ainslie T. Embree, ed., *1857 in India: Mutiny or War of Independence?* (Lexington, MA: D. C. Heath, 1963); Rudrangshu Mukherjee, *Awadh in Revolt, 1857–1858: A Study of Popular Resistance* (New Delhi: Oxford University Press, 1984); Biswamoy Pati, ed., *The 1857 Rebellion* (New Delhi: Oxford University Press, 2007); and Eric Stokes, *The Peasant and the Raj: Studies in Agrarian Society and Peasant Rebellion in Colonial India* (Cambridge: Cambridge University Press, 1978).
2. Katherine Bartrum, *A Widow's Reminiscence of the Siege of Lucknow* (London: James Nisbet, 1858), 68.
3. On January 30, 1858, Polehampton remarked, "Mrs. Bartrum's little boy (her only child) is very ill, and I fear will die." He died on February 11, 1858. Emily Polehampton's Diary, reprinted in Henry Polehampton, *A Memoir, Letters, and Diary*, ed. Edward Polehampton and Thomas Stedman Polehampton (London: Richard Bentley, 1858), 374.
4. Bartrum, *A Widow's Reminiscence* (February 11, 1858), 70, emphasis in original. Also see Katherine Bartrum, Manuscript Copy of Diary,

February 11, 1858, British Library, India Office Select Materials, MSS Eur. A69 1857–58.
5. Emmie and Henry Polehampton's son was born on December 30, 1857, and died days later in early January. The great importance of postmortem photographs is suggested by Henry Polehampton's note in his diary that before leaving their home for the Residency, "Emmie then came; having first secured a little box containing daguerreotypes of our darling in Heaven." After helping Bartrum through the burial of her son, Polehampton remarked, "All this brought back my own losses too vividly to my mind!" See Henry Polehampton, letter to his mother (January 7, 1857), 166–71, Extracts from the Diary of the Rev. H. S. Polehampton (May 21, 1857), 259, and Emily Polehampton's Diary (February 11, 1858), 376, all in Polehampton, *Memoir, Letters, and Diary*.
6. Emily Polehampton's Diary (February 11, 1858), in Polehampton, *Memoir, Letters, and Diary*, 376.
7. Bartrum, *Widow's Reminiscence* (February 11, 1858), 70.
8. Bartrum, Manuscript Copy of Diary, February 11, 1858, British Library, India Office Select Materials, MSS Eur. A69 1857–58; Emily Polehampton's Diary (February 11, 1858), in Polehampton, *Memoir, Letters, and Diary*, 376–77.
9. Bartrum, Manuscript Copy of Diary, February 12, 1858, British Library, India Office Select Materials, MSS Eur. A69 1857–58; Bartrum, *Widow's Reminiscence* (February 12, 1858), 72.
10. Alison Blunt also suggests that on the death of her husband Bartrum suffered from a loss of domestic and imperial identity, and Claudia Klaver explores how British women at Lucknow negotiated the tensions between their symbolic domestic roles as representatives of empire and the material conditions of the siege, focusing on their use of narrative subjectivities to retain their domestic identities. See Alison Blunt, "The Flight From Lucknow: British Women Travelling and Writing Home, 1857–8," in *Writes of Passage: Reading Travel Writing*, ed. James Duncan and Derek Gregory (London: Routledge, 1999), 106; Caludia Klaver, "Domesticity Under Siege: British Women and Imperial Crisis at the Siege of Lucknow, 1857," *Women's Writing* 8, no. 1 (2001).
11. Katherine Bartrum, letter to her father, December 27, 1857, British Library, India Office Select Materials, MSS Eur. A67/2.
12. Bartrum, letter to her father, February 12, 1858, British Library, India Office Select Materials, MSS Eur. A67/3.
13. Philippe Ariès, *The Hour of Our Death*, trans. Helen Weaver (New York: Alfred A. Knopf, 1981). Also see Philippe Ariès, *Western Attitudes Toward Death: From the Middle Ages to the Present*, trans. Patricia M. Ranum (Baltimore: Johns Hopkins University Press, 1974).

14. George L. Mosse, *Fallen Soldiers: Reshaping the Memory of the World Wars* (Oxford: Oxford University Press, 1990), 41; see also 38–50. Thomas Laqueur provides the most detailed analysis of this transition; see *The Work of the Dead: A Cultural History of Mortal Remains* (Princeton, NJ: Princeton University Press, 2015).
15. Drew Gilpin Faust, *This Republic of Suffering: Death and the American Civil War* (New York: Alfred A. Knopf, 2008), 17. Also see Gillian Avery and Kimberley Reynolds, eds., *Representations of Childhood Death* (Houndmills, Basingstoke, Hampshire: Macmillan Press, 2000); Nicola Brown, "Empty Hands and Precious Pictures: Post-Mortem Portrait Photographs of Children," *Australasian Journal of Victorian Studies* 14, no. 2 (2009): 8–24; David Cannadine, "War and Death, Grief and Mourning in Modern Britain," in *Mirrors of Mortality: Studies in the Social History of Death*, ed. Joachim Whaley (New York: St. Martin's Press, 1981), 187–242; James Curl, *The Victorian Celebration of Death* (Devon: David and Charles, 1972); Pat Jalland, *Death in the Victorian Family* (Oxford: Oxford University Press, 1996); Audrey Linkman, *Photography and Death* (London: Reaktion Books, 2011); John Morley, *Death, Heaven and the Victorians* (London: Studio Vista, 1971); and Julie-Marie Strange, *Death, Grief and Poverty in Britain, 1870–1914* (Cambridge: Cambridge University Press, 2005).
16. Lara Kriegel, *The Crimean War and Its Afterlife: Making Modern Britain* (Cambridge: Cambridge University Press, 2022), 124–25.
17. Judith Butler, *Precarious Life: The Powers of Mourning and Violence* (London: Verso, 2004), 22.
18. See, for example, Thomas R. Metcalf, *Ideologies of the Raj* (Cambridge: Cambridge University Press, 1995), 28–65.
19. The photographs of Felice Beato included public hangings and the corpses of Indian soldiers. On Beato's work in India, see Zahid Chaudhary, "Phantasmagoric Aesthetics: Colonial Violence and the Management of Perception," *Cultural Critique* 59 (Winter 2005): 63–119; John Fraser, "Beato's Photograph of the Interior of the Sikandarbagh at Lucknow," *Journal of the Society for Army Historical Research* 59, no. 237 (Spring 1981): 51–55; Peter Harrington, "Lucknow after the Indian Mutiny: The Photographs of Felice Beato," *Military Heritage* 6, no. 4 (February 2005): 68–71, 82; David Harris, "Topography and Memory: Felice Beato's Photographs of India, 1858–1859," in *India through the Lens: Photography, 1840–1911*, ed. Vidya Dehejia (Washington, DC: Freer Gallery of Art and Arthur M. Sackler Gallery, 2000), 119–47; Laqueur, *Work of the Dead*, 342–43; Ben Lifson, "Beato in Lucknow," *Artforum International* 26, no. 9 (May 1988): 98–103; and Jim Masselos and Narayani Gupta, *Beato's Delhi, 1857, 1997* (Delhi: Ravi Dayal, 1997).

20. Robert Bartrum, letter to his mother, written in General Outram and Queen's 90th camp between Allahabad and Kanpur, September 7, 1857, in Bartrum, *Widow's Reminiscence*, 86.
21. See David Arnold, *Colonizing the Body: State Medicine and Epidemic Disease in Nineteenth-Century India* (Berkeley: University of California Press, 1993); Bernard S. Cohn, "Representing Authority in Victorian India," in *The Invention of Tradition*, ed. Eric Hobsbawm and Terence Ranger (Cambridge: Cambridge University Press, 1983), 165–209; Nicholas Dirks, *Castes of Mind: Colonialism and the Making of Modern India* (Princeton, NJ: Princeton University Press, 2001); John Falconer, "'A Pure Labor of Love': A Publishing History of *The People of India*," in *Colonialist Photography: Imag(in)ing Race and Place*, ed. Eleanor M. Hight and Gary D. Sampson (London: Routledge, 2002), 51–83; Peter Hoffenberg, *An Empire on Display: English, Indian, and Australian Exhibitions from the Crystal Palace to the Great War* (Berkeley: University of California Press, 2001); Christopher Pinney, *Camera Indica: The Social Life of Indian Photographs* (London: Reaktion, 1997). For an interpretation stressing the importance of class divides over race, see David Cannadine, *Ornamentalism: How the British Saw Their Empire* (Oxford: Oxford University Press, 2001).
22. Jenny Sharpe, *Allegories of Empire: The Figure of Woman in the Colonial Text* (Minneapolis: University of Minnesota Press, 1993), 68. For other discussions of British women representing the values of British imperialism, see Alison Blunt, "Embodying War: British Women and Domestic Defilement in the Indian 'Mutiny,' 1857–8," *Journal of Historical Geography* 26, no. 3 (July 2000): 403–28; Klaver, "Domesticity Under Siege"; Nancy L. Paxton, *Writing Under the Raj: Gender, Race, and Rape in the British Colonial Imagination, 1830–1947* (New Brunswick, NJ: Rutgers University Press, 1999); Penelope Tuson, "Mutiny Narratives and the Imperial Feminine: European Women's Accounts of the Rebellion in India in 1857," *Women's Studies International Forum* 21, no. 3 (May–June 1998): 291–303. In recent decades, there has been significant scholarship on British women and imperialism. For select examples, see Antoinette Burton, *Burdens of History: British Feminists, Indian Women, and Imperial Culture, 1865–1915* (Chapel Hill: University of North Carolina Press, 1994); Nupur Chaudhuri and Margaret Strobel, eds., *Western Women and Imperialism: Complicity and Resistance* (Bloomington: Indiana University Press, 1992); Anna Davin, "Imperialism and Motherhood," *History Workshop Journal* 5, no. 1 (Spring 1978): 9–66; Margaret MacMillan, *Women of the Raj: The Mothers, Wives, and Daughters of the British Empire in India* (New York: Thames and Hudson, 1988); Clare Midgley, *Feminism and Empire: Women Activists in Imperial Britain, 1790–1865* (London: Routledge, 2007); Mary Procida, *Married to the Empire: Gender, Politics, and Imperialism in India, 1883–1947* (Manchester:

Manchester University Press, 2002); Rosemary Raza, *In Their Own Words: British Women Writers and India, 1740–1857* (Oxford: Oxford University Press, 2006); Robinson, *Angels of Albion;* Mrinalini Sinha, *Specters of Mother India: The Global Restructuring of an Empire* (Durham, NC: Duke University Press, 2006); Indrani Sen, *Woman and Empire: Representations in the Writings of British India (1858–1900)* (New Delhi: Orient Longman, 2002); Margaret Strobel, *European Women and the Second British Empire* (Bloomington: Indiana University Press, 1991); and Alison Twells, *The Civilising Mission and the English Middle Class, 1792–1850: The "Heathen" at Home and Overseas* (New York: Palgrave Macmillan, 2009). Clare Midgley provides a useful overview of this literature, distinguishing the earlier works that often tended to focus on independent women travelers or the memsahibs connected with "Raj nostalgia" from studies emerging in the 1990s exploring the connections between Western feminist movements, racism, and empire. See *Feminism and Empire*, 2–3.

23. See Rosemary Marangoly George, "Homes in the Empire, Empires in the Home," *Cultural Critique* 26 (Winter 1993–94): 95–127.
24. Georgina Harris, *A Lady's Diary of the Siege of Lucknow, Written for the Perusal of Friends at Home* (London: John Murray, 1858), 173.
25. For an example of this image being used for military recruitment, see "Willing Hands for India," *Punch*, August 29, 1857, 88–89, in which Tenniel's cartoon is reproduced on the flag rallying new recruits.
26. Charles Ball, *The History of the Indian Mutiny: Giving A Detailed Account of the Sepoy Insurrection in India; and a Concise History of the Great Military Events Which Have Tended to Consolidate British Empire in Hindostan*, 2 vols. (London: London Printing and Publishing, 1858–59).
27. See Edward Said, *Orientalism* (New York: Vintage Books, 1979). Ball's text acknowledges the much more fluid racial and cultural makeup of Anglo-Indian communities, recognizing that Europeans often lived with "half-castes," native Christians, and Indian servants. See, for example, his description of the massacre of Jhansi, in *History of the Indian Mutiny*, 1: 271–72.
28. Thanks to James Merrell for helping me make this connection.
29. Harriet Tytler, *An Englishwoman in India: The Memoirs of Harriet Tytler, 1828–1858* (Oxford: Oxford University Press, 1986), 172.
30. On these new meanings associated with childhood, see in particular Philippe Ariès, *Centuries of Childhood: A Social History of Family Life*, trans. Robert Baldick (New York: Alfred A. Knopf, 1962); Hugh Cunningham, *Children and Childhood in Western Society Since 1500* (London: Longman, 1995); and Carolyn Steedman, *Strange Dislocations: Childhood and the Idea of Human Interiority* (London: Virago, 1995). Hugh Cunningham's "Review Essay: Histories of Childhood," *American Historical Review* 103,

no. 4 (October 1998): 1195–208, is a particularly helpful introduction to the debates sparked by Ariès's classic work on the invention of modern childhood.

31. The Home and Foreign Missionary Record for the Free Church of Scotland, 1845–46, 2: 356, as quoted in Midgley, *Feminism and Empire*, 115, see also 111–16; *A Domestic Guide to Mothers in India*, 2nd ed. (Bombay: American Mission Press, 1848), 62.

32. See Alison Blunt, *Domicile and Diaspora: Anglo-Indian Women and the Spatial Politics of Home* (Oxford: Blackwell, 2005), and "Imperial Geographies of Home: British Domesticity in India, 1886–1925," *Transactions of the Institute of British Geographers* 24, no. 4 (1999): 421–40; Elizabeth Buettner, *Empire Families: Britons and Late Imperial India* (Oxford: Oxford University Press, 2004); Nupur Chaudhuri, "Memsahibs and Motherhood in Nineteenth Century Colonial India," *Victorian Studies* 31, no. 4 (Summer 1988): 517–35; E. M. Collingham, *Imperial Bodies* (Malden, MA: Blackwell, 2001); Durba Ghosh, *Sex and the Family in Colonial India: The Making of Empire* (Cambridge: Cambridge University Press, 2006); Indrani Sen, "Colonial Domesticities, Contentious Interactions: Ayahs, Wet-Nurses and Memsahibs in Colonial India," *Indian Journal of Gender Studies* 16, no. 3 (November 2009): 299–328. For other works exploring childhood and imperial identity, see David Arnold, "European Orphans and Vagrants in India in the Nineteenth Century," *Journal of Imperial and Commonwealth History* 7, no. 2 (January 1979): 104–27; Satadru Sen, *Colonial Childhoods: The Juvenile Periphery of India, 1850–1945* (London: Anthem Press, 2005); Ann Laura Stoler, *Carnal Knowledge and Imperial Power: Race and the Intimate in Colonial Rule* (Berkeley: University of California Press, 2002), and *Race and the Education of Desire: Foucault's History of Sexuality and the Colonial Order of Things* (Durham, NC: Duke University Press, 1995).

33. For a general account of the siege of Lucknow, see Christopher Hibbert, *The Great Mutiny: India, 1857* (New York: Viking Press, 1978), 216–66, 327–66. Jane Robinson estimates there were 2,000 people at the beginning of the siege, including 237 European women with 260 of their children. I have found no estimates for Indian women and children. See Robinson, *Angels of Albion*, 153–54. Citing M. Innes, *Lucknow and Oude in the Mutiny: A Narrative and A Study* (London, 1895), Alison Blunt provides the estimate of 3,000 people—the extra thousand likely being troops added during the September 25 reinforcement. Innes recorded that 1,392 of these were Indian and 1,608 were British or from other parts of Europe, and that there were 1,720 combatants and 1,280 noncombatants. See Blunt, "Embodying War," 426–27 n. 76. For other breakdowns of the besieged population, see Money Collection: Album of Views of Lucknow, British Library, India Office Select Materials, Photo 499, 1.

34. Blunt, "Embodying War," 418.
35. "English Captives at Cabul," *Bentley's Miscellany* (1843), reprinted in Antoinette Burton, ed., *The First Anglo-Afghan Wars: A Reader*, with a foreword by Andrew Bacevich (Durham, NC: Duke University Press, 2014), 101. Thanks to Devaansh Singh for this reference. On the publication of private letters, see Ellen Smith, "'Pregnant with the Interests of Life and Death': Family Correspondence and the British Imperial News Sphere during the 1857 Indian Rebellion," *Journal of British Studies* (March 2025), 1–22, https://doi.org/10.1017/jbr.2025.1.
36. See Robert Patrick Anderson, *A Personal Journal of the Siege of Lucknow* (London: W. Thacker, 1858); Bartrum, *Widow's Reminiscence*; Adelaide Case, *Day by Day at Lucknow: A Journal of the Siege of Lucknow* (London: Richard Bentley, 1858); Martin Richard Gubbins, *An Account of the Mutinies in Oudh, and of the Siege of the Lucknow Residency* (London: Richard Bentley, 1858); Harris, *Lady's Diary of the Siege of Lucknow*; Major Macbean and J. Hogarth, *Views in Lucknow from Sketches Made During the Siege* (London: J. Hogarth, 1858); Clifford Henry Mecham and George Ebenezer Wilson Couper, *Sketches and Incidents of the Siege of Lucknow: From Drawings Made During the Siege* (London: Day and Son, 1858); Polehampton, *Memoir, Letters, and Diary*; L. E. Ruutz Rees, *A Personal Narrative of the Siege of Lucknow from Its Commencement to Its Relief by Sir Colin Campbell* (London: Longman, Brown, Green, Longmans, and Roberts, 1858); Thomas Fourness Wilson, *The Defence of Lucknow: A Diary Recording the Daily Events During the Siege of the European Residency, from 31st May to 25th September, 1857* (London: Smith, Elder, 1858). Also in 1858, Julia Inglis printed a version of her diary for private circulation that was reviewed along with published memoirs in *The Albion: A Journal of News, Politics, and Literature* 36, no. 14 (April 3, 1858): 160–61. Inglis later published her Lucknow diary as *The Siege of Lucknow: A Diary* (1892). In addition to those works published in 1858, I draw on two other women's memoirs published well after the events: Colina Brydon's *Diary of the Doctor's Lady* (1857), compiled by Geoffrey Moore (Huntingdon: Geoffrey Moore, 1979), and Maria Germon's *Journal of the Siege of Lucknow: An Episode of the Indian Mutiny* (London: Constable, 1958), edited by Michael Edwardes. Germon's original manuscript is in the British Library, and a privately printed edited version of Germon's journal appeared as *A Diary Kept by Mrs. R. C. Germon at Lucknow, Between the Months of May and December 1857* (London, 1870).
37. Harris, *Lady's Diary of the Siege of Lucknow*, iii, emphasis in original.
38. *The Times*, March 24, 1892, 4.
39. For reviews of *A Widow's Reminiscence of the Siege of Lucknow*, by Katherine Bartrum, see *The Athenaeum*, April 2, 1859, 449, and *Tait's Edinburgh Magazine*, May 1859, 307. For reviews of *A Memoir, Letters, and Diary*,

by Henry Polehampton, that primarily focus on the materials related to Henry Polehampton, see *The Athenaeum*, October 9, 1858, 451–52; *The Examiner*, October 9, 1858, 644–45; *The Leader*, November 6, 1858, 1186; *New Quarterly Review*, November 1858, 288; and *The Saturday Review*, November 20, 1858, 507–8.

40. For reviews of *Day by Day at Lucknow*, by Adelaide Case, see *The Athenaeum*, July 3, 1858, 12–13; *The Critic*, July 24, 1858, 420; *The Leader*, June 26, 1858, 619–20; *London Journal*, July 31, 1858, 366; and *The Rambler*, November 1858, 360.

41. See reviews of *A Lady's Diary of the Siege of Lucknow*, by Georgina Harris, in *The Athenaeum*, April 24, 1858, 523, and *The Examiner*, April 24, 1858, 260; and review of *Day by Day at Lucknow*, by Adelaide Case, in *The Critic*, July 24, 1858, 411.

42. Review of *A Lady's Diary of the Siege of Lucknow*, by Georgina Harris, *The Examiner*, April 24, 1858, 260.

43. Review of *Day by Day at Lucknow*, by Adelaide Case, *The Critic*, July 24, 1858, 411.

44. Review of *The Siege of Lucknow*, by Julia Inglis, *The Academy*, April 16, 1892, 370. For a similar linking of the virtues of a female survivor of Lucknow with English values, see review of *Day by Day at Lucknow*, by Adelaide Case, *The Critic*, July 24, 1858, 411.

45. Review of *A Lady's Diary of the Siege of Lucknow*, by Georgina Harris, *The Athenaeum*, April 24, 1858, 523.

46. Review of *Day by Day at Lucknow*, by Adelaide Case, *The Rambler*, November 1858, 360.

47. Review of Case in *The Rambler*, November 1858, 360.

48. Harris, *Lady's Diary of the Siege of Lucknow* (June 20, 1857), 60. In May, after the fall of Delhi, Lawrence told Julia Inglis at dinner that "he considered the annexation of Oude the most unrighteous act that was ever committed." Inglis, *Siege of Lucknow* (May 18, 1857), 11.

49. See, for example, the class tensions in the conflict between Lucknow survivors Martin Gubbins and L. E. Rees in *The Times*, July 23, 1858, 9, and July 27, 1858, 11.

50. Germon, *Journal of the Siege of Lucknow* (May 25, 1857), 27.

51. On the organization of women's night watches during the siege, see Harris, *Lady's Diary of the Siege of Lucknow* (July 25 and August 9, 1857), 90, 97.

52. Germon, *Journal of the Siege of Lucknow* (May 26 and 31, 1857), 28, 29, 34. See Klaver, "Domesticity Under Siege," 31.

53. Case, *Day by Day at Lucknow*, 22.

54. Rees, *Personal Narrative of the Siege of Lucknow*, 93.

55. See, for example, Bartrum, Manuscript Copy of Diary, June 28, 1857, British Library, India Office Select Materials, MSS Eur. A69; Maria Germon,

Journal of Maria Germon, July 9 and 18, 1857, 25, 30, British Library, India Office Select Materials, MSS Eur. B134; Harris, *Lady's Diary of the Siege of Lucknow*, 46–47; Polehampton, *Memoir, Letters, and Diary*, 344–45; Klaver, "Domesticity Under Siege," 32–34.

56. Bartrum, letter to her father, December 27, 1857, 6, British Library, India Office Select Materials, MSS Eur. A67/2, emphasis in original. She directly followed this statement with a discussion of servants.
57. Harris, *Lady's Diary of the Siege of Lucknow* (June 16, 1857), 51. This event was also reported in *The Athenaeum*, April 24, 1858, 523.
58. Bartrum, Manuscript Copy of Diary, August 20 and September 18, 1857, British Library, India Office Select Materials, MSS Eur. A69; Bartrum, *Widow's Reminiscence of the Siege of Lucknow* (August 19, 1857), 41; Brydon, *Diary of the Doctor's Lady* (September 5 and 15, 1857), 39, 41; Case, *Day by Day at Lucknow* (September 8 and 29, 1857), 186, 216; Harris, *Lady's Diary of the Siege of Lucknow* (September 5 and 15, 1857), 108, 112–13; Captain Birch as quoted in Inglis, *Siege of Lucknow*, 80; Inglis, *Siege of Lucknow* (September 5, 1857), 143.
59. Inglis, *Siege of Lucknow* (August 11, 1857), 116. Also see Inglis (July 28, 1857), 100–101; Case, *Day by Day at Lucknow* (July 28, 1857), 118; Klaver, "Domesticity Under Siege," 41.
60. Domo [Miss Moore], Painted Memorial Scroll, Twenty-Six Coloured Views . . . of Buildings, etc. in Delhi, Cawnpore, Lucknow, Benares, Agra, and Amritsar, Connected with the Indian Mutiny, British Library, Add. MSS 37153. Other accounts note that there were sixty-nine British "ladies" present. See Blunt, "Embodying War," 417.
61. "List of Officers and Non-Military Men and Their Families Present Before and During the Whole of the Siege of Lucknow," in Rees, *Personal Narrative of Lucknow*, 365–80. Maria Germon recorded a list of "European" and "Native" military personnel killed and wounded during the siege from June 30 to September 26, 1857. According to her record, which does not include civilians or those who died from sickness, 73 "Native" and 139 "European" rank and file, sergeants, and officers died during these months. See Germon, *Diary Kept by Mrs. R. C. Germon at Lucknow*, 144–45.
62. Inglis, *Siege of Lucknow*, 77, 227.
63. Bartrum, Manuscript Copy of Diary, July 8, 1857, British Library, MSS Eur. A69 1857–58. For a slightly different wording of this account, see Bartrum, *Widow's Reminiscence*, 30.
64. Inglis, *Siege of Lucknow* (October 20, 1857), 185.
65. Brydon, *Diary of the Doctor's Lady* (July 8, 1857), 21.
66. Harris, *Lady's Diary of the Siege of Lucknow* (June 27, 1857), 73.
67. Brydon, *Diary of the Doctor's Lady* (September 12, 1857), 40. Colina Brydon's husband, William Brydon, was initially falsely claimed to be the sole

survivor of General Elphinstone's retreat from Kabul in the First Anglo-Afghan War of 1842.
68. Case, *Day by Day at Lucknow* (September 17, 1857), 196.
69. Inglis, *Siege of Lucknow* (July 23, 1857), 87.
70. Captain Birch as quoted in Inglis, *Siege of Lucknow,* 79–80.
71. Bartrum, Manuscript Copy of Diary, August 11, 1857, British Library, India Office Select Materials, MSS Eur. A69.
72. Case, *Day by Day at Lucknow* (August 14, 1857), 151–53, quotations at 151, 152.
73. Inglis, *Siege of Lucknow* (August 14, 1857), 117.
74. Case, *Day by Day at Lucknow* (August 14, 1857), 152–53.
75. See Brydon, *Diary of the Doctor's Lady* (August 26, 1857), 37.
76. Hibbert, *Great Mutiny,* 250.
77. Bartrum, Manuscript Copy of Diary, July 31 and August 1, 1857, British Library, India Office Select Materials, MSS Eur. A69.
78. Harris, *Lady's Diary of the Siege of Lucknow* (August 2, 1857), 93–94.
79. Harris, *Lady's Diary of the Siege of Lucknow* (August 2, 1857), 93–94. For other accounts of arrowroot and sugar mixtures being given to children, see Bartrum, Manuscript Copy of Diary, July 20 and August 17, 1857, British Library, India Office Select Materials, MSS Eur. A69.
80. Harris, *Lady's Diary of the Siege of Lucknow* (August 15 and 19, 1857), 100–102.
81. Brydon, *Diary of the Doctor's Lady* (August 15, 1857), 33.
82. Hadow Papers, Worcester College, Oxford, as quoted in Hibbert, *Great Mutiny,* 249.
83. Harris, *Lady's Diary of the Siege of Lucknow* (August 9, 1857), 97.
84. Brydon, *Diary of the Doctor's Lady* (June 25, 1857), 17.
85. Inglis, *Siege of Lucknow* (August 12 and 13, 1857), 117.
86. Brydon, *Diary of the Doctor's Lady* (June 30, 1857), 18.
87. Germon, *Journal of the Siege of Lucknow* (July 16, 1857), 64.
88. Germon, *Journal of the Siege of Lucknow* (September 13, 1857), 92.
89. Brydon, *Diary of the Doctor's Lady* (August 19, 1857), 35.
90. Bartrum, Manuscript Copy of Diary, 8 August 1857, British Library, India Office Select Materials, MSS Eur. A69.
91. Harris, *Lady's Diary of the Siege of Lucknow* (September 13, 1857), 110–11.
92. See David Arnold, *Burning the Dead: Hindu Nationhood and the Global Construction of Indian Tradition* (Oakland: University of California Press, 2021).
93. Germon, *Journal of the Siege of Lucknow* (August 19, 1857), 82; Inglis, *Siege of Lucknow* (October 1, 1857), 173.
94. Bartrum, *Widow's Reminiscence* (August 8, 1857), 36; Case, *Day by Day at Lucknow* (August 20, 1857), 162; Inglis, *Siege of Lucknow* (August 20, 1857), 130.

95. Germon, *Journal of the Siege of Lucknow* (August 19, 1857), 82; Harris, *Lady's Diary of the Siege of Lucknow* (July 20, 1857), 87; Inglis, *Siege of Lucknow* (October 1, 1857), 173.
96. Inglis, *Siege of Lucknow* (October 1, 1857), 173.
97. Rees, *Personal Narrative of the Siege of Lucknow*, 103.
98. Germon, Journal of Maria Germon, July 4, 1857, 25, British Library, India Office Select Materials, MSS Eur. B134; Harris, *Lady's Diary of the Siege of Lucknow* (July 20, 1857), 86–87; Extract from the Diary of the Rev. H. S. Polehampton, July 1, 1857, in Polehampton, *Memoir, Letters, and Diary*, 321.
99. Laqueur, *Work of the Dead*, 314.
100. Harris, *Lady's Diary of the Siege of Lucknow* (August 2, 1857), 94.
101. Harris, *Lady's Diary of the Siege of Lucknow* (August 14, 1857), 99.
102. Case, *Day by Day at Lucknow* (July 13, 1857), 91.
103. Case, *Day by Day at Lucknow* (September 2, 1857), 179. Also see Inglis, *Siege of Lucknow* (September 2, 1857), 140.
104. See Elizabeth Buettner, "Cemeteries, Public Memory and Raj Nostalgia in Postcolonial Britain and India," *History and Memory* 18, no. 1 (Spring–Summer 2006): 5–42; Laqueur, *Work of the Dead*, 265–71; Robert Travers, "Death and the Nabob: Imperialism and Commemoration in Eighteenth-Century India," *Past and Present*, no. 196 (August 2007): 83–124; Melissa S. Turoff, "'Told by the Tombs': British Death and Cemeteries in Colonial India" (history thesis, Vassar College, 2007).
105. Emily Polehampton, Letter to Mrs. Wood (Henry Polehampton's mother), Letter to Rev. Edward Polehampton, and Diary (November 18, 1857), in Polehampton, *Memoir, Letters, and Diary*, 333, 347, 350; Harris, *Lady's Diary of the Siege of Lucknow* (November 8, 1857), 152.
106. Boileau Papers, Cambridge, September 13, 1857, as quoted in Hibbert, *Great Mutiny*, 250.
107. Emily Polehampton's Diary (January 11, 13, and 14, 1858), in Polehampton, *Memoir, Letters, and Diary*, 370. The cemetery and bazaar function as two forms of what Michel Foucault termed heterotopias. See Michel Foucault, "Of Other Spaces," trans. Jay Miskowiec, *Diacritics* 16, no. 1 (1986): 22–27.
108. Mary Martha Sherwood, *The Life of Mrs. Sherwood (Chiefly Autobiographical) with Extracts from Mr. Sherwood's Journal During His Imprisonment in France and Residence in India*, ed. by her daughter, Sophia Kelly (London, 1854), as quoted in Sen, "Colonial Domesticities, Contentious Interactions," 310. On Sherwood's fictional death scenes, see Laqueur, *Work of the Dead*, xi, 409; Lerner, *Angels and Absences*, 129–40.
109. Harris, *Lady's Diary of the Siege of Lucknow* (December 11, 1857), 192. Some women sewed or donated mourning dresses for others during the siege, but the majority of women deeply felt the loss of mourning attire. See Bartrum,

Widow's Reminiscence, 50; Harris, *Lady's Diary of the Siege of Lucknow* (July 29, 1857), 92–93; Inglis, *Siege of Lucknow*, 227.
110. *The Athenaeum*, April 24, 1858, 524.
111. *The Athenaeum*, April 24, 1858, 523. This passage is also quoted in *The Examiner*, April 24, 1858, 260. Reviewers included other details from Harris's diary demonstrating the best possible fulfillment of conventional mourning practices in Herbert's case: "We closed his pretty blue eyes, and crossed his little hands over his breast, and there he lay by his mother's side till daylight; then she washed the body herself, and put him on a white nightgown, and I tied a lace handkerchief round his face, as she had no caps. Charlie D. came over to see her, and we left her quite with him and the dead baby till eleven, when I was obliged to go in and ask her to part with it. She let me take it away, and I sewed the little sweet one up myself in a clean white cloth, and James carried it over to the hospital to wait there for the evening burials." See Harris, *Lady's Diary of the Siege of Lucknow* (August 19, 1857), 101–2.
112. Brian Allen, "The Indian Mutiny and British Painting," *Apollo* 132 (1990): 156; Blunt, "Embodying War," 416–17; Julia Thomas, "A Tale of Two Stories: Joseph Noel Paton's *In Memoriam*," in *Pictorial Victorians: The Inscription of Values in Word and Image* (Athens: Ohio University Press, 2004), 125–43.
113. *The Times*, May 1 and 22, 1858, as quoted in Blunt, "Embodying War," 416.
114. *Illustrated London News*, May 15, 1858, as quoted in Blunt, "Embodying War," 416.
115. Andrew Ward, *Our Bones Are Scattered: The Cawnpore Massacres and the Indian Mutiny of 1857* (London: John Murray, 1996), 550.
116. William Butler, *The Land of the Veda*, 310, as quoted in Ward, *Our Bones Are Scattered*, 551. On Marochetti's memorial at Scutari, see Kriegel, *Crimean War and Its Afterlife*, 143–45.
117. Stephen Heathorn, "Angel of Empire: The Cawnpore Memorial Well as a British Site of Imperial Remembrance," *Journal of Colonialism and Colonial History* 8, no. 3 (Winter 2007): 18, 33.
118. Review of Inglis, *The Siege of Lucknow*, in *The Academy*, April 16, 1892, 370.
119. See Manu Goswami, "'Englishness' on the Imperial Circuit: Mutiny Tours in Colonial South Asia," *Journal of Historical Sociology* 9, no. 1 (March 1996): 54–84.
120. Sophie Gordon, "'A Silent Eloquence': Photography in 19th-Century Lucknow," in *Lucknow: Then and Now*, ed. Rosie Llewellyn-Jones (Mumbai: Marg Publications for the National Centre for the Performing Arts, 2003), 142; Rosie Llewellyn-Jones, "The Residency and the River," in *Lucknow: City of Illusion*, ed. Rosie Llewellyn-Jones (Munich: Prestel, 2006), 197–99.
121. Editors' note in reference to Polehampton's nursing work on board the ship from Calcutta to Plymouth (*Memoir, Letters, and Diary*, 378).

122. See, for example, Collingham, *Imperial Bodies*; William Dalrymple, *White Mughals: Love and Betrayal in Eighteenth-Century India* (London: Penguin, 2004); MacMillan, *Women of the Raj*; Metcalf, *Ideologies of the Raj*, 92–112; Procida, *Married to the Empire*. In *Sex and the Family in Colonial India*, Durba Ghosh provides an essential corrective to histories emphasizing a lack of racial hierarchy and segregation in the pre-1858 colonial era.
123. Christopher Herbert, *War of No Pity: The Indian Mutiny and Victorian Trauma* (Princeton, NJ: Princeton University Press, 2008), quotations at 186, 136, 163; see 203–4.

4. "A Loud and Bitter Cry"

1. Mark Clement, "Rothery, Mary Catherine Hume- (1824–1885)," *Oxford Dictionary of National Biography* (Oxford University Press, online ed., 2004), https://doi.org/10.1093/ref:odnb/49483. On Hume-Rothery's objection to the Contagious Diseases Acts, see Mary Hume-Rothery, *A Letter Addressed to the Right Hon. W. E. Gladstone, M.P.* (Manchester: Abel Heywood and Son; London: Simpkin, Marshall, 1870).
2. Mary Hume-Rothery, *Women and Doctors: Or, Medical Despotism in England* (n.p., 1871), 1. These local proposals led to the national Infectious Diseases (Notification) Acts of 1889 and 1899. Eventually, the Notification of Births (Extension) Act (1915) applied to all districts the Notification of Births Act (1907) requirement that medical officers be notified of any birth, whether alive or stillborn, after the twenty-eighth week of pregnancy. On the rise of and popular responses to national education and public health legislation, see Sascha Auerbach, "'The Law Has No Feeling for Poor Folks Like Us!': Everyday Responses to Legal Compulsion in England's Working-Class Communities, 1871–1904," *Journal of Social History* 45, no. 3 (Spring 2012): 686–708; Nadja Durbach, *Bodily Matters: The Anti-Vaccination Movement in England, 1853–1907* (Durham, NC: Duke University Press, 2005); R. M. MacLeod, "Law, Medicine and Public Opinion: The Resistance to Compulsory Health Legislation, 1870–1907," *Public Law* (1967): 107–28, 189–211; Graham Mooney, *Intrusive Interventions: Public Health, Domestic Space, and Infectious Disease Surveillance in England, 1840–1914* (Rochester, NY: University of Rochester Press, 2015); Dorothy Porter and Roy Porter, "The Politics of Prevention: Anti-Vaccinationism and Public Health in Nineteenth-Century England," *Medical History* 32 (1988): 231–52.
3. Hume-Rothery, *Women and Doctors*, 1.
4. Hume-Rothery, *Women and Doctors*, 2.
5. Hume-Rothery, *Women and Doctors*, 5.
6. Hume-Rothery, *Women and Doctors*, 13–14.
7. Hume-Rothery, *Women and Doctors*, 6–7.

8. Hume-Rothery, *Women and Doctors*, Appendix B, 16.
9. Hume-Rothery, *Women and Doctors*, 11.
10. Hume-Rothery, *Women and Doctors*, 2.
11. Hume-Rothery, *Women and Doctors*, 15.
12. Christopher Bischof, "A 'Rich Crop of Nervousness': Childhood, Expertise, and the State in the Mid-1880s Over-Pressure Controversy," *English Historical Review* 131, no. 553 (December 2016): 1418. The scholarship detailing this late Victorian politics of childhood is extensive. See, for example, Margaret Arnot, "Infant Death, Child Care and the State: The Baby-Farming Scandal and the First Infant Life Protection Legislation of 1872," *Continuity and Change* 9, no. 2 (1994): 271–311; Christopher Bischof, *Teaching Britain: Elementary Teachers and the State of the Everyday, 1846–1906* (Oxford: Oxford University Press, 2019); George Behlmer, *Child Abuse and Moral Reform in England, 1870–1908* (Stanford, CA: Stanford University Press, 1982); George Behlmer, *Friends of the Family: The English Home and Its Guardians, 1850–1940* (Stanford, CA: Stanford University Press, 1998); Anna Davin, *Growing Up Poor: Home, School, and Street in London, 1870–1914* (London: Rivers Oram Press, 1996); Monica Flegel, *Conceptualizing Cruelty to Children in Nineteenth-Century England: Literature, Representation, and the NSPCC* (Burlington, VT: Ashgate, 2009); Lydia Murdoch, *Imagined Orphans: Poor Families, Child Welfare, and Contested Citizenship in London* (New Brunswick, NJ: Rutgers University Press, 2006); Ellen Ross, *Love and Toil: Motherhood in Outcast London, 1870–1918* (Oxford: Oxford University Press, 1993); Carolyn Steedman, *Childhood, Culture and Class in Britain: Margaret McMillan, 1860–1931* (New Brunswick, NJ: Rutgers University Press, 1990).
13. Thomas Laqueur, *The Work of the Dead: A Cultural History of Mortal Remains* (Princeton, NJ: Princeton University Press, 2015), 1, 8.
14. William Reddy, *Navigation of Feeling: A Framework for the History of Emotions* (Cambridge: Cambridge University Press, 2001), 124, 129.
15. Antoinette Burton, "Who Needs the Nation? Interrogating 'British History,'" *Journal of Historical Sociology* 10, no. 3 (1997): 237, emphasis in original.
16. See Anthony Wohl, introduction to *The Bitter Cry of Outcast London*, ed. Andrew Mearns (New York: Humanities Press, 1970), 18.
17. Wohl, introduction to *The Bitter Cry*, 34.
18. Andrew Mearns, *The Bitter Cry of Outcast London* (1883), reprinted in Peter Keating, ed., *Into Unknown England, 1866–1913: Selections from the Social Explorers* (Manchester: Manchester University Press, 1976), 97.
19. Wohl, introduction to *The Bitter Cry*, 16–17. Also see Anthony Wohl, "Sex and the Single Room: Incest Among the Victorian Working Classes," in *The Victorian Family: Structure and Stresses*, ed. Anthony Wohl (London: Croom Helm, 1978), 197–216.

20. Friedrich Engels, *The Condition of the Working Class in England*, ed. with a foreword by Victor Kiernan (Harmondsworth, UK: Penguin Books, 1987), 137.
21. Engels, *Condition of the Working Class in England*, 132.
22. *The Times*, September 5, 1848, as quoted in Anthony Wohl, *Endangered Lives: Public Health in Victorian Britain* (Cambridge, MA: Harvard University Press, 1983), 117.
23. T. E. Kebbel, ed., *Selected Speeches of the Late Right Honourable the Earl of Beaconsfield*, vol. 2 (London: Longmans, Green, 1882), 533.
24. See Anna Davin's classic essay "Imperialism and Motherhood," *History Workshop Journal* 5, no. 1 (Spring 1978): 9–66, and Michael S. Teitelbaum and Jay M. Winter, *The Fear of Population Decline* (Orlando, FL: Academic Press, 1985).
25. Similar legislation made the registration of births and deaths compulsory in Scotland in 1855, and Irish officials began registering births and deaths in 1864, though the practice was not always enforced. Registration of stillbirths after twenty-eight weeks became compulsory in 1915. See Deborah Dwork, *War Is Good for Babies and Other Young Children* (London: Tavistock, 1987), 3–4; T. W. Grimshaw, "An Address Delivered at the Opening of the Section of Public Medicine," *British Medical Journal* 2, no. 972 (August 16, 1879): 242–43; Edward Higgs, *Life, Death and Statistics: Civil Registration, Censuses and the Work of the General Register Office, 1836–1952* (Hatfield, Hertfordshire: Local Population Studies, 2004), 17–21, 86–88; Wohl, *Endangered Lives*, 11.
26. Higgs, *Life, Death and Statistics*, 218 quotation; see 86–87.
27. F. B. Smith, *The People's Health, 1830–1910* (New York: Holmes and Meier, 1979), 69.
28. Wohl, *Endangered Lives*, 10–42. On efforts to provide public mortuaries and curtail wakes, specifically targeting Irish Roman Catholics, see Lydia Murdoch, "'The Dead and the Living': Child Death, the Public Mortuary Movement, and the Spaces of Grief and Selfhood in Victorian London," *Journal of the History of Childhood and Youth* 8, no. 3 (Fall 2015): 378–402.
29. Judith Walkowitz, *City of Dreadful Delight: Narratives of Sexual Danger in Late-Victorian London* (Chicago: University of Chicago Press, 1992), 26–27; Wohl, introduction to *The Bitter Cry*, 16.
30. George Sims, *How the Poor Live and Horrible London* (London: Chatto and Windus, 1889), 1.
31. Sims, *How the Poor Live*, 62.
32. Julie-Marie Strange, *Death, Grief and Poverty in Britain, 1870–1914* (Cambridge: Cambridge University Press, 2005), 66.
33. Sims, *How the Poor Live*, 60, 61, 62.
34. Sims, *How the Poor Live*, 60.

35. Mearns, *Bitter Cry*, reprinted in Keating, *Into Unknown England*, 103, emphasis in original.
36. Sims, *How the Poor Live*, 94.
37. Mearns, *Bitter Cry*, reprinted in Keating, *Into Unknown England*, 103.
38. Mearns, *Bitter Cry*. reprinted in Keating, *Into Unknown England*, 95–96.
39. Mearns, *Bitter Cry*, reprinted in Keating, *Into Unknown England*, 109.
40. Mearns, *Bitter Cry*, reprinted in Keating, *Into Unknown England*, 104.
41. Mearns, *Bitter Cry*, reprinted in Keating, *Into Unknown England*, 106.
42. Mearns, *Bitter Cry*, reprinted in Keating, *Into Unknown England*, 95.
43. Mearns, *Bitter Cry*, reprinted in Keating, *Into Unknown England*, 110.
44. Wohl, introduction to *The Bitter Cry*, 17.
45. Mearns, *Bitter Cry*, reprinted in Keating, *Into Unknown England*, 99.
46. Steedman, *Strange Dislocations*.
47. Mearns, *Bitter Cry*, reprinted in Keating, *Into Unknown England*, 93.
48. Sims, preface to *How the Poor Live* [n.p.].
49. George Godwin, *London Shadows: A Glance at the "Homes" of the Thousands* (London: George Routledge & Co., 1854), 27.
50. Mearns, *Bitter Cry*, reprinted in Keating, *Into Unknown England*, 102.
51. Mearns, *Bitter Cry*, reprinted in Keating, *Into Unknown England*, 92.
52. Mearns, *Bitter Cry*, reprinted in Keating, *Into Unknown England*, 105.
53. Mearns, *Bitter Cry*, reprinted in Keating, *Into Unknown England*, 106.
54. Josephine Butler, *Recollections of George Butler*, 5th ed. (Bristol: J. W. Arrowsmith; London: Simpkin, Marshall, Hamilton, and Kent., 1896), 183; Josephine Butler, *Josephine E. Butler: An Autobiographical Memoir*, ed. George W. and Lucy A. Johnson (Bristol: J. W. Arrowsmith; London: Simpkin, Marshall, Hamilton, and Kent, 1909), 58–59. See Laurence Lerner, *Angels and Absences: Child Deaths in the Nineteenth Century* (Nashville: Vanderbilt University Press, 1997), 22–23.
55. For major biographical studies of Josephine Butler and her role in the campaign against the Contagious Diseases Acts, see Nancy Boyd, *Three Victorian Women Who Changed Their World: Josephine Butler, Octavia Hill, Florence Nightingale* (Oxford: Oxford University Press, 1982); A. S. G. Butler, *Portrait of Josephine Butler* (London: Faber and Faber, 1954); Barbara Caine, *Victorian Feminists* (Oxford: Oxford University Press, 1992); Jenny Daggers and Diana Neal, ed., *Sex, Gender, and Religion: Josephine Butler Revisited* (New York: Peter Lang, 2006); Jane Jordan, *Josephine Butler* (London: John Murray, 2001); Glen Petrie, *A Singular Iniquity: The Campaigns of Josephine Butler* (New York: Viking Press, 1971); Judith Walkowitz, *Prostitution and Victorian Society* (Cambridge: Cambridge University Press, 1980). Butler's main autobiographical writings are *Personal Reminiscences of a Great Crusade* [1896] (Westport, CT: Hyperion Press, 1976; reprint of 1911 edition) and *Recollections of George*

Butler. *Josephine E. Butler: An Autobiographical Memoir*, edited by George and Lucy Johnson, reprints material from these two sources along with Butler's other published writings.
56. Walkowitz, *Prostitution and Victorian Society*, 192–213.
57. Walkowitz, *City of Dreadful Delight*, 23.
58. William Acton, as quoted in Walkowitz, *Prostitution and Victorian Society*, 49.
59. Hugh Jones, "The Perils and Protection of Infant Life," *Journal of the Royal Statistical Society* 57, no. 1 (March 1894): 65.
60. "The Contagious Diseases Acts," *The Examiner* (October 31, 1874): 1181–82.
61. W. T. Stead, *Josephine Butler: A Life Sketch* (London: Morgan and Scott, 1886), 10, as quoted in A. S. G. Butler, *Portrait of Josephine Butler*, 54. Butler's grandson refuted this characterization that Butler "like Saint Paul . . . had undergone a sudden conversion" (54).
62. W. T. Stead, "The Progress of the World: Josephine Butler," *The Review of Reviews* 35 (January 1907): 10.
63. On Butler's Evangelicalism, see Helen Mathers, "The Evangelical Spirituality of a Victorian Feminist: Josephine Butler, 1828–1906," *Journal of Ecclesiastical History* 52, no. 2 (April 2001): 282–312, quotation on 312.
64. Stead, "Progress of the World," 10.
65. "Obituary, Mrs. Josephine Butler," *The Times*, January 2, 1907, 8.
66. "Obituary, Mrs. Josephine Butler."
67. Josephine Butler, *Memoir of John Grey of Dilston* (Edinburgh, 1869), as quoted in Caine, *Victorian Feminists*, 165.
68. "Obituary, Mrs. Josephine Butler."
69. "Obituary, Mrs. Josephine Butler." See Walkowitz, *Prostitution and Victorian Society*, 116.
70. Canon Henry Scott Holland, as quoted in Judith R. Walkowitz, "Butler [née Grey], Josephine Elizabeth (1828–1906)," *Oxford Dictionary of National Biography* (Oxford University Press, online ed., 2006), https://doi.org/10.1093/ref:odnb/32214.
71. Mary Priestman (accompanied by Mary Estlin), as quoted in Walkowitz, *Prostitution and Victorian Society*, 114.
72. Anna Garlin Spencer, as quoted in *The Review of Reviews* 48 (July 1913): 51.
73. Rev. Thomas Phillips, "The Late Mrs. Josephine Butler," *The Christian*, January 17, 1907, 15 [excerpts from an address at Bloomsbury Baptist Church, January 6, 1907], in file "Material Relating to the Death of Josephine Butler," 3AMS/J/03, Women's Library, London School of Economics.
74. See, for example, "Mrs. Josephine Butler," *The Woman at Home* (n.d., publication ran 1894–1900), for a discussion of her effect on audiences.
75. Josephine Butler, letter from Cheltenham, August 1864, reprinted in Josephine Butler, *Recollections of George Butler*, 153–55. The August 1864 letter is also reproduced in *Josephine E. Butler: An Autobiographical Memoir*, 49–52.

76. Josephine Butler, letter from Cheltenham, August 1864, reprinted in *Josephine E. Butler: An Autobiographical Memoir*, 49.
77. Josephine Butler, letter from Cheltenham, August 1864, reprinted in *Josephine E. Butler: An Autobiographical Memoir*, 49.
78. *Josephine E. Butler: An Autobiographical Memoir*, 52.
79. For contrasting interpretations of Butler's account of Eva's death, see Jane Jordan, *Josephine Butler*, 55–65; Jane Jordan, "'Trophies of the Saviour': Josephine Butler's Biographical Sketches of Prostitutes," *Sex, Gender, and Religion: Josephine Butler Revisited*, 21–36; Lisa Nolland, "Josephine Butler and the Historian: Critic and Friend," in *Sex, Gender, and Religion*, 113–33.
80. Josephine Butler, letter from Cheltenham, August 1864, reprinted in *Josephine E. Butler: An Autobiographical Memoir*, 52.
81. NRO (Northumberland Record Office), MSS Butler, ZBU.E3/A10, Letter, "A Memory of Child Sorrow," Josephine Butler to George, undated, as quoted in Nolland, "Josephine Butler and the Historian," 117.
82. *Josephine E. Butler: An Autobiographical Memoir*, 52.
83. Josephine Butler, as quoted in A. S. G. Butler, *Portrait of Josephine Butler*, 54.
84. Josephine Butler, letter from Cheltenham, August 1864, reprinted in *Josephine E. Butler: An Autobiographical Memoir*, 51.
85. *Josephine E. Butler: An Autobiographical Memoir*, 56, 57.
86. *Josephine E. Butler: An Autobiographical Memoir*, 58, 59.
87. *Josephine E. Butler: An Autobiographical Memoir*, 53.
88. *Josephine E. Butler: An Autobiographical Memoir*, 60.
89. This second bust of Butler by Alexander Munro was completed in 1865 and contrasts with his earlier 1855 sculpture of Butler that evoked Dante Gabriel Rossetti's "The Blessed Damozel," with her hair down, one shoulder bared, eyes looking forward, and starred halo. Butler started using a photograph of the 1865 Munro bust as a carte de visite by the 1870s. See Jordan, *Josephine Butler*, 41–42.
90. Stead, *Josephine Butler: A Life Sketch*, 17–18.
91. *An Appeal to the People of England on the Recognition and Superintendence of Prostitution by Governments* (1870), as quoted in Stead, *Josephine Butler: A Life Sketch*, 38.
92. Josephine Butler, "The Dark Side of English Life: Illustrated in a Series of True Stories," *The Methodist Protest* 2 (January 1877): 3–4; (February 1877): 15–16; (March 1877): 27–28; (April 1877): 39–40; (May 1877): 51–52; the "Story of Marion" reprinted in *Recollections of George Butler* (1896), 189–194; Walkowitz, *City of Dreadful Delight*, 88.
93. Butler, "Dark Side of English Life," 3.
94. Walkowitz, *Prostitution and Victorian Society*, 117. See Josephine Butler, "A Mother to Mothers," *The Christian Commonwealth*, December 18, 1902, in

"Printed Material by Josephine Butler, 1888–1902," 3AMS/J/02, Women's Library, London School of Economics.
95. Josephine Butler, *The Hour Before the Dawn: An Appeal to Men* (London: Trübner, 1876), 1, 7, 8; selections also quoted in Stead, *Josephine Butler: A Life Sketch*, 15.
96. Josephine Butler, letter to the British, Continental and General Federation for the Abolition of Government Regulation of Prostitution, meeting at Neuchâtel (1905), in *Josephine E. Butler: An Autobiographical Memoir*, 300–301, emphasis in original.
97. Butler, "Dark Side of English Life," 27; Elizabeth Barrett Browning, "The Runaway Slave at Pilgrim's Point," in *The Complete Works of Elizabeth Barrett Browning*, vol. 3, ed. Charlotte Porter and Helen Clarke (New York: Thomas Y. Crowell, 1900), stanza 18.
98. Butler, "Dark Side of English Life," 27.
99. Butler, "Dark Side of English Life," 28. A slight misquoting of Elizabeth Barrett Browning, *Casa Guidi Windows* (1851).
100. See Walkowitz, *Prostitution and Victorian Society*, 108–10.
101. Hume-Rothery, *Women and Doctors*, 4.
102. Josephine Butler, letter to London meeting of the World's Women's Christian Temperance Union (1892), in *Josephine E. Butler: An Autobiographical Memoir*, 205.
103. Josephine Butler, letter to London meeting of the World's Women's Christian Temperance Union (1892), in *Josephine E. Butler: An Autobiographical Memoir*, 206.
104. Hadley, *Melodramatic Tactics*, 212.
105. "Anti-Vaccination Demonstration at Leicester," *The Times*, March 24, 1885, 10; Durbach cites estimates of crowds of between 80,000 and 100,000; see Durbach, *Bodily Matters*, 51.
106. "The Procession," *Vaccination Inquirer and Health Review* 7 (April 1885): 5; "The Leicester Demonstration," *Vaccination Inquirer and Health Review* 7 (April 1885): 4.
107. "Anti-Compulsory Vaccination Demonstration at Leicester," *Daily News*, March 24, 1885, 6.
108. "The Procession," 4.
109. T. Biggs, *Sanitation vs. Vaccination* (London: N.A.V.L., 1912), as quoted in MacLeod, "Law, Medicine and Public Opinion," 196.
110. "The Procession," 4.
111. For an example of children's postmortem photographs used for the antivaccinationist cause, see William J. Furnival, *Alleged Vaccinal Injuries: Illustrated* (Stone: William J. Furnival, 1907).
112. Manon Nouvian, "Defiant Mourning: Public Funerals as Funeral Demonstrations in the Chartist Movement," *Journal of Victorian Culture* 24, no. 2

(2019): 208–26; Thomas Laqueur, "Bodies, Death, and Pauper Funerals," *Representations* 1, no. 1 (February 1983): 109–31. Emily Davison's funeral procession on June 14, 1913, drew thousands of women suffrage activists, including contingents of hunger strikers, brass bands, and Elsie Howey dressed as Joan of Arc riding a white horse.

113. Durbach, *Bodily Matters*.
114. Durbach, *Bodily Matters*, 3.
115. Durbach, *Bodily Matters*, 43–44.
116. Durbach, *Bodily Matters*, 190. On the Vaccination Acts, also see MacLeod, "Law, Medicine and Public Opinion"; Dorothy and Roy Porter, "The Politics of Prevention"; and J. R. Smith, *The Speckled Monster: Smallpox in England, 1670–1970* (Chelmsford: Essex Record Office, 1987), 117–41.
117. Durbach, *Bodily Matters*, 41–47.
118. On Jessie Craigen's anti-vaccination organizing, see Lydia Murdoch, "Anti-Vaccination and the Politics of Grief for Children in Late Victorian England," in *Childhood, Youth and Emotions in Modern History: National, Colonial and Global Perspectives*, ed. Stephanie Olsen (New York: Palgrave Macmillan, 2015), 242–60.
119. "Our London Letter," *Sheffield and Rotherham Independent*, August 6, 1884, 2; "House of Lords," *The Times*, August 6, 1884, 6.
120. Jalland, *Death in the Victorian Family*, 221; Strange, *Death, Grief and Poverty in Britain*, 123–24.
121. "Death in the Household," *Cassell's Household Guide: Being a Complete Encyclopaedia of Domestic and Social Economy, and Forming A Guide to Every Department of Practical Life*, vol. 3 (London: Cassell, Petter, and Galpin, 1869), 344–46, here 344, as quoted in Jalland, *Death in the Victorian Family*, 221.
122. "Our London Letter."
123. *National Anti-Compulsory Vaccination Reporter* (September 1884), 198, as quoted in Durbach, *Bodily Matters*, 63.
124. "Our London Letter." For other regional reports, see "London Correspondence," *Western Times*, August 6, 1884, 4; "A Novel Deputation," *Lancaster Gazette and General Advertiser for Lancashire, Westmorland, and Yorkshire*, August 9, 1884; "A Sensational Deputation," *Sunderland Daily Echo and Shipping Gazette*, August 6, 1884, 3; "Correspondence," *Huddersfield Daily Chronicle*, August 7, 1884, 3; "Anti-Vaccination Demonstration," *Western Mail*, August 7. 1884; *Dundee Courier and Argus and Northern Warder*, August 8, 1884; "Summary of the Week's News," *Leicester Chronicle and the Leicester Mercury*, August 9, 1884, 3; "News in Brief," *York Herald*, August 9, 1884, 11; "Notes of the Week," *Bury and Norwich Post, and Suffolk Herald*, August 12, 1884, 3.
125. *Dundee Courier and Argus and Northern Warder*, August 8, 1884.

126. "How Parents May Protect Their Offspring from the Dangers and Injuries of Vaccination," *Vaccination Inquirer and Health Review* 1 (April 1879): 14.
127. Mary Hume-Rothery, ed., *150 Reasons for Disobeying the Vaccination Law, by Persons Prosecuted Under It* (Cheltenham: George F. Poole, 1878), 3.
128. Hume-Rothery, *150 Reasons for Disobeying the Vaccination Law*, 4.
129. "As the Wind Blows," *Vaccination Inquirer and Health Review* 6, no. 67 (October 1884): 130.
130. "Vaccination-Funeral Ode," *Vaccination Inquirer and Health Review* 6, no. 71 (February 1885): 206.
131. On the Old Liberalism of anti-vaccinationists, see Durbach, *Bodily Matters*, 69–90.
132. Jessie Craigen, "A Peckham Disaster," *Vaccination Inquirer and Health Review* 6, no. 66 (September 1884): 116.
133. Lord Salisbury, *Times*, August 5, 1898, as quoted in Millicent Garret Fawcett, "The Vaccination Act of 1898," *Contemporary Review* 75 (March 1899): 334; see Murdoch, *Imagined Orphans*, 107.
134. Hadley, *Melodramatic Tactics*, 183–84.
135. "A Procession Across London," *Vaccination Inquirer and Health Review* 6, no. 70 (January 1885): 193.
136. "Procession Across London."
137. "Anti-Vaccination Demonstration," *York Herald*, December 27, 1884, 8. The Third Reform Act received royal assent on December 6, 1884.
138. "London Letter," *Sheffield Daily Telegraph*, December 22, 1884, 2.
139. "London Letter."
140. "Procession Across London"; Durbach, *Bodily Matters*, 63.
141. "What Are We Coming To!," *The Globe*, December 22, 1884, 1.
142. "What Are We Coming To!"
143. "What Are We Coming To!"
144. "London Letter," *Berrow's Worcester Journal*, December 27, 1884, 4.
145. "London Letter," *Sheffield Daily Telegraph*, December 22, 1884, 2.
146. "Anti-Vaccination Demonstration at Leicester"; King James Bible: Matt. 9:12; Mark 2:17; Luke 5:31.
147. "The Procession," 5.
148. "The Procession," 4.

5. "A Life of Her Own"

1. Virginia Woolf, *A Room of One's Own* (San Diego: Harcourt, 1989), 65.
2. Letter from Virginia Woolf to Margaret Llewelyn Davies, August 31, 1915, in Nigel Nicolson, ed., *The Letters of Virginia Woolf*, vol. 2: 1912–1922 (London: Hogarth Press, 1975), 63. On this exchange, also see Patricia Laurence, "'Holding Her Pen Like a Broom': Virginia Woolf's Anxieties About

Working-Class Women," *Études Britanniques Contemporaines* (Montpellier: Presses Universitaires de Montpellier, 1999), 16, http://ebc.chez-alice.fr/ebc16b1.html. On Davies's friendship with Leonard and Virginia Woolf and their involvement with the WCG, also see Mary Jean Corbett, *Behind the Times: Virginia Woolf in Late-Victorian Contexts* (Ithaca, NY: Cornell University Press, 2020), 190–225; Mariza Corrêa, "Feminist Letters," *Vibrant* 8, no. 2 (2011): 4–23; Clara Jones, *Virginia Woolf: Ambivalent Activist* (Edinburgh: Edinburgh University Press, 2016), 108–53; Sybil Oldfield, "Margaret Llewelyn Davies and Leonard Woolf," 3–32, in *Women in the Milieu of Leonard and Virginia Woolf: Peace, Politics, and Education*, ed. Wayne Chapman and Janet Manson (New York: Pace University Press, 1998); Alice Wood, "Facing *Life as We Have Known It*: Virginia Woolf and the Women's Co-operative Guild," *Literature and History* 23, no. 2 (Autumn 2014): 18–34.

3. Margaret Llewelyn Davies, introduction to *Maternity: Letters from Working Women*, edited by Margaret Llewelyn Davies (New York: W. W. Norton, 1978), 15. All references to *Maternity* are from this edition unless otherwise noted.

4. Davies, introduction to *Maternity*, 1; Gillian Scott, *Feminism and the Politics of Working Women: The Women's Co-operative Guild, 1880s to the Second World War* (London: UCL Press, 1998), xii. On the history of the WCG, also see Barbara J. Blaszak, *The Matriarchs of England's Cooperative Movement: A Study in Gender Politics and Female Leadership, 1883–1921* (Westport, CT: Greenwood Press, 2000), which offers a critical assessment of Margaret Llewelyn Davies's leadership, arguing that "the general secretary's class prejudices and possible sexual orientation warped her ability to identify with the married working-class women who constituted the rank-and-file membership of the Guild" (116); Ruth Cohen, "'Mothers First': The Women's Co-operative Guild's Campaign for Maternity Care, 1906–18," *Women's History Magazine* 4 (Spring 2016): 11–19; Gloden Dallas, introduction to *Maternity: Letters from Working-Women, Collected by the Women's Co-Operative Guild* (London: Virago, 1978); Catherine Webb, *The Woman with the Basket: The History of the Women's Co-operative Guild, 1883–1927* (Manchester: Co-operative Society's Printing Works, 1927).

5. *Thirty-Second Annual Report of the Women's Co-operative Guild* (May 1914–May 1915), Bishopsgate Institute (BI) WCG/1/26, 1.

6. See especially Cohen, "'Mothers First': The Women's Co-operative Guild's Campaign for Maternity Care, 1906–18."

7. Margaret Llewelyn Davies and Margaret G. Bondfield, "Maternity Benefit," *The Times*, August 9, 1913, 5. For the WCG's position on these reforms, see Margaret Llewelyn Davies, "Wives and Mother Under the Insurance Bill," *The Times*, October 31, 1911, 13; Margaret Llewelyn Davies

and Margaret G. Bondfield, "The Insurance Act," *The Times*, July 10, 1913, 10; Margaret Llewelyn Davies, "War And the Care Of Motherhood," *The Times*, August 13, 1914, 7.
8. Susan Pedersen, *Family, Dependence, and the Origins of the Welfare State: Britain and France, 1914–1945* (Cambridge: Cambridge University Press, 1993), 57.
9. "National Scheme Proposed by the Women's Co-operative Guild," in *Maternity*, 209–12. The WCG proposed increasing the 30s. maternity benefit to "£3 10s. in weekly payments of 10s. for three weeks before and four weeks after confinement" (209).
10. Regenia Gagnier, *Subjectivities: A History of Self-Representation in Britain, 1832–1920* (New York: Oxford University Press, 1991), 63.
11. Carolyn Tilghman, "Autobiography as Dissidence: Subjectivity, Sexuality, and the Women's Co-operative Guild," *Biography* 26, no. 4 (Fall 2003): 583–606.
12. Anthony Wohl, *Endangered Lives: Public Health in Victorian Britain* (Cambridge, MA: Harvard University Press, 1983), 10–11
13. Ellen Ross, *Love and Toil: Motherhood in Outcast London, 1870–1918* (Oxford: Oxford University Press, 1993), 182–83.
14. Ross, *Love and Toil*, 182–83.
15. See, for example, Anna Davin, "Imperialism and Motherhood," *History Workshop Journal* 5, no. 1 (Spring 1978): 9–66; Deborah Dwork, *War Is Good for Babies and Other Young Children* (London: Tavistock, 1987); Carol Dyhouse, "Working-Class Mothers and Infant Mortality in England, 1895–1914," *Journal of Social History* 12, no. 2 (Winter 1978): 248–67; Lara Marks, *Metropolitan Maternity: Maternal and Infant Welfare Services in Early Twentieth Century London, 1870–1939* (Amsterdam: Rodopi, 1996); Susan Pedersen, *Eleanor Rathbone and the Politics of Conscience* (New Haven, CT: Yale University Press, 2004); Ross, *Love and Toil*, 195–221; Melanie Reynolds, *Infant Mortality and Working-Class Child Care, 1850–1899* (New York: Palgrave Macmillan, 2016). For international perspectives on early twentieth-century campaigns to improve infant mortality and maternal health in Europe and the United States, see Miriam Cohen, *Julia Lathrop: Social Service and Progressive Government* (Boulder, CO: Westview Press, 2017); Seth Koven and Sonya Michel, eds., *Mothers of a New World: Maternalist Politics and the Origins of Welfare States* (New York: Routledge, 1993); Pedersen, *Family, Dependence, and the Origins of the Welfare State*.
16. On the 1906 Education (Provision of Meals) Act, see Nadja Durbach, *Many Mouths: The Politics of Food in Britain from the Workhouse to the Welfare State* (Cambridge: Cambridge University Press, 2020), 146–77, quotation at 152.

17. Ellen Ross, ed., *Slum Travelers: Ladies and London Poverty, 1860–1920* (Berkeley: University of California Press, 2007), 208; Maud Pember Reeves, *Family Life on a Pound a Week*, Fabian Tract, no. 162 (London: The Fabian Society, 1912); *Round About a Pound a Week* (London: George Bell and Sons, 1913); reprint ed., *Round About a Pound a Week*, introduction by Sally Alexander (London: Virago, 1979).
18. Ross, *Slum Travelers*, 208–209.
19. Maud Pember Reeves, *Round about a Pound a Week*, 2nd ed. (London: George Bell and Sons, 1914), 194.
20. Reeves, *Round About a Pound a Week*, 2nd ed., 177–78.
21. Reeves, *Round About a Pound a Week*, 2nd ed., 215.
22. Reeves, *Round About a Pound a Week*, 2nd ed., 74. See Sally Alexander, "Reeves [*née* Robison], Magdalen Stuart [*known as* Maud Pember Reeves]," *Oxford Dictionary of National Biography* (Oxford University Press, online ed., 2004), https://doi.org/10.1093/ref:odnb/41214.
23. Most histories of the WCG give the dates of 1913 and 1914 for the member survey on childbirth, but there are earlier references to a survey of guild members in preparation for a meeting with Attorney General Sir Rufus Isaacs to discuss maternity insurance in 1911. *Twenty-Eighth Annual Report of the Women's Co-operative Guild*, May 1910–May 1911, BI WCG/1/22, 17. See also Margaret Llewelyn Davies, Central Committee Circular (March 13, 1911), Circulars and Internal Papers, Women's Co-operative Guild, BI WCG/4/1.
24. Linda Gordon, introduction to *Maternity: Letters from Working Women*, ed. Margaret Llewelyn Davies (New York: W. W. Norton, 1978), vi.
25. *Thirty-First Annual Report of the Women's Co-operative Guild* (May 1913–May 1914), BI WCG/1/25, 24.
26. *Thirty-Second Annual Report of the Women's Co-operative Guild* (May 1914–May 1915), BI WCG/1/26, 16–17.
27. Letter 721, from Virginia Woolf to Margaret Llewelyn Davies, February 22, 1915, in Nicolson, *Letters of Virginia Woolf*, 2: 59.
28. Letter from G. Bell and Sons, Ltd., Ernest Bell, to Margaret Llewelyn Davies, May 14, 1915, BI WCG/4/3, letter 1.
29. Clementina Black, ed., *Married Women's Work: Being the Report of an Enquiry Undertaken by the Women's Industrial Council* (London: George Bell and Sons, 1915), 5.
30. Barbara Hutchins, *Women in Modern Industry* (London: George Bell and Sons, 1915), 74. Also see B. L. Hutchins, *The Working Life of Women*, Fabian Tract, no. 157 (London: The Fabian Society, 1911).
31. Introduction to Davies, *Maternity*, 1.
32. "Method of Inquiry," in *Maternity*, 191.
33. "Method of Inquiry," in *Maternity*, 194. Davies notes, "Of the 400 cases, 26 were childless, and 26 did not give definite figures."

34. *Maternity*, 195.
35. "Occupations of Husbands," in *Maternity*, 192–93.
36. "Method of Inquiry," in *Maternity*, 192.
37. *Maternity*, 212.
38. I have been unable to find the original letters in various archival collections related to the WCG; Margaret Davies and her partner, Lillian Harris; and Virginia and Leonard Woolf, including the Bishopsgate Institute, London School of Economics Archives (WCG Collection), the WCG archive at Hull, the National Co-operative Archive (Manchester), Girton College, the British Library, Yale University Beinecke Rare Book and Manuscript Library (Llewelyn Davies Family Papers), University of Reading (George Bell and Sons Archive), University of Sussex (Leonard and Virginia Woolf Papers), New York Public Library (Woolf papers). In *Matriarchs of England's Cooperative Movement* Blaszak notes that Davies and Lillian Harris likely destroyed most of their personal papers (120).
39. *Maternity*, 2. Facsimiles of letters published along with the 1915 edition and the 1978 W. W. Norton edition show an example of the type of medical details omitted. See Letter 36, "Many Miscarriages," and "Facsimile of Extract from Letter 36," in *Maternity*, 62–63. The published version includes the letter writer's description of "a misplaced womb" brought on by many pregnancies, but leaves out her mention of "having to wear an inside article."
40. *Maternity*, 29, 36, 43, 62, 70, 72, 73, 98, 114, 119.
41. Letter 2, "Out of Bed on the Third Day," in *Maternity*, 20.
42. Letter 6, "Healthy and Strong," in *Maternity*, 25.
43. Letter 9, "Bad Confinements," in *Maternity*, 28.
44. Letter 39, "Benefit from Hearts of Oak," in *Maternity*, 66.
45. Letter 84, "Two Children Under the Year," in *Maternity*, 109.
46. Letter 16, "A Nightmare Yet," in *Maternity*, 39.
47. Letter 51, "Shun Patent Foods," in *Maternity*, 78.
48. Letter 10, "I am a Ruined Woman," in *Maternity*, 29.
49. Letter 32, "Restriction Advocated," in *Maternity*, 60.
50. Letter 1, "Twenty Years of Child-Bearing," in *Maternity*, 18. On working women's food consumption, see, for example, Emma Griffin, *Bread Winner: An Intimate History of the Victorian Economy* (New Haven, CT: Yale University Press, 2020); Pedersen, *Family, Dependence, and the Origins of the Welfare State*, 159–60; and Ross, *Love and Toil*, 27–55.
51. Letter 15, "Oh, the Horrors We Suffer!," in *Maternity*, 37.
52. Letter 8, "Men Need Education," in *Maternity*, 27.
53. Letter 30, "Mother Last," in *Maternity*, 58.
54. Letter 2, "Out of Bed on the Third Day," in *Maternity*, 20.
55. Letter 5, "A Half-Starved Pregnancy," in *Maternity*, 24.
56. See, for example, Letter 4, "All Day Washing and Ironing," in *Maternity*, 22.

57. Letter 62, "State Maternity Homes Wanted," in *Maternity*, 88.
58. Letter 132, "The Terrible Suffering I Endured," in *Maternity*, 161.
59. Letter 128, "Often Went Short of Food," in *Maternity*, 158.
60. Letter 12, "I Dragged About in Misery," in *Maternity*, 33.
61. Letter 12, "I Dragged About in Misery," in *Maternity*, 34.
62. Letter 77, "Care and Attention," in *Maternity*, 104.
63. Letter 20, "Stead's Penny Poets," in *Maternity*, 45.
64. Letter 21, "How a Woman May Suffer," in *Maternity*, 48.
65. Letter 73, "Suffering and Hard Work," in *Maternity*, 99.
66. Letter 8, "Men Need Education," in *Maternity*, 27–28.
67. Letter 37, "Against Large Families," in *Maternity*, 65–66.
68. Letter 41, "Over-Child-Bearing," in *Maternity*, 68.
69. In England, couples who married between 1860 and 1869 gave birth on average to just over six children, but for those who married in the 1890s the average family size decreased to just over four children. For early studies of middle-class family limitation, see J. A. Banks, *Prosperity and Parenthood: A Study of Family Planning Among the Victorian Middle Classes* (London: Routledge and Kegan Paul, 1954); J. A. Banks and O. Banks, *Feminism and Family Planning in Victorian England* (Liverpool: Liverpool University Press, 1964); and J. A. Banks, *Victorian Values: Secularism and the Size of Families* (London: Routledge and Kegan Paul, 1981). For revisionist works that place greater emphasis on women's agency in limiting fertility as well as regional and occupational variations, rather than class as the principal factor, see, for example, Michael Anderson, "The Social Implications of Demographic Change," in *The Cambridge Social History of Britain, 1750–1950*, ed. F. M. L. Thompson, vol. 2 (Cambridge: Cambridge University Press, 1990), 38–44; Eilidh Garrett, Alice Reid, Kevin Schürer, and Simon Szreter, *Changing Family Size in England and Wales: Place, Class and Demography, 1891–1911* (Cambridge: Cambridge University Press, 2001); Alison Mackinnon, "Was There a Victorian Demographic Transition?," in *The Victorian World*, ed. Martin Hewitt (London: Routledge, 2013), 276–90; Angus McLaren, *Birth Control in Nineteenth-Century England* (London: Croom Helm, 1978); Simon Szreter, *Fertility, Class and Gender in Britain, 1860–1940* (Cambridge: Cambridge University Press, 1996); R. I. Woods, "Approaches to the Fertility Transition in Victorian England," *Population Studies* 41, no. 2 (July 1987): 283–311.
70. Letter 62, "State Maternity Homes Wanted," in *Maternity*, 89.
71. Letter 24, "Utterly Overdone," in *Maternity*, 50.
72. Judith Allen, "The Rise and Fall of the Abortion Prosecutrix, 1780–1861," conference paper, North American Conference on British Studies, Minneapolis, MN, 2014; see McLaren, *Birth Control in Nineteenth-Century England*; John Keown, *Abortion, Doctors and the Law: Some Aspects of the Legal*

Regulation of Abortion in England from 1803 to 1982 (Cambridge: Cambridge University Press, 1998).
73. "The Murder-Monger," *The Lancet* 146, issue 3772 (December 14, 1895): 1518. Also see "The Traffic in Abortifacients," *British Medical Journal* 1, no. 1985 (January 14, 1899): 110–11. Thanks to Izzy Kaufman-Sites for these references.
74. Letter 20, "Stead's Penny Poets," in *Maternity*, 45.
75. Letter 20, "Stead's Penny Poets," in *Maternity*, 46. For other references to preventatives, see 25, 38, 40, 42, 52, 59, 60–61, 94–95, 100, 105, 115, 146, 159, 160, 169.
76. Letter 136, "I Wonder How I Lived," in *Maternity*, 166–67.
77. Davies, introduction to *Maternity*, 15.
78. Letter 2, "Out of Bed on the Third Day," in *Maternity*, 20–21.
79. Letter 10, "I Am a Ruined Woman," in *Maternity*, 29.
80. Letter 9, "Bad Confinements," in *Maternity*, 28, 29.
81. Letter 83, "A Wage-Earning Mother," in *Maternity*, 108.
82. Letter 107, "Felt Like Giving in Altogether," in *Maternity*, 140. Also see 142–43, 144–45.
83. Letter 95, "Husband Who Was Nurse and Mother," in *Maternity*, 119.
84. Letter 96, "Injury at Confinement," in *Maternity*, 122.
85. Letter 15, "Oh, the Horrors We Suffer!," in *Maternity*, 38.
86. Letter 58, "Inefficient Doctor," in *Maternity*, 84.
87. Letter 40, "Neglect by Doctors," in *Maternity*, 66.
88. Letter 40, "Neglect by Doctors," in *Maternity*, 67; also see 172–73. For a case of a neglectful nurse who put off calling the doctor, see 125–27.
89. See especially Letter 67, "A Steady and Regular Income," in *Maternity*, 92.
90. Ross, *Love and Toil*, 191; Strange, *Death, Grief and Poverty in Britain*, 259.
91. Letter 136, "I Wonder How I Lived," in *Maternity*, 166.
92. Letter 115, "Proper Care," in *Maternity*, 147.
93. Letter 84, "Two Children Under the Year," in *Maternity*, 108–9.
94. *Maternity*, 180, 101, 146.
95. Letter 87, "Struggles of a Miner's Wife," in *Maternity*, 111.
96. Letter 120, "Sock-Making at Twopence a Pair," in *Maternity*, 152.
97. *Maternity*, 39, 48, 54, 168.
98. Letter 34, "Delicate Children," in *Maternity*, 61.
99. Letter 35, "Continual Pregnancy for Fifteen Years," in *Maternity*, 62. For a variation on the theme of unled lives, see Andrew Miller, *On Not Being Someone Else: Tales of Our Unled Lives* (Cambridge, MA: Harvard University Press, 2020).
100. Letter 136, "I Wonder How I Lived," in *Maternity*, 167.
101. Letter 5, "A Half-Starved Pregnancy," in *Maternity*, 23.
102. Letter 5, in *Maternity*, 24.

103. Letter 5, in *Maternity*, 24. On the loss of the ability to nurse linked to physical and emotional strain, see also 102, 111.
104. Letter 15, "Lack of Food and Bad Housing," in *Maternity*, 42.
105. Letter 5, "A Half-Starved Pregnancy," in *Maternity*, 24.
106. Letter 5, "A Half-Starved Pregnancy," in *Maternity*, 25.
107. Letter 160, "Eight to Keep on Eleven Shillings and Threepence," in *Maternity*, 190.
108. Letter 5, "A Half-Starved Pregnancy," in *Maternity*, 24.
109. Letter 5, in *Maternity*, 25, emphasis in original.
110. Letter 122, "Ironing and Kneading in Bed," in *Maternity*, 154.
111. Letter 100, "A Wreck at Thirty," in *Maternity*, 129.
112. Ellen Ross, "Mothers and the State in Britain, 1904–1914," in *The European Experience of Declining Fertility, 1850–1970*, ed. John Gillis, Louise Tilly, and David Levine (Cambridge, MA: Blackwell, 1992), 63.
113. Letter 20, "Stead's Penny Poets," in *Maternity*, 47.
114. Samuel, preface to *Maternity*, xv.
115. Samuel, preface to *Maternity*, xv.
116. Letter 125, "Worked Too Hard as a Girl," in *Maternity*, 156.
117. Letter 157, "Thought We Must Put Up With It," in *Maternity*, 183–84.
118. Letter 136, "I Wonder How I Lived," in *Maternity*, 167.
119. Letter 132, "The Terrible Suffering I Endured," in *Maternity*, 162.
120. Letter 127, "Wine Lodges Should Be Closed," in *Maternity*, 157.
121. Judith Butler, *Precarious Life: The Powers of Mourning and Violence* (London: Verso, 2004), 22, emphasis in original.
122. Butler, *Precarious Life*, 23.
123. Butler, *Precarious Life*, 27.
124. Butler, *Precarious Life*, 22.
125. Letter 134, "An Awful Struggle," in *Maternity*, 164–65.
126. See Letters from G. Bell and Sons, Ltd., Ernest Bell to Margaret Llewelyn Davies (May 14, 1915; April 27, 1915; March 27, 1916; October 24, 1916), BI WCG/4/3.
127. Letter 729, Virginia Woolf to Margaret Llewelyn Davies, September 30, 1915, *Letters of Virginia Woolf*, 2: 65.
128. *The Thirty-Third Annual Report of the Women's Co-operative Guild* (May 1915–May 1916), BI WCG/1/27, 2.
129. *The Thirty-Second Annual Report of the Women's Co-operative Guild* (May 1914–May 1915), BI WCG/1/26, 12.
130. "Maternity from the Woman's Side," *British Medical Journal* 2, no. 2862 (November 6, 1915): 680.
131. "Maternity: Letters from Working Women (Book Review)," *The New Statesman*, October 9, 1915, 20. The review was anonymous, but may have

been written by Leonard Woolf, who by this point was a regular author for the magazine and had previously contributed essays on the guild.
132. "The Crucifixion of Motherhood," *Votes for Women*, October 8, 1915, 13.
133. "Mothers & Votes," *Votes for Women*, October 29, 1915, 36.
134. "Mothers & Votes," *Votes for Women*, October 29, 1915, 36, emphasis in original.
135. "Peaceful Campaigns by Two Old Campaigners," Women's Co-operative Guild Collection, London School of Economics Archives (LSEA), COLL MISC 0268/1, vol. 1, 119, 127. Also see Margaret Llewelyn Davies, ed., *Life as We Have Known It* [1931] (New York: W. W. Norton, 1975), 50. From these testimonies, the exact date of the Whitehall action is unclear.
136. Women's Co-operative Guild, "Hints for Speakers on Special Subjects, National Care of Maternity, 1916–1917," BI WCG/6/2.
137. Women's Co-operative Guild, "Memorandum on the National Care of Maternity," BI WCG/4/3, 5–6.
138. John Williams, "Thomas, David Alfred, First Viscount Rhondda (1856–1918)," *Oxford Dictionary of National Biography* (Oxford University Press, online ed., 2008), https://doi.org/10.1093/ref:odnb/36470.
139. "Peaceful Campaigns by Two Old Campaigners," Women's Co-operative Guild Collection, LSEA, COLL MISC 0268/1, vol. 1, 126, also see 119. For this speech by Mrs. Taylor, see Women's Co-operative Guild, "Memorandum on the National Care of Maternity," BI WCG/4/3, 7.
140. Women's Co-operative Guild, "Memorandum on the National Care of Maternity," BI WCG/4/3, 8.
141. Women's Co-operative Guild, "Memorandum on the National Care of Maternity," BI WCG/4/3, 8.
142. Dwork, *War Is Good for Babies and Other Young Children*, 214. On the campaigns for family allowances, see Pedersen, *Family, Dependence, and the Origins of the Welfare State*, 138–223.
143. *The Thirty-Fourth Annual Report of the Women's Co-operative Guild* (May 1916–1917), BI WCG/1/28; *The Thirty-Sixth Annual Report of the Women's Co-operative Guild* (May 1918–1919), BI WCG/1/29.
144. *The Thirty-Second Annual Report of the Women's Co-operative Guild* (May 1914–1915), BI WCG/1/26, 35.
145. *The Thirty-Eighth Annual Report of the Women's Co-operative Guild* (May 1920–1921), BI WCG/1/31, 10–11.
146. *The Twenty-Eighth Annual Report of the Women's Co-operative Guild* (May 1910–1911), BI WCG/1/22, 26. Also see "Hints for Speakers on Special Subjects, Adult Suffrage" (1912), BI WCG/6/2.
147. Karen Vallgårda, Kristine Alexander, and Stephanie Olsen, "Emotions and the Global Politics of Childhood," in *Childhood, Youth and Emotions in*

Modern History: National, Colonial and Global Perspectives, ed. Stephanie Olsen (New York: Palgrave Macmillan, 2015), 22–26.
148. Carolyn Steedman, *Landscape for a Good Woman: A Story of Two Lives* (New Brunswick, NJ: Rutgers University Press, 1987), 7.
149. "Peaceful Campaigns by Two Old Campaigners," Women's Co-operative Guild Collection, LSEA, COLL MISC 0268/1, vol. 1, 121.
150. Anonymous guildswomen, as quoted in "Peaceful Campaigns by Two Old Campaigners," Women's Co-operative Guild Collection, LSEA, COLL MISC 0268/1, vol. 1, 131.
151. Mrs. F. H. Smith, "In a Mining Village," in *Life as We Have Known It*, 67; Deborah Smith as quoted in Emma Griffin, *Bread Winner*, 287.

Conclusion

1. Kate Manzo, "Imaging Humanitarianism: NGO Identity and the Iconography of Childhood," *Antipode* 40, no. 4 (2008): 632–57, quotation at 639.
2. On child-centered protests against the British blockade, see Emily Baughan, *Saving the Children: Humanitarianism, Internationalism, and Empire* (Oakland: University of California Press, 2022), 22–25. On the international campaign against Leopold's atrocities in the Belgian Congo, see Kevin Grant, *A Civilised Savagery: Britain and the New Slaveries in Africa, 1884–1926* (New York: Routledge, 2005); Adam Hochschild, *King Leopold's Ghost: A Story of Greed, Terror, and Heroism in Colonial Africa* (1998; Boston: Mariner Books, 1999); E. D. Morel, *The Treatment of Women and Children in the Congo State, 1895–1904: An Appeal to the Women of the United States of America* (Boston: Congo Reform Association, 1904); Dean Pavlakis, *British Humanitarianism and the Congo Reform Movement, 1896–1913* (Burlington, VT: Ashgate, 2015). Photographs of killed or maimed children played an essential role in these campaigns. See, for example, works on the English Protestant missionary Alice Seeley Harris's photographs: Kevin Grant, "Anti-Slavery, Refugee Relief, and the Missionary Origins of Humanitarian Photograph ca. 1900–1960," *History Compass* 15.5 (2017): 1–24; Kevin Grant, "Christian Critics of Empire: Missionaries, Lantern Lectures, and the Congo Reform Campaign in Britain," in *The Rise and Fall of Modern Empires*, ed. Martin Shipway, vol. 4 (Burlington, VT: Ashgate, 2013), 91–122; Marouf Hasian, "Alice Seeley Harris, the Atrocity Rhetoric of the Congo Reform Movements, and the Demise of King Léopold's Congo Free State," *Atlantic Journal of Communication* 23 (2015): 178–92; Sharon Sliwinski, "The Childhood of Human Rights: The Kodak on the Congo," *Journal of Visual Culture* 5, no. 3 (2006): 333–63; Christina Twomey, "The Incorruptible Kodak: Photography, Human Rights and the Congo Campaign," in *The Violence of the Image: Photography and International Conflict*, ed. Liam Kennedy and Caitlin

Patrick (London: I. B. Tauris, 2014), 9–33; Christina Twomey, "Severed Hands: Authenticating Atrocity in the Congo, 1904–13," in *Picturing Atrocity: Photography in Crisis*, ed. Jay Prosser et al. (London: Reaktion Books, 2012), 39–50.
3. Lynn Hunt, *Inventing Human Rights: A History* (New York: W. W. Norton, 2007); Jenny Martinez, *The Slave Trade and the Origins of International Human Rights Law* (Oxford: Oxford University Press, 2012). For an overview of the vast literature on British imperialism and human rights, see Kevin Grant, "The British Empire, International Government, and Human Rights," *History Compass* 11, no. 8 (2013): 573–83.
4. Hunt, *Inventing Human Rights*, 23–24.
5. Hunt, *Inventing Human Rights*, 34.
6. Baughan, *Saving the Children*, 3.
7. Baughan, *Saving the Children*, 18, 214.
8. Judith Butler, *Precarious Life: The Powers of Mourning and Violence* (London: Verso, 2004), xii.
9. For an account of high mortality among South Asian children and adults as they traveled to the Caribbean as enforced indentured laborers in the aftermath of 1857, see Captain and Mrs. E. Swinton, *Journal of a Voyage with Coolie Emigrants, from Calcutta to Trinidad* (London: A. W. Bennett, 1859).
10. Elizabeth Barrett Browning, *Casa Guidi Windows*, in *The Complete Works of Elizabeth Barrett Browning*, vol. 3, ed. Charlotte Porter and Helen Clarke (New York: Thomas Y. Crowell, 1900), part 2: lines 638–39.

BIBLIOGRAPHY

Special Collections and Archives

Armstrong Browning Library, Baylor University (Digital Collections)
Bishopsgate Institute (BI)
British Library (BL)
Center for Research Libraries (CRL)
London School of Economics Archives (LSEA) and The Women's Library
The National Archives, United Kingdom (TNA)
Royal Holloway, University of London (RHUL)
Vassar College Special Collections and Archives

Parliamentary Papers and Government Publications

Children's Employment Commission. *First Report of the Commissioners on the Employment of Children (Mines)*. London: HMSO, 1842.
Factories Inquiry Commission. *First Report of the Central Board of His Majesty's Commissioners Appointed to Collect Information in the Manufacturing Districts, as to the Employment of Children in Factories, and as to the Propriety and Means of Curtailing the Hours of Their Labour*. House of Commons, June 28, 1833.
———. *Second Report of the Central Board of His Majesty's Commissioners Appointed to Collect Information in the Manufacturing Districts, as to the Employment of Children in Factories*. House of Commons, July 15, 1833.
Hansard Parliamentary Debates, House of Commons.
Report from the Committee on the Bill to Regulate the Labour of Children in the Mills and Factories of the United Kingdom. House of Commons, August 8, 1832.
Select Committee on Public Petitions. *Second Report from the Select Committee on Public Petitions: February 26–March 1, 1833*. House of Commons, n.d.
———. *Fourth Report from the Select Committee on Public Petitions*. House of Commons, March 12, 1833.
———. *Sixth Report from the Select Committee on Public Petitions*. House of Commons, March 19, 1833.
———. *Seventh Report from the Select Committee on Public Petitions*. House of Commons, March 22, 1833.
———. *Eighth Report from the Select Committee on Public Petitions*. House of Commons, March 26, 1833.

———. *Tenth Report from the Select Committee on Public Petitions*. House of Commons, April 2, 1833.
———. *Eleventh Report from the Select Committee on Public Petitions*. House of Commons, April 19, 1833.
———. *Twelfth Report from the Select Committee on Public Petitions*. House of Commons, April 19, 1833.
———. *Thirteenth Report from the Select Committee on Public Petitions*. House of Commons, April 23, 1833.
———. *Fourteenth Report from the Select Committee on Public Petitions*. House of Commons, April 29, 1833.
———. *Twentieth Report from the Select Committee on Public Petitions*. House of Commons, May 23, 1833.
———. *Twenty-First Report from the Select Committee on Public Petitions*. House of Commons, May 23, 1833.
———. *Twenty-Third Report from the Select Committee on Public Petitions*. House of Commons, May 31, 1833.
———. *Twenty-Fourth Report from the Select Committee on Public Petitions*. House of Commons, June 5, 1833.
———. *Twenty-Fifth Report from the Select Committee on Public Petitions*. House of Commons, June 7, 1833.
———. *Thirty-First Report from the Select Committee on Public Petitions*. House of Commons, June 28, 1833.
———. *Thirty-Third Report from the Select Committee on Public Petitions*. House of Commons, July 5, 1833.
———. *Thirty-Fourth Report from the Select Committee on Public Petitions*. House of Commons, July 10, 1833.
———. *Thirty-Seventh Report from the Select Committee on Public Petitions*. House of Commons, July 26, 1833.
———. *Thirty-Eighth Report from the Select Committee on Public Petitions*. House of Commons, August 5, 1833.
———. *Thirty-Ninth Report from the Select Committee on Public Petitions*. House of Commons, August 12, 1833.
———. *Fortieth Report from the Select Committee on Public Petitions*. House of Commons, August 16, 1833.
———. *Forty-First Report from the Select Committee on Public Petitions*. House of Commons, August 28, 1833.
———. *Forty-Second Report from the Select Committee on Public Petitions*. House of Commons, August 29, 1833.

Periodicals

The Academy
The Albion: A Journal of News, Politics, and Literature

The Aldine
The Anti-Slavery Advocate
The Athenaeum
Berrow's Worcester Journal
Blackwood's Edinburgh Magazine
British Medical Journal
Bury and Norwich Post, and Suffolk Herald
Contemporary Review
The Critic
Daily News
Derbyshire Courier
Dundee Courier and Argus and Northern Warder
English Woman's Journal
The Examiner
The Freed-Man
Freeman's Journal and Daily Commercial Advertiser (Dublin)
The Globe
Huddersfield Daily Chronicle
Journal of the Royal Statistical Society
Lancaster Gazette and General Advertiser for Lancashire, Westmorland, and Yorkshire
The Lancet
The Leader
Leeds Anti-Slavery Juvenile Series
Leicester Chronicle and the Leicester Mercury
The Liberator
The Liberty Bell
London Journal
The Methodist Protest
The Morning Chronicle
National Anti-Slavery Standard
New Quarterly Review
The New Statesman
Punch
The Rambler
Reading Mercury, Oxford Gazette, Newbury Herald and Berks County Paper, etc.
The Religious Intelligencer
The Review of Reviews
The Saturday Review
Sheffield Daily Telegraph
Sheffield and Rotherham Independent
The Standard
Sunderland Daily Echo and Shipping Gazette
Tait's Edinburgh Magazine

The Times
Universal Magazine of Knowledge and Pleasure
Vaccination Inquirer and Health Review
Votes for Women
The Ware Patriot
Waterford Mail
The Weekly True Sun
Western Mail
Western Times
The Woman at Home
Workingman's Advocate
York Herald

Published Primary Sources

Alfred (Samuel Kydd). *The History of the Factory Movement from the Year 1802, to the Enactment of the Ten Hours' Bill in 1847.* Vol. 1. London: Simpkin, Marshall, 1857.

Anderson, Robert Patrick. *A Personal Journal of the Siege of Lucknow.* London: W. Thacker, 1858.

Anti-Slavery Scrap Book. London: Bagster and Thoms, 1829. JSTOR Wilson Anti-Slavery Collection.

An Appeal to the Christian Women of Sheffield, from the Association for the Universal Abolition of Slavery. Sheffield: R. Leader, 1837.

Ball, Charles. *The History of the Indian Mutiny: Giving a Detailed Account of the Sepoy Insurrection in India; and a Concise History of the Great Military Events Which Have Tended to Consolidate British Empire in Hindostan.* 2 vols. London: London Printing and Publishing, 1858–59.

Barbauld, Anna Lætitia. *Hymns in Prose for Children.* London: J. Johnson, 1781.

Bartrum, Katherine. *A Widow's Reminiscences of the Siege of Lucknow.* London: James Nisbet, 1858.

Benham, William, ed. *Catharine and Craufurd Tait, Wife and Son of Archibald Campbell, Archbishop of Canterbury: A Memoir.* London: Macmillan, 1882.

Bernier, Celeste-Marie, and Hannah-Rose Murray, eds. *Nineteenth-Century African American Speeches in Britain and Ireland.* Edinburgh: University of Edinburgh Press, 2024.

Black, Clementina, ed. *Married Women's Work: Being the Report of an Enquiry Undertaken by the Women's Industrial Council.* London: George Bell and Sons, 1915.

Browning, Elizabeth Barrett. *The Complete Works of Elizabeth Barrett Browning.* Vol. 3. Edited by Charlotte Porter and Helen A. Clarke. New York: Thomas Y. Crowell, 1900.

Brydon, Colina. *Diary of the Doctor's Lady*. 1857. Compiled by Geoffrey Moore. Huntingdon: Geoffrey Moore, 1979.
Butler, Josephine. *The Hour Before the Dawn: An Appeal to Men*. London: Trübner, 1876.
———. *Josephine E. Butler: An Autobiographical Memoir*. Edited by George W. and Lucy A. Johnson. Bristol: J. W. Arrowsmith; London: Simpkin, Marshall, Hamilton, Kent, 1909.
———. *Personal Reminiscences of a Great Crusade*. 1896. Westport, CT: Hyperion Press, 1976; reprint of 1911 edition.
———. *Recollections of George Butler*. 5th ed. Bristol: J. W. Arrowsmith; London: Simpkin, Marshall, Hamilton, and Kent. 1896.
Buxton, Thomas Fowell. *The African Slave Trade*. London: J. Murray, 1839.
Case, Adelaide. *Day by Day at Lucknow: A Journal of the Siege of Lucknow*. London: Richard Bentley, 1858.
Clark, George W. *The Liberty Minstrel*. New York: Leavitt and Alden, 1845.
Clarkson, Thomas. *An Essay on the Slavery and Commerce of the Human Species, Particularly the African, Translated from a Latin Dissertation Which Was Honoured with the First Prize in the University of Cambridge in the Year 1785*. 2nd ed. London: J. Phillips, 1788.
Cobbe, Frances Power. *Life of Frances Power Cobbe as Told by Herself*. London: Swan Sonnenschein, 1904.
Cugoano, Ottobah. *Thoughts and Sentiments on the Evil of Slavery*. 1787. London: Dawsons of Pall Mall, 1969.
Darwin, Charles. "Charles Darwin's Memorial of Anne Elizabeth Darwin." April 30, 1851. *Darwin Correspondence Project*. University of Cambridge. https://www.darwinproject.ac.uk/people/about-darwin/family-life/death-anne-elizabeth-darwin.
Davies, Margaret Llewelyn, ed. *Life as We Have Known It*. 1931. New York: W. W. Norton, 1975.
———. *Maternity: Letters from Working Women*. 1915. Introduction by Linda Gordon. New York: W. W. Norton, 1978.
Dickens, Charles. *A Christmas Carol*. 1843. London: Penguin Books, 1984.
A Domestic Guide to Mothers in India. 2nd ed. Bombay: American Mission Press, 1848.
Douglass, Frederick. *Frederick Douglass: Autobiographies*. Edited by Henry Louis Gates Jr. New York: Library of America, 1994.
Engels, Friedrich. *The Condition of the Working Class in England*. Edited by Victor Kiernan. New York: Penguin Books, 1987.
The First Report of the Female Society, for Birmingham, West-Bromwich, Wednesbury, Walsall, and Their Respective Neighbourhoods, for the Relief of British Negro Slaves. Birmingham: Richard Peart, 1826. JSTOR Wilson Anti-Slavery Collection.

Five Hundred Thousand Strokes for Freedom: A Series of Anti-Slavery Tracts, of Which Half a Million Are New First Issued by the Friends of the Negro. London: W. and F. Cash, 1853.

Follen, Eliza Lee Cabot. *Hymns, Songs, and Fables for Young People.* 1831. Rev. ed. Boston: William Crosby and H. P. Nichols, 1848.

Forten, Charlotte L. *The Journal of Charlotte L. Forten.* Introduction and notes by Ray Allen Billington. New York: Dryden Press, 1953.

The Fourth Annual Report, of the Ladies' Association, for Salisbury, Calne, Melksham, Devizes, &c. in Aid of the Cause of Negro Emancipation. Calne: T. P. Baily, 1829. JSTOR Wilson Anti-Slavery Collection.

Furnival, William J. *Alleged Vaccinal Injuries: Illustrated.* Stone, Staffordshire, UK: William J. Furnival, 1907.

Gaskell, Elizabeth. *Mary Barton*, 1848. Edited by Macdonald Daly. London: Penguin, 1996.

Germon, Maria. *A Diary Kept by Mrs. R. C. Germon, at Lucknow, Between the Months of May and December, 1857.* London: Waterlow and Sons, 1870.

———. *Journal of the Siege of Lucknow: An Episode of the Indian Mutiny.* Edited by Michael Edwardes. London: Constable, 1958.

Godwin, George. *London Shadows: A Glance at the "Homes" of the Thousands.* London: George Routledge, 1854.

The Good Little Boy. London: Religious Tract Society, n.d.

Gubbins, Martin Richard. *An Account of the Mutinies in Oudh, and of the Siege of the Lucknow Residency.* London: Richard Bentley, 1858.

Harris, Georgina. *A Lady's Diary of the Siege of Lucknow, Written for the Perusal of Friends at Home.* London: John Murray, 1858.

Hill, Matthew Davenport, ed. *Our Exemplars, Poor and Rich; or, Biographical Sketches of Men and Women Who Have, by an Extraordinary Use of the Opportunities, Benefited Their Fellow Creatures.* Introduction by Lord Brougham. London: Cassell, Petter, and Galpin, 1861.

Hume-Rothery, Mary, ed. *150 Reasons for Disobeying the Vaccination Law, by Persons Prosecuted Under It.* Cheltenham: George F. Poole, 1878.

Hume-Rothery, Mary. *A Letter Addressed to the Right Hon. W. E. Gladstone, M.P.* Manchester: Abel Heywood and Son; London: Simpkin, Marshall, 1870.

———. *Women and Doctors: Or, Medical Despotism in England.* N.p., 1871.

Hutchins, Barbara. *Women in Modern Industry.* London: George Bell and Sons, 1915.

———. *The Working Life of Women.* Fabian Tract, no. 157. London: The Fabian Society, 1911.

Inglis, Julia. *The Siege of Lucknow: A Diary.* London: James R. Osgood, McIlvaine, 1892.

Jacobs, Harriet. *Incidents in the Life of a Slave Girl.* Boston: For the author, 1861.

Jones, William. *The Jubilee Memorial of the Religious Tract Society: Containing a Record of Its Origin, Proceedings, and Results, A.D. 1799 to A.D. 1849*. London: Religious Tract Society, 1850.

Kebbel, T. E., ed. *Selected Speeches of the Late Right Honourable the Earl of Beaconsfield*. Vol. 2. London: Longmans, Green, 1882.

Kelley, Philip, and Ronald Hudson, eds. *The Brownings' Correspondence*. Vol. 7. Winfield, KS: Wedgestone Press, 1989.

Kelley, Philip, and Scott Lewis, eds. *The Brownings' Correspondence*. Vol. 9. Winfield, KS: Wedgestone Press, 1991.

———. *The Brownings' Correspondence*. Vol. 10. Winfield, KS: Wedgestone Press, 1992.

———. *The Brownings' Correspondence*. Vol. 11. Winfield, KS: Wedgestone Press, 1993.

———. *The Brownings' Correspondence*. Vol. 14. Winfield, KS: Wedgestone Press, 1998.

Kelley, Philip, Scott Lewis, and Edward Hagan, eds. *The Brownings' Correspondence*. Vol. 16. Winfield, KS: Wedgestone Press, 2007.

———. *The Brownings' Correspondence*. Vol. 17. Winfield, KS: Wedgestone Press, 2010.

Kelley, Philip, Scott Lewis, Edward Hagan, Joseph Phelan, and Rhian Williams, eds. *The Brownings' Correspondence*. Vol. 22. Winfield, KS: Wedgestone Press, 2015.

Ladies' New York City Anti-Slavery Society. *Appeal to the Christian Women of America*. New York: William S. Dorr, 1836.

Macbean, George Scougal, and J. Hogarth. *Views in Lucknow from Sketches Made During the Siege*. London: J. Hogarth, 1858.

Mearns, Andrew. *The Bitter Cry of Outcast London*. 1883. Reprinted in Peter Keating, ed., *Into Unknown England, 1866–1913: Selections from the Social Explorers*, 91–111. Manchester: Manchester University Press, 1976.

Mecham, Clifford Henry, and George Ebenezer Wilson Couper. *Sketches and Incidents of the Siege of Lucknow: From Drawings Made During the Siege*. London: Day and Son, 1858.

[More, Hannah.] Cheap Repository. *The Sorrows of Yamba; or, the Negro Woman's Lament*. London: J. Marshall, 1795.

Morel, E. D. *The Treatment of Women and Children in the Congo State, 1895–1904: An Appeal to the Women of the United States of America*. Boston: Congo Reform Association, 1904.

Nicolson, Nigel, ed. *The Letters of Virginia Woolf*. Vol. 2: 1912–1922. London: Hogarth Press, 1975.

Petition to Her Majesty, Queen Victoria, from the Ladies of Glasgow and Its Vicinity, Adopted at the Public Meeting Held in the Rev. David King's Chapel,

1st August, 1837. Glasgow: Glasgow Chronicle, 1837. JSTOR Wilson Anti-Slavery Collection.

Polehampton, Henry S. *A Memoir, Letters, and Diary, of the Rev. Henry S. Polehampton, M.A. Chaplain of Lucknow*. Edited by Edward Polehampton and Thomas Stedman Polehampton. London: Richard Bentley, 1858.

["Prayer About a Negro Slave."] N.t., n.p., 1840. JSTOR Wilson Anti-Slavery Collection.

Prince, Mary. *The History of Mary Prince: A West Indian Slave*. 1831. Edited by Moira Ferguson. Ann Arbor: University of Michigan Press, 1997.

———. *The History of Mary Prince: A West Indian Slave*. 1831. Edited by Sara Salih. London: Penguin Books, 2004.

Rees, L. E. Ruutz. *A Personal Narrative of the Siege of Lucknow from Its Commencement to Its Relief by Sir Colin Campbell*. London: Longman, Brown, Green, Longmans, and Roberts, 1858.

Reeves, Maud Pember. *Family Life on a Pound a Week*. Fabian Tract, no. 162. London: The Fabian Society, 1912.

———. *Round About a Pound a Week*. London: George Bell and Sons, 1913.

———. *Round About a Pound a Week*. 2nd ed. London: George Bell and Sons, 1914.

———. *Round About a Pound a Week*. Introduction by Sally Alexander. London: Virago, 1979.

"Remember the Slave!" N.p., 1830. JSTOR Wilson Anti-Slavery Collection.

Ripley, C. Peter, ed. *The Black Abolitionist Papers*. Vol. 1: *The British Isles, 1830–1865*. Chapel Hill: University of North Carolina Press, 1985.

Ross, Ellen, ed. *Slum Travelers: Ladies and London Poverty, 1860–1920*. Berkeley: University of California Press, 2007.

Rousseau, Jean Jacques. *The Emile of Jean Jacques Rousseau*, 1762. Translated and edited by William Boyd. New York: Teachers College Press, 1956.

Sadler, Michael Thomas. *Speech of Michael Thomas Sadler, Esq. in the House of Commons, Friday, March 16, 1832, on Moving the Second Reading of the Factories' Regulation Bill*. 3rd ed. London: Seeley and Sons, Hatchard and Son, 1832.

Seeley, Robert Benton. *Memoirs of the Life and Writings of Michael Thomas Sadler, Esq. M.P. F.R.S. &c*. London: R. B. Seeley and W. Burnside, 1842.

Sims, George. *"How the Poor Live" and "Horrible London."* London: Chatto and Windus, 1889.

Sixth Annual Report of the Boston Female Anti-Slavery Society. Boston: Dow and Jackson, 1839.

Stead, W. T. *Josephine Butler: A Life Sketch*. London: Morgan and Scott, 1886.

Swinton, Captain, and Mrs. E. *Journal of a Voyage with Coolie Emigrants, from Calcutta to Trinidad*. London: A. W. Bennett, 1859.

Three Years' Female Anti-Slavery Effort, in Britain and America: Being A Report of the Proceedings of the Glasgow Ladies' Auxiliary Emancipation Society, Since Its

Formation in January, 1834. Glasgow: Aird and Russell, 1837. JSTOR Wilson Anti-Slavery Collection.

Tytler, Harriet. *An Englishwoman in India: The Memoirs of Harriet Tytler, 1828–1858.* Edited by Anthony Sattin. Oxford: Oxford University Press, 1986.

Victoria and Albert Museum. "Reticule, ca. 1827 (made)." https://collections.vam.ac.uk/item/O68954/reticule-lines-samuel/.

Watts, Isaac. *Divine and Moral Songs for Children.* London: M. Lawrence, 1715.

Wilson, Thomas Fourness. *The Defence of Lucknow: A Diary Recording the Daily Events During the Siege of the European Residency, from 31st May to 25th September, 1857.* London: Smith, Elder, 1858.

Wing, Charles. *Evils of the Factory System Demonstrated by Parliamentary Evidence.* London: Saunders and Otley, 1837.

Woolf, Virginia. *A Room of One's Own.* 1929. San Diego: Harcourt, 1989.

Wordsworth, William. *Selected Poems and Prefaces.* Edited by Jack Stillinger. Boston: Houghton Mifflin, 1965.

Secondary Sources

Ablow, Rachel. "Introduction: Victorian Emotions." *Victorian Studies* 50, no. 3 (Spring 2008): 375–77.

Agathocleous, Tanya. *Disaffected: Emotion, Sedition, and Colonial Law in the Anglosphere.* Ithaca, NY: Cornell University Press, 2021.

Ahmed, Sara. *The Cultural Politics of Emotion.* 2nd ed. New York: Routledge, 2015.

Alexander, Sally. "Reeves [*née* Robison], Magdalen Stuart [*known as* Maud Pember Reeves]." *Oxford Dictionary of National Biography.* Oxford University Press, online ed., 2004. https://doi.org/10.1093/ref:odnb/41214.

Allen, Brian. "The Indian Mutiny and British Painting." *Apollo* 132, no. 343 (September 1990): 152–58.

Allen, Judith. "The Rise and Fall of the Abortion Prosecutrix, 1780–1861." Conference paper, North American Conference on British Studies, Minneapolis, MN, 2014.

Anderson, Michael. "The Social Implications of Demographic Change." In *The Cambridge Social History of Britain, 1750–1950,* edited by F. M. L. Thompson, vol. 2: 38–44. Cambridge: Cambridge University Press, 1990.

Ariès, Philippe. *Centuries of Childhood: A Social History of Family Life.* Translated by Robert Baldick. New York: Alfred A. Knopf, 1962.

———. *The Hour of Our Death.* Translated by Helen Weaver. New York: Alfred A. Knopf, 1981.

———. *Western Attitudes Toward Death: From the Middle Ages to the Present.* Translated by Patricia M. Ranum. Baltimore: Johns Hopkins University Press, 1974.

Arnold, David. *Burning the Dead: Hindu Nationhood and the Global Construction of Indian Tradition.* Oakland: University of California Press, 2021.

———. *Colonizing the Body: State Medicine and Epidemic Disease in Nineteenth-Century India.* Berkeley: University of California Press, 1993.

———. "European Orphans and Vagrants in India in the Nineteenth Century." *Journal of Imperial and Commonwealth History* 7, no. 2 (January 1979): 104–27.

Arnot, Margaret. "Infant Death, Child Care and the State: The Baby-Farming Scandal and the First Infant Life Protection Legislation of 1872." *Continuity and Change* 9, no. 2 (1994): 271–311.

Auerbach, Sascha. "'The Law Has No Feeling for Poor Folks Like Us!': Everyday Responses to Legal Compulsion in England's Working-Class Communities, 1871–1904." *Journal of Social History* 45, no. 3 (Spring 2012): 686–708.

Avery, Gillian, and Kimberley Reynolds, eds. *Representations of Childhood Death.* Houndmills, Basingstoke, Hampshire: Macmillan Press, 2000.

Banks, J. A. *Prosperity and Parenthood: A Study of Family Planning Among the Victorian Middle Classes.* London: Routledge and Kegan Paul, 1954.

———. *Victorian Values: Secularism and the Size of Families.* London: Routledge and Kegan Paul, 1981.

Banks, J. A., and O. Banks. *Feminism and Family Planning in Victorian England.* Liverpool: Liverpool University Press, 1964.

Battles, Elizabeth H. "Slavery Through the Eyes of a Mother: *The Runaway Slave at Pilgrim's Point.*" *Studies in Browning and His Circle* 19 (1991): 93–100.

Baughan, Emily. *Saving the Children: Humanitarianism, Internationalism, and Empire.* Oakland: University of California Press, 2022.

Behlmer, George. *Child Abuse and Moral Reform in England, 1870–1908.* Stanford, CA: Stanford University Press, 1982.

———. *Friends of the Family: The English Home and Its Guardians, 1850–1940.* Stanford, CA: Stanford University Press, 1998.

Bernstein, Robin. *Racial Innocence: Performing American Childhood from Slavery to Civil Rights.* New York: New York University Press, 2011.

Berry, Helen. *Orphans of Empire: The Fate of London's Foundlings.* Oxford: Oxford University Press, 2019.

Bhadra, Gautam. "Four Rebels of Eighteen-Fifty-Seven." In *Selected Subaltern Studies,* edited by Ranajit Guha and Gayatri Chakravorty Spivak, 129–75. Oxford: Oxford University Press, 1988.

Bischof, Christopher. "A 'Rich Crop of Nervousness': Childhood, Expertise, and the State in the mid-1880s Over-Pressure Controversy." *English Historical Review* 131, no. 553 (December 2016): 1418.

———. *Teaching Britain: Elementary Teachers and the State of the Everyday, 1846–1906.* Oxford: Oxford University Press, 2019.

Blackett, R. J. M. *Building an Antislavery Wall: Black Americans in the Atlantic Abolitionist Movement, 1830–1860*. Baton Rouge: Louisiana State University Press, 1983; Ithaca, NY: Cornell University Press, 1989.

Blaszak, Barbara J. *The Matriarchs of England's Cooperative Movement: A Study in Gender Politics and Female Leadership, 1883–1921*. Westport, CT: Greenwood Press, 2000.

Blouet, Olwyn Mary. "Buxton, Sir Thomas Fowell, First Baronet (1786–1845), Politician and Philanthropist." *Oxford Dictionary of National Biography*. Oxford University Press, online ed., 2010. https://doi.org/10.1093/ref:odnb/4247.

Blunt, Alison. *Domicile and Diaspora: Anglo-Indian Women and the Spatial Politics of Home*. Oxford: Blackwell, 2005.

———. "Embodying War: British Women and Domestic Defilement in the Indian 'Mutiny,' 1857–8." *Journal of Historical Geography* 26, no. 3 (July 2000): 403–28.

———. "*The Flight from Lucknow*: British Women Travelling and Writing Home, 1857–8." In *Writes of Passage: Reading Travel Writing*, edited by James Duncan and Derek Gregory, 92–113. London: Routledge, 1999.

———. "Imperial Geographies of Home: British Domesticity in India, 1886–1925." *Transactions of the Institute of British Geographers* 24, no. 4 (1999): 421–40.

Boddice, Rob. *The History of Emotions*. Manchester: Manchester University Press, 2018.

Boucher, Ellen. *Empire's Children: Child Emigration, Welfare, and the Decline of the British World, 1869–1967*. Cambridge: Cambridge University Press, 2014.

Boyd, Nancy. *Three Victorian Women Who Changed Their World: Josephine Butler, Octavia Hill, Florence Nightingale*. Oxford: Oxford University Press, 1982.

Brewer, Holly. *By Birth or Consent: Children, Law, and the Anglo-American Revolution in Authority*. Chapel Hill: University of North Carolina Press, 2005.

Brody, Jennifer DeVere. *Impossible Purities: Blackness, Femininity, and Victorian Culture*. Durham, NC: Duke University Press, 1998.

Bronstein, Jamie. *The Happiness of the British Working Class*. Stanford, CA: Stanford University Press, 2023.

Brooks, Peter. *The Melodramatic Imagination: Balzac, Henry James, Melodrama, and the Mode of Excess*. New Haven, CT: Yale University Press, 1976.

Brophy, Sarah. "Elizabeth Barrett Browning's 'The Runaway Slave at Pilgrim's Point' and the Politics of Interpretation." *Victorian Poetry* 36, no. 3 (Fall 1998): 273–88.

Brown, Nicola. "Empty Hands and Precious Pictures: Post-Mortem Portrait Photographs of Children." *Australasian Journal of Victorian Studies* 14, no. 2 (2009): 8–24.

Brownlee, Sibyl Ventress. "Out of the Abundance of the Heart: Sarah Ann Parker Remond's Quest for Freedom." PhD diss., University of Massachusetts, Amherst, 1997.

"Brutal Exposure: The Congo." Exhibition at the International Slavery Museum, 2015. National Museums Liverpool. https://www.liverpoolmuseums.org.uk/whatson/international-slavery-museum/exhibition/brutal-exposure-congo#section--the-exhibition.

Buettner, Elizabeth. "Cemeteries, Public Memory and Raj Nostalgia in Postcolonial Britain and India." *History and Memory* 18, no. 1 (Spring–Summer 2006): 5–42.

———. *Empire Families: Britons and Late Imperial India*. Oxford: Oxford University Press, 2004.

Burton, Antoinette. *Burdens of History: British Feminists, Indian Women, and Imperial Culture, 1865–1915*. Chapel Hill: University of North Carolina Press, 1994.

———, ed. *The First Anglo-Afghan Wars: A Reader*, with a foreword by Andrew Bacevich. Durham, NC: Duke University Press, 2014.

———. "Who Needs the Nation?: Interrogating 'British' History." *Journal of Historical Sociology* 10, no. 3 (1997): 227–48.

Butler, A. S. G. *Portrait of Josephine Butler*. London: Faber and Faber, 1954.

Butler, Judith. *Precarious Life: The Powers of Mourning and Violence*. London: Verso, 2004.

Caine, Barbara. *Victorian Feminists*. Oxford: Oxford University Press, 1992.

Cannadine, David. *Ornamentalism: How the British Saw Their Empire*. Oxford: Oxford University Press, 2001.

———. "War and Death, Grief and Mourning in Modern Britain." In *Mirrors of Mortality: Studies in the Social History of Death*, edited by Joachim Whaley, 187–242. New York: St. Martin's Press, 1981.

Carby, Hazel V. *Reconstructing Womanhood: The Emergence of the Afro-American Woman Novelist*. New York: Oxford University Press, 1987.

Cardwell, Donald. "Ure, Andrew (1778–1857)." *Oxford Dictionary of National Biography*. Oxford University Press, online ed., 2004. https://doi.org/10.1093/ref:odnb/28013.

Chakravarty, Gautam. *The Indian Mutiny and the British Imagination*. Cambridge: Cambridge University Press, 2005.

Chatani, Sayaka. "A Man at Twenty, Aged at Twenty-Five: The Conscription Exam Age in Japan." *American Historical Review* 125, no. 2 (April 2020): 427–37.

Chatterjee, Ronjaunee, Alicia Christoff, and Amy Wong. "Undisciplining Victorian Studies." *Victorian Studies* 62, no. 3 (2020): 369–91.

Chaudhary, Zahid. "Phantasmagoric Aesthetics: Colonial Violence and the Management of Perception." *Cultural Critique* 59 (Winter 2005): 63–119.

Chaudhuri, Nupur. "Memsahibs and Motherhood in Nineteenth-Century Colonial India." *Victorian Studies* 31, no. 4 (Summer 1988): 517–35.
Chaudhuri, Nupur, and Margaret Strobel, eds. *Western Women and Imperialism: Complicity and Resistance*. Bloomington: Indiana University Press, 1992.
Clapp, Elizabeth J., and Julie Roy Jeffrey, eds. *Women, Dissent, and Anti-Slavery in Britain and America, 1790–1865*. Oxford: Oxford University Press, 2011.
Clark, Anna. *The Struggle for the Breeches: Gender and the Making of the British Working Class*. Berkeley: University of California Press, 1995.
Clark, Elizabeth B. "'The Sacred Rights of the Weak': Pain, Sympathy, and the Culture of Individual Rights in Antebellum America." *Journal of American History* 82, no. 2 (September 1995): 463–93.
Clement, Mark. "Rothery, Mary Catherine Hume- (1824–1885)." *Oxford Dictionary of National Biography*. Oxford University Press, online ed., 2004. https://doi.org/10.1093/ref:odnb/49483.
Cohen, Miriam. *Julia Lathrop: Social Service and Progressive Government*. Boulder, CO: Westview Press, 2017.
Cohen, Ruth. "'Mothers First': The Women's Co-operative Guild's Campaign for Maternity Care, 1906–18." *Women's History Magazine* 4 (Spring 2016): 11–19.
Cohn, Bernard S. "Representing Authority in Victorian India." In *The Invention of Tradition*, edited by Eric Hobsbawm and Terence Ranger, 165–209. Cambridge: Cambridge University Press, 1983.
Coleman, Willi. "'Like Hot Lead to Pour on the Americans . . .': Sarah Parker Remond—From Salem, Mass., to the British Isles." In *Women's Rights and Transatlantic Antislavery in the Era of Emancipation*, edited by Kathryn Kish Sklar and James Brewer Stewart, 173–88. New Haven, CT: Yale University Press, 2007.
———. "Remond, Sarah Parker (1826–1894), Slavery Abolitionist and Medical Practitioner." *Oxford Dictionary of National Biography*. Oxford University Press, online ed., 2022. https://doi.org/10.1093/ref:odnb/100414.
Collingham, E. M. *Imperial Bodies: The Physical Experience of the Raj, c. 1800–1947*. Malden, MA: Blackwell, 2001.
Corbett, Mary Jean. *Behind the Times: Virginia Woolf in Late-Victorian Contexts*. Ithaca, NY: Cornell University Press, 2020.
Corrêa, Mariza. "Feminist Letters." *Vibrant* 8, no. 2 (2011): 4–23.
Crawford, Elizabeth. *The Women's Suffrage Movement: A Reference Guide, 1866–1928*. London: Routledge, 1999.
———. "Taylor [née Doughty], Clementina (1810–1908), Women's Activist." *Oxford Dictionary of National Biography*. Oxford University Press, online ed., 2004. https://doi.org/10.1093/ref:odnb/45468.
Cunningham, Hugh. *Children and Childhood in Western Society Since 1500*. London: Longman, 1995.

———. "Review Essay: Histories of Childhood." *American Historical Review* 103, no. 4 (October 1998): 1195–208.

Curl, James. *The Victorian Celebration of Death*. Devon: David and Charles, 1972.

Daggers, Jenny, and Diana Neal, eds. *Sex, Gender, and Religion: Josephine Butler Revisited*. New York: Peter Lang, 2006.

Dallas, Gloden. Introduction to *Maternity: Letters from Working-Women, Collected by the Women's Co-operative Guild*. London: Virago, 1978.

Dalrymple, William. *White Mughals: Love and Betrayal in Eighteenth-Century India*. London: Penguin, 2004.

Davenport, Romola. "Urbanization and Mortality in Britain, c. 1800–50." *Economic History Review* 73, no. 2 (2020): 455–85.

Davidoff, Leonore. *Thicker Than Water: Siblings and Their Relations, 1780–1920*. Oxford: Oxford University Press, 2012.

Davin, Anna. *Growing Up Poor: Home, School, and Street in London, 1870–1914*. London: Rivers Oram Press, 1996.

———. "Imperialism and Motherhood." *History Workshop Journal* 5, no. 1 (Spring 1978): 9–66.

Davis, Angela Y. *Women, Race and Class*. New York: Vintage Books, 1983.

Decker, Corrie. "A Feminist Methodology of Age-Grading and History in Africa." *American Historical Review* 125, no. 2 (April 2020): 418–26.

De Rosa, Debora C. *Domestic Abolitionism and Juvenile Literature, 1830–1865*. Albany: State University of New York Press, 2003.

Dirks, Nicholas. *Castes of Mind: Colonialism and the Making of Modern India*. Princeton, NJ: Princeton University Press, 2001.

Dixon, Thomas. *Weeping Britannia: Portrait of a Nation in Tears*. Oxford: Oxford University Press, 2015.

Duane, Anna Mae, ed. *Child Slavery Before and After Emancipation: An Argument for Child-Centered Slavery Studies*. New York: Cambridge University Press, 2017.

Durbach, Nadja. *Bodily Matters: The Anti-Vaccination Movement in England, 1853–1907*. Durham, NC: Duke University Press, 2005.

———. *Many Mouths: The Politics of Food in Britain from the Workhouse to the Welfare State*. Cambridge: Cambridge University Press, 2020.

Dwork, Deborah. *War Is Good for Babies and Other Young Children*. London: Tavistock Publications, 1987.

Dyhouse, Carol. "Working-Class Mothers and Infant Mortality in England, 1895–1914." *Journal of Social History* 12, no. 2 (Winter 1978): 248–67.

Edelman, Lee. *No Future: Queer Theory and the Death Drive*. Durham, NC: Duke University Press, 2004.

Elbourne, Elizabeth. *Empire, Kinship and Violence: Family Histories, Indigenous Rights and the Making of Settler Colonialism, 1770–1842*. Cambridge: Cambridge University Press, 2022.

Embree, Ainslie T., ed. *1857 in India: Mutiny or War of Independence?* Lexington, MA: D. C. Heath, 1963.

Eustace, Nicole. "Emotion and Political Change." In *Doing Emotions History*, edited by Susan J. Matt and Peter N. Stearns, 163–83. Urbana: University of Illinois Press, 2014.

———. *Passion Is the Gale: Emotion, Power, and the Coming of the American Revolution*. Chapel Hill: University of North Carolina Press for the Omohundro Institute of Early American History and Culture, 2008.

Falconer, John. "'A Pure Labor of Love': A Publishing History of *The People of India*." In *Colonialist Photography: Imag(in)ing Race and Place*, edited by Eleanor M. Hight and Gary D. Sampson, 51–83. London: Routledge, 2002.

Faust, Drew Gilpin. *This Republic of Suffering: Death and the American Civil War*. New York: Alfred A. Knopf, 2008.

Ferguson, Moira. *Subject to Others: British Women Writers and Colonial Slavery, 1670–1834*. New York: Routledge, 1992.

Ficke, Sarah H. "Crafting Social Criticism: Infanticide in 'The Runaway Slave at Pilgrim's Point' and *Aurora Leigh*." *Victorian Poetry* 51, no. 2 (Summer 2013): 249–67.

Field, Corinne T. *The Struggle for Equal Adulthood: Gender, Race, Age, and the Fight for Citizenship in the Antebellum America*. Chapel Hill: University of North Carolina Press, 2014.

Field, Corinne T., and Nicholas L. Syrett. "Age and the Construction of Gendered and Raced Citizenship in the United States." *American Historical Review* 125, no. 2 (April 2020): 438–50.

———. "Introduction." *American Historical Review* 125, no. 2 (April 2020): 371–84.

Fisch, Audrey A. *American Slaves in Victorian England: Abolitionist Politics in Popular Literature and Culture*. Cambridge: Cambridge University Press, 2000.

Flanders, Judith. *Rites of Passage: Death and Mourning in Victorian Britain*. London: Picador, 2024.

Flegel, Monica. *Conceptualizing Cruelty to Children in Nineteenth-Century England: Literature, Representation, and the NSPCC*. Burlington, VT: Ashgate, 2009.

Fletcher, Anthony. *Growing Up in England: The Experience of Childhood, 1600–1914*. New Haven, CT: Yale University Press, 2008.

Foucault, Michel. "Of Other Spaces." Translated by Jay Miskowiec. *Diacritics* 16, no. 1 (Spring 1986): 22–27.

Fraser, John. "Beato's Photograph of the Interior of the Sikandarbagh at Lucknow." *Journal of the Society for Army Historical Research* 59, no. 237 (Spring 1981): 51–55.

Gagnier, Regenia. *Subjectivities: A History of Self-Representation in Britain, 1832–1920*. New York: Oxford University Press, 1991.

Garrett, Eilidh, Alice Reid, Kevin Schürer, and Simon Szreter. *Changing Family Size in England and Wales: Place, Class and Demography, 1891–1911*. Cambridge: Cambridge University Press, 2001.

Gates, Henry Louis, Jr. "History the Slaveholders Wanted Us to Forget." *The New York Times*, February 5, 2017.

George, Rosemary Marangoly. "Homes in the Empire, Empires in the Home." *Cultural Critique* 26 (Winter 1993–94): 95–127.

Ghosh, Durba. *Sex and the Family in Colonial India: The Making of Empire*. Cambridge: Cambridge University Press, 2006.

Goose, Nigel, and Katrina Honeyman, eds. *Childhood and Child Labour in Industrial England: Diversity and Agency, 1750–1914*. Surrey: Ashgate Publishing, 2013.

Goswami, Manu. "'Englishness' on the Imperial Circuit: Mutiny Tours in Colonial South Asia." *Journal of Historical Sociology* 9, no. 1 (March 1996): 54–84.

Grant, Kevin. "Anti-Slavery, Refugee Relief, and the Missionary Origins of Humanitarian Photograph ca. 1900–1960." *History Compass* 15, no. 5 (2017): 1–24.

———. "The British Empire, International Government, and Human Rights." *History Compass*, 11, no. 8 (2013): 573–83.

———. "Christian Critics of Empire: Missionaries, Lantern Lectures, and the Congo Reform Campaign in Britain." In *The Rise and Fall of Modern Empires*, edited by Martin Shipway, vol. 4: 91–122. Burlington, VT: Ashgate, 2013.

———. *A Civilised Savagery: Britain and the New Slaveries in Africa, 1884–1926*. New York: Routledge, 2005.

Gray, Robert. *The Factory Question and Industrial England, 1830–1860*. Cambridge: Cambridge University Press, 1996.

Gregory, Melissa Valiska. "Race and the Dramatic Monologue." *Victorian Studies* 62, no. 2 (Winter 2020): 213–18.

Grey, Daniel. "Creating the 'Problem Hindu': *Sati*, Thuggee and Female Infanticide in India, 1800–60." *Gender and History* 25, no. 3 (November 2013): 498–510.

———. "'It Is Impossible to Judge the Extent to Which the Crime is Prevalent': Infanticide and the Law in India, 1870–1926." *Women's History Review* 30, no. 6 (2021): 1028–46.

Griffin, Emma. *Bread Winner: An Intimate History of the Victorian Economy*. New Haven, CT: Yale University Press, 2020.

Hall, Catherine. "Anti-Slavery Society (act. 1823–1833)." *Oxford Dictionary of National Biography*. Oxford University Press, online ed., 2008. https://doi.org/10.1093/ref:odnb/96359.

Hammond, J. L., and Barbara Hammond. *The Town Labourer, 1760–1832: The New Civilisation*. London: Longmans, Green, 1919.

Hansen, Debra Gold. *Strained Sisterhood: Gender and Class in the Boston Female Anti-Slavery Society*. Amherst: University of Massachusetts Press, 1993.

Harratt, Simon. "Sadler, Michael Thomas (1780–1835)." *The History of Parliament: The House of Commons, 1820–1832.* Edited by D. R. Fisher. Cambridge: Cambridge University Press, 2009. https://www.historyofparliamentonline.org/volume/1820-1832/member/sadler-michael-1780-1835.

Harrington, Peter. "Lucknow After the Indian Mutiny: The Photographs of Felice Beato." *Military Heritage* 6, no. 4 (February 2005): 68–71, 82.

Harris, David. "Topography and Memory: Felice Beato's Photograph's of India, 1858–1859." In *India Through the Lens: Photography, 1840–1911*, edited by Vidya Dehejia, 119–47. Washington, DC: Freer Gallery of Art and Arthur M. Sackler Gallery, 2000.

Hasian, Marouf. "Alice Seeley Harris, the Atrocity Rhetoric of the Congo Reform Movements, and the Demise of King Léopold's Congo Free State." *Atlantic Journal of Communication* 23 (2015): 178–92.

Heathorn, Stephen. "Angel of Empire: The Cawnpore Memorial Well as a British Site of Imperial Remembrance." *Journal of Colonialism and Colonial History* 8, no. 3 (Winter 2007). https://doi.org/10.1353/cch.2008.0009.

Hendrick, Harry. *Children, Childhood and English Society, 1880–1990.* Cambridge: Cambridge University Press, 1997.

Henry, Peaches. "The Sentimental Artistry of Barrett Browning's 'The Cry of the Children.'" *Victorian Poetry* 49, no. 4 (Winter 2011): 535–56.

Herbert, Christopher. *War of No Pity: The Indian Mutiny and Victorian Trauma.* Princeton, NJ: Princeton University Press, 2008.

Hibbert, Christopher. *The Great Mutiny: India 1857.* New York: Viking Press, 1978.

Higgs, Edward. *Life, Death and Statistics: Civil Registration, Censuses and the Work of the General Register Office, 1836–1952.* Hatfield, Hertfordshire: Local Population Studies, 2004.

Higonnet, Anne. *Pictures of Innocence: The History and Crisis of Ideal Childhood.* New York: Thames and Hudson, 1998.

———. "What Do You Want to Know About Children?" In *Picturing Children: Constructions of Childhood Between Rousseau and Freud*, edited by Marilyn R. Brown, 200–206. Burlington, VT: Ashgate, 2002.

Hochschild, Adam. *King Leopold's Ghost: A Story of Greed, Terror, and Heroism in Colonial Africa.* Boston: Mariner Books, 1999.

Hoffenberg, Peter H. *An Empire on Display: English, Indian, and Australian Exhibitions from the Crystal Palace to the Great War.* Berkeley: University of California Press, 2001.

Honeyman, Katrina. *Child Workers in England, 1780–1820: Parish Apprentices and the Making of the Early Industrial Labour Force.* Burlington, VT: Ashgate, 2007.

Howard, June. "What Is Sentimentality?" *American Literary History* 11, no. 1 (Spring 1999): 63–81.

Humphries, Jane. *Childhood and Child Labour in the British Industrial Revolution.* Cambridge: Cambridge University Press, 2010.

Hunt, Lynn. *Inventing Human Rights: A History.* New York: W. W. Norton, 2007.

Huzzey, Richard, and Henry Miller. "Petitions, Parliament and Political Culture: Petitioning the House of Commons, 1780–1918." *Past and Present* 248, no. 1 (2020): 123–64.

Huzzey, Richard, Henry Miller, and Ciara Stewart. "Petitioning and the Politics of Nation, Gender, and Empire." Conference panel, North American Conference on British Studies, Providence, RI, 2018.

Jalland, Pat. *Death in the Victorian Family.* Oxford: Oxford University Press, 1996.

Johnson, Patricia. *Hidden Hands: Working-Class Women and Victorian Social-Problem Fiction.* Athens: Ohio University Press, 2001.

Jones, Catherine. *Intimate Reconstructions: Children in Postemancipation Virginia.* Charlottesville: University of Virginia Press, 2015.

Jones, Clara. *Virginia Woolf: Ambivalent Activist.* Edinburgh: Edinburgh University Press, 2016.

Jordan, Jane. *Josephine Butler.* London: John Murray, 2001.

Joseph, Gerhard, and Herbert F. Tucker. "Passing On: Death." In *A New Companion to Victorian Literature and Culture,* edited by Herbert F. Tucker, 110–23. Chichester, UK: Wiley-Blackwell, 2014.

Joyce, Patrick. *Democratic Subjects: The Self and the Social in Nineteenth-Century England.* Cambridge: Cambridge University Press, 1994.

Kaplan, Fred. *Sacred Tears: Sentimentality in Victorian Literature.* Princeton, NJ: Princeton University Press, 1987.

Keown, John. *Abortion, Doctors and the Law: Some Aspects of the Legal Regulation of Abortion in England from 1803 to 1982.* Cambridge: Cambridge University Press, 1998.

Keynes, Randal. *Annie's Box: Charles Darwin, His Daughter and Human Evolution.* London: Fourth Estate, 2001.

King, Wilma. "'Mad' Enough to Kill: Enslaved Women, Murder, and Southern Courts." *Journal of African American History* 92, no. 1 (Winter 2007): 37–56.

———. *Stolen Childhood: Slave Youth in Nineteenth-Century America.* 2nd ed. Bloomington: Indiana University Press, 2011.

———. "'Suffer with Them till Death': Slave Women and Their Children in Nineteenth-Century America." In *More Than Chattel: Black Women and Slavery in the Americas,* edited by David Barry Gaspar and Darlene Clark Hine, 147–68. Bloomington: Indiana University Press, 1996.

Kirby, Peter. *Child Labour in Britain, 1750–1870.* Basingstoke: Palgrave Macmillan, 2003.

———. *Child Workers and Industrial Health in Britain, 1780–1850.* Woodbridge, Suffolk: Boydell Press, 2013.

Klaver, Claudia. "Domesticity Under Siege: British Women and Imperial Crisis at the Siege of Lucknow, 1857." *Women's Writing* 8, no. 1 (2001): 21–58.

Knott, Sarah. *Sensibility and the American Revolution*. Chapel Hill: University of North Carolina Press for the Omohundro Institute of Early American History and Culture, 2009.

Koven, Seth, and Sonya Michel, eds. *Mothers of a New World: Maternalist Politics and the Origins of Welfare States*. New York: Routledge, 1993.

Kriegel, Lara. *The Crimean War and Its Afterlife: Making Modern Britain*. Cambridge: Cambridge University Press, 2022.

Laqueur, Thomas. "Bodies, Death, and Pauper Funerals." *Representations* 1, no. 1 (February 1983): 109–31.

———. *The Work of the Dead: A Cultural History of Mortal Remains*. Princeton, NJ: Princeton University Press, 2015.

Lassonde, Stephen. "Age and Authority: Adult-Child Relations During the Twentieth Century in the United States." *Journal of the History of Childhood and Youth* 1, no. 1 (Winter 2008): 95–105.

Laurence, Patricia. "'Holding Her Pen Like a Broom': Virginia Woolf's Anxieties about Working-Class Women." *Études Britanniques Contemporaines*, 5–18. Montpellier: Presses Universitaires de Montpellier, 1999. http://ebc.chez-alice.fr/ebc16b1.html.

Lee, Debbie. *Slavery and the Romantic Imagination*. Philadelphia: University of Pennsylvania Press, 2002.

Lerner, Laurence. *Angels and Absences: Child Deaths in the Nineteenth Century*. Nashville: Vanderbilt University Press, 1997.

Levene, Alysa. *Childcare, Health and Mortality in the London Foundling Hospital, 1741–1800: "Left to the Mercy of the World."* Manchester: Manchester University Press, 2007.

Levene, Alysa, and Jean Webb. "Depictions of the 'Ideal Child' in Nineteenth-Century British Literature and Legislature." *Journal of the History of Childhood and Youth* 12, no. 1 (Winter 2019): 26–44.

Lifson, Ben. "Beato in Lucknow." *Artforum International* 26, no. 9 (May 1988): 98–103.

Linkman, Audrey. *Photography and Death*. London: Reaktion Books, 2011.

Llewellyn-Jones, Rosie, ed. *Lucknow: City of Illusion*. Munich: Prestel, 2006.

———, ed. *Lucknow: Then and Now*. Mumbai: Marg Publications for the National Centre for the Performing Arts, 2003.

Lovett, Laura L. "Age: A Useful Category of Historical Analysis." *Journal of the History of Childhood and Youth* 1, no. 1 (Winter 2008): 89–90.

Lutz, Deborah. *Relics of Death in Victorian Literature and Culture*. Cambridge: Cambridge University Press, 2015.

Lydon, Jane. *Imperial Emotions: The Politics of Empathy Across the British Empire*. Cambridge: Cambridge University Press, 2020.

Mackinnon, Alison. "Was There a Victorian Demographic Transition?" In *The Victorian World*, edited by Martin Hewitt, 276–90. London: Routledge, 2013.

MacLeod, R. M. "Law, Medicine and Public Opinion: The Resistance to Compulsory Health Legislation, 1870–1907." *Public Law* (1967): 107–28, 189–211.

MacMillan, Margaret. *Women of the Raj: The Mothers, Wives, and Daughters of the British Empire in India*. New York: Thames and Hudson, 1988.

Mallipeddi, Ramesh. "Political Rights and the Printed Word." In "The End of Print: A Roundtable," special issue, *Journal of British Studies* (March 4, 2025). https://doi.org/10.1017/jbr.2024.187.

Manzo, Kate. "Imaging Humanitarianism: NGO Identity and the Iconography of Childhood." *Antipode* 40, no. 4 (2008): 632–57.

Marks, Lara. *Metropolitan Maternity: Maternal and Infant Welfare Services in Early Twentieth Century London, 1870–1939*. Amsterdam: Rodophi, 1996.

Martinez, Jenny. *The Slave Trade and the Origins of International Human Rights Law*. Oxford: Oxford University Press, 2012.

Masselos, Jim, and Narayani Gupta. *Beato's Delhi 1857, 1997*. Delhi: Ravi Dayal, 1997.

Mathers, Helen. "The Evangelical Spirituality of a Victorian Feminist: Josephine Butler, 1828–1906." *Journal of Ecclesiastical History* 52, no. 2 (April 2001): 282–312.

Matt, Susan J., and Peter N. Stearns, eds. *Doing Emotions History*. Urbana: University of Illinois Press, 2014.

Maynes, Mary Jo. "Age as a Category of Historical Analysis: History, Agency, and Narratives of Childhood." *Journal of the History of Childhood and Youth* 1, no. 1 (Winter 2008): 114–24.

Maza, Sarah. "The Kids Aren't All Right: Historians and the Problem of Childhood." *American Historical Review* 125, no. 4 (October 2020): 1261–85.

McAllister, David. *Imagining the Dead in British Literature and Culture, 1790–1848*. Cham, Switzerland: Palgrave Macmillan, 2018.

McClelland, Keith. "Redefining the West India Interest: Politics and the Legacies of Slave-Ownership." In *Legacies of British Slave-Ownership: Colonial Slavery and the Formation of Victorian Britain*, edited by Catherine Hall, Nicholas Draper, Keith McClelland, Katie Donington, and Rachel Lang, 127–62. Cambridge: Cambridge University Press, 2014.

McFeely, William S. *Frederick Douglass*. New York: W. W. Norton, 1991.

McLaren, Angus. *Birth Control in Nineteenth-Century England*. London: Croom Helm, 1978.

Metcalf, Thomas R. *Ideologies of the Raj*. Cambridge: Cambridge University Press, 1995.

Midgley, Clare. *Feminism and Empire: Women Activists in Imperial Britain, 1790–1865*. London: Routledge, 2007.

———. *Women Against Slavery: The British Campaigns, 1780–1870.* London: Routledge, 1992.
Miller, Andrew. *On Not Being Someone Else: Tales of Our Unled Lives.* Cambridge, MA: Harvard University Press, 2020.
Miller, Henry. *A Nation of Petitioners: Petitions and Petitioning in the United Kingdom, 1780–1918.* Cambridge: Cambridge University Press, 2023.
Miller, John MacNeill. "Slavish Poses: Elizabeth Barrett Browning and the Aesthetics of Abolition." *Victorian Poetry* 52, no. 4 (Winter 2014): 637–59.
Mintz, Steven. "Reflections on Age as a Category of Historical Analysis." *Journal of the History of Childhood and Youth* 1, no. 1 (Winter 2008): 91–94.
Mitchell, B. R. *British Historical Statistics.* Cambridge: Cambridge University Press, 1988.
Mooney, Graham. *Intrusive Interventions: Public Health, Domestic Space, and Infectious Disease Surveillance in England, 1840–1914.* Rochester, NY: University of Rochester Press, 2015.
Morley, John. *Death, Heaven and the Victorians.* London: Studio Vista, 1971.
Mosse, George L. *Fallen Soldiers: Reshaping the Memory of the World Wars.* Oxford: Oxford University Press, 1990.
Mukherjee, Rudrangshu. *Awadh in Revolt, 1857–1858: A Study of Popular Resistance.* New Delhi: Oxford University Press, 1984.
Murdoch, Lydia. "Anti-Vaccination and the Politics of Grief for Children in Late Victorian England." In *Childhood, Youth and Emotions in Modern History: National, Colonial and Global Perspectives*, edited by Stephanie Olsen, 242–60. New York: Palgrave Macmillan, 2015.
———. "'The Dead and the Living': Child Death, the Public Mortuary Movement, and the Spaces of Grief and Selfhood in Victorian London." *Journal of the History of Childhood and Youth* 8, no. 3 (Fall 2015): 378–402.
———. *Imagined Orphans: Poor Families, Child Welfare, and Contested Citizenship in London.* New Brunswick, NJ: Rutgers University Press, 2006.
Nardinelli, Clark. *Child Labour and the Industrial Revolution.* Bloomington: Indiana University Press, 1990.
Noakes, Lucy. *Dying for the Nation: Death, Grief and Bereavement in Second World War Britain.* Manchester: Manchester University Press, 2020.
Nouvian, Manon. "Defiant Mourning: Public Funerals as Funeral Demonstrations in the Chartist Movement." *Journal of Victorian Culture* 24, no. 2 (2019): 208–26.
Oldfield, Sybil. "Margaret Llewelyn Davies and Leonard Woolf." In *Women in the Milieu of Leonard and Virginia Woolf: Peace, Politics, and Education*, edited by Wayne Chapman and Janet Manson, 3–32. New York: Pace University Press, 1998.
Olsen, Stephanie. "The History of Childhood and the Emotional Turn." *History Compass* (August 25, 2017). https://doi.org/10.1111/hic3.12410.

Pande, Ishita. "Power, Knowledge, and the Epistemic Contract on Age: The Case of Colonial India." *American Historical Review* 125, no. 2 (April 2020): 407–17.

Paris, Leslie."Through the Looking Glass: Age, Stages, and Historical Analysis." *Journal of the History of Childhood and Youth* 1, no. 1 (Winter 2008): 106–13.

Parry, Ann. "Sexual Exploitation and Freedom: Religion, Race, and Gender in Elizabeth Barrett Browning's 'The Runaway Slave at Pilgrim's Point.'" *Studies in Browning and His Circle* 16 (1988): 114–26.

Pati, Biswamoy, ed. *The 1857 Rebellion*. New Delhi: Oxford University Press, 2007.

———, ed. *The Great Rebellion of 1857 in India: Exploring Transgressions, Contests and Diversities*. London: Routledge, 2010.

Paugh, Katherine. *The Politics of Reproduction: Race, Medicine, and Fertility in the Age of Abolition*. Oxford: Oxford University Press, 2017.

Paxton, Nancy L. *Writing Under the Raj: Gender, Race, and Rape in the British Colonial Imagination, 1830–1947*. New Brunswick, NJ: Rutgers University Press, 1999.

Pavlakis, Dean. *British Humanitarianism and the Congo Reform Movement, 1896–1913*. Burlington, VT: Ashgate, 2015.

Pedersen, Susan. *Eleanor Rathbone and the Politics of Conscience*. New Haven, CT: Yale University Press, 2004.

———. *Family, Dependence, and the Origins of the Welfare State: Britain and France, 1914–1945*. Cambridge: Cambridge University Press, 1993.

Peterson, Carla L. *"Doers of the Word": African-American Women Speakers and Writers in the North (1830–1880)*. New York: Oxford University Press, 1995.

Peterson, M. Jeanne. *Family, Love, and Work in the Lives of Victorian Gentlewomen*. Bloomington: Indiana University Press, 1989.

Petrie, Glen. *A Singular Iniquity: The Campaigns of Josephine Butler*. New York: Viking Press, 1971.

Pinney, Christopher. *Camera Indica: The Social Life of Indian Photographs*. London: Reaktion, 1997.

Plamper, Jan. *The History of Emotions: An Introduction*. Oxford: Oxford University Press, 2012.

Pollock, Linda. *Forgotten Children: Parent-Child Relations from 1500–1900*. Cambridge: Cambridge University Press, 1983.

Pomfret, David. *Youth and Empire: Trans-Colonial Childhoods in British and French Asia*. Stanford, CA: Stanford University Press, 2015.

Poovey, Mary. *Making a Social Body: British Cultural Formation, 1830–1864*. Chicago: University of Chicago Press, 1995.

Porter, Dorothy, and Roy Porter."The Politics of Prevention: Anti-Vaccinationism and Public Health in Nineteenth-Century England." *Medical History* 32 (1988): 231–52.

Porter, Dorothy B. "Sarah Parker Remond, Abolitionist and Physician." *Journal of Negro History* 20, no. 3 (July 1935): 287–93.
Premo, Bianca. "Meticulous Imprecision: Calculating Age in Colonial Spanish American Law." *American Historical Review* 125, no. 2 (April 2020): 396–406.
Procida, Mary A. *Married to the Empire: Gender, Politics and Imperialism in India, 1883–1947.* Manchester: Manchester University Press, 2002.
Pryor, Elizabeth Stordeur. *Colored Travelers: Mobility and the Fight for Citizenship Before the Civil War.* Chapel Hill: University of North Carolina Press, 2016.
Rahikainen, Marjatta. *Centuries of Child Labour: European Experiences from the Seventeenth to the Twentieth Century.* Aldershot, UK: Ashgate Publishing, 2004.
Raza, Rosemary. *In Their Own Words: British Women Writers and India, 1740–1857.* Oxford: Oxford University Press, 2006.
Razzell, Peter, and Christine Spence. "The History of Infant, Child and Adult Mortality in London, 1550–1850." *London Journal* 32, no. 3 (November 2007): 271–92.
Reddy, William. *The Navigation of Feeling: A Framework for the History of Emotions.* Cambridge: Cambridge University Press, 2001.
Reinhardt, Mark. *Who Speaks for Margaret Garner?* Minneapolis: University of Minnesota Press, 2010.
Reynolds, Melanie. *Infant Mortality and Working-Class Child Care, 1850–1899.* New York: Palgrave Macmillan, 2016.
Richardson, Alan. "'The Sorrows of Yamba,' by Eaglesfield Smith and Hannah More: Authorship, Ideology, and the Fractures of Antislavery Discourse." *Romanticism on the Net* 28 (November 2002). https://doi.org/10.7202/007209ar.
Richardson, Ruth. *Death, Dissection and the Destitute.* 2nd ed. Chicago: University of Chicago Press, 2001.
Robinson, Jane. *Angels of Albion: Women of the Indian Mutiny.* London: Penguin Books, 1996.
Rosenwein, Barbara. *Emotional Communities in the Early Middle Ages.* Ithaca, NY: Cornell University Press, 2006.
Ross, Ellen. *Love and Toil: Motherhood in Outcast London, 1870–1918.* Oxford: Oxford University Press, 1993.
———. "Mothers and the State in Britain, 1904–1914." In *The European Experience of Declining Fertility, 1850–1970,* edited by John Gillis, Louise Tilly, and David Levine, 48–65. Cambridge, MA: Blackwell, 1992.
Sabatos, Terri. "Images of Death and Domesticity in Victorian Britain." PhD diss., Indiana University, 2001.
Said, Edward. *Orientalism.* New York: Vintage Books, 1979.
Salenius, Sirpa. *An Abolitionist Abroad: Sarah Parker Remond in Cosmopolitan Europe.* Amherst: University of Massachusetts Press, 2016.

---. "Interracial Networks of Transatlantic Activism: Sarah Parker Remond Reassessing Black Womanhood." In *Connecting Women: National and International Networks During the Long Nineteenth Century*, edited by Barton C. Hacker, Joanne Paisana, Margarida Esteves Pereira, Jaime Costa, and Margaret Vining, 47–61. Washington, DC: Smithsonian Scholarly Press, 2021.

Sánchez-Eppler, Karen. *Touching Liberty: Abolition, Feminism, and the Politics of the Body*. Berkeley: University of California Press, 1993.

Schaub, Melissa. "The Margins of the Dramatic Monologue: Teaching Elizabeth Barrett Browning's 'The Runaway Slave at Pilgrim's Point.'" *Victorian Poetry* 49, no. 4 (Winter 2011): 557–68.

Schor, Esther. *Bearing the Dead: The British Culture of Mourning from the Enlightenment to Victoria*. Princeton, NJ: Princeton University Press, 1994.

Schwartz, Marie Jenkins. *Born in Bondage: Growing Up Enslaved in the Antebellum South*. Cambridge, MA: Harvard University Press, 2000.

Scott, Gillian. *Feminism and the Politics of Working Women: The Women's Cooperative Guild, 1880s to the Second World War*. London: UCL Press, 1998.

Scott, Joan Wallach. *Gender and the Politics of History*. New York: Columbia University Press, 1988.

Semmel, Bernard. *The Governor Eyre Controversy*. London: MacGibbon and Kee, 1962.

Sen, Indrani. "Colonial Domesticities, Contentious Interactions: Ayahs, Wet-Nurses and Memsahibs in Colonial India." *Indian Journal of Gender Studies* 16, no. 3 (November 2009): 299–328.

---. *Woman and Empire: Representations in the Writings of British India (1858–1900)*. New Delhi: Orient Longman, 2002.

Sen, Satadru. *Colonial Childhoods: The Juvenile Periphery of India, 1850–1945*. London: Anthem Press, 2005.

Sharpe, Jenny. *Allegories of Empire: The Figure of Woman in the Colonial Text*. Minneapolis: University of Minnesota Press, 1993.

Sinha, Mrinalini. *Specters of Mother India: The Global Restructuring of an Empire*. Durham, NC: Duke University Press, 2006.

Sklar, Kathryn Kish, and James Brewer Stewart, eds. *Women's Rights and Transatlantic Antislavery in the Era of Emancipation*. New Haven, CT: Yale University Press, 2007.

Sliwinski, Sharon. "The Childhood of Human Rights: The Kodak on the Congo." *Journal of Visual Culture* 5, no. 3 (2006): 333–63.

Smith, Andrew. *Gothic Death, 1740–1914: A Literary History*. Manchester: Manchester University Press, 2016.

Smith, Ellen. "'Pregnant with the Interests of Life and Death': Family Correspondence and the British Imperial News Sphere During the 1857 Indian Rebellion." *Journal of British Studies* (March 2025): 1–22. https://doi.org/10.1017/jbr.2025.1.

Smith, F. B. *The People's Health, 1830–1910*. New York: Holmes and Meier, 1979.
Smith, J. R. *The Speckled Monster: Smallpox in England, 1670–1970*. Chelmsford, UK: Essex Record Office, 1987.
Smith, Thomas W., and Helen Killick, eds. *Petitions and Strategies of Persuasion in the Middle Ages: The English Crown and the Church, c. 1200–c. 1550*. Woodbridge, UK: York Medieval Press, 2018.
Solomon, Robert C. *In Defense of Sentimentality*. New York: Oxford University Press, 2004.
Stauffer, Andrew. "Elizabeth Barrett Browning's (Re)visions of Slavery." *English Language Notes* 34, no. 4 (June 1997): 29–48.
Stearns, Carol, and Peter. "Emotionology: Clarifying the History of Emotions and Emotional Standards." *American Historical Review* 90, no. 4 (October 1985): 813–36.
Stedman-Jones, Gareth. *Languages of Class*. Cambridge: Cambridge University Press, 1983.
Steedman, Carolyn. *Childhood, Culture and Class in Britain: Margaret McMillan, 1860–1931*. New Brunswick, NJ: Rutgers University Press, 1990.
———. *Landscape for a Good Woman: A Story of Two Lives*. New Brunswick, NJ: Rutgers University Press, 1987.
———. *Strange Dislocations: Childhood and the Idea of Human Interiority, 1780–1930*. London: Virago, 1995.
Sterling, Dorothy. *We Are Your Sisters: Black Women in the Nineteenth Century*. New York: W. W. Norton, 1984.
Stokes, Eric. *The Peasant and the Raj: Studies in Agrarian Society and Peasant Rebellion in Colonial India*. Cambridge: Cambridge University Press, 1978.
Stoler, Ann Laura. *Carnal Knowledge and Imperial Power: Race and the Intimate in Colonial Rule*. Berkeley: University of California Press, 2002.
———. *Race and the Education of Desire: Foucault's History of Sexuality and the Colonial Order of Things*. Durham, NC: Duke University Press, 1995.
Stone, Lawrence. *The Family, Sex and Marriage in England, 1500–1800*. New York: Harper and Row, 1977.
Stone, Marjorie. "Between Ethics and Anguish: Feminist Ethics, Feminist Aesthetics, and Representations of Infanticide in 'The Runaway Slave at Pilgrim's Point' and *Beloved*." In *Between Ethics and Aesthetics: Crossing the Boundaries*, edited by Dorota Glowacka and Stephen Boos, 131–58. Albany: State University of New York Press, 2002.
———. "Browning [née Moulton Barrett], Elizabeth Barrett (1806–1861)." *Oxford Dictionary of National Biography*. Oxford University Press, online ed., 2008. https://doi.org/10.1093/ref:odnb/3711.
———. "Cursing as One of the Fine Arts: Elizabeth Barrett Browning's Political Poems." In *Critical Essays on Elizabeth Barrett Browning*, edited by Sandra Donaldson, 184–201. New York: G. K. Hall, 1999.

———. "Elizabeth Barrett Browning and the Garrisonians: 'The Runaway Slave at Pilgrim's Point,' the Boston Female Anti-Slavery Society, and Abolitionist Discourse in the *Liberty Bell*." In *Victorian Women Poets (Essays and Studies, 56)*, edited by Alison Chapman, 33–55. Cambridge: D. S. Brewer, 2003.

———. "Witness Narratives and Working-Class Suffering: 'The Cry of the Children,' *Corn Law Rhymes*, and Elizabeth Barrett Browning's Unpublished Hunger Ballad." *Victorian Studies* 62, no. 4 (Summer 2020): 616–43.

Strange, Julie-Marie. *Death, Grief and Poverty in Britain, 1870–1914*. Cambridge: Cambridge University Press, 2005.

Strobel, Margaret. *European Women and the Second British Empire*. Bloomington: Indiana University Press, 1991.

Surridge, Lisa. "Working-Class Masculinities in *Mary Barton*." *Victorian Literature and Culture* 28, no. 2 (2000): 331–43.

Sussman, Charlotte. *Consuming Anxieties: Consumer Protest, Gender and British Slavery, 1713–1833*. Stanford, CA: Stanford University Press, 2000.

Szreter, Simon. *Fertility, Class and Gender in Britain, 1860–1940*. Cambridge: Cambridge University Press, 1996.

Szreter, Simon, and Graham Mooney. "Urbanization, Mortality, and the Standard of Living Debate: New Estimates of the Expectation of Life at Birth in Nineteenth-Century Cities." *Economic History Review* 51, no. 1 (February 1998): 84–112.

Tambe, Ashwini. "The Moral Hierarchies of Age Standards: The UN Debates a Common Minimum Marriage Age, 1951–1962." *American Historical Review* 125, no. 2 (April 2020): 451–59.

Taylor, Lou. *Mourning Dress: A Costume and Social History*. London: George Allen and Unwin, 1983.

Taylor, Nikki M. *Driven Toward Madness: The Fugitive Slave Margaret Garner and Tragedy on the Ohio*. Athens: Ohio University Press, 2016.

Teitelbaum, Michael S., and Jay M. Winter. *The Fear of Population Decline*. Orlando, FL: Academic Press, 1985.

Thane, Pat. "Old Age in European Cultures: A Significant Presence from Antiquity to the Present." *American Historical Review* 125, no. 2 (April 2020): 385–95.

Thomas, Julia. *Pictorial Victorians: The Inscription of Values in Word and Image*. Athens: Ohio University Press, 2004.

Thompson, E. P. *The Making of the English Working Class*. New York: Pantheon Books, 1963.

Tilghman, Carolyn. "Autobiography as Dissidence: Subjectivity, Sexuality, and the Women's Co-operative Guild." *Biography* 26, no. 4 (Fall 2003): 583–606.

Tompkins, Jane. *Sensational Designs: The Cultural Work of American Fiction, 1790–1860*. New York: Oxford University Press, 1985.

Travers, Robert. "Death and the Nabob: Imperialism and Commemoration in Eighteenth-Century India." *Past and Present* 196 (August 2007): 83–124.

Turner, Sasha. *Contested Bodies: Pregnancy, Childrearing, and Slavery in Jamaica.* Philadelphia: University of Pennsylvania Press, 2017.

———. "The Nameless and the Forgotten: Maternal Grief, Sacred Protection, and the Archive of Slavery." *Slavery and Abolition* 38, no. 2 (2017): 232–50.

Turoff, Melissa. "'Told by the Tombs': British Death and Cemeteries in Colonial India." History thesis, Vassar College, 2007.

Tuson, Penelope. "Mutiny Narratives and the Imperial Feminine: European Women's Accounts of the Rebellion in India in 1857." *Women's Studies International Forum* 21, no. 3 (May–June 1998): 291–303.

Twells, Alison. *The Civilising Mission and the English Middle Class, 1792–1850: The "Heathen" at Home and Overseas.* New York: Palgrave Macmillan, 2009.

Twomey, Christina. "The Incorruptible Kodak: Photography, Human Rights and the Congo Campaign." In *The Violence of the Image: Photography and International Conflict*, edited by Liam Kennedy and Caitlin Patrick, 9–33. London: I. B. Tauris, 2014.

———. "Severed Hands: Authenticating Atrocity in the Congo, 1904–13," in *Picturing Atrocity: Photography in Crisis*, edited by Jay Prosser et al., 39–50. London: Reaktion Books, 2012.

Vallgårda, Karen, Kristine Alexander, and Stephanie Olsen. "Emotions and the Global Politics of Childhood." In *Childhood, Youth and Emotions in Modern History: National, Colonial and Global Perspectives*, edited by Stephanie Olsen, 12–34. New York: Palgrave Macmillan, 2015.

Vasconcellos, Colleen. *Slavery, Abolition, and Childhood in Jamaica, 1788–1838.* Athens: University of Georgia Press, 2015.

Vincent, David. "Love and Death and the Nineteenth-Century Working Class." *Social History* 5, no. 2 (May 1980): 223–47.

Walkowitz, Judith. "Butler [née Grey], Josephine Elizabeth (1828–1906)." *Oxford Dictionary of National Biography*. Oxford University Press, online ed., 2006. https://doi.org/10.1093/ref:odnb/32214.

———. *City of Dreadful Delight: Narratives of Sexual Danger in Late-Victorian London.* Chicago: University of Chicago Press, 1992.

———. *Prostitution and Victorian Society.* Cambridge: Cambridge University Press, 1980.

Walvin, James. *The Zong: A Massacre, the Law and the End of Slavery.* New Haven, CT: Yale University Press, 2011.

Ward, Andrew. *Our Bones Are Scattered: The Cawnpore Massacres and the Indian Mutiny of 1857.* London: John Murray, 1996.

Ward, J. T. *The Factory Movement, 1830–1855.* London: Macmillan; New York: St. Martin's Press, 1962.

———. *The Factory System*. Vol. 2: *The Factory System and Society*. New York: Barnes and Noble, 1970.

Webb, Catherine. *The Woman with the Basket: The History of the Women's Co-operative Guild, 1883–1927*. Manchester: Co-operative Society's Printing Works, 1927.

Weisenburger, Steven. *Modern Medea: A Family Story of Slavery and Child-Murder from the Old South*. New York: Hill and Wang, 1998.

Wheeler, Michael. *Death and the Future Life in Victorian Literature and Theology*. Cambridge: Cambridge University Press, 1990.

Williams, John. "Thomas, David Alfred, First Viscount Rhondda (1856–1918)." *Oxford Dictionary of National Biography*. Oxford University Press, online ed., 2008. https://doi.org/10.1093/ref:odnb/36470.

Wohl, Anthony. *Endangered Lives: Public Health in Victorian Britain*. Cambridge, MA: Harvard University Press, 1983.

———. Introduction to *The Bitter Cry of Outcast London*, by Andrew Mearns, edited by Anthony Wohl, 9–50. New York: Humanities Press, 1970.

———. "Sex and the Single Room: Incest Among the Victorian Working Classes." In *The Victorian Family: Structure and Stresses*, edited by Anthony Wohl, 197–216. London: Croom Helm, 1978.

Woo, Ilyon. *Master Slave Husband Wife: An Epic Journey from Slavery to Freedom*. New York: Simon and Schuster, 2023.

Wood, Alice. "Facing *Life as We Have Known It*: Virginia Woolf and the Women's Co-operative Guild." *Literature and History* 23, no. 2 (Autumn 2014): 18–34.

Woods, R. I. "Approaches to the Fertility Transition in Victorian England." *Population Studies* 41, no. 2 (July 1987): 283–311.

Woods, Robert. *Children Remembered: Responses to Untimely Death in the Past*. Liverpool: Liverpool University Press, 2006.

———. *The Demography of Victorian England and Wales*. Cambridge: Cambridge University Press, 2000.

Wrigley, E. A., and R. S. Schofield. *The Population History of England, 1541–1871: A Reconstruction*. Cambridge: Cambridge University Press, 1981.

Yee, Shirley J. *Black Women Abolitionists: A Study in Activism, 1828–1860*. Knoxville: University of Tennessee, 1992.

Yellin, Jean Fagan, and John C. Van Horne. *The Abolitionist Sisterhood: Women's Political Culture in Antebellum America*. Ithaca, NY: Cornell University Press, 1994.

Zackodnik, Teresa C. *The Mulatta and the Politics of Race*. Jackson: University Press of Mississippi, 2004.

INDEX

Italicized page numbers refer to illustrations.

abolitionism. *See* antislavery campaign
abortion, 132, 136, 143–44, 155
abuse. *See* child abuse; sexual abuse and assault
Acton, William, 112
affect. *See* emotions
agency: child factory labor and, 24, 173n71; free, 13, 23, 29, 33; political, 11–12, 160; of women, 155, 179n3, 222n69
Ahmed, Sara, 8
Allen, William G., 64
American Anti-Slavery Society, 56, 64, 65
Anatomy Act of 1832, 15, 170n23
Anderson, Elizabeth Garrett, 112
antislavery campaign, 36–71; on apprenticeship system, 19, 39–40, 43, 51, 181n19; Christianity and, 44–45, 48, 50–53, 69; on death of enslaved children, 36–39, 47–61, 63, 66–70; gradualist approach of, 42, 183n34; infanticide accounts utilized by, 37–39, 55–61, 63, 66–70, 159, 195n147; material objects utilized in, 48–50, *49*, 187n70; petitioning in, 19, 46, 171n45; public grief and mourning evoked by, 36–38; on resurrected childhood, 53–55, 58–61, 63, 69; on rights of childhood for enslaved children, 41, 43–47, 53, 69; songs used in, 44–45, 52, 184n44; women in, 36–39, 41–46, 49–70, 181n16; World Anti-Slavery Convention (1840), 64; on *Zong* murders, 40, 181n21
Anti-Slavery Society, 41–42, 179n3
anti-vaccinationist movement, 120–30; on child death, 120, 123–29; emotions in, 126–29; funeral processions as political protest used by, 120–29; liberalism of, 126, 217n131; music utilized by, 125–27; postmortem photographs used by, 122, 215n111; public grief and mourning by, 120, 122, 124, 127–30; women in, 102, 121, 123–29; working class and, 123, 125–28
apprenticeship system, 6, 19, 39–40, 43, 51, 181nn19–20
Ariès, Philippe: *The Hour of Our Death*, 74
Arnold, Matthew, 3
Artisans' Dwellings Act of 1875, 108
Ashley, Lord, 13, 15, 21, 24, 25, 30
assault. *See* sexual abuse and assault

Ball, Charles: *History of the Indian Mutiny*, 78–81, *80–81*, 83, 201n27
Barbauld, Anna Lætitia, 49–50, 186n68
Bartrum, Bobbie, 72–74, 197n3
Bartrum, Katherine, 72–74, 83–84, 87, 89–92, 99, 198n10
Bartrum, Robert, 72, 76
Baughan, Emily, 158
Beato, Felice, 199n19
Beeton, Isabella, 3
Behn, Aphra, 132
bereavement. *See* grief and mourning
Bernstein, Robin, 37–39, 185n53, 187n69
birth control, 143–44, 152, 155
Births and Deaths Registration Act of 1874, 105
Black, Clementina: *Married Women's Work*, 137, 153
Blake, William, 41, 185n53
Blunt, Alison, 198n10, 202n33
Boileau, Ina, 92, 94

257

Boston Female Anti-Slavery Society, 45–46, 50–51, 55, 57, 65, 185nn49–50
Boucicault, Dion: *Jessie Brown; or, The Relief of Lucknow*, 83
Brewer, Holly, 6
Bright, Ursula, 123
British Medical Journal, 4, 152
Brontë, Charlotte: *Jane Eyre*, 3–4
Brown, Henry "Box," 64
Brown, William Wells, 64, 65
Browning, Elizabeth Barrett: antislavery activism of, 38–39, 54–62, 70; *Aurora Leigh*, 55, 62; "The Cry of the Children," 30–33, 62, 178n119; "A Curse for a Nation," 55, 188n86; "A Dead Rose," 62; in discourse of child death, 13; Douglass's *Narrative* as influence on, 58, 190n104; family background, 55, 56, 189n90; "Hiram Powers' 'Greek Slave,'" 55; on infanticide by enslaved parents, 55–61, 70, 189n94; "An Ode to America," 55; politics and, 30, 55, 61, 62, 177n113; sentimentalism in works by, 14, 30, 32, 177n112; "The Runaway Slave at Pilgrim's Point," 55–62, 118–19, 188nn86–87, 190n100, 190n102, 190–91nn106–11
Browning, Robert, 56
Brownlee, Sibyl Ventress, 195n147
Brydon, Colina, 90, 91, 205–6n67
Brydon, William, 205–6n67
burial practices: cemetery reconfiguration and, 74, 199n14; class status and, 9, 106; during First World War, 74; during Indian Rebellion, 73, 75, 92–94; public health reforms and, 106
Burton, Antoinette, 103
Butler, Evangeline, 109, 113–16, 117, 120, 214n79
Butler, George, 113, 115, 118
Butler, Josephine: CD Acts opposed by, 102, 109–13, 116, 118–20, 212n55; characterizations of, 113–15, 213n61; child death experienced by, 109, 110, 113–16, 214n79; "The Dark Side of English Life," 116, 118; Evangelicalism of, 113, 115, 213n63; grief and mourning by, 110, 112–16, 118, 120, 159; *The Hour Before the Dawn*, 118; on infanticide, 118–19, 160; Munro's sculpture of, 116, 117, 214n89; *Recollections of George Butler*, 115; Watts's portrait of, *110*
Butler, Judith: on grief and mourning, 8, 75, 151; *Precarious Life*, 151
Button, James, 125
Buxton, Charles, 41, 196n167
Buxton, Dorothy, 158
Buxton, Thomas Fowell, 41–43, 54, 61, 68, 182n23, 183n34

Campbell, Colin, 83
Canning, Charles, 77, 79
Canning, George, 42, 183n37
capitalism, 8, 19, 148, 160
Carby, Hazel, 38
Cardwell, Donald, 171n37
Carlyle, Thomas, 71
Carpenter, Mary, 71
Case, Adelaide: *Day by Day at Lucknow*, 84–87, 89–91, 94, 98
Case, William, 84
Cawnpore massacres. *See* Kanpur massacres
CD Acts. *See* Contagious Diseases (CD) Acts
Chadwick, Edwin, 15, 17, 103
Chapman, Maria Weston, 45, 55–56, 62, 63, 188n87
Chartists, 13, 19, 26, 29, 122, 169n16
Child, Lydia Maria, 45
child abuse, 16, 24, 102, 104, 135, 173n69
child death: anti-vaccinationist movement on, 120, 123–29; in Christian good death tradition, 74, 75, 89, 92–95, 115; city dangers resulting in, 104; emotional regimes centered around, 8, 131; factory labor and, 11–14, 18–19, 23–35, 169n14; fatalistic views of, 5–6; *The Good Little Boy* instructional on, 1, 2, 3, 5; during Indian Rebellion, 72–82, 78–80, 88–99, 159; medical neglect and mistreatment as causes of, 144–45, 223n88; militaristic representations

of, 76–82; politicization of, 13, 39, 101, 102; public health reforms and, 101–2, 105–6, 130; slavery and, 36–39, 47–61, 63, 66–70; treatment of corpses following, 106–7, 130, 154; wishes and prayers for, 48, 50–53, 56, 188n79; working-class women and, 139–52. *See also* burial practices; child mortality rates; grief and mourning; infanticide

child factory labor, 11–35; abuse in, 16, 24, 173n69; agency and, 24, 173n71; defenders of, 13, 16–18, 21, 23; industrialization and, 7, 12–14, 17–19, 169n15; literature related to, 11, 30–33; mortality rates and, 25, 169n14; petitions on regulation of, 14, 18–31, 22, 33–35, 159–60, 171n38, 173n69; public grief and mourning for workers, 11–12, 14, 30, 33–35; reform movement, 11, 13–21, 23–25, 27–29, 31; Sadler on, 11–13, 15–16, 25, 168n8; slavery compared to, 34–35; standards of living and, 13, 16

childhood: denial of, 24, 26–27, 37, 46, 69; domesticity and, 2, 5, 82–88; emotions in, 14, 18, 38, 40, 122; enslaved people's experiences of, 46–47, 185n53; human rights in, 27, 35, 45, 70, 158; imperialism and, 82, 202n32; lost, 14, 29–30, 33, 35, 37, 53, 59; politicization of, 13, 39, 101–2, 130, 160, 210n12; resurrected, 53–55, 58–61, 63, 69; rhetoric of, 42, 161; rights of, 6–7, 18, 41, 43–47, 53, 69; Romantic, 31, 46, 48, 180n12, 185n55; stolen, 37, 39, 179n7; as universal experience, 34. *See also* education; ideals of childhood; innocence of childhood

child life: Butler's valuing of, 113, 120; celebrations of, 13, 101, 131; emotional regimes centered around, 8, 103, 131; preciousness of, 37, 70, 103, 160; reproductive futurism and, 2, 58, 163n9; state protection of, 102, 112, 136, 154

child mortality rates: class status and, 4, 103, 105, 134–35; for enslaved children, 37, 40; factory labor and, 25, 169n14; improvement of, 7, 134, 157; indentured laborers and, 227n9; parental bonds of affection and, 5, 165n22. *See also* infant mortality rates

Children's Acts (1889, 1908), 102, 135, 138
child welfare movement, 20, 47, 172n51
cholera, 4, 72, 91–92, 104, 171n37
Christianity: antislavery campaign and, 44–45, 48, 50–53, 69; British civilizing mission and, 77; child factory labor in opposition to, 27; Evangelicals, 6–7, 41, 52, 113; good death in, 7, 73–75, 89, 92–95, 115, 118, 145; industrialization in undermining of, 31; missionary work and, 42; resurrected childhood and, 53, 58, 59, 63, 69; urban housing reform and, 108. *See also* Evangelicalism

citizenship: claims to, 34, 63, 109, 120, 155; models of, 13, 134; naturalized, 70, 196–97n169; reimagining of, 2, 8; rights of, 3, 9, 70, 108–9, 120, 122, 134, 155
Clark, George: *The Liberty Minstrel,* 52
Clarkson, Thomas, 40
class status: burial practices and, 9, 106; mortality rates and, 4, 103, 105, 134–35; racial hierarchies and, 76, 200n21; siege of Lucknow and, 86, 204n49; suffrage and, 13, 19, 29. *See also* middle class; upper class; working class
Cobbe, Frances Power, 63, 64, 71, 123
Coleman, Willi, 193n128
Coleridge, Samuel Taylor, 41
collective grief and mourning. *See* public grief and mourning
Congo Free State, 157, 226n2
contagious diseases. *See* infectious diseases
Contagious Diseases (CD) Acts (1864, 1866, 1869), 100–102, 109–13, 116, 118–19, 130, 209n1, 212n55
contraception. *See* birth control
Corn Laws, 19, 30, 32, 62, 112
Cowper, William, 41
Craft, Ellen, 64, 65, 194n136
Craft, William, 64, 194n136
Craigen, Jessie, 123, 126, 127, 216n118
Crimean War, 74, 96

Criminal Law Amendment Act of 1885, 102
Croft, Richard, 101
Cugoano, Ottobah, 40–41

Darwin, Charles, 3
Dashwood, Herbert, 91, 95, 208n111
Davies, Emily, 133
Davies, Margaret Llewelyn: introduction to *Maternity* by, 132, 138, 144; survey research conducted by, 136–38, 220n33; Women's Co-operative Guild and, 132–33, 136–39, 153–56, 218n4; Woolf's friendship with, 132, 152, 218n2
Davin, Anna, 135
Davis, Eunice, 45
Davison, Emily, 216n112
death. *See* burial practices; child death; grief and mourning; mortality rates
Declaration of the Rights of the Child (1959), 157
Dickens, Charles: child death in works by, 1–2, 4, 13, 163n9; *A Christmas Carol*, 1–2, 9, 10, 163n9; *Dombey and Son*, 107; family deaths experienced by, 3
diseases. *See* infectious diseases
Disraeli, Benjamin, 104–5
domesticity, 2, 5, 77, 82–88, 98, 159
Douglass, Frederick: antislavery campaign and, 64, 180n9, 185n54; lecture tour of United Kingdom, 46, 185n54; *Life and Times of Frederick Douglass*, 46; *My Bondage and My Freedom*, 46–47; *Narrative of the Life of Frederick Douglass*, 46, 58, 190n104; on Romantic boyhood, 46, 48, 185n55; visit to Remond, 62–63
Dred Scott decision (1857), 68, 70
Duane, Anna Mae, 38, 39
Duckworth, Gerald, 137
Durbach, Nadja, 122, 123
Dwork, Deborah, 154
Dyhouse, Carol, 135
dysentery, 91

East India Company, 16, 76, 181n18
Edelman, Lee, 58, 163n9

education: for child factory workers, 18, 26, 28; national system of, 6, 7, 101, 136, 209n2; religious, 14, 27, 42, 82; on reproductive health, 142, 143; for women, 64, 110, 133, 150
Elbourne, Elizabeth, 42
elites. *See* upper class
Ellenborough Act of 1803, 143
Elmy, Elizabeth Wolstenholme, 112, 123
emotional regimes, 8, 10, 103, 120, 130–31
emotions: in anti-vaccinationist movement, 126–29; appeals to, 37, 108, 124, 131; in childhood, 14, 18, 38, 40, 122; history of, 5, 166n39; normative order for, 103; political rights and, 37–38, 180n10. *See also* grief and mourning
enfranchisement. *See* suffrage
Engels, Friedrich: *The Condition of the Working Class in England*, 104; in discourse of child death, 13; on rights of working class, 34; on social murder of children, 14
enslaved children: death of, 36–39, 47–61, 63, 66–70; emotional capabilities of, 38, 40; mortality rates for, 37, 40; parents of, 36–44, 47–63, 66–70, 159, 184n44, 189n94, 195n147; public grief and mourning for, 36–38; resurrected childhood and, 53–55, 58–61, 63, 69; right of childhood for, 41, 43–47, 53, 69; stolen childhood of, 37, 39, 179n7; transport from Africa, 41, 182n26; *Zong* murders and, 40. *See also* antislavery campaign
Equiano, Olaudah, 40, 46, 47
Estlin, Mary, 64
Eustace, Nicole, 37–38, 180n10
Evangelicalism: in antislavery campaign, 41, 52; of Butler, 113, 115, 213n63; childhood as reimagined in, 6; good death envisioned by, 7, 115
Eyre, Edward John, 41, 70–71, 196n167

Fabian Women's Group, 135, 137, 152
Factories Act of 1847 (Ten Hours Act), 16, 26, 30

INDEX

Factories' Regulation Bill (Ten Hours Bill), 11, 12, 15, 21, 23–25
Factory Act of 1833, 16–17, 21, 29
Factory Act of 1844, 30
factory children. *See* child factory labor
Factory Commission, 15–16, 21, 23, 168–69n14
Farr, William, 103
Farre, John, 25
Faust, Drew Gilpin, 74
Fawcett, Millicent Garret, 123
feelings. *See* emotions
Female Society for Birmingham, 36, 42–43, 49, 49–50, 186n67, 187n70
feminism, 62, 111, 133, 136–37, 154, 201n22
Ficke, Sarah, 56, 57, 191n108
Fielden, John, 25–26, 34
First World War, 9, 74, 137, 152–53, 155, 157
Follen, Eliza Lee Cabot: Browning and, 56, 188n87; "The Little Slave's Wish," 52, 187n77; "Remember the Slave!," 44–45, 51
Forten, Charlotte, 62, 191n119
Foucault, Michel, 207n107
Fox, Rebecca, 49
Foxe, John: *Book of Martyrs*, 81
Fry, Elizabeth, 3, 41
Fugitive Slave Act of 1850, 66–67
funeral processions as political protest, 120–29, 216n112

Gagnier, Regenia: *Subjectivities*, 133–34
Garner, Margaret, 63, 66–69, 159, 160, 195n147, 195nn149–50
Garner, Robert, 66, 195n150
Garrison, William Lloyd, 64, 65, 189–90n96
Gaskell, Elizabeth: child death experienced by, 3; in discourse of child death, 13; *Mary Barton*, 12
Gates, Henry Louis, Jr., 180n12
Geneva Declaration of the Rights of the Child (1924), 157
George IV, King, 49
Germon, Maria, 86–87, 205n61
Ghosh, Durba, 209n122

Gladstone, William, 3, 104
Glasgow Ladies' Auxiliary Emancipation Society, 57
Godwin, George, 105, 108
good death, 7, 73–75, 89, 92–95, 115, 118, 145
Good Little Boy, The (Religious Tract Society), 1, 2, 3, 5
Gordon, Linda, 136
Great Rebellion. *See* Indian Rebellion
Great Reform Act of 1832, 13, 15, 19
Great War. *See* First World War
Gregory, Melissa Valiska, 58
grief and mourning: commercialization of, 8; democratization of, 8, 158, 160; language of, 24–25, 120, 160; nationalistic expressions of, 99; politicization of, 2, 10, 101, 102, 158, 160; private, 5, 8, 25, 110, 115, 128; rituals of, 8, 73–75, 91–92, 94, 99, 103; suppressed, 89, 92, 124. *See also* child death; maternal grief and mourning; public grief and mourning
Grimké, Angelina: *Appeal to the Christian Women of the South*, 187n72; Glasgow Ladies' Auxiliary Emancipation Society and, 57
Gubbins, Martin, 204n49

Hadley, Elaine, 120, 127
Hadow, Gilbert, 91
Hanway, Jonas, 4
Harper, Francis: "The Slave Mother, a Tale of the Ohio," 190n97
Harris, Georgina, 83–86, 91, 92, 95, 208n111
Harris, James, 93
Harris, José, 5
Harris, Lilian, 153, 156
Havelock, Henry, 83
health reforms. *See* public health reforms
Heathorn, Stephen, 96
Henry, Peaches, 31, 177n112
Herbert, Christopher, 99
heterotopias, 207n107
Higgs, Edward, 105
Higonnet, Anne, 180n12
Holland, Henry Scott, 114

Hope, John, 13
Hopwood, Charles, 124
Horne, Richard Hengist, 30, 31, 34
Housing Act of 1885, 103–4
housing reform, 102–9, 159
Howey, Elsie, 216n112
human rights: abstract language of, 134; in childhood, 27, 35, 45, 70, 158; equal treatment under law and, 119; feminist and socialist vision of, 137; global campaign for, 157; imperialism and, 71, 227n3; slavery's impact on, 68; transnational nature of debates about, 63; universal, 34, 40, 157
Hume, Joseph, 19, 100
Hume-Rothery, Mary Catherine: anti-vaccinationist movement and, 102, 123, 125; CD Acts opposed by, 100–101, 119, 209n1; death of child experienced by, 101; *Women and Doctors*, 100–101
Hunt, Leigh, 3
Hunt, Lynn, 157–58
Hutchins, Barbara: *Women in Modern Industry*, 137
Huzzey, Richard, 19

ideals of childhood: as basis for natural rights, 44; comfort, 26; dependence, 2, 6, 40; freedom, 17–19, 37, 44, 45, 52–53, 69; happiness, 26, 69, 130; joy, 40, 44, 45, 48, 52; leisure, 18, 33; love, 44, 45, 48, 53, 69; play, 17, 18, 26, 33, 44, 69; politicization of, 13; protection, 2, 5–6, 19, 26, 37, 44, 48, 52, 69; slavery in shaping of, 39
imperialism: childhood and, 82, 202n32; civilizing mission and, 77, 97, 98; human rights and, 71, 227n3; infanticide and, 26, 175n88; justification through domestic ideals, 75; liberal reformist rhetoric of, 76; propaganda and, 99; racism and, 70, 201n22; women and values of, 77, 81, 85–86, 200n22
Indian Rebellion (1857), 72–99; British retaliation and suppression of, 76–79, 83; burial practices during, 73, 75, 92–94; child death during, 72–82, 78–80, 88–99, 159; Jhansi massacre, 78–79, 80, 201n27; Kanpur massacres, 76–78, 81, 81–83, 96–97, 97; military recruitment during, 78, 201n25; photographs of, 76, 199n19; public grief and mourning during, 77, 78, 81, 95, 99; public memorials for, 96–99, 97; public memory of, 75–76, 88, 90, 96, 99; *Punch* magazine cartoons and, 77–78, 78–80; terminology considerations, 197n1. *See also* Lucknow, siege of
industrialization: capitalism and, 8, 19, 148, 160; child factory labor and, 7, 12–14, 17–19, 169n15; Christianity undermined by, 31; environmental impact of, 169n14; mortality rates and, 4, 104, 164n16, 169n14; standards of living and, 14, 164n16, 168–69n14
infanticide: Butler on, 118–19, 160; child factory labor as, 25–26, 28, 31; by enslaved parents, 37–39, 55–61, 63, 66–70, 159, 189n94, 195n147; imperialism and, 26, 175n88; legislation targeting, 102
Infant Life Protection Acts (1872, 1897), 102
infant mortality rates: class status and, 105, 134–35; for enslaved infants, 37; in industrial towns, 169n14; international perspectives on, 219n15; syphilis and, 112, 130; trends related to, 4, 105, 134, 164n17
infectious diseases: cholera, 4, 72, 91–92, 104, 171n37; dysentery, 91; notification requirements, 100, 209n2; scarlet fever, 1, 5, 106, 127; smallpox, 91–92, 100, 102, 120, 122–23; venereal, 111, 112, 122, 130, 154. *See also* Contagious Diseases (CD) Acts
Inglis, Julia: *The Siege of Lucknow*, 84, 85, 87–93, 97, 203n36
Inglis, Robert, 19
Innes, M., 202n33
innocence of childhood: antislavery activists on, 37–40, 42, 44, 53–55, 60, 69–70; appeals to human rights shaped

by, 157, 158; blankness associated with, 42, 53, 58; factory labor regulation and, 26; middle-class interpretations of, 82; in reconceptualizations of childhood, 2, 5–6, 82; unknowingness and, 55, 58, 180n12; whiteness associated with, 37, 180n9

Jacobs, Harriet, 47, 48
Jalland, Pat, 5, 74
Jamaican Rebellion (1865), 42, 70, 99, 196n167
Jebb, Eglantyne, 158
Jenner, Edward, 120, 122, 129
Jhansi massacre (1857), 78–79, 80, 201n27

Kanpur massacres (1857), 76–78, 81, 81–83, 96–97, 97
Kemble, Fanny, 63
King, Wilma: on childhoods of enslaved people, 46; *Stolen Childhood*, 39, 179n7, 182n26
Kirby, Peter, 21, 169n14
Klaver, Claudia, 198n10
Knight, Joseph, 181n17
Knott, Sarah, 180n10
Kriegel, Lara, 74

labor: apprenticeship system, 6, 19, 39–40, 43, 51, 181nn19–20; as form of property, 13, 29, 33; industrial, 14, 16, 19, 24–26, 30–34, 104, 135, 169n14. *See also* child factory labor; slavery; working class
Ladies' London Emancipation Society, 64, 65
Ladies' National Association for the Repeal of the Contagious Diseases Acts (LNA), 112
Ladies' New York City Anti-Slavery Society: *Appeal to the Christian Women of America*, 45, 51, 185n48, 187n72; on separation of enslaved children from parents, 44
Laqueur, Thomas: on erasure of poor from community of the dead, 15; on transition from churchyards to cemeteries, 8, 199n14; on treatment of the dead, 93, 102; *The Work of the Dead*, 102
Lawrence, Henry, 86, 87, 204n48
Layton, Elizabeth, 154
League of Nations, 157
Leech, John, 9
Leeds Anti-Slavery Juvenile Series, 52, 53, 54
Lenox, Nancy, 63, 192n125
Leopold II, King, 157, 226n2
Lewis, Edmonia, 64
Liberty Bell, The (giftbook), 55, 57–58, 61–62, 188nn86–87, 189n94
Lines, Samuel, 49, 187n70
Lloyd George, David, 133, 136, 153
LNA (Ladies' National Association for the Repeal of the Contagious Diseases Acts), 112
Lowell, James Russell, 55–57, 61
Lowell, Maria: "The Slave Mother," 57, 190n97
Lucas, Margaret Bright, 64
Lucknow, siege of (1857): child death during, 75, 88–95, 98–99; class tensions during, 86, 204n49; evacuation of survivors, 83, 85, 87, 88; memoirs and diaries of survivors, 73, 75, 83–94, 203n36; military deaths during, 205n61; public memorials for, 97–98; public memory of, 88, 99; suppressed grief at, 89; women at, 72–73, 82–95, 98, 198n10, 202n33, 204n51, 205n60
Lugard, Lord, 158

Macaulay, Thomas Babington, 15, 16, 76, 170n26
Malthus, Thomas, 3
Manning, Charlotte, 64
Mansfield, Lord Justice, 39, 40, 182n22
Marochetti, Carlo, 96, 97, 208n116
Marshall, John, 12, 13, 15
Marshall, William, 12, 13
Martineau, Harriet, 42, 63, 64
Martinez, Jenny, 157

maternal grief and mourning: of Butler, 110, 112–16, 118, 120, 159; public accounts of, 132–34, 139–40, 145–52, 155; of working-class women, 133–34, 139–40, 145–52, 155

Maternity: Letters from Working Women (Women's Co-operative Guild): collecting letters for, 136–38; introduction by Davies, 132, 138, 144; letters selected for inclusion in, 139–51, 147, 221n39; on maternal grief and mourning, 133–34, 139–40, 145; preface by Samuel, 138, 150; public reactions to, 152–56, 224–25n131; publisher selected for, 137

Maternity and Child Welfare Act of 1918, 154

maternity care, 133, 134, 137–45, 149, 152–55

Mathers, Helen, 113

Mathews, Cornelius, 61

Maza, Sarah, 7

Mazzini, Giuseppe, 197n169

Mearns, Andrew: *Bitter Cry of Outcast London*, 102–9, 120, 134; on urban housing reform, 102–9, 159

middle class: childhood as viewed by, 82, 89; child mortality rates among, 4; death as experienced by, 72–73; family size and, 222n69; at siege of Lucknow, 88; suffrage for, 13; on women at funeral services, 124

Midgley, Clare, 183n40, 201n22

midwives, 101, 133, 138, 154

Mill, John Stuart, 64, 71, 76, 196n167

Miller, Henry, 19–20

Mines and Collieries Act of 1842, 16, 30, 34

Mitford, Mary Russell, 61–62, 188n87

More, Hannah: *The Sorrows of Yamba*, 41, 50, 182n28

Morrison, Toni: *Beloved*, 63, 190n97

mortality rates: class status and, 4, 103, 105, 134–35; industrialization and, 4, 104, 164n16, 169n14; urbanization and, 4, 164n16. See also child mortality rates; infant mortality rates

Mosse, George, 74

mourning. See grief and mourning

mourning dress, 8, 89, 95, 110, 124, 207n109

Munro, Alexander, 116, 117, 214n89

Nana Sahib, 76–77

National Association for the Repeal of the Contagious Diseases Acts, 112

nationalism, 86, 99, 132, 137, 155

National Society for the Prevention of Cruelty to Children (NSPCC), 6, 47, 102, 186n62

"Negro Mother's Appeal, The" (poem), 43–44, 44, 183n40

"Negro Woman's Lamentation over Her Child, A" (poem), 50–51

New Poor Law of 1834, 2, 19, 112

Nightingale, Florence, 111

Notification of Births (Extension) Act of 1915, 138

Nye, Charles Washington, 125

Oastler, Richard, 15

O'Connell, Daniel, 19

Offences Against the Person Act of 1861, 143

Oliphant, Margaret, 3

Outram, James, 83

parents: bonds of affection formed by, 5, 165n22; of enslaved children, 36–44, 47–63, 66–70, 184n44, 189n94, 195n147. See also maternal grief and mourning

Parker, Theodore, 63

Paton, Joseph Noel: *In Memoriam*, 96

Pattison, James, 16

Pease, Elizabeth, 185n50

Pedersen, Susan, 133

Peel, Robert, 19

personal grief and mourning. See private grief and mourning

Peterson, M. Jeanne, 5
petitioning: in antislavery campaign, 19, 46, 171n45; on child factory labor regulation, 14, 18–31, 22, 33–35, 159–60, 171n38, 173n69; on compulsory vaccination laws, 123; political participation through, 19–21; on public health reforms, 101, 112; for women's suffrage, 64, 193n131
Phillips, Thomas, 114
Phillips, Wendell, 65
Pintor, Lazario, 64
Poe, Edgar Allan, 32
Polehampton, Emmie, 73, 83–84, 94, 98, 197n3, 198n5
Polehampton, Henry, 84, 198n5
political rights: Butler's view of, 110, 120; Chartist demands for, 169n16; emotions and, 37–38, 180n10; feminist movement and, 111; public grief and mourning as means for demanding, 2, 14, 30, 103, 113; of women, 122, 135; of working class, 14, 122, 133. *See also* petitioning; suffrage
poor laws, 2, 19, 112
postmortem photographs, 8, 73, 122, 198n5, 215n111
Prince, John Critchley: "The Death of a Factory Child," 30
Prince, Mary, 36–37, 39, 44, 69, 70, 179n3
Pringle, Thomas, 179n3
private grief and mourning, 5, 8, 25, 110, 115, 128
pronatalism, 150, 152, 155
prostitution, 100, 101, 109, 111, 113, 118, 130
protests: by antislavery campaign, 38, 44; by anti-vaccinationist movement, 102, 120–30; child death and, 2, 38, 120–21; child factory labor and, 24; funeral processions as, 120–29, 216n112. *See also* Indian Rebellion
public grief and mourning: by anti-vaccinationist movement, 120, 122, 124, 127–30; for child factory workers, 11–12, 14, 30, 33–35; connections formed through, 94–95; emotional regimes and, 130–31; for enslaved children, 36–38; in global human rights campaigns, 157; during Indian Rebellion, 77, 78, 81, 95, 99; maternal, 132–34, 139–40, 145–52, 155; as means for demanding political rights, 2, 14, 30, 103, 113; national action inspired by, 24, 160; public health reforms and, 102–3, 114; reimagining of childhood and, 5, 6; value of life asserted through, 8, 159; as voice for political resistance, 101, 159–61
public health reforms, 100–131; burial practices and, 106; campaign against CD Acts, 102, 109–13, 116, 118–20; child death and, 101–2, 105–6, 130; emotional regimes and, 103; Hume-Rothery's opposition to, 100–101; legislation related to, 100, 102, 131, 209nn1–2; petitioning on, 101, 112; public grief and mourning and, 102–3, 114; urban housing reform, 102–9, 159; urban sanitation reform, 104–5. *See also* infectious diseases; vaccination
Punch magazine cartoons, 77–78, 78–80

Quincey, Thomas de, 7–8

race: exclusionary policies and, 97; hierarchies based on, 53, 76, 209n122; interracial relationships, 82, 98; superiority beliefs and, 77, 78
racism, 58–60, 70, 201n22
rape. *See* sexual abuse and assault
Reddy, William, 103
Rees, L. E. Ruutz, 87, 88, 204n49
Reeves, Maude Pember: *Round About a Pound a Week*, 135–37
registration of births and deaths, 100, 105, 138, 211n25
Reid, Elizabeth Jesser, 64, 193n128
religious education, 14, 27, 42, 82. *See also* Christianity
Religious Tract Society, 1, 2, 3, 163n1
Remond, Charles Lenox, 64
Remond, John, 63, 192n125

Remond, Sarah Parker, 66; antislavery activism of, 38–39, 54–55, 62–71; British citizenship of, 70, 71, 196–97n169; Browning as influence on, 62, 191n119; call for political transformation, 63, 68; denial of U.S. passport for, 70, 196n164; discrimination experienced by, 196n157; family background, 63–64, 192n125; on infanticide by enslaved parents, 63, 66–70, 159, 195n147; lectures by, 62, 64–69, 118, 159, 193n128, 194n136, 194–95n147, 195n153, 195n156; in medical profession, 64, 71, 193n132; at Taylor residence, 64, 71, 193n130; visit by Douglass, 62–63
reproductive futurism, 2, 58, 163n9
Rhondda, Lord, 153–54
rights: of bodily autonomy, 119, 126; of childhood, 6–7, 18, 41, 43–47, 53, 69; of citizenship, 3, 9, 70, 108–9, 120, 122, 134, 155; equal, 53, 68, 70, 126, 160; natural, 33, 37, 43, 44; universal, 7, 34, 40, 47, 157, 158; of women, 111–13, 122–23, 130, 133, 135, 152. *See also* human rights; political rights
Robinson, Jane, 202n33
Ross, Ellen, 5, 134, 135, 145, 150
Rossetti, Dante Gabriel, 214n89
Rousseau, Jean-Jacques: *Émile, or On Education*, 6, 46, 158; *The Social Contract*, 157–58
Ruskin, John, 55

Sadler, Michael: on child factory labor, 11–13, 15–16, 25, 168n8; in discourse of child death, 13, 101; Factories' Regulation Bill and, 11, 12, 15, 21, 23; "The Factory Girl's Last Day," 11, 30; public grief and mourning evoked by, 11–12, 14; report issued by, 13, 15–16, 21, 24, 34, 168–69n14
Salenius, Sirpa, 192n125, 193n132
Salisbury, Lord, 123, 126–27
Samuel, Herbert, 138, 150, 153
Save the Children Fund, 158
scarlet fever, 1, 5, 106, 127
schooling. *See* education

Sen, Indrani, 94
Senior, Nassau: *Letters on the Factory Act*, 16–17; opposition to child factory labor regulation, 21
Sepoy Mutiny. *See* Indian Rebellion
sexual abuse and assault: of child factory workers, 16, 24, 173n69; of enslaved women, 45, 47, 56–58, 60, 67–68, 190n102, 195n147; forced medical examinations as, 119; vulnerability of women to, 100–101
sex work. *See* prostitution
shared grief and mourning. *See* public grief and mourning
Sharp, Granville, 40
Sheffield Association for the Universal Abolition of Slavery, 44, 51, 183–84n43, 185n50
Shelley, Mary, 3
Sherwood, Mary Martha: *The Fairchild Family*, 94–95, 163n1; fictional scenes of child death by, 94–95, 207n108
Sims, George: *How the Poor Live*, 105–6, 108
Slave Emancipation Act of 1833, 36, 39–40, 181n18
"Slave Mother, The" (poem), 56–57, 189–90n96
slavery: child factory labor compared to, 34–35; commodification of bodies in, 170n23; economic and political structures of, 61, 67; gradualist approach to end of, 42, 183n34; human rights impacted by, 68; ideals of childhood shaped by, 39; judicial challenges to, 39, 181n17; legacies of, 38, 53, 55, 58, 60; process of forgetting, 38, 54, 180n12; *Zong* murders, 40, 181–82nn21–23. *See also* antislavery campaign; enslaved children
smallpox, 91–92, 100, 102, 120, 122–23
Smith, Eaglesfield, 41, 182n28
Smith, Thomas Southwood, 15
social class. *See* class status
socialism, 105, 133, 135–37, 154
Society for the Preservation of Infant Life, 102

Somerset, James, 39, 70
Stansfeld, Carolyn Ashurst, 64
Stead, William T., 104, 113, 116
Steedman, Carolyn, 108, 155
Stewart, Ciara, 19
Stone, Marjorie, 30, 57–58, 62, 63, 178n119, 188n87, 190n97
Stowe, Harriet Beecher, 63, 64, 187n69, 193n128
Strange, Julie-Marie, 5, 8–9, 145
Strickland, Susanna, 179n3
suffrage: class status and, 13, 19, 29; property requirements for, 6; universal adult, 133. *See also* women's suffrage
syphilis, 112, 122, 130

Tait, Catherine and Archibald, 5
Taylor, Clementia (Mentia), 63, 64, 71, 193nn130–31, 197n169
Taylor, Peter, 64, 71, 193n130, 197n169
Ten Hours Act of 1847 (Factories Act), 16, 26, 30
Ten Hours Bill. *See* Factories' Regulation Bill
Tenniel, John, 77–78, 80, 201n25
Third Reform Act of 1884, 20, 103, 123, 127, 217
Thomas, Margaret Haig, 154
Thompson, George and Anne Erskine, 45
Tonna, Charlotte Elizabeth: "The Slave and Her Babe," 52–53
Tooke, Thomas, 15
Trollope, Frances, 13
Tytler, Harriet, 81–82
Tytler, Robert, 81

United Nations Declaration of the Rights of the Child (1959), 157
upper class: child mortality rates among, 4, 105; domestic sphere as place of protection for, 72; grief and mourning among, 5; at siege of Lucknow, 83–85, 87, 88; on women at funeral services, 124
urban housing reform, 102–9, 159
urbanization, 4, 164n16

Ure, Andrew: opposition to child factory labor regulation, 21; *The Philosophy of Manufactures*, 17–18, 171n37

vaccination: compulsory, 7, 100, 102, 121, 122–26, 130, 159; for smallpox, 100, 102, 120, 122–23. *See also* anti-vaccinationist movement
Vaccination Acts (1853, 1861, 1867, 1871), 100, 101, 111, 120–26, 216n116
venereal diseases, 111, 112, 122, 130, 154
Victoria, Queen, 49, 77, 78, 134
voting rights. *See* suffrage

Walkowitz, Judith, 111, 112, 118
Waterhouse, E., 185n50
Watts, George Frederic, 110
Watts, Isaac: "Against Idleness and Mischief," 16; *Divine and Moral Songs for Children*, 5–6
Waugh, Benjamin, 6
Wheatley, Phillis, 46, 47
whiteness, child innocence associated with, 37, 180n9
Wilberforce, William, 41
Wilson, Charlotte, 135
Wohl, Anthony, 107
women: abortion and, 132, 136, 143–44, 155; agency of, 155, 179n3, 222n69; age of consent for girls, 102; in antislavery campaign, 36–39, 41–46, 49–70, 181n16; in anti-vaccinationist movement, 102, 121, 123–29; birth control for, 143–44, 152, 155; bodily autonomy of, 119, 150; education for, 64, 110, 133, 150; enslaved, 40–63, 66–69, 190n102, 195n147; feminism and, 62, 111, 133, 136–37, 154, 201n22; imperial values and, 77, 81, 85–86, 200n22; in Kanpur massacres, 76–78, 81, 82, 96–97; maternity care for, 133, 134, 137–45, 149, 152–55; maternity insurance benefit for, 133, 136, 138, 150, 153, 219n9; as midwives, 101, 133, 138, 154; mourning dress for, 8, 89, 95, 110, 124, 207n109; in prostitution, 100, 101, 109, 111, 113, 118, 130; rights of,

women (*continued*) 111–13, 122–23, 130, 133, 135, 152; at siege of Lucknow, 72–73, 82–95, 98, 198n10, 202n33, 204n51, 205n60; vulnerability to sexual assault, 100–101. *See also* maternal grief and mourning; working-class women

Women's Co-operative Guild: on access to birth control, 144; campaigns undertaken by, 133; Davies and, 132–33, 136–39, 153–56, 218n4; establishment and growth of, 133; *Life as We Have Known It*, 154; maternity insurance benefit and, 133, 136, 138, 150, 153, 219n9; National Maternity Scheme, 138–39, 153–54; political campaigns coordinated by, 153–54, 225n142; survey research with members, 136–38, 220n23, 220n33; on women's suffrage, 154, 159, 161; Woolf and, 10, 132–33, 137, 154, 218n2. *See also Maternity: Letters from Working Women*

Women's Social and Political Union (WSPU), 152–53

women's suffrage: age requirements for, 20; Butler's support for, 110, 119; funeral processions as political protest used by, 122, 216n112; Hume-Rothery's support for, 100; as means to guarantee constitutional rights, 111; petitioning for, 64, 193n131; Women's Co-operative Guild on, 154, 159, 161; Women's Social and Political Union on, 153

Woolf, Leonard, 132, 218n2, 225n131

Woolf, Virginia: on Browning, 62; Davies's friendship with, 132, 152, 218n2; on maternal health, 10; *A Room of One's Own*, 132; Women's Co-operative Guild and, 10, 132–33, 137, 154, 218n2

Wordsworth, William: antislavery activism of, 41; "The Mad Mother," 56; "We Are Seven," 3

working class: anti-vaccinationist movement and, 123, 125–28; burial practices and, 9, 106; child mortality rates among, 4, 103, 105, 135; grief and mourning among, 5; housing for, 103–9; political rights of, 14, 122, 133; suffrage for, 19, 29; systemic exploitation of, 12. *See also* child factory labor

working-class women: abortion among, 143–44; agency of, 155; child death experienced by, 139–52; child workers, 17, 23, 24, 28, 34, 173n69; domestic labor of, 141, 142, 149; food consumption of, 140–41, 146, 148, 221n50; in funeral processions, 124; as government officials, 139; loss of ability to nurse, 148, 224n103; maternal grief and mourning of, 133–34, 139–40, 145–52, 155; parenting skills of, 135; political rights of, 133; regulation of labor for, 16, 34; suffering of, 120. *See also Maternity: Letters from Working Women*

World Anti-Slavery Convention (1840), 64

World War I. *See* First World War

WSPU (Women's Social and Political Union), 152–53

Zong murders, 40, 181–82nn21–23

RECENT BOOKS IN THE
Victorian Literature and Culture Series

Confessing the Flesh: Reading Hopkins in Context
Lesley Higgins

Victorian Nightshades: How the Solanaceae Shaped the Modern World
Elizabeth A. Campbell

Haunting Ecologies: Victorian Conceptions of Water
Ursula Kluwick

The Turn of Rhythm: How Victorian Poetry Shaped a New Concept
Ewan Jones

Narrative and Its Nonevents: The Unwritten Plots That Shaped Victorian Realism
Carra Glatt

Victorian Metafiction
Tabitha Sparks

Strangers in the Archive: Literary Evidence and London's East End
Heidi Kaufman

Evangelical Gothic: The English Novel and the Religious War on Virtue from Wesley to "Dracula"
Christopher Herbert

Reading with the Senses in Victorian Literature and Science
David Sweeney Coombs

Parting Words: Victorian Poetry and Public Address
Justin A. Sider

The Physics of Possibility: Victorian Fiction, Science, and Gender
Michael Tondre

Willful Submission: Sado-Erotics and Heavenly Marriage in Victorian Religious Poetry
Amanda Paxton

Pirating Fictions: Ownership and Creativity in Nineteenth-Century Popular Culture
Monica F. Cohen

Mathilde Blind: Late-Victorian Culture and the Woman of Letters
James Diedrick

Poetry and the Thought of Song in Nineteenth-Century Britain
Elizabeth K. Helsinger

*The Antagonist Principle: John Henry Newman and
the Paradox of Personality*
Lawrence Poston

*Personal Business: Character and Commerce in
Victorian Literature and Culture*
Aeron Hunt

*Second Person Singular: Late Victorian Women Poets
and the Bonds of Verse*
Emily Harrington

The Ghost behind the Masks: The Victorian Poets and Shakespeare
W. David Shaw

Victorian Poets and the Changing Bible
Charles LaPorte

Liberal Epic: The Victorian Practice of History from Gibbon to Churchill
Edward Adams

Supposing "Bleak House"
John O. Jordan

*Feeling for the Poor: Bourgeois Compassion, Social Action,
and the Victorian Novel*
Carolyn Betensky

The Science of Religion in Britain, 1860–1915
Marjorie Wheeler-Barclay

Reading for the Law: British Literary History and Gender Advocacy
Christine L. Krueger

*The Dynamics of Genre: Journalism and the Practice of Literature
in Mid-Victorian Britain*
Dallas Liddle

The Fowl and the Pussycat: Love Letters of Michael Field, 1876–1909
Edited by Sharon Bickle

Victorian Prism: Refractions of the Crystal Palace
Edited by James Buzard, Joseph W. Childers, and Eileen Gillooly

Nostalgia in Transition, 1780–1917
Linda M. Austin

www.ingramcontent.com/pod-product-compliance
Lightning Source LLC
Chambersburg PA
CBHW030611230426
43661CB00053B/1943